The
Forgotten
People

The Forgotten People

Cane River's Creoles of Color

GARY B. MILLS

Louisiana State University Press
Baton Rouge and London

Manufactured in the United States of America
Designer: Albert Crochet
Typeface: VIP Times Roman
Typesetter: The Composing Room of Michigan, Inc.

Publication of this book was assisted by the
American Council of Learned Societies under a grant
from the Andrew W. Mellon Foundation.
Ninth printing (February, 1997)

LIBRARY OF CONGRESS CATALOGING IN PUBLICATION DATA

Mills, Gary B
    The forgotten people : Cane River's Creoles of color

    Bibliography: p.
    Includes index.
    1. Creoles. 2. Cane River Lake region, La.—History.
I. Title
F377.N4M54   976.3'65   77-452
ISBN 0-8071-0279-2 (cloth)
ISBN 0-8071-0287-3 (paper)

The paper in this book meets the guidelines for permanence
and durability of the Committee on Production Guidelines for
Book Longevity of the Council on Library Resources. ∞

To Elizabeth, Clay,
Donna, and Danny

Contents

Illustrations

following page 54

Charts

Preface

Cane River's Creoles of color were, despite their unique and separate way of life, a component of a larger social order which was a confraternity peculiar to Louisiana. Known as *gens de couleur libre,* the men and women of this society were neither black nor white. They successfully rejected identification with any established racial order and achieved recognition as a distinct ethnic group. From the diverse cultures which spawned them was developed a unique ideology, conceived of necessity, nurtured by hope, and jealously guarded against changing mores of society. The status which they enjoyed, however, was not entirely of their own making. The growth of this singular people was fostered by the attitude of a society not common to North America.

The fact that most free men or women of color bore some degree of white blood was of little consequence in most of the United States. By law and social custom, the Negro and the part-Negro, whether slave or free, were usually relegated to the same social status and frequently displayed the same life-style and personal philosophy. The primary exception to this general rule was found in Louisiana.

From the time of the introduction of African slaves into the Louisiana colony, a distinctive and complex caste system existed for Creoles of African descent. Special terminology denoted the ratio of Negro blood to Caucasian blood which each nonwhite possessed. The classifications most commonly found in colonial and antebellum records of Louisiana are:

Negro . . . . applied usually to one
of full Negro blood
Sacatra . . . . ⅞ Negro–⅛ white
Griffe . . . . ¾ Negro–¼ white
Mulatto . . . . ½ Negro–½ white

Quadroon or Quarteron . . ¼ Negro–¾ white
Octoroon or sang-mele . . ⅛ Negro–⅞ white

The degree of privilege or degradation which a nonwhite, whether slave or free, was accorded by society in general was frequently dependent upon that individual's placement upon this caste scale.

The racial philosophy of the white Creoles who dominated Louisiana society also contained a counterpoint to this caste system. Upon obtaining freedom, a nonwhite classified as sacatra or above entered into a separate but complementary racial category, an intermediate class between white and black that was seldom recognized outside Louisiana. Under the title of *gens de couleur libre,* free part-white Creoles were accorded special privileges, opportunities, and citizenship not granted to part-Negroes in other states.

Preservation of this third racial class in Louisiana society was contingent upon strict adherence to the caste system by its members. Just as the whites entertained feelings of superiority to Negroes, so did Louisiana's *gens de couleur libre.* Often possessing more white blood than black, and quite often on good terms with and publicly recognized by their white relatives, most members of this third caste in Louisiana were reared to believe that they were a race apart from the blacks, who occupied the lowest stratum of society. Countless testimonials reveal their inherent pride in their French or Spanish heritage and their identification with the white rather than the black race.

Into this complex caste system still another factor injected itself: economic status. Louisiana's legal code provided a wider berth of economic opportunities to free people of color than could be found in any of the other states. As is the case with any given society, the *gens de couleur libre* displayed varying degrees of initiative, industry, and aptitude. The extent to which individual members of this third class utilized their opportunities often determined their degree of social acceptability in society as a whole.

As a consequence of these factors, this third class in Louisiana advanced socially, economically, and politically to a level unknown among nonwhites in North American society. Yet few efforts have been made to examine the depth of their success or the scope of the factors which produced it. As early as 1917 Alice Dunbar-Nelson lamented, "There is no state in the Union, hardly any spot of like size on the globe, where the man of color has lived so intensely, made so much progress, been of such historical importance and yet about whom so comparatively little is known."

More than half a century has elapsed since that observation was made, but the condition which prompted the remark still exists. Rodolphe Lucien Desdunes' *Nos Hommes et nos Histoire* was a pioneer work; it had, in fact, already appeared in Canada several years before Ms. Nelson pointed to the need for more study of the subject. Desdunes' presentation, however, emphasized the *gens de couleur libre* of the New Orleans area and excluded a number of worthy Creoles of color who resided in the backcountry of the state.

Unfortunately, Desdunes' focus upon New Orleanians is typical of most studies made of the third caste in Louisiana society. More recent studies, such as Charles B. Rousseve's interesting monograph, *The Negro in Louisiana: Aspects of His History and His Literature,* and a sizable number of journal articles, doctoral dissertations, and master's theses have all displayed this shortcoming. To some extent, the emphasis upon New Orleans' Creoles of color is justified, since that metropolis possessed more men and women of this caste than any city in the nation. But, such urban-oriented studies reveal little of the life-style of the many rural *gens de couleur libre* and the role they played in the development of Louisiana as a whole.

The most extensive effort yet made to fill this void is that of H. E. Sterkx in his *The Free Negro in Ante-Bellum Louisiana.* Sterkx has provided some degree of coverage of the rural free nonwhite as a much needed counterpoint to the more usual emphasis that is placed upon New Orleanians. Because of the broad geographical area that he covered, however, only superficial treatment could be given to many aspects of his subject. Sterkx's greatest contribution is his broad and solid base upon which more in-depth analyses of Louisiana's third caste may be built.

Existing studies of *gens de couleur libre* leave three primary areas in need of considerable amplification. First, most of the studies mentioned above fail to show distinctly the caste barriers which stood between the slave, the free Negro, and the free man of color in Creole society. Their failure to do so has made it more difficult for those historians who attempt broader studies. Ira Berlin's *Slaves Without Masters* is an excellent example. Although Berlin has filled a definite need in bringing together a series of less-known publications and unpublished doctoral dissertations into one comprehensive study, his examination of "The Free People of Color in Louisiana and the Gulf Ports" completely ignored the chasm that existed between the black and the part-black in Creole society and treated these two diverse cultures as a single entity. Apparently the modern emphasis upon "black brotherhood" leads many to think that all nonwhites feel, and have always felt, a bond of unity—that the color of their skin, which sets them apart from white Americans, has forged a spiritual bond between Americans of African descent that has always transcended less consequential social and economic differences. This assumption is fallacious.

Then, too, as Carl N. Degler points out in his excellent study, *Neither Black Nor White,* studies in United States history have traditionally presented the nonwhite "primarily as a problem, not as a contributor to the making of the society."[1] The more recent focus upon the history of minorities is slowly reversing traditional views, and several of the studies discussed above have contributed to the reordering of previously accepted ideas. Much more basic research must be done, however, if the historical role of minorities is to be justly compared to that of the extensively researched dominant race in American history.

A third consideration for the historian is the need to recognize that nonwhite Americans *do* have a *traceable* ancestry. For too long it has been accepted *de rigueur* that sexual incontinency and a lack of family stability (both of which of course impede genealogical research) have been basic traits of nonwhite society in America. Fogel and Engerman's controversial *Time on the Cross* blasted this accepted viewpoint, but their statistical conclusions were challenged immediately. Considerable reinforcement, on the most basic level, undoubtedly will be needed before their findings succeed in replacing traditional concepts which have discouraged pursuit of this field of inquiry.

Moreover, the conduct of nonwhite genealogical research also has been handicapped by a general unawareness of the type and volume of records available on the nonwhite family. Alex Haley, with the publication of his historical novel *Roots,* not only has sparked an interest in Afro-American

1. Carl N. Degler, *Neither Black Nor White: Slavery and Race Relations in Brazil and the United States* (New York, 1971), 7.

genealogy, but has made significant progress toward spotlighting the problems involved and many of their solutions. But Haley's Afro-American family existed in a society much different from that of Creole Louisiana. Many of the resources used by Haley would have little bearing on Louisiana's Creoles of color, and many records exist on the *gens de couleur libre* that were not available to Haley in his search for ancestral roots.

This study aspires to fill some of these voids. In one respect its scope is purposefully narrow; it is confined to one family group concentrated in an area roughly thirty miles by five miles in the heart of Louisiana. In another sense, however, it is much broader than any yet presented, for it examines critically every aspect of the private and public lives and feelings of the subject colony and relates their development to the progress of the community as a whole. It is hoped that such a detailed examination of the evolution of one minority group—its difficulties, its achievements, its heartaches, and its pride—will make manifest the contribution to society that has been made by minorities and some of the forces which have motivated them.

The Cane River colony of Creoles of color is not entirely unknown to Louisiana's scholars. One recent major sociological study, Sister Frances Jerome Woods's *Marginality and Identity: A Colored Creole Family Through Ten Generations,* has discussed that aspect of the colony's makeup in considerable detail. However, the nature and scope of this study necessarily focus it upon the modern colony. Sister Frances Jerome's coverage of the colony's very significant historical role is only nominal, and even that degree of historical reconstruction which was attempted, regrettably, suffers from inaccuracy of detail. Considering the amount of historical data through which it would have been necessary to sift in order to correctly reconstruct the colony's past, and recognizing that the presentation of history was not her primary purpose, it is easy to understand this one shortcoming of her otherwise excellent study. Nonetheless, the inadequacy of her background material makes an historical analysis of the colony even more imperative if one is to fully understand the nature of the twentieth-century Creoles of color whose psyche Sister Frances Jerome has so meticulously analyzed.

In addition to *Marginality and Identity,* several well-known studies of an historical nature have included references to various individuals of the colony and their wealth. None of these studies, however, have come close to showing the extent of the prosperity of the people of Cane River or the role which they played in the maturation of central Louisiana society.

In terms of prosperity, the Creoles of Cane River were not completely unique in American society. Every southern state had a few men of color of comparable wealth. Missouri and Louisiana boasted a sizable number. No *individual* in the Cane River colony can be touted as the wealthiest of his class in antebellum society. However, no *family* group yet has been found, in Louisiana or in any other of the United States, which boasted as many prosperous men and women or which retained such a degree of affluence and status for so long a period of time.

Moreover, despite the migratory patterns of the past two centuries, this colony has to a great extent remained intact on the same plantations that their ancestors carved from the Louisiana wilderness almost two hundred years ago. Despite the technological advances with which they have kept abreast, the people have maintained the same values which guided their forefathers and have preserved with pride the old customs. Most significantly, they are still recognized by area society in general as "the third caste," separate and apart from either the blacks or the whites, and they still pride themselves on this status.

In yet another way, the people of the Cane River colony are especially significant historically. In general, far fewer historical records exist on non-white Americans than on the dominant white society, a factor which undeniably limits the depth of research that can be done. Yet, in the present study, this proved to be no problem. Although many documents have been lost in the course of the past two centuries, countless others remain to chronicle almost every aspect of the colony's past. There are, in fact, more documents dealing with them in public and private collections than can be found on most of the white families that settled their area.

The main difficulty encountered in a thorough study of this Cane River colony was occasioned by the nature of the people themselves. The social uncertainty which members of this third caste have felt, and especially the events and attitudes that have prevailed since the emancipation of all people of color, have produced a closely knit and closemouthed society. Betrayals by those they considered to be their friends quite naturally have left them suspicious of the motives of all "outsiders." Many of the people are hesitant to talk to writers for fear they may be misrepresented or that their statements may be misquoted in such a way as to offend their family and friends. A few, apparently, are still afraid that whites in their area may take offense at suggestions of close friendship or even a blood relationship between their ancestors.

Still others among Cane River's Creoles of color shun the whites who come among them for a much more personal reason: they dislike hearing themselves referred to by the terms which are indiscriminately applied to people of their racial origins, specifically *Negro* and *mulatto*. As will be seen, these people have consistently refused to identify themselves as Negro, and the term *mulatto* is particularly detested by many of them, despite the fact that it has been a universally applied term from the time the first children of mixed ancestry appeared in the colonies. Since the word *mulatto* is a derivative of the French and Spanish words for mule, its connotation is especially offensive. Therefore, in the presentation of this study, the feelings of the people will be respected to every extent possible. No confidence will be intentionally betrayed. Offensive nomenclature will be avoided, except in the case of direct quotes from legal documents or from the published works of others.

While the issue of terminology is being discussed, it should be noted that considerable disagreement exists regarding the exact definition of the term *Creole* and the elements of Louisiana society to which this term should be applied. In this study, the term is used to signify any person born in the colony of French or Spanish descent (with the sole exclusion of the Acadian exiles—popularly called Cajuns—who settled in south Louisiana and maintained a distinct ethnic identity). *Creole* will not be limited herein to Louisianians of pure-white descent, to the wealthy aristocracy of the state, or to the residents of the New Orleans-Baton Rouge area exclusively, as has often been the restrictive usage.

In a spirit of respect for the people of the Cane River colony and for their story, every effort has been made here to present as objective a view as possible of the socioeconomic history of this exceptional group. Should any inadvertent bias appear, it must be in favor of the society which attained such achievements against such great odds.

Acknowledgments

Light is the task where many
share the toil—HOMER

While I would never assert that the completion of this study was a light or easy task, I do humbly admit that the work was lightened immeasurably by the generous assistance given by many of my friends and colleagues. My debt to each of these must be acknowledged.

It was Mr. Arthur Chopin Watson of Natchitoches who sparked my interest in the Cane River Creoles of color. A leading force in Louisiana's development for several decades, Mr. Watson has labored tirelessly to promote and perpetuate the rich heritage of the Cane River area. Without his encouragement and support, as well as that of the Association for the Preservation of Historic Natchitoches and its president, Dr. Ora V. Watson, who funded the initial part of this research, this study never would have materialized.

Special thanks are due to several of my colleagues for assistance, professional criticism, and encouragement. The perceptive and analytical suggestions of Dr. Arvarh E. Strickland of the University of Missouri and Dr. John Marszalek of Mississippi State University proved invaluable in shaping the manuscript. Dr. Jan Vansina of the University of Wisconsin provided vital assistance in pinpointing the African origins of the colony's matriarch, and Dr. Jack D. L. Holmes of the University of Alabama at Birmingham generously assisted in locating elusive documents. Deep appreciation also is owed to Professors Roy V. Scott, Harold S. Snellgrove, and Glover Moore of Mississippi State University for their technical guidance throughout all the period in which this study evolved.

Equally vital to this project was the interest, assistance, and cooperation of various descendants of the Cane River colony. I must express my sincerest thanks to Mr. and Mrs. Lewis Emory Jones, Mrs. Lee Etta Vaccarini Coutii, Mr. and Mrs. Tillman Chelettre, Sr., and Mrs. Noble Morin, all of Natchez, Louisiana; to Mr. Hugh LaCour, Sr., of Shreveport, Louisiana; and to those many others who assisted me in understanding their heritage but wished to remain anonymous.

I am heavily indebted to Mr. Irby Knotts, the clerk of court for Natchitoches Parish, and to his very capable deputies, Mrs. Elaine Smith, Mr. Eddie Gallien, and Mr. Douglas Knotts, as well as to the pastors of several Roman Catholic churches of the area: Monsignor Henry F. Beckers, the Reverend John Cunningham, and the Reverend Russell Lemoine, former pastors of the Immaculate Conception Church of Natchitoches; Monsignor Milburn Broussard of the Church of St. John the Baptist, Cloutierville; and the Reverend William J. McElroy, former pastor of the Church of St. Augustine on Isle Brevelle. For years these individuals not only patiently tolerated my persistent presence in their archives but attempted, in every possible way, to facilitate my use of them.

I also deeply appreciate the contributions of those people who, prompted by friendship and an interest in history, offered whatever they could in the way of materials, labor, encouragement, and hospitality: Mr. and Mrs. Robert B. De Blieux, Mr. and Mrs. E. G. Mahan, Jr., Mrs. Arthur C. Watson, Mr. François Mignon, and Mrs. Ora G. Williams, all of Natchitoches; Mrs. Mildred McCoy of the Bayou Folk Museum, Cloutierville; Mr. and Mrs. E. A. Rachal of Baton Rouge; and Mrs. Rowena E. Mulhern of Rayville, Louisiana.

Much assistance was provided by the staff of Mitchell Memorial Library, Mississippi State University, and especially by Mrs. Martha Irby of that library's interlibrary loan department. A special debt is also owed to Mr. John Price of the Eugene P. Watson Memorial Library at Northwestern State University of Louisiana, Mrs. Connie Griffith, formerly of the Howard-Tilton Memorial Library at Tulane University, Mrs. Alberta Ducoté of the Louisiana State Archives and Records Service, and Mrs. Helen Olivier, lands administrator of the Louisiana State Land Office. The staffs of the Louisiana State University Library, the New Orleans Public Library, the Louisiana State Museum Library, the Office of the Keeper of the Notarial Archives, the Office of the District Court, and the Catholic Life Center of Baton Rouge also deserve special thanks for their assistance. Equally appreciated is the unlimited cooperation of the National Archives, Washington, D.C., the Archivo General de Indias at Seville, the Bibliothèque Nationale of Paris, and the Archives of the Departments of Charente-Maritime and the Marne, France.

Foremost is the gratitude that I owe to my research assistant, genealogical consultant, typist, and keenest critic, my wife Elizabeth Shown Mills. Fortunate indeed have I been to have an assistant who is not only willing, versatile, and adept, but who is equally familiar with and interested in the history of the Cane River area.

GARY B. MILLS

Prologue

The Chicago Tribune
August 1, 1943

Will someone please give me information about a little place called Cane River Lake, Louisiana? It's in the open country. The nearest towns are Natchitoches, Louisiana, and Cloutierville, Louisiana. While on maneuvers we had occasion to pass or travel on the bank of this river, or lake as it is called.

The people there were so nice to us. They gave us coffee and hot biscuits, creole gumbo, filet, [sic] and rice. They were a bit shy and they spoke French and broken English, and one old lady read eighteenth century French for us in her prayer book and gave us her blessing. They call her Aunt Louise—Looy for short to everyone who knows her.

Their names are all old French names such as Du Pre, Chevalier, LeCaure, Mullon, Sarpy, Laubieu, Metoyer, St. Ville, Rachal, Monette, and Balthazar. They live in an old world, off to themselves, and have their own church, school and places of amusement. When asked who they were, one lady answered in French, "We are the forgotten people of America." That's all we could get out of them. I am on furlough in Chicago for ten days visiting my parents. Will some one please give me this information before I leave? I am very anxious to know as I am called Nosey by all my friends.

Pvt. James Holloway

The "forgotten people" who so intrigued Private Holloway were the legendary colony of Creoles who have made the Isle Brevelle area of Louisiana's Cane River country their home for almost two centuries. The origins of the colony are reflected not only in the names which the people bear but also in the gentle color which often, but not always, tints their skin. Cane River's "forgotten people" claim a variety of racial origins: French, Spanish, Indian, and African. Their blend of cultures has been so assiduously cultivated and perpetuated that they have long been considered a distinct ethnic group within Louisiana's culture. Neither Caucasian nor Negroid, the families

xxv

which comprise this Cane River colony of Creoles are known among themselves, and by outsiders as well, simply as "the People" or "the people of Isle Brevelle."

When cotton was king in the South, the people of Isle Brevelle were noble subjects. Their plantations, stretching for thousands of acres along the Cane and graced by large and stately homes, were tilled by men and women held in bondage according to the custom of the times. But their wealth, prestige, and privilege vanished in the smoke of war and the upheaval of Reconstruction. Their unique status disappeared in the flood of freedmen. The memory of their former prominence faded from the minds of the dominant white society. It was then that the people of Isle Brevelle begat to consider themselves the "forgotten people."

Within the confines of their own community, however, the past has never been forgotten. Indeed, the story of the colony's origins and the recollections of life as it was once enjoyed have been proudly, almost religiously, immortalized. From *grandpère* to *demi-fille,* from *marraine* to *filleul,* the legend of their past has been handed down, by word of mouth alone, through the successive generations.

Like most legends, the story of this Cane River colony has taken several deviant forms. Every teller of tales does so in his own manner, and the natural infirmities of age often result in a blurring of time and events. Even greater digression occurred when popular writers of the twentieth century became intrigued with the story of the forgotten people and repeated it with their own embellishments. The composite legend, however, is not only an extraordinary story but also an unusually valid one, and even those aspects of the legend which differ from the documented facts are replaced by details even more interesting.

According to the legend, the Cane River colony owes its beginnings to a woman known as Marie Thérèze, or Coincoin. Of African origins, she was from her childhood a slave in the household of the commandant of the Natchitoches post, Sieur Louis Juchereau de St. Denis. The legendary Coincoin was outstanding even as a slave; her natural intelligence, her loyalty, and her devotion to duty soon made her a favored servant in the St. Denis household. Ultimately, these qualifications were to earn for her the one thing she most desired: freedom.

Supposedly the event which gave her the chance to break the bonds of slavery and take the first step toward becoming the founder of this unique society was the illness of her mistress. Mme. de St. Denis was in bad health, and the local physician could find no cure. Others were brought in from New Orleans, Mexico, and even France; their efforts were to no avail. The family was counseled to accept the will of God. But one member of the household refused to despair. Marie Thérèze, who had gained from her African parents a knowledge of herbal medicines, begged for an opportunity to save the dying mistress whom she loved deeply. In desperation the family yielded to her entreaties, and to the bafflement of the educated physicians she accomplished her purpose. In appreciation the St. Denis family rewarded her with the ultimate gift a slave can receive.

The gratitude of the St. Denis family, according to the legend, did not end with Marie Thérèze's manumission. Through their influence, she applied for and received a grant of land which contained some of the most fertile soil in the colony. With two slaves given to her by the family and many more whom she was to purchase later, this African woman carved from the wilderness a magnificent plantation.

These accomplishments did not come easily. Marie Thérèze had worked hard as a slave and she continued to do so as a free woman. Trees were cut and converted into barrel staves which would be used in the West Indian sugar trade. As the land was cleared, tobacco and probably indigo were planted for exportation to Europe. According to legend, Marie Thérèze was the first in the area to recognize the suitability of Natchitoches soil for the cultivation of the lucrative indigo plant. Only this dye, it was said, produced the desired depth of blue for the uniforms of European armies. Other products of a nonagricultural nature were also produced by the former slave. She and her slaves went into the woods to hunt native bears, not only for their hides but also for their grease, which was in demand in Europe to lubricate the axles of carriages and artillery pieces.

The center of this emerging agricultural empire was Yucca Plantation, still extant and more commonly known as Melrose. It was here, allegedly, that Marie Thérèze erected her home and auxiliary plantation buildings, and here again she seems to have exhibited her individuality, constructing her buildings, supposedly, in African style, adapted to Louisiana conditions and native materials.

Marie Thérèze was a family woman. All of her actions were calculated to benefit the offspring she left behind. At least one of her daughters was born into slavery; Marie Thérèze purchased that daughter and the daughter's son in order to give them their freedom. Most of her children, however, were of Franco-African descent, resulting from an alliance with a Frenchman at the Natchitoches post. Not just any Frenchman did she choose to share her life, but a man reputed to be the scion of a noble family, Claude Thomas Pierre Metoyer. As her children entered adolescence and made their First Communion, according to religious customs of that time, Marie Thérèze carved for each of them a wooden rosary. At least one such rosary was treasured by her descendants until well into the twentieth century.

Before her death Marie Thérèze divided her extensive holdings among the children she had borne to Metoyer. For almost a half century following her death, the Metoyers of Cane River enjoyed a wealth and prestige that few whites of their era could match. Gracious and impressive manor homes were erected on every plantation, furnished not only with the finest pieces that local artisans could make but also with imported European articles of quality and taste. Private tutors provided the children with studies in the classics, philosophy, law, and music. The young men of many families were sent abroad for the "finishing touches" which only a continental university could provide.

In spite of the racial limbo into which their origins placed them, the men of the family were accepted and accorded equality in many ways by the white planters. It was not uncommon to find prominent white men at dinner in Metoyer homes, and the hospitality was returned. White planters brought their families to worship in the church erected by the colony, the only one in its area for many decades. In a time and place in which there were no banking institutions, the Metoyers freely lent and borrowed, advised, and stood *in solido* with their white friends and neighbors. They were known as "French citizens" long after Louisiana was sold to the United States, and they held themselves aloof from the waves of "red-necked Americans" who settled in the poor pine woods that surrounded the rich Cane River plantations.

The colony was founded by Metoyers, but each successive generation saw the introduction of two or three new family names. *Gens de couleur libre* from Haiti and New Orleans settled on the Isle, and those whose background passed inspection intermarried with the community. Wealthy white planters of the parish arranged marriages for their own "children of color" with the offspring of their Metoyer friends. This new blood, carefully chosen, did much to protect the colony from the genetic hazards of too frequent intermarriage.

For more than a half century this self-contained colony flourished on Cane River. The people founded not only their own schools and church but also their own businesses and places of entertainment. The family's patriarch, Grandpère Augustin, who was the eldest Metoyer son of Marie Thérèze, served for decades as judge and jury; his word was law and went unquestioned. It was his dream to make of the Isle a place for his people, not merely a home but a refuge against the new breed of greedy Americans. By the end of their era of affluence, the family had almost totally achieved the goal laid out for them by Grandpère Augustin.

A nationwide economic depression and increasingly restrictive legislation began to curtail the economic activities of the colony in the mid-1800s. Several of their plantations were lost, one of the first of which was the one known as Yucca. According to legend it was a white man who caused its downfall. After the death of Marie Thérèze the central portion of her plantation had been inherited by her son Louis, who in turn had bequeathed it to his son, Louis, Jr. It was Louis, Jr., who had cosigned a note for a white planter, as he had cosigned many notes before. This time, however, the friend failed to meet his very sizable obligation. Louis, Jr., was held liable for the debt, and his plantation was lost at public auction.

Despite occasional individual bankruptcies, the colony as a whole continued to prosper until the eruption of the Civil War. Cane River's *gens de couleur libre,* like other southern planters, supported the doomed cause of the Confederacy; and they, like most planters, suffered the depredations of war and the financial ruin of Reconstruction. Unlike their white neighbors, however, they found that after Reconstruction their ruin was complete, since the reactionary political climate of the Redeemer period throttled their economic opportunities. The "liberation of all men" shackled the people of Isle Brevelle with anonymity; the equality proclaimed by the Union lost for them their special prestige. The colony turned inward even more, finding now that they must not only protect themselves against status-conscious whites but also against ambitious black freedmen.

Throughout the remainder of the nineteenth century and well into the twentieth, the people of Isle Brevelle were definitely, in a sense, forgotten people.

They were forgotten by their former white friends who now saw all men of color as a threat, forgotten by the American government which had promised nonwhites so much but provided so little, forgotten by society which now sacrilegiously abandoned the French heritage of which the people of Isle Brevelle were so proud in favor of the American way of life that had brought them nothing but despair.

The Second World War which thrust Private Holloway into the heart of Cane River country accompanied a new era for the forgotten people of Isle Brevelle. The new and more mobile society of the twentieth century brought more strangers, often cosmopolitan strangers, into their midst, strangers who were also curious about the origins of the people and who succeeded in obtaining from them answers to their questions that Private Holloway did not obtain. Themselves storytellers by profession, many of these outsiders listened with delight to the stories that had been so proudly preserved and hastened to repeat them to their audiences and readers. No serious attempt was made to document the stories; on the contrary, more interesting threads of fancy were often interwoven with the fabric of the legend.

Although no longer forgotten, the people of Isle Brevelle are faced today with a new threat, a threat against the memories that they have so proudly cherished. The variations on the theme which have appeared in recent years have contained statements of such obvious fancy that a reaction has set in; other writers have begun to disclaim the entire legend as fiction. The survival of this legend as true oral history is now dependent upon its ability to withstand documentation. Consequently, every facet of the legend, as the people and others have told it, has been scrutinized and compared to actual historical evidence and contemporary conditions. The story which has emerged is, itself, as phenomenal as any claim of the embroidered legend.

The
Forgotten
People

Chapter ONE

A Fusion of Roots

It was in 1714 that the intrepid French Canadian Louis Juchereau de St. Denis founded the first military post and colonial settlement in the region now known as northwest Louisiana. It was a strategic location which St. Denis chose. Situated on the Red River[1] at the site of the old Natchitoches Indian village, the post of St. Jean Baptiste des Natchitoches coexisted in harmony with the friendly natives. Located just fifteen miles from the presidio of Los Adaes, the easternmost outpost of Spanish Texas, Natchitoches served as a bulwark against Spanish agression into French Louisiana and as a convenient base for private and surreptitious trade between the two nations.

The inevitable social intercourse between French, Spanish, and Indian neighbors resulted in an amalgamation of bloodlines that ultimately affected the racial composition of the Cane River colony, as well as that of the region as a whole. Among the colonial ancestors of the colony were numbered at least one commandant each of the Natchitoches and Los Adaes posts, a number of French and Spanish *habitants,* and members of more than one Indian tribe.

The traditions of the people of Isle Brevelle, relative to their ancestry, contain one fundamental paradox. Of their four primary bloodlines—French, African, Indian, and Spanish—it is the French heritage in which they have professed the most pride; yet it is an African woman whom they invariably identify as the nucleus around which their society developed. Proud, aristocratic, and,

---

1. After a series of changes in course which the Red River made in the 1760s and 1830s, the two waterways at whose juncture Natchitoches was established were abandoned by the Red. The larger of these courses was subsequently renamed Cane River. In the 1930s, this river was dammed and has since been known as Cane River Lake.

above all, free, the colony perpetually disdained that element of society which lived in servitude, but they never lost their admiration or respect for the exceptional black woman who generated their Cane River dynasty.

The African heritage of the people may be traced to the year 1735, when the earliest known progenitor was baptized, as an adult, at the Natchitoches post. Since the Roman Catholic society of Louisiana insisted that all slaves be instructed in the Christian catechism and promptly and regularly administered the sacraments,[2] the fact that this slave was an adult not yet baptized indicates that he was a new arrival in the colony.

The presence of such a slave is particularly curious, in that eight years earlier the French colonial government had suspended the African slave trade. Slaves in the service of the crown were growing older and those still of childbearing years could not reproduce sufficient numbers to satisfy the demands of the swelling colonial population.[3]

Commandant St. Denis, however, was an entrepreneur of the first rank. Few men in the colony were as adept at legal commercial activities or at the fine art of smuggling. For three dozen years the ingenious St. Denis had been valued by his French superiors and both respected and feared by the Spanish and Indians for his ability to achieve that which seemed impossible and to procure that which appeared unobtainable. In the 1730s, when fresh supplies of Negro slaves were by law nonexistent, Commandant St. Denis and another prominent Natchitoches trader with Spanish connections succeeded in procuring several adult Negro slaves.[4]

On December 26, 1735, Pierre Vitry, priest of the Company of Jesus serving the parish of St. François des Natchitoches, baptized one such slave for the commandant and gave to him the Christian name of François after the man

2. B. F. French (ed.), *Historical Collections of Louisiana* (5 vols.; New York, 1851), III, 89.

3. N. M. Miller Surrey, *The Commerce of Louisiana During the French Regime, 1699–1763* (New York, 1916), 239–40.

4. Book 1 of the Registers of the Parish of St. François des Natchitoches (Immaculate Conception Church, Natchitoches) contains several baptismal entries for adult slaves belonging to the St. Denis family and to one Jean Baptiste Derbanne. Like St. Denis, young Derbanne was married to the daughter of a Spanish official, his father-in-law being José Maria Gonzales, the commandant of the nearby Spanish post of Los Adaes. St. Denis' wife was the granddaughter of Captain Diego Ramon, commandant of the Presidio del Norte on the Río Grande. This source is hereinafter cited as Natchitoches Registers; the pages are not uniformly numbered but dates are given when available.

who had agreed to be his godfather, the surgeon François Goudeau.[5] The Negro's new master was a man who conscientiously attended to the religious welfare of the men and women he held in bondage. Thus, a wife was found for François from the small slave household of St. Denis; less than two weeks after his baptism, François was married in the small, crude, mission church at Natchitoches to a young black named Marie Françoise.[6]

In some periods of Louisiana history the recorders of ecclesiastical and civil documents noted the tribal origins of the African slaves who received the sacraments or were involved in legal transactions. It is unfortunate that no such information was recorded for François and Marie Françoise. The only clues to their origins are the African names which they gave to three of their eleven children.[7] Documents in the successions of both St. Denis and his wife often refer to Marie Gertrude by the name of Dgimby; François, Jr., was known by a name written variously in these sources as Choera or Kiokera; and Marie Thérèze was repeatedly identified as Coincoin, Quoinquin, KuenKuoin, or other variant spellings.[8]

One authority in African linguistics believes that these names, however corrupted by French and Spanish spellers, belong in all probability to a linguistic group in the Gold Coast/Dahomey region. The name Coincoin is considered the most conclusive clue; its phonetic equivalent, Ko Kwē, is the name reserved for second-born daughters by the Glidzi dialect of the Ewe linguistic group which occupied the coastal region of Togo.[9] Marie Thérèze, called Coincoin, was, according to the church and civil records of the Natchitoches post, the second-born daughter of François and Marie Françoise.

5. *Ibid.*, December 26, 1735.
6. *Ibid.*, January 8, 1736.
7. The children of François and Marie Françoise were: (1) Marie Gertrude, called Dgimby, baptized November 18, 1736; (2) François, Jr., called Kiokera or Choera, born about 1738; (3) Jean Baptiste, born about 1740; (4) Marie Thérèze, called Coincoin, baptized August 24, 1742; (5) Barnabé, born September 9, 1744; (6) Marie Jeanne, baptized June 25, 1746; (7) Marie Louise, born about 1748 or 1749; (8) Bonaventure, baptized June 18, 1751; (9) Hyacinthe, baptized September 13, 1753; (10) Marguerite, born 1755 or 1756; and (11) François, baptized April 21, 1758. Natchitoches Registers, Books 1 and 2; Succession of St. Denys and Succession of Wife of St. Denys, in Natchitoches Parish Records (Office of the Clerk of Court, Natchitoches), Docs. 176–78, 203–206.
8. Natchitoches Registers, Books 1 and 2; Natchitoches Parish Records, Docs. 176–78, 203–206.
9. Dr. Jan Vansina to author, May 12, 1973.

Regardless of their tribal origins, it is obvious that the parents clung to their native heritage in the midst of an alien environment. The African names which they gave to at least three of their children are used with greater frequency than, and in obvious preference to, the Christian names which were bestowed upon them by their masters. It has not been possible to trace the life of Dgimby past late adolescence, but several later records exist on Choera, and the career of Marie Thérèze Coincoin is mapped in many civil and ecclesiastical documents. For the remainder of their lives, these latter two continued to be known by their African names. Moreover, the descendants of Marie Thérèze continued to use the name of Coincoin as late as the fourth generation.[10] Tradition among the descendants of Marie Thérèze also insists that, in addition to the official languages of her time, French and Spanish, Marie Thérèze was fluent in an African dialect and that she was well trained by her parents in the native use and application of medicinal herbs and roots.[11]

The retention of some degree of African culture by François and Marie Françoise is typical of the reaction of many transported blacks in colonial America. According to one authority, a number of first-generation African slaves "consistently refused to abandon their linguistic tie with their homeland."[12] Those slaves who were determined to survive in the New World, however, found it necessary to acquire some degree of fluency in the master language, if for no other reason than to be able to understand and follow commands. Yet, it seems there were a fair number who only grudgingly acquiesced to their subjection and who stubbornly refused to accept a new name.[13]

The report of the authority just cited is reinforced by records at the Natchitoches post. Civil and ecclesiastical documents from the colonial and territorial periods record the existence of several such slaves in the area. François

10. Intestate Succession of Mr. St. Denis [Jr.], in Laura L. Porteous (trans.), "Index to the Spanish Judicial Records of Louisiana," *Louisiana Historical Quarterly,* XIII (January, 1930), 183. Ms. Porteous has erroneously transcribed the name of Choera or Choeras as Chocras. Mrs. Lee Etta Vaccarini Coutii of Isle Brevelle, the great-great-great-granddaughter of Marie Thérèze, well remembers Coinquan Metoyer, son of Neres Pierre, who was given this nickname in memory of his great-grandmother. Mrs. Coutii to author, March 21, 1974.

11. Interview with Mrs. Coutii, March 24, 1974.

12. John W. Blassingame, *The Slave Community: Plantation Life in the Antebellum South* (New York, 1972), 22.

13. *Ibid.,* 21.

and Marie Françoise, however, provided a curious variation to the general rule. While they taught the African language to their offspring, gave African names to at least three of these, and obviously insisted upon the use of these names in preference to Christian counterparts, there is no indication that they continued to use their own African names.

Not only did François and Marie Françoise instill in their children a respect for their African heritage, but they were also able to provide the family solidarity which characterized their descendants for the next two and a half centuries. In this respect at least partial credit must be given to the particular system of slavery under which they served. One of the unfortunate aspects of many slave systems was the lack of opportunity for bonded men and women to establish permanent relationships and solid family ties. In most eras and locales slaves could be sold at the will of their masters. If economic considerations necessitated, husbands were separated from wives, children were taken from their parents. In French Louisiana, however, this evil was curtailed. Article XLIII of the *Code Noir* proclaimed by Governor Bienville in 1724 specifically stated:

> Husbands and wives shall not be seized and sold separately when belonging to the same master; and their children, when under fourteen years of age, shall not be separated from their parents, and such seizures and sales shall be null and void. The present article shall apply to voluntary sales, and in case such sales should take place in violation of the law, the seller shall be deprived of the slave he has illegally retained, and said slave shall be adjudged to the purchaser without any additional price being required.[14]

In early Natchitoches this regulation, in general, was respected. Consequently, from the time of their marriage until their concurrent deaths, François and Marie Françoise were never separated by sale from each other or from their children. As their oldest daughter matured and became a mother herself, she remained in her parents' household, and the older couple were blessed with the opportunity of experiencing the day-to-day growth of their first grandchild.

Commandant Louis Juchereau de St. Denis died at the Natchitoches post on June 11, 1744, and was buried within the parish church.[15] In the last years of

---

14. French (ed.), *Historical Collections of Louisiana,* III, 94.
15. Natchitoches Registers, Book 1, June 12, 1744.

his life the free-spending St. Denis had suffered serious financial reverses. As a consequence, the much entangled estate that he left behind was not settled for twelve years. The final partition of his slaves was executed in September, 1756, and by its terms the entire family of François and Marie François was inherited by the widow.[16]

Less than two years later an apparent epidemic struck the St. Denis household. On April 16, 1758, the widow St. Denis was buried at the Natchitoches post. Three days later her slaves, François and Marie Françoise, were also interred.[17] The cause of their deaths and that of their mistress was not recorded.

Soon the slaves of the St. Denis household were partitioned again, this time among the children and grandchildren of the deceased commandant and his wife. There was no alternative now to separating the orphaned children of François and Marie Françoise. By lot, each of the six heirs was assigned one or two of the slave children. Marie Thérèze, called Coincoin, and her brother Jean Baptiste were inherited by Pierre Antoine Juchereau de St. Denis, the youngest son of the deceased commandant.[18]

Of the eleven children born to François and Marie Françoise, nine were destined to live and die in the state of anonymity from which few slaves ever rose. The tenth, Marie Jeanne, who had been inherited by a St. Denis son-in-law named Athanase Fortune Christophe De Mézières, was to become the matriarch of a community of *gens de couleur libre* by that surname who enjoyed a small measure of affluence in the Campti area of Natchitoches Parish. Only Marie Thérèze Coincoin, however, could be correctly termed successful. With loyalty, determination, foresight, ingenuity, and a considerable degree of business acumen, this exceptional black woman and the children she produced overcame the stigma of slavery that had been branded upon them by birth. By engineering their own fate, she and her remarkable family were to become the respected and renowned proprietors of an imposing and, ultimately, legendary plantation operation.

Marie Thérèze's success was not easily or quickly accomplished. The records contradict the legend that she was given her freedom by the widow St. Denis, along with a vast grant of land from the king himself. Marie Thérèze

16. Partition of Slaves of St. Denys, in Natchitoches Parish Records, Doc. 176.
17. Natchitoches Registers, Book 2.
18. Succession of Wife of St. Denys, in Natchitoches Parish Records, Docs. 203–205.

was still a slave at the death of the widow in 1758 and was to remain in bondage for twenty more years. Nothing is known of her life during the first ten of these years, except the scanty information that is provided in the records of the church.

The registers of the parish of St. François des Natchitoches clearly reflect the general state of religion at the post. In short, religious fervor was sporadic. The French who settled there were Roman Catholic by birth, and Catholicism was the state religion. However, the Natchitoches settlement was twenty years old before the mother church was able to assign a priest there. Natchitoches should not, however, be considered the wayward child of the Louisiana colony, since colonial society as a whole suffered from inadequate religious as well as civil leadership. Louisiana was, in this period, *"sans religion, sans justice, sans discipline, sans ordre, et sans police."* [19] Although Louisiana society underwent considerable improvement throughout the colonial period, organized religion still suffered, especially at Natchitoches. Indeed, for over a century after its settlement, under French, Spanish, and American regimes, there were to be a number of periods when the inhabitants had no clergyman to baptize their infants, marry their youth, bury their dead, hear confession, or offer regular mass. [20]

Commandant and Mme. de St. Denis were bulwarks of the local religious congregation during their lives, and their efforts to promote piety were directed toward nonwhites as well as the local French society. They insisted upon the practice of Christian principles among their slaves, both those of Indian and African descent and, when priests were available, saw to it that their slaves were regularly administered the sacraments. Thus it was that François had been provided with a wife shortly after his arrival at the post. Most area residents followed the example set by the commandant and his wife, but the custom did not long outlive the St. Denis hegemony. By the 1760s the registers of the church reflect a significant decrease in slave marriages. [21]

19. George W. Cable, *The Creoles of Louisiana* (New York, 1884), 24–25.

20. Roger Baudier, *The Catholic Church in Louisiana* (New Orleans, 1939), 147–51, 198–99; Henry F. Beckers *et al.*, *A History of Immaculate Conception Catholic Church, Natchitoches, Louisiana, 1717–1973* (Natchitoches, 1973). Immaculate Conception is the modern name of the old parish of St. François.

21. Baudier, *The Catholic Church in Louisiana*, 147–51, 198–99; Beckers *et al.*, *A History of Immaculate Conception Catholic Church*; Natchitoches Registers, Books 1 and 2.

Like most female slaves who reached maturity during this period, Marie Thérèze was not provided with a husband by her owners. Nor was she encouraged to adhere to the Christian moral code by which even the white colonists often had difficulty living. Although the elder St. Denis and wife have been lauded for their piety, some of their children fell short of the parents' example, and the moral laxity they displayed had a significant effect upon their slaves. As one authority points out, when members of the self-proclaimed superior race violated their own sexual morality with impunity, it is not surprising that their slaves did not display a higher personal standard.[22] Upon reaching maturity Marie Thérèze was left to work out her own code of behavior.

Economic conditions were in part responsible for the moral relaxation that occurred in the slave households of the younger members of the St. Denis family. The wealth which the commandant had once enjoyed had provided him with a number of slaves of all ages, which made pairing relatively easy. After his reversal of fortunes, he died leaving only a small estate; when this was divided between six heirs, the portions were small. Moreover, under the new Spanish political regime,[23] the sons and the daughter did not fare as well as had their father under the French. Their slave households were exceedingly small. Pierre Antoine, for example, owned no males of appropriate age with whom he could pair young Marie Thérèze, except her own brother. Apparently he could not afford to purchase a husband for her, and marriages between slaves belonging to different masters was not a common practice at Natchitoches.

At the same time, however, it was a fundamental principle of the institution of slavery in North America that much of a young female slave's value was dependent upon her ability to produce more slaves. Marie Thérèze well fulfilled this duty. In 1759, the year following her acquisition by young St. Denis, the seventeen-year-old girl gave birth to her first child. This daughter, Marie Louise, was described by colonial records as being of full Negro blood. In

22. Blassingame, *The Slave Community,* 82.

23. By the terms of the Treaty of Fontainbleau in 1762, Louis XV of France ceded the Louisiana colony to his cousin, Charles III of Spain.

1761, while still the property of St. Denis, Marie Thérèze produced her second daughter; this one, also black, was named for the mother, Thérèze.[24]

At some point between 1761 and 1766 Marie Thérèze and her two daughters became the property of her master's youngest sister, Marie des Nieges de St. Denis, wife of Antoine Manuel Bermudez y de Soto; but no record of the conveyance is extant. During this period a visiting priest, Father Ygnacio Maria Laba, baptized her third child, Françoise; the infant's racial composition was not specified.[25] Again in 1766 Marie Thérèze gave birth, this time to a son, Jean Joseph. The baptismal record of this child indicates an improvement in Marie Thérèze's status, for this time she was allowed to choose his godparents herself. The godfather was her brother Jean Baptiste, still the slave of Pierre Antoine de St. Denis. The godmother was Marie Louise, Marie Thérèze's oldest daughter.[26]

It had been at least three decades since the progenitors of this family had been herded onto a slave ship on the coast of Africa. It would be another one hundred years before the majority of black men in America would again know the taste of freedom. But Marie Thérèze Coincoin did not passively accept her lot. Never did she resign herself and the children she had borne to that which a legion of other blacks accepted as fate. Within the next three decades Marie Thérèze and her children would be free.

The legend insists that Marie Thérèze was given her freedom as a reward for saving the life of her dying mistress. No records can be found which either completely support or completely contradict this claim. It is known that her last mistress, Marie de St. Denis (as she invariably called herself throughout her long marriage to de Soto) was bedridden for at least the last ten years of her life,[27] and it is possible that in earlier years she was also in poor health. It is obvious from several relevant documents that the hard-nosed daughter of the old commandant held a tender spot in her heart for this slave. For the remainder of her life the lady was to grant Marie Thérèze and her children a

24. Baptism of Marie Louise, slave of M. de St. Denis, September 8, 1759, and Baptism of Thérèze, September 24, 1761, Natchitoches Registers, Book 2; Marie Thérèze to Marie Louise, and Marie St. Denis to Marie Thérèze Coincoin, in Natchitoches Parish Records, Docs. 2596, 2804.
25. Baptism of Françoise, July 8, 1763, in Natchitoches Registers, Book 1.
26. Baptism of Jean Joseph and others, March 29, 1766, *ibid*.
27. Marie St. Denis to Marie Thérèze Coincoin, in Natchitoches Parish Records, Doc. 2804.

number of special favors, and at one point she vigorously defended her slave against detractors. In view of this attitude which Marie de St. Denis exhibited, it may be possible that she did owe to Marie Thérèze a debt of gratitude for service rendered in one way or another.

The actual accomplishment of this slave's freedom, however, may be more validly accredited to another factor. It was apparently in 1767 that the most significant event in the life of Marie Thérèze occurred. There appeared at the Natchitoches post a young Frenchman named Claude Thomas Pierre Metoyer. Together with a brother he had emigrated to the colonies and, reportedly, settled for a while at New Orleans. There the brother remained, but Pierre wound his way upriver to Natchitoches where a friend, Étienne Pavie, had already established himself as a merchant. At Natchitoches Metoyer entered this same vocation, while serving in the reserve militia.[28]

Tradition among the descendants of Pierre Metoyer, both those of pure French blood and those of Franco-African origins, boasts that Metoyer was a member of a "noble" French family. The records which can be obtained from France do not support this tradition. In actuality, Metoyer belonged to a family of the merchant class, although apparently they were well-to-do bourgeoisie. Claude Thomas Pierre Metoyer was born at La Rochelle on March 12, 1744; his father, however, had migrated there from Rheims in the province of Champagne.[29]

Attempts to trace the Metoyer family at Rheims have been unsuccessful.

---

28. Agreement between Merchants, in Natchitoches Parish Records, Doc. 739; Register of the Company of Infantry of the Natchitoches Militia, inspected January 1, 1780 (MS in Jack D. L. Holmes Collection, Eugene P. Watson Memorial Library, Northwestern State University of Louisiana, Natchitoches) Reel 5.

29. Claude Thomas Pierre's father, Baptiste Nicolas François Metoyer, was born in the parish of St. Denis de Rheims in 1715, the son of the merchant Jean Metoyer and his wife Françoise Galloteau. At the age of twenty-six, Baptiste Nicolas François migrated to La Rochelle and established himself in trade there in the parish of Notre-Dame. Two years later he married the twenty-nine-year-old Marie Anne Drapron, a native of Chaignoller, Parish of Dompierre, in the province of Aunis. Mlle. Drapron was also from a merchant family, being the daughter of the deceased merchant Sieur François Drapron and his widow, Anne Naudin. At the time of her marriage to Metoyer, Mlle. Drapron was living in the parish of St. Sauveur.

Genealogical information on the Metoyer family of France is provided in the baptismal record of Claude Thomas Pierre Metoyer, dated May 14, 1744, in the marriage record of his parents, dated February 20, 1743, and in the burial record of his father, dated May 15, 1766. All are preserved in the Archives Départementales de Charente-Maritime at La Rochelle. Copies in possession of author.

The only information on their economic or social status there is provided in the will which Metoyer drew at Natchitoches in 1801. In this document he referred to a chateau of eleven rooms, some miles distant from the town of Rheims, which he had inherited from a late uncle, the priest Jorge Metoyer. Father Metoyer had also bequeathed to him a set of silver flatwear and dishes on which was engraved Claude Thomas Pierre Metoyer's entire name.[30] It thus appears that the Metoyers of Rheims did enjoy some measure of affluence. However, given the meaning of the surname which this family bore, the traditional claims of nobility do not appear likely.[31]

In a small post the size of Natchitoches, it was probably not long before Pierre Metoyer met the slave of Mme. de Soto. No accounts of Marie Thérèze's personal characteristics have been found, but it is obvious that her appearance was comely and her personality appealing. She was already twenty-five years of age and the mother of four children, and feminine beauty was short-lived in her society. Imported creams, lotions, and soaps were so costly that few women in colonial Louisiana could afford these to wash and smooth away the inevitable results of the hard life they led, and soap that was made at home of ashes and waste fats was so harsh that the colonial dames were forced to rub their faces and hands with bear or sheep fat to soften them.[32] Yet, despite her years and the factors that prematurely aged colonial women, Marie Thérèze was to attract the affection of this sophisticated, city-bred Frenchman who was, in fact, two years her junior, and was to hold his affection until she was well into the fifth decade of her life.

It was not long before Metoyer had persuaded Mme. de Soto to lease to him her Negro slave. In payment for her services he promised her owners to provide her room and board, and Marie Thérèze moved into the home of Metoyer.[33] In 1771 this arrangement was made illegal when the Cabildo at

---

30. The 1801 will of Claude Thomas Pierre Metoyer, which should be among the official records in the Office of the Clerk of Court for the Parish of Natchitoches, cannot be found there. However, a photocopy of the original is available at the Natchitoches Parish Library.

31. The variant spellings of Metoyer, Metayer, Mettoyer, and Mettayer, which appear at Natchitoches and in European records dealing with the family, translate as *sharecropper* or *small farmer*.

32. Edwin A. Davis, *Louisiana: A Narrative History* (Baton Rouge, 1961), 87.

33. Pierre Metoyer to Athanase De Mézières, *Rex* v. *de Soto,* in Natchitoches Parish Records, Doc. 1227.

New Orleans ruled that owners of slaves were henceforth prohibited from hiring them out.[34] As in the case of many such regulations, however, enforcement at posts as distant as Natchitoches was extremely lax. In this instance the parties involved had a double advantage, for the commandant at the post was the brother-in-law of Mme. de Soto, Athanase Christophe Fortune De Mézières. The de Soto-Metoyer lease agreement was not canceled after the passage of the new law.

It was Claude Thomas Pierre Metoyer and Marie Thérèze Coincoin who were the immediate progenitors of the Cane River Creoles of color. The first children of this French-African alliance were born in January of 1768, a set of twins. The boy was given the name of Nicolas Augustin, apparently after his grandfather, Nicolas François Metoyer, and the girl was given the name of Marie Suzanne, the name borne by her father's stepmother in France, Susanne Vinault.[35] Both children were baptized into the Catholic faith the following month, and Catholic the family has remained, for the most part, throughout the two centuries that have followed.

The baptismal records for the parish of Natchitoches between 1769 and 1776 are no longer extant. It was in this period, when no priest was in residence at the post, that three more of the Franco-African Metoyer children were born. As best can be determined by later records, Louis was born in 1770, Pierre in 1772, and Dominique in 1774. In June 1775 a new Spanish priest was assigned to the Natchitoches post; it was he who baptized the sixth Metoyer child, Marie Eulalie, the following January. With the deceit that convention demanded, the new priest, Father Luis de Quintanilla, entered into his register the customary statement: "father unknown."[36]

Within a year of his arrival, Father Quintanilla left Natchitoches. Since no priest was available to take his place, Commandant De Mézières petitioned for his return, and Father Quintanilla arrived at the Natchitoches post the second time about August of 1777. The reason for his departure from the post in 1776 is not known, but the letter which he brought with him upon his

34. Works Progress Administration, Survey of the Federal Archives in Louisiana: Alphabetical and Chronological Digest of the Acts and Deliberations of the Cabildo, 1769–1803 (Ten-volume typescript in New Orleans Public Library), I, 65.

35. Natchitoches Registers, Book 2, February 1, 1768.

36. *Ibid.*, January 28, 1776.

second arrival, addressed by Governor Bernardo de Galvez to the commandant, hinted at a possible explanation. After praising the priest as a worthy
man, Galvez closed his letter with the suggestion: "I therefore recommend
that you treat him well and protect him as far as you can in order that he may
remain willingly in that district."[37] Galvez did not make it clear what protection Father Quintanilla needed, or from whom he needed it. However, the
events of the year to come clearly indicated that his major foes were his own
zealousness and his own flock.

By early fall Father Quintanilla was embroiled in a raging controversy, and
his would-be protector, Commandant De Mézières, was caught in the middle.
During his previous brief stay, Father Quintanilla had baptized one child for
Marie Thérèze and entered into his books the phrase, "father unknown,"
despite public knowledge to the contrary. Upon his second arrival at the post
he found that Marie Thérèze was again pregnant, and his conscience could no
longer let him ignore the situation at which the community winked so blithely.

Indeed, the concubinage of Metoyer and Marie Thérèze which so upset
Father Quintanilla was but one case of what many priests of that era considered
to be a growing plague. One contemporary bishop officially complained that
"a good many inhabitants live almost publicly with colored concubines," and
that they did not even "blush" when they carried their illegitimate offspring
"to be recorded in the registries as their natural children."[38] A later judicial
decision explained the primary reason for this social condition: "[Since] there
were at that time but few of the white women in the colony, and hardly any of
equal condition with the officers of the government and of the troops stationed
here, the inevitable consequence was that these gentlemen formed connections with women of color. This custom coming as it did from the ruling class
soon spread throughout the colony."[39]

Lest it be concluded that such circumstances were typical of Louisiana social conditions but atypical of the remainder of American society, it should be

37. Herbert Eugene Bolton, *Athanase De Mézières and the Louisiana-Texas Frontier,
1768–1780* (2 vols.; Cleveland, 1914), II, 134–35.
38. Quoted in Laura Foner, "The Free People of Color in Louisiana and St. Dominigue: A
Comparative Portrait of Two Three-Caste Societies," *Journal of Social History,* III (Summer,
1970), 411.
39. *Badillo* v. *Tio,* 6 King La., 129 (1848).

noted that the factors which promoted miscegenation in Louisiana also prevailed in the earliest days of the eastern seaboard colonies. One authority, who commented on the scarcity of white women in the English colonies, noted that "the intermixture of races had become so extensive by the end of the colonial period that many mulattoes seem to have lost all the distinguishing physical features of the Negro." [40] Despite drastic efforts to control interracial sex in the English colonies, the amalgamation of races continued, if to a somewhat lesser degree than that which occurred in Louisiana. "The process of miscegenation was part of the system of slavery," another authority explains; "the dynamics of race contact and sex interest were stronger than prejudice, theory, law or belief. . . . Every traveler in the South before the Civil War commented on the widespread miscegenation." [41]

Natchitoches society was typical of most, with only one significant exception to the general rule of early miscegenation. At the time that Metoyer and Marie Thérèze initiated their alliance, there was no great disparity between the number of male adults and females above puberty. On the contrary, the census of 1766 enumerated 55 men to 54 women who were classified as white. [42] Despite the adequate supply of white women, however, the baptismal registers of the parish of St. François des Natchitoches contain numerous references to slave children whose fathers were white. In these other cases, apparently, the men involved exercised a certain amount of discretion. Pierre Metoyer, however, lived in open concubinage with the Negro slave of his choice and it was he, and Marie Thérèze, of whom the priest chose to make an example.

Two months after his second arrival at the post, Father Quintanilla filed a formal complaint with Commandant de Mézières:

> Fr. Luis de Quintanilla, Capuchin Religious and Parish curé of the abovesaid Post, has the honor of representing to His Majesty that, perceiving himself compelled by virtue of his ministry to eradicate the vices and relate the scandals as these originate, not having been able after much diligence to place a control on the scandalous concubinage of a Negress named Cuen Cuen, slave of Dn. Manuel de Soto,

40. James Hugo Johnston, *Race Relations in Virginia and Miscegenation in the South, 1776–1860* (Amherst, Mass., 1970), 190.
41. Frank Tannenbaum, *Slave and Citizen* (New York, 1947), 121–23.
42. Katherine Bridges and Winston DeVille, "Natchitoches in 1766," *Louisiana History,* IV (Spring, 1963), 156–59.

hired for many years to the named Metoyer in whose house and company the said Negress has produced (not being married) five or six mulattoes and mulattresses, not including in this number the one with whom she is now pregnant; and as this cannot happen in the house of an unmarried man and an unmarried woman without the public thinking and judging there to be illicit intercourse between the two partners in cohabitation, from which ensues a great scandal and damage to the souls; and according to the mandate sent to the petitioner by his Superior, the Most Illustrious Senor, Bishop of Cuba, that "in case these concubinages do not cease after apostolic counsel the concubines must deliver themselves to the Royal Court of Justice so that they can be coerced and punished ... these concubines should make use, Your Reverence, of the apostolic means, they should be persuaded to sanctify their bad concubinage by the union of matrimony and, if after all this, they persist, denounce them, Your Reverence, to the Royal Court of Justice so that they can be forced to do so and the scandal can be removed"—

The petitioner, in consideration of this, denounces to Your Majesty the aforesaid Negress Cuen Cuen as a public concubine in order that Your Majesty deign to castigate her according to the law, prohibiting her under grave punishment ever to go into the house of the mentioned Metoyer in order to avoid public scandal, having commanded her owner to look after that, so that she not bring more upon herself by similar sins, because of other ways of exposing herself to losing her Negress. Justice, which waits for the conscientiousness of Your Majesty, October 23, 1777.

Fr. Luis de Quintanilla, who is supreme[43]

In response to the curé's request, Commandant de Mézières issued a ruling that same day ordering Pierre Metoyer to abandon Marie Thérèze, to expel her permanently from his home and his service, never to buy her, and to affirm that he had no desire to cause further scandal or disgrace. Upon receipt of the commandant's order, Metoyer reluctantly complied, then petitioned de Mézières to release him from the contract which he had made with Mme. de Soto, under the terms of which he was to furnish Marie Thérèze's board as payment of the rent for her services.[44]

The Spanish priest apparently had succeeded. Marie Thérèze had been expelled from Metoyer's household, their public concubinage was prohibited, and the scandal was eradicated, officially. His success, however, was short-lived. Early in 1778 the duties of de Mézière's office as commandant and

43. Father Quintanilla to A. De Mézières, *Rex* v. *de Soto,* in Natchitoches Parish Records, Doc. 1227.
44. De Mézières to Metoyer and Metoyer to De Mézières, *ibid.*

lieutenant governor called him into the Texas region. A letter was posted by him in February, 1778, from the presidio of San Antonio de Bexar, and from there he led an expedition to the Indian nations on the upper Trinity, Brazos, and Red rivers. It was at least three months before de Mézières returned to the Natchitoches post; Marie Thérèze and Metoyer apparently took advantage of the opportunity afforded them by his extended absence, and once again she moved into Metoyer's home.[45]

In June the outraged Father Quintanilla greeted the newly returned commandant with a second protest. The first had been directed mainly against Metoyer and had brought no permanent results. This time the curé demanded that Marie Thérèze's owner, Mme. de Soto, be commanded to "put away" her slave in her house and forbid any further resumption of this unsanctioned alliance with the Frenchman. Moreover, Father Quintanilla took this opportunity to castigate Metoyer for his failure to perform his obligations as a true Christian and a Catholic; it had been, he swore, at least two years since Metoyer had complied with the requirement of annual confession and communion. The curé's indignant statement ended with a threat to take the matter to higher authorities, the governor or even the viceroy, if De Mézières (because of his relationship to the recalcitrant Mme. de Soto) was not willing or able to see that justice was done. Again the priest authoritatively signed his protest "Fr. Luis de Quintanilla, who is supreme."[46]

With his directly involving Marie de Nieges de St. Denis de Soto in this delicate issue, Father Quintanilla made a grave mistake. This youngest daughter of Natchitoches' founder was a woman of very formidable character. The notarial records of both the Natchitoches post, where she was born, and the Opelousas post, where she died, contain many examples of her forcefulness and determination. Like her father, Mme. de Soto usually accomplished that which she set out to accomplish.

The basic issue raised by Father Quintanilla, the "scandalous conduct" of her African slave and this French gentleman, was certainly not a serious issue in the eyes of Mme. de Soto. Prejudice against the African races did not reach

45. Father Quintanilla to A. De Mézières, *ibid.;* Bolton, *Athanase De Mézières,* II, 172, 214–15.
46. Father Quintanilla to A. De Mézières, *Rex* v. *de Soto,* in Natchitoches Parish Records, Doc. 1227.

any degree of intensity in French society until the late eighteenth century, and even then it was short-lived, since the French Revolution immediately restored full citizenship to all French-born residents. It was not until 1778 that France forbade marriage between the races. Prior to this period, African members of French society were considered more or less "exotic," and even the illustrious King Louis XIV reportedly once had a Negro mistress.[47]

In true French tradition, Mme. de Soto obviously considered *l'amour* to be a private affair, beyond the understanding of holy priests whose hearts were armored by their vows of celibacy and lives of constant prayer. Scandal, moreover, was not exactly a new experience to the lady, for she had weathered the storms of gossip that undoubtedly resulted when she bore a child out of wedlock in 1750.[48] As in the case of other such unfortunate girls at the Natchitoches post, the incident had not prevented her from making an acceptable marriage and she had long since resumed her role as a respectable member of Natchitoches society.

Moreover, Marie de St. Denis de Soto was in 1778 a very lonely lady who had been thwarted in love by Spanish authority. Her husband, Don Manuel Bermudez y de Soto, prior to his settlement at the French post, had been secretary to the governor of the Texas region but had committed the crime of treason against the Spanish government. To escape punishment he sought refuge in French Louisiana. Upon his marriage to the daughter of the late St. Denis, who was also the sister-in-law of two of the most respected leaders of French colonial government, Athanase De Mézières and Cesar De Blanc, de Soto's position in the French colony was virtually secure. After so many years of Franco-Spanish rivalry in the colonies, the French certainly were not inclined to hold a grudge against a gentleman for an offense against the Spanish government.[49]

47. Shelby T. McCloy, "Negroes and Mulattoes in Eighteenth-Century France," *Journal of Negro History,* XXX (July, 1945), 276–92. Although intermarriage between the races was not illegal in France before 1778, and then only briefly, it was outlawed in the colonies in 1724 as a means of maintaining the all-important caste barrier and power structure between free men and slaves.

48. Baptism of Marie Éleonore de St. Denis, November 5, 1750, Natchitoches Registers, Book 1.

49. David K. Bjork (ed.), "Documents Relating to Alexandro O'Reilly and an Expedition Sent Out by Him from New Orleans to Natchitoches, 1769–1770," *Louisiana Historical Quarterly,* VII (January, 1924), 23; Bridges and DeVille, "Natchitoches in 1766," 146–47.

In 1762 Don Manuel's position changed drastically. When Louis XV, King of France, ceded the Louisiana colony to his cousin, Charles III of Spain, the country in which de Soto had sought refuge against Spanish justice suddenly came under Spanish control. It was not until 1769, however, that Spain's military genius, General Alexandro O'Reilly, established the first authoritative Spanish regime in Louisiana, and it was in that year that de Soto's political game was lost. In late 1769 O'Reilly wrote: "The Viceroy of New Spain has sent me a legal order requesting the arrest of Don Manuel Bermudez de Soto, secretary of the former Governor of the Province of Texas. This man, Bermudez, knew the province well and had many friends there, none of whom, however, was of any help to him. Due to my orders he was arrested and delivered to the Commander of the Presidio of Adaes."[50] From Los Adaes, de Soto was transferred to Mexico, where he was to spend a number of years in political confinement. Documents executed by Mme. de Soto for the next ten years or so indicate that he was still absent from his home at Natchitoches.

The affair of her slave and Pierre Metoyer, therefore, was an opportunity for Mme. de Soto to vent her anger against the Spanish authorities, and it was certainly exploited by her to the fullest. In a lengthy and scorching redress that was directed to de Mézières, Mme. de Soto came to the defense of her slave and the man whom Marie Thérèze had chosen.

Father Quintanilla's latest charges were described by her as "willfull" and "inflammatory," designed to "attack her honor and trouble the tranquility of the Post." It was obvious, Mme. de Soto contended, in view of the commandant's order of last October barring the slave from Metoyer's home, that Marie Thérèze would not have resumed living with the gentleman even during the commandant's absence. But if Father Quintanilla chose to believe local wagging tongues rather than her own testimony, then he must consider well at this point the degree of support which she, Mme. de Soto, was providing to Father Quintanilla's church. There was the matter of a furnace and a mill, which she had donated, apparently, to the parish.[51] Moreover, she also was providing a residence for the members of the religious community of St. An-

---

50. Bjork (ed.), "Documents Relating to Alexandro O'Reilly," 23.
51. This mill which Mme. de Soto furnished the parish was of considerable value since it was one of only two mills in the entire colony. Davis, *Louisiana,* 133.

toine, and she had every legal right to require them to do work for her in payment for their living expenses.[52]

The fact that Marie Thérèze had produced seven children of mixed blood while living in Metoyer's home and the fact that Metoyer had already purchased four of these children from Mme. de Soto were both irrelevant, the lady felt. Was the Reverend Father ready to accuse all masters whose slaves had produced such children? Moreover, "public belief" in the existence of a concubinage between this couple did not constitute certain knowledge and certainly not legal proof; without better proof, Father Quintanilla surely had no case.[53]

The curé's charge that Metoyer lacked religious devotion was likewise of little import to Mme. de Soto. If Metoyer failed to approach the confessional, he was merely following the example of almost all of the post. She, herself, made a practice of leaving mass before the commencement of Father Quintanilla's tedious and disagreeable sermons, delivered for two to three hours in atrociously mispronounced French idioms and violent, scandalous language.[54]

The Reverend Father also had two faces, the lady challenged. While he preached against avarice, he simultaneously indulged in it. No longer did he affix to the door of the church, as had been customary, the tax on burials, thereby concealing the fact that he charged more than his predecessors. It was also worth noting, she felt, that he followed unfair practices of taxation by which poor people were disproportionately charged, and their taxes were distributed among the more fortunate inhabitants whose labors did provide sufficient means upon which to live.[55]

The temerity of the Spanish priest, Mme. de Soto charged, even extended to the encroachment upon civil powers, exercising "with despotism a right that does not belong to him." To support this charge, a number of instances were cited in which Father Quintanilla had, at least in her estimation, meddled in other affairs that should not have concerned him.[56] On behalf of the be-

---

52. Marie de St. Denis de Soto to Commandant, *Rex* v. *de Soto,* in Natchitoches Parish Records, Doc. 1227.
53. *Ibid.*
54. *Ibid.*
55. *Ibid.*
56. *Ibid.*

leaguered priest, it must be noted that at least some of the cited instances represented situations in which Father Quintanilla had stepped on the lady's toes, rather than overstepped the bounds of his office.[57] In summary, Mme. de Soto requested that Commandant De Mézières refer both Father Quintanilla's charges and her own to his religious superior, the vicar general of the colony.[58]

The only other existing document filed in this case is the curé's reply to the lady's attack. Father Quintanilla acknowledged receipt of De Mézières' letter informing him of Mme. de Soto's remarks. He was not worried and had no objection to a review of the facts by the vicar general. He did, however, want to know just what the commandant intended to do about his sister-in-law, her slave, and the Sieur Metoyer. This time, for the first time, Father Quintanilla signed his petition in a drastically less confident manner. This time he was "Your Majesty's attentive servant and chaplain, Fr. Luis de Quintanilla, *humble* Capuchin."[59] The Spanish curé had been subdued. No longer did he proclaim himself supreme.

The legal disposition of this case is no longer a matter of record. It is apparent from the events which followed, however, that Quintanilla had no success in severing the alliance between Marie Thérèze Coincoin and Pierre Metoyer. Yet he may well be credited with achieving for the slave a great measure of good, even though it was not quite that which he had set out to achieve.

Father Quintanilla strove to assist Marie Thérèze in obtaining the end which he deemed the most important goal in any Christian life: salvation of the soul.

57. Mme. de Soto and Quintanilla had already come into conflict, for example, over the succession of her late brother, Louis Juchereau de St. Denis, Jr. Prior to his death, St. Denis had requested the commandant to draw up a will for him leaving his estate to his half-Indian wife, Marie Derbanne Barbier, by whom he had no children. De Mézières refused, for under colonial law St. Denis' siblings or their heirs (which included the heirs of the late Mme. De Mézières) should inherit his estate. After De Mézières' refusal, St. Denis, almost as a dying request, asked the priest to help his wife obtain the inheritance. Father Quintanilla did just that, and by so doing he earned the enmity of Mme. de Soto, who subsequently went to great lengths to have her brother's wish disallowed so that she might inherit a share of the estate. Porteous (trans.), "Index to the Spanish Judicial Records of Louisiana," 177–93.

58. Marie de St. Denis de Soto to Commandant, *Rex* v. *de Soto,* in Natchitoches Parish Records, Doc. 1227.

59. Father Quintanilla to A. De Mézières, *ibid.* Italics mine.

Tradition among her descendants holds that this was not a consideration which she took lightly; her descendants strongly assert that she remained as faithful to Metoyer as any Christian wife was expected to be and that she died a devout Catholic. Yet, she was not his wife and, in defiance of Christian precepts, she clung tenaciously to this man whom she had chosen.

Father Quintanilla had counseled Marie Thérèze and Metoyer to marry, but his advice was not practical. Pierre Metoyer was French; Marie Thérèze was African. Had they lived in France and had Marie Thérèze not been a slave, there would have been no legal impediment to the marriage. Under the terms of the *Code Noir* of colonial Louisiana, however, any marriage between a white and a black slave would have resulted in their expulsion from the colony.[60] Perhaps Quintanilla was ignorant of the law or else he placed moral precepts above legal and financial considerations. At any rate, the priest's advice was ignored and the couple continued to live in concubinage.

The expulsion of Marie Thérèze from Metoyer's household presented additional problems for Metoyer. The children born to him and Marie Thérèze were legally the property of the mother's owner, Mme. de Soto. As noted in Father Quintanilla's first complaint, Metoyer had already purchased four of these children in order to prevent their sale in the event something should happen to their mistress.[61] The children were now legally a part of Metoyer's household, but their mother was not. Reestablishment of a normal family relationship could never be affected as long as Marie Thérèze remained the property of Mme. de Soto and Father Quintanilla continued his opposition.

Therefore, in July, 1778, Metoyer reached an agreement with Mme. de Soto for the purchase of Marie Thérèze and the son who had been born to her since her expulsion, Joseph Antoine. The complete purchase price of 1,500 *livres* could not be immediately met; Metoyer paid only half and agreed to assume responsibility for the payment of a financial obligation of Mme. de

---

60. Article 6 of the *Code Noir* stated: "It must be absolutely prohibited to all white subjects of either sex to contract marriage with any blacks or mulattoes, upon pain of being dishonorably expelled from the Colony." *Code Noir ou Loi Municipal Servant de Reglement* (New Orleans, 1778), 2.

61. The purchase of his four oldest children was executed by Metoyer on March 31, 1776; Mrs. Manuel de Soto to Pierre Metoyer, Sale of Slaves, in Natchitoches Parish Records, Doc. 1161.

Soto that was equal to the remainder which he owed to her.[62] Although Commandant De Mézières had ordered Metoyer not to purchase the woman at the time that he expelled her from Metoyer's household, this order was ignored and no legal recriminations resulted.

The purchase of Marie Thérèze by Metoyer enabled the couple to resume their cohabitation; however, it presented still more problems. A further article of the *Code Noir* demanded that any master who fathered children by his own slave should suffer the loss of the slave and the child; both would be sold for the benefit of the hospital and never be allowed freedom.[63] Metoyer's alliance with Marie Thérèze had already produced seven children; future cohabitation would undoubtedly result in still more, and it was obviously not Metoyer's desire to forfeit Marie Thérèze and the next child born to them for the benefit of the hospital. Therefore, shortly after the execution of the purchase of 1778, Metoyer called in two friends and neighbors; taking advantage of the liberal manumission policy of the Spanish government, he declared, in a private document drawn before his friends, that Marie Thérèze and their infant son Joseph were henceforth free.[64]

Marie Thérèze was now thirty-eight years of age. Although she was free, she had no money or property of her own. In contrast to many other former slaves whose white benefactors gave them homes or other property, Marie Thérèze received nothing at this time except her freedom. She was no longer young, but her legendary success was still many years away. Before its attainment the freed woman still had a hard row to hoe.

---

62. Marie de St. Denis to Pierre Metoyer, *ibid.,* Doc. 1312; Baptism of Antoine Joseph, February 8, 1778, in Natchitoches Registers, Book 4, p. 312.

63. *Code Noir,* Article 10, p. 3.

64. Testament of Claude Thomas Pierre Metoyer, February 26, 1783, Acts of Leonardo Mazange, No. 7 (January 2–April 7, 1783), in New Orleans Notarial Archives (Civil Courts Building, New Orleans), 188–91.

Chapter TWO

The Life and Labors
of a Former Slave

In 1778 free nonwhites were a very small minority at the Natchitoches post. The census of 1776, the last one taken before Marie Thérèze's manumission, indicated that of a total population of 1,021 there were 430 nonwhites and only 8 of these were free. Three of the free people of color enumerated on that census died or moved away shortly afterward; by 1785 there were still only eight free nonwhites at the post. Marie Thérèze, Antoine Joseph, and the two additional sons born to her after her manumission constituted half of this free nonwhite population in 1785.[1]

The attainment of freedom, initially, had little effect on the life-style of Marie Thérèze Coincoin. For a half dozen more years she remained with Metoyer under roughly the same status that she had held before Father Quintanilla's interference. The now complacent priest had withdrawn his opposition to the alliance, and the controversy had subsided. Metoyer did not bother to make public the fact that the woman in his household was no longer his slave and that she remained there by mutual agreement. When their eighth child, Marie Françoise Roselie, was born in 1780 and when her brother Pierre was born two years later, Father Quintanilla identified their mother on the occasion of both baptisms as "the slave of Metoyer."[2]

In 1780 Metoyer purchased from Mme. de Soto his two remaining children whom the lady still owned: Dominique, aged six, and Eulalie, aged four.[3] As in the case of the four eldest children whom he purchased in 1776, Metoyer

---

1. Bolton, *Athanase De Mézières*, 134–135; *An Account of Louisiana, Being an Abstract of Documents in the Offices of the Department of State and of the Treasury* (Philadelphia, 1803), 45.

2. Baptism of Maria Francisca Rosalia, December 24, 1780, and Baptism of Pedro Todos Santos, November 10, 1782, in Natchitoches Registers, Book 4, pp. 322, 330.

3. Marie de St. Denis to Pierre Metoyer, in Natchitoches Parish Records, Doc. 1473.

did not give these children their freedom. He did, however, soon indicate his intention to do so.

Pierre Metoyer was a regular visitor to the colonial seat of government, the burgeoning city of New Orleans. Not only did he still have a brother there[4]— the only relative that he seems to have had in the colonies—but he was also a man of growing means by this time and regularly conducted business in the provincial capital. On one such journey to the city he visited a notary and requested a document to be drawn up for him, a document which he apparently was hesitant to file in the small and gossiping post where he made his home.

In February, 1783, before the royal notary Leonardo Mazange, Metoyer executed his last will and testament. It is obvious from the document that he was not willing to acknowledge legally the paternity of his children; yet his sense of justice required him to arrange for the future financial security of his offspring and of the woman who had served him in every possible way for some sixteen years. In a later, public, and less incriminating will, Metoyer was to go into great detail about his family background and his relatives, both living and dead. In this 1783 document, however, which he quietly filed in a distant city, Metoyer obviously sought to avoid unnecessary embarrassment to his blood ties by identifying none of them by name. Not even his place of origin was specified.[5]

The will began with the customary acknowledgment of his faith and his unworthiness, the commendation of his soul to God, and the specifications of desired funeral arrangements. Then, apparently unwilling to embarrass his

---

4. In his will of 1801 Metoyer referred to his brother at New Orleans but did not name him. The 1790 militia roll of the city includes the name of only one Metoyer, Nicolas. Since this was the name of Pierre's father in France, the Nicolas of New Orleans may be assumed to be the brother whom Pierre had in that city. See Summaria formada sobre un Memorial que intentaban presentar los Milicianos del batallon de la Nueva Orleans, Legajo 168e, in Papeles Procedentes de Cuba, Archivo General de Indias, Seville, Spain.

5. Acts of Leonardo Mazange, in New Orleans Notarial Archives, No. 7, 188–91. Although Pierre Metoyer stated in this will that he "had no children," his paternity of the children of Marie Thérèze was, and has since been, widely recognized in the area. In 1883, for example, a white granddaughter of Metoyer, Mme. Valery Gaiennie, made a sworn statement to their family attorney that her grandfather *was* the father of "a colored son, Augustin," and of Augustin's siblings. See "Notes," Safford Collection (Eugene P. Watson Memorial Library, Northwestern State University, Natchitoches), Box 2, Folder 12.

family publicly and irrevocably by acknowledging his sixteen years of public concubinage, the usually verbose Metoyer next wrote one paragraph of uncharacteristic terseness. In its entirety it stated, "I declare to be a bachelor and not to have any children." With his name forever cleared, he proceeded to devote the remainder, and major part, of his testament to arrangements providing for the future needs of the black woman with whom he lived and the Franco-African children whom she had borne during the years of their cohabitation.[6]

First, an acknowledgment was made of the still-private paper by which he had freed Marie Thérèze in 1778. His wish was expressed that this paper be as completely binding as it would have been if executed before proper authorities, and he requested his executors not to put any obstacle in the way of her enjoyment of complete liberty. Second, the six Franco-African children born to Marie Thérèze prior to her purchase and subsequent freedom were promised their freedom upon his death.[7]

Metoyer also took steps to provide these children with a measure of security. To them and their free-born brothers Metoyer bequeathed a tract of land of five *arpents*[8] frontage on both sides of Red River (later Cane River) bordering his own tract that the Spanish crown had granted him. Finally, Metoyer proclaimed that after his death, should the value of his estate in the colonies exceed the debts which he owed, two-thirds of the remainder would go to his family in France (still unnamed) as the law required, and the remaining third must be divided among the Franco-African children of Marie Thérèze Coincoin. As long as she lived, however, the mother was to have the use and enjoyment of whatever estate her children inherited from him.[9]

On September 26 of the following year, 1784, Marie Thérèze gave birth to her last child, François. By this time her manumission had become public knowledge.[10] Within the next four years her emancipation was to become complete.

6. *Ibid.*

7. *Ibid.*, 189.

8. An *arpent* during this period was equal to slightly less than one acre.

9. Acts of Leonardo Mazange, in New Orleans Notarial Archives, No. 7, 189–90.

10. Baptism of François, October 4, 1784, in Natchitoches Registers, Book 4, p. 345. This entry identifies Marie Thérèze as a "*free* Negress."

Pierre and Marie Thérèze were now in their forties. For Metoyer the accumulation of years had brought new desires, new cares, and new wisdom. Enslaved by moral principles that were undoubtedly weighing more heavily upon his mind and by the deeply ingrained consciousness of his family's social position, he could not free himself to recognize the illegitimate children which he must have wanted to acknowledge. Pierre Metoyer was now entering the last third of his life and he had no sons to whom he could legally bequeath the considerable fortune that he was now accumulating. Moreover, the captivating woman whose charms had lifted her from the hopeless station of her birth was now a matronly forty-two years of age.

It was apparently in 1786 that Pierre Metoyer and Marie Thérèze Coincoin agreed to end their alliance. In November of that year he gave to her the land that he had bequeathed to her children in the will of 1783. Marie Thérèze promptly petitioned the Spanish government for full title, and on January 18, 1787, the concession was confirmed in her name.[11]

It was also promised, apparently at this same time, that Metoyer would pay to her a lifetime stipend of 120 piasters per year.[12] This land and annuity, he felt, would be sufficient for the basic needs of Marie Thérèze and their children. It was not an overly generous sum; in Spanish Louisiana the unpretentious rank of military drummer brought an income of 200 piasters annually.[13] Moreover, Metoyer stipulated that upon the death of Marie Thérèze the property and cash that he had donated to her must be divided among her surviving Franco-African children. The black offspring whom she had borne before their alliance should not inherit the products of Metoyer's labor. As was the case with her manumission, this contract was privately drawn. Not until October, 1788, was a copy filed with the commandant of the post.[14]

Having provided sufficiently, according to his own conscience, for the

11. Book of Patents, 17–18, and File A1679, Maria Thereza, Free Negress, in State Land Records (State Land Office, Baton Rouge). This land is identified on American survey maps as Sections 18 and 89 of Township 8 North, Range 6 West in the Côte Joyeuse area of lower Natchitoches Parish.

12. The existence of this document is noted in the Index to French Archives, Natchitoches Parish Records, as Pierre Metoyer to Marie Thérèze Coincoin, Donation, Doc. 2119. The actual document is missing. In his will of 1801, Metoyer reiterates the terms of the document.

13. Bolton, *Athanase De Mézières*, II, 122.

14. Metoyer to Marie Thérèze, Donation, in Natchitoches Parish Records, Doc. 2119; 1801 will of Claude Thomas Pierre Metoyer (MS in Natchitoches Parish Library).

needs of Marie Thérèze and her children, Metoyer chose for himself a legal wife of his own race and social background, a woman who also bore the same name as his mistress. The wife whom he chose was Marie Thérèze Buard, the widow of his old friend from La Rochelle, Étienne Pavie. In October, 1788, Pierre drew up his contract of marriage with the widow.

Although he was still reluctant to publicly and legally acknowledge the existence of illegitimate children, Metoyer nevertheless exercised extreme caution in the draft of his marriage contract in order to protect the rights of those children. It was clearly specified that the Franco-African children of Marie Thérèze whom he still held in slavery would not become part of the community property shared by himself and his new wife. Moreover, by the terms of this document, he reserved for himself the right to free those offspring at his discretion.[15]

With the Widow Pavie, Metoyer began a new life and soon assumed a place of leadership in the economic, civic, and even ecclesiastical affairs of the community. As syndic, he took the church census in 1790[16] and handled the church's preemption claim against the United States Land Office in the early 1800s.[17] His plantations flourished, he enlarged his original grant with the acquisition of a number of tracts, and the census of 1810 shows him to be, by far, the largest slaveholder in the parish, owning 103 men, women, and children.[18] But the greatest blessing that came to him in those years was one that

15. This document, which is listed in the Index to French Archives, Natchitoches Parish Records, as Pierre Metoyer and Vve. Étienne Pavie, Marriage Contract, Doc. 2121, is also missing. Some of the terms of the document were reiterated in Metoyer's will of 1801.

16. Répartition a L'ocasion de 75 p. que La Comunote de Mes^{rs} Les habitants son Convenu de Payer a Mr J. B^{te} Maurin fette le l^r Mars 1790, in Natchitoches Parish Records Collection (Department of Archives, Louisiana State University, Baton Rouge), Folder 1. Hereinafter cited as Natchitoches Parish Records Collection, LSU.

Syndics in Spanish Louisiana were justices of the peace, appointed to office, and established at distances of three leagues apart. Subordinate to the commandant, they were permitted to hold court and render decisions in small cases and held police authority over roads, taxes, Negroes, and travelers. *An Account of Louisiana*, 35.

17. File 260–873, Congregation of the Roman Catholic Church, *American State Papers: Documents Legislative and Executive of the Congress of the United States* (38 vols.; Washington, D.C.: Gales & Seaton, 1832–1861), *Public Lands*, III, 195; Section Map, Township 9 North, Range 7 West, Section 43, Lot 26, State Land Records.

18. Third Census of the United States, 1810. Numerous entries for purchases of land by Metoyer are entered in French Archives Index and Index to Conveyances, 1800–1880, Natchitoches Parish Records.

he could never have enjoyed with Marie Thérèze Coincoin. The new Marie Thérèze, who was a number of years younger than her predecessor, gave Metoyer the offspring he could acknowledge, two sons and a daughter.[19]

In 1786 Marie Thérèze Coincoin was forty-four years of age. Most of her life, apparently, had been spent as a house servant. Almost two decades had been dedicated to serving the French gentleman who had found her attractive and who was willing to shelter her and provide for her needs in return for her service and devotion. Now in the middle of the fifth decade of her life, Marie Thérèze was a free woman, legally and emotionally, dependent for the most part upon her own abilities and resources for the present and future welfare of her offspring. Despite her age and apparent inexperience, Marie Thérèze took to the fields.[20]

For the newly freed black woman and her children these years were undoubtedly lean ones. There was an infinity of difference between the absolute dependency of a slave and the responsibilities of a free citizen; the chasm could not be bridged in a day or even a year. Although Marie Thérèze had been legally free for eight years, she had remained sheltered, protected, and provided for by Metoyer. Not until the dissolution of their relationship was she forced to accept the responsibilities of her new station. Overnight she was given a tract of land, and along with it was thrust upon her the sole responsibility for its success or failure. Such a transition was not an easy one. Numerous slaves in that era were freed and given tracts of land upon which they lived and died in drudging poverty. Marie Thérèze Coincoin, however, was destined to succeed where the others failed.

Marie Thérèze settled in a small cabin on the sixty-eight acres given to her by Metoyer and began the cultivation of tobacco, an important industry in this Spanish colony. When properly grown and cured, Louisiana tobacco was of such excellent quality that it was used in the manufacture of the famed Havana cigars. The Natchitoches crop, although it represented only a fraction of the total produced in the colony, was noted especially for its superior quality.[21] It

19. Metoyer's will of 1801 identifies his three legitimate children (MS in Natchitoches Parish Library).
20. It is hardly surprising that Marie Thérèze turned to agriculture as a livelihood. An agrarian-based culture was a predominant characteristic of the Ewe linguistic group to which Marie Thérèze's parent(s) belonged. Blassingame, *The Slave Community,* 2.
21. Lewis C. Gray, *History of Agriculture in the Southern United States to 1860* (2 vols.; reprinted Gloucester, Mass., 1958), I, 73.

was the dark, aromatic leaves from Natchitoches that Longfellow mentally savored when he penned his famous *Evangeline:*

> Then from his station aloft, at the head of the table, the herdsman
> Poured forth his heart and his wine together in endless profusion
> Lighting his pipe, that was filled with sweet Natchitoches tobacco. . . .

The tobacco industry of Spanish Louisiana was controlled rigorously by specifications designed to maintain this famed quality. In 1777 Galvez issued a seventeen-point set of regulations covering every aspect of tobacco production, planting, harvesting, shipping, and marketing. Severe penalties were exacted upon all who deliberately or carelessly violated the regulations.[22]

Meeting minute and rigid governmental regulations was but a small part of the difficulties faced by Marie Thérèze in the operation of her tobacco farm. Production of the crop was even more complex than the governmental marketing regulations. Le Page du Pratz provided an excellent description of tobacco farming in colonial Louisiana. According to his account, the extremely small seed was first sown very thinly in a prepared bed of the best soil available, then covered with ashes to the thickness of a small coin to discourage worms. As soon as each tobacco plant sprouted four leaves it was transplanted in prepared holes a foot broad and three feet apart. If the transplanting was not done immediately after a rain, the seedlings had to be watered.[23]

Until the young plants fully took root they were lightly covered during the day with leaves plucked the night before, and each plant was examined daily throughout its growing season to keep it free of caterpillars. Weeding was a cautious process, with growers taking great care not to touch the hoe to the plant; with each weeding new earth was pulled to the plant to provide it with more nourishment. When the plant began to sprout suckers, these must be pulled; if they were permitted to form branches the leaves would be undernourished. Similar care was taken, for the same reason, not to let a plant form more than twelve leaves.[24]

At harvest, the leaves were stripped from the stalk, strung, and hung in the

22. *Annual Report of the American Historical Association, 1945,* II; Lawrence Kinnaird (ed.), *Spain in the Mississippi Valley, 1765–1794,* Part I, *The Revolutionary Period, 1765–1781* (Washington, 1949), 297–98.

23. Antoine-Simon Le Page du Pratz, *The History of Louisiana* (trans. from the French, London, 1774, reprinted at New Orleans,1947), 172.

24. *Ibid.*

air. When dry they were usually piled in heaps to make them sweat out still more moisture. At the proper stage of dryness they were rolled into bundles, wrapped in a cloth, and bound. Twenty-four hours later each cloth was untied and each bundle rolled still more tightly in order to meet market regulations.[25]

In view of the exacting and personal attention which had to be given to each plant individually, it is surprising that a woman alone, with no slaves and no labor other than that of her children, should have attempted the cultivation of tobacco. But this was the crop which Marie Thérèze chose to plant. With experience her harvest grew until, by 1792, her annual production was of such size that she was sending her own barge to New Orleans, loaded with rolls of tobacco for sale in the markets of the provincial capital. One passport for shipment, issued by the commandant to Marie Thérèze, has been preserved. In April, 1792, Louis De Blanc checked out a barge load for the former slave and granted it a pass to New Orleans in company with a bateau belonging to Pierre Metoyer. Exclusive of other commodities, this shipment of Metoyer and Marie Thérèze contained 9,900 *carotes,* or rolls, of tobacco.[26]

The legend of Marie Thérèze has not preserved any details of her experiences in planting this popular crop, but it has preserved reports of more venturesome endeavors to accumulate capital. For generations her descendants have recounted how their family's matriarch trapped the wild bears in the Natchitoches wilderness and sent bear grease to market in large stone jars brought from the Mediterranean. Although the exportation of bear grease was a thriving business in early Natchitoches, by the Spanish period it was not widely practiced. According to one authority, the New Orleans market was normally supplied with shipments from the St. Francis River Valley.[27] Yet the passport for the 1792 barge sent by Marie Thérèze to New Orleans included shipment of three hundred hides and two barrels of grease.[28]

In all probability it was her older sons who did the trapping for Marie Thérèze, for it is definitely known that she did not yet own slaves at this point

25. *Ibid.,* 173.

26. État de la Cargaison d'un Bateau Apartenant a Pierre Metoyer et d'un Gabarre a Marie Thérèze, in Holmes Collection, Reel 1.

27. Gray, *Agriculture in Southern United States,* I, 78; Heloize H. Cruzat (trans.), "Louisiana in 1724," *Louisiana Historical Quarterly,* XII (January, 1929), 122.

28. État de la Cargaison, in Holmes Collection.

of her career. Hunting quite possibly was a major source of provision and income for Marie Thérèze and her family. Not only bears but a variety of animals and fowl proliferated in the parish, and the 1801 will of Pierre Metoyer notes that he was indebted to Marie Thérèze for some turkeys that she had furnished him.[29]

Another tradition among the people holds that the main crop Marie Thérèze produced was indigo. The records which provide information on her economic endeavors mention only tobacco; yet it is not outside the realm of possibility that she did cultivate a second crop. It would hardly have been possible for Marie Thérèze to have planted her entire sixty-eight acres in such a crop as tobacco that demanded careful attention to each individual plant, and, despite the legend of the matriarch's innovation, indigo had been a factor in the economy of Natchitoches for many years. Moreover, both of Marie Thérèze's neighbors, Claude Thomas Pierre Metoyer and Jean Baptiste Ailhaud de Ste. Anne, operated indigo processing sheds.[30] For Marie Thérèze indigo would have been a convenient crop. Moreover, the succession inventory of Pierre Metoyer, the son who took over the operation of her plantation after her retirement, included an indigo sower.[31]

A fourth, very probable, source of income for Marie Thérèze was the manufacture of medicine. Descendants of this enterprising woman relate the tradition that she was extremely knowledgeable in the use and application of native medicinal herbs and roots. Medicine was perenially short in colonial Louisiana, and much of what was available for use was actually manufactured in the northwestern section of the colony from plants that grew in the area.[32] In view of the prevalence of this enterprise in her region, it seems safe to assume that a

29. Natchitoches Parish Library.

30. File A1714, J. B. Ailhaud Ste. Anne, and File A1684, Pierre Metoyer, State Land Records.

31. File A1679, Maria Thereza, Free Negress, *ibid.;* Succession of Pierre Metoyer, f. m. c., in Natchitoches Parish Records, No. 193.

32. Davis, *Louisiana,* 134. In colonial days, all settlers of the "northwestern section" were habitants of the area broadly known as Natchitoches. In fact, the original parish of Natchitoches covered an area that was roughly 120 miles long by seventy broad and included all or part of the present parishes of Caddo, Claiborne, Webster, Bossier, Lincoln, Sabine, De Soto, Bienville, Winn, Red River, and Grant; *Biographical and Historical Memoirs of Northwest Louisiana* (Nashville, 1890), 293.

woman of Marie Thérèze's alleged talent and initiative would not have ignored such a likely source of income.

By 1793 Marie Thérèze had succeeded in establishing an efficient plantation operation on her small tract and she desired to extend her holdings. Much unclaimed land still lay within the parish, and the colonial government encouraged increased production by its citizens by freely granting lands of reasonable quantities to deserving heads of households. It was probably in late 1793 that Marie Thérèze petitioned for a grant of land; on May 14, 1794, that petition was answered with the grant of a concession of twenty *arpents* frontage by a depth of forty, located on the west bank of the Old River branch of the Red River.[33]

It has long been believed by the descendants of Marie Thérèze that she was the recipient of a grant of land from the king of France or Spain, a grant which she received through the influence of her former master. Upon this land she supposedly labored, alongside her slaves, clearing it and developing it, and upon her death the royal grant was divided among her many children. Although details of the legend vary, the basic story appears to be grounded upon fact.

The statement that Marie Thérèze received a grant "from the King," is also one of the most disputed points of the legend. One newspaper feature article which denied the validity of the legend in general and the existence of any such grant, asserted: "She never received a land grant from the King. . . . I repeat, the King . . . never even knew of the existence of Marie Thérèze Coincoin."[34] The point is arguable. Marie Thérèze was definitely the recipient of a sizable grant of land in the Spanish colonial era, and all actions taken by the colonial government were taken in the monarch's name. O'Reilly's land ordinance of 1770, which remained in effect until 1798, specifically stated: "All grants shall be made in the name of the King."[35]

---

33. File B2146, Maria Therese Metoyer, State Land Records. This land is identified on section maps as Section 55 of Township 8 North, Range 7 West, in the southern half of Natchitoches Parish.

34. Louis R. Nardini, Sr., "Legends about Marie Therese Disputed by Local Historian and Author," Natchitoches *Times,* October 22, 1972.

35. "O'Reilly's Ordinance of 1770," *Louisiana Historical Quarterly,* XI (April, 1928), 240.

The person of influence who assisted Marie Thérèze in obtaining her grant is usually identified as Mme. de St. Denis; it appears more probable, however, that it was Pierre Metoyer who provided the assistance. Mme. de St. Denis had been dead for many years. Moreover, this grant was issued in the name of "Maria Therese Metoyer," which is the only instance on record that this surname was assigned to Marie Thérèze. Further indication is provided by the fact that a request of Metoyer for a grant of land was approved by the colonial government at the same time that Marie Thérèze's was approved. In all probability the two petitions were submitted simultaneously.[36]

Grants made in Spanish Louisiana were basically free, but certain regulations nevertheless were to be followed by all recipients. A small but immediate cash outlay was required in the form of a surveyor's fee, based upon the actual size of the grant, and no title to a grant was complete until the survey was made. At many posts, however, the enforcement of this requirement was lax and those who lacked the required cash remained in possession of the land without benefit of survey, without a complete title, and without disturbance. Some 75 percent of the grants in the Natchitoches area, it has been estimated, remained in this state of legal limbo.[37] Marie Thérèze's concession was included among this number.

In other respects, however, the law was more rigorously enforced. The first matter to be attended was, of necessity, the clearance of the land. Within the first three years of possession, grantees were required to clear the entire front of their tract to the depth of two *arpents*. Every inhabitant was bound to enclose, within this same period, the front of his land, and for the enclosure of the remainder of his property he had to reach an agreement with his neighbors.

It was also required of all grantees that they construct and repair roads, bridges, and embankments where necessary and keep them in good repair; this requirement was rigorously enforced since it was levied in lieu of taxes. If the lands granted were used for grazing, all cattle had to be branded. Failure to meet the required conditions would result in the forfeiture of the entire grant.[38]

36. File A1684, Pierre Metoyer, State Land Records.
37. *An Account of Louisiana*, 26–27.
38. "O'Reilly's Ordinance of 1770," 237–40; *An Account of Louisiana*, 38.

The obligation which Marie Thérèze assumed in accepting this grant of land was not a small one. In meeting her responsibilities, she, her sons, and the slaves she eventually purchased undoubtedly expended every bit of the labor attributed to them by the legend.

The grant which Marie Thérèze obtained was not high-quality farm land. It was not sought for the establishment of a family residence or plantation, and apparently neither she nor her family ever used it as such. Initially, Marie Thérèze utilized the land as a *vacherie,* a grazing range for her cattle. Herding had already become a major industry in central Louisiana, especially on such rolling hill land as her grant included. About 1797, after making the improvements required of her in the first three years of possession, Marie Thérèze hired a Spaniard named José Maré to move upon the *vacherie* for her. For ten years he oversaw her cattle business and cultivated the land in corn and other crops. By 1807 the Spaniard either died or developed wanderlust, and no other hirelings were employed.[39]

In these first years of economic growth, Marie Thérèze had one overriding goal: the liberation of her still enslaved children. She had brought fourteen children into the world. Two of her living children, Pierre Toussaint and François, were free from birth. A third free-born, Marie Françoise Roselie, had not survived infancy, and a fourth, Marie Eulalie, had died in her teens.[40] A fifth, Antoine Joseph, had been bought and freed by his father as a nursing baby. Five more were now the property of their father: Nicolas Augustin, Marie Suzanne, Louis, Pierre, and Dominique. But for these children there was no immediate need for concern. As long as Claude Thomas Pierre Metoyer was alive, their enslavement was little more than a legality. It was to her other children, the black ones, that Marie Thérèze first turned her attention.

The first of her children whom Marie Thérèze purchased was her eldest daughter, Marie Louise. In the fall of 1786, Marie Thérèze entered into an

39. File B2146, Maria Therese Metoyer, State Land Records. Gray notes that the potential of the cattle industry was recognized and encouraged by officials of Louisiana as early as 1770; see his *Agriculture in Southern United States,* I, 150.

40. The 1783 will of Metoyer did not mention Marie Françoise Roselie, who had been born in 1780; apparently she had died within that brief interim. In his will of 1801, Metoyer noted that Marie Eulalie was still alive in 1788 but had since died.

agreement with a resident of the parish, Sieur Pierre Dolet, for the purchase of this daughter. Inasmuch as Marie Louise was a cripple, the result of a gun accident, Dolet agreed to a price of only three hundred piasters, a very small sum for a twenty-seven-year-old female slave. Since Marie Thérèze had not yet begun her plantation operation and was of limited means, Dolet agreed further to accept payment in three annual installments. He also stated that he was freeing Marie Louise at that time.[41] Apparently, some technicality or legal difficulty subsequently arose, since nine years later Marie Thérèze appeared before the commandant and again declared Marie Louise to be free.[42]

As a free woman, Marie Louise remained close to her mother and half-siblings, undoubtedly assisting them in the development of their estates. The contention is sometimes made that the half-French children of Marie Thérèze were ashamed of their African ancestry and severed all ties with that part of their past. The records do not support this idea; Marie Louise *dit* Mariotte is often mentioned in the church records as godmother to Metoyer nieces and nephews.[43] Census and legal records indicate that she lived with them in the Isle Brevelle community,[44] and her grandchildren intermarried with their Metoyer cousins.[45]

In the years since Mme. de Soto had sold Marie Thérèze to Metoyer, the de Sotos had moved from Natchitoches. Don Manuel had finally been freed by Spanish authorities and together he, his wife, and younger children started a new life at the post of St. Landry des Opelousas in south Louisiana. With them they took Thérèze, the second daughter of Marie Thérèze. By 1790, young Thérèze was herself almost thirty and the mother of at least one child. Unlike her own mother, she had failed to find a French gentleman to provide

---

41. Pierre Dolet to Marie Thérèze Coincoin (MS in Cammie G. Henry Collection, Eugene P. Watson Memorial Library, Northwestern State University of Louisiana, Natchitoches), Old Natchitoches Data, II, 289.

42. Marie Thérèze to Marie Louise, in Natchitoches Parish Records, Doc. 2596.

43. For example, see Baptism of Marie Susanne, daughter of Dominique and Marguerite [Metoyer], June 6, 1802, in Natchitoches Registers, Book 5.

44. For example, see Third Census of the United States, 1810.

45. For example, see *Philippe Valsain* v. *Cloutier,* in Natchitoches Parish Records, District Court Record Book 3, pp. 118–26, and Marie Louise Doralise Dupre to C. F. Benoist, Mortgage, in Natchitoches Parish Records Collection, LSU, Box 14, Folder 62. The first document identifies Marie Doralise Dupre as the granddaughter of Marie Louise Mariotte; the second document indicates that Marie Doralise married J. B. D. Metoyer, grandson of Marie Thérèze.

her with the opportunity for social and economic advancement. Moreover, her mistress, Mme. de Soto, was now an invalid and aging woman. The future which faced young Thérèze was an uncertain one.[46]

After completing payment of the debt she had assumed in the purchase of her first daughter, Marie Thérèze began to save again for the purchase of her second-born. In the fall of 1790 she set out for Opelousas, a distance of 120 miles by way of prairies and forests, with only fifty dollars and the infinite hope that spurs mothers to action. Marie Thérèze was determined to make arrangements with her former mistress for the freedom of her daughter and grandson. Mme. de Soto, the shrewd, dominant, and hard-bitten matron whom few people ever bested, not only accepted the small downpayment that was proffered but agreed to a total price for the two slaves that was surprisingly small. In the fall of 1790, Mme. de Soto personally penned her own deed of sale:

> On this day . . . I, Dona Maria Nieves de St. Denis, legitimate wife of Don Manuel de Soto, in presence of the undersigned witnesses, declare to my Negress named Teresa, for her prompt and faithful service which at all times she has rendered me, and especially rendered me in my infirmities, inasmuch as it is she who has handled everything, I have conceded her the privilege of being sold by me, with her mulatto son Joseph Mauricio of the age of nine years, to her mother Maria Teresa, free Negress, for the sum of seven hundred dollars.[47]

The stipulation was made, however, that young Thérèze and her son must continue to serve Mme. de Soto in her illness until her death occurred. At that time the two slaves would become the property of Thérèze's mother and would remain so as long as they paid to the de Soto heirs the remaining amount due within a year and a half after Mme. de Soto's demise. In the meantime, in order to help Thérèze and Marie Thérèze raise the money to pay the remaining $650, Mme. de Soto agreed to permit Thérèze to raise cattle in partnership with one Maria del Marger. No statements were made as to how the young black slave would obtain the necessary stock to enter the cattle business; apparently, the stock or requisite capital was also furnished by her mother.[48]

46. Marie St. Denis to Marie Thérèze Coincoin, in Natchitoches Parish Records. Doc. 2804.
47. *Ibid.*
48. *Ibid.*

In the years that followed, Mme. de Soto made further entries on the document. No additional receipts for actual cash are included, but on two separate occasions the physically deteriorating Mme. de Soto recorded that she was allowing Thérèze and her son a discount on their debt in appreciation for the "continuous and prompt solicitude" that they had shown in the "protracted infirmities which for almost ten years I have been suffering in this bed without hope of any health."[49]

Marie de St. Denis de Soto lingered on for seven years after she agreed to sell Thérèze and the child to Marie Thérèze. The last rites of the church were finally administered to the dying woman at her home near Opelousas in the summer of 1797.[50] As promised, Marie Thérèze's daughter and her grandson were passed to her for manumission. There still remained on the debt a balance of $490. Mme. de Soto's heirs and executors accepted from Thérèze the payment of six head of cattle, valued at $40, to be applied toward this debt, but no record can be found of how the mother or the daughter cleared the balance. The following month Thérèze and Joseph Mauricio became the property of their mother and grandmother, and by the old matriarch they were freed.[51]

The circumstances of the manumission of young Thérèze bear striking resemblance to one facet of the legend of Marie Thérèze Coincoin. In exchange for her solicitous care and nursing abilities, allegedly, Marie Thérèze was given her freedom by Mme. de St. Denis. However, the family that preserved this story did not preserve the memory of a younger Thérèze, a daughter who bore her mother's name. It is easy to speculate that over the years the identities of these two individuals have become fused into a single personality, and that the story of the manumission of young Thérèze has been inadvertently attributed to the mother.

Little is known of the life of young Thérèze after her manumission. As a free woman she apparently adopted as a surname the name favored by her master, Don Manuel, because documents relating to the partition of Marie Thérèze's grant among her children identify one of the recipients of this land

49. *Ibid.*
50. August 10, 1797, Registers of the Parish of St. Landry des Opelousas (St. Landry Catholic Church, Opelousas, Louisiana), Book 1, p. 33.
51. Marie St. Denis to Marie Thérèze Coincoin, Natchitoches Parish Records, Doc. 2804.

as Marie Thérèze Don Manuel. Thérèze remained at the Opelousas post, where two additional children were apparently born to her after her purchase by her mother. In 1820 she and her oldest son, Joseph, were both free heads of households in St. Landry Parish.[52] In all probability their descendants remain there.

Late in 1794 Marie Thérèze executed another slave purchase and manumission. This fourth recipient of her love and generosity was also a grandchild, the natural daughter of her still single and still enslaved Metoyer son, Louis.[53] From Widow Jean Baptiste LeComte, Marie Thérèze purchased for $150 cash a small Franco-American girl named "Catiche, or Catherine, age of five years or about." It was noted that Catiche was already living in Marie Thérèze's home, having been "entrusted to her at the age of two." Three days after the purchase, Marie Thérèze manumitted little Catiche.[54]

Marie Thérèze had now purchased two daughters and two grandchildren. The fate of her other two non-Metoyer children is not completely known. The third daughter, Françoise, who was born in 1763, had been sold by Mme. de Soto when the child was but nine years old, despite the specific regulation of the *Code Noir* that children under the age of fourteen were not to be separated from their mothers. The purchaser, Sieur Delissard Jouhannis, resold Françoise almost immediately to a local *habitant* named Baptiste Dupre for 1,200 piasters, a handsome price for so young a child.[55]

52. Théophile L. Metoyer to J. B. Prudhomme, in Natchitoches Parish Records, Mortgage Records, Vol. 28, p. 395; Fourth Census of the United States, 1820, Parish of Opelousas.

53. Father A. Dupre, Metoyer Family Genealogy, in St. Augustine Parish Records, Parish Rectory, Melrose, Louisiana. Father Dupre was pastor of St. Augustine Church (the Catholic church founded by the Isle Brevelle colony) from 1878 to 1889. His informal genealogy was based partly upon records in the Natchitoches Registers and partly on information provided him by the family. Since the Natchitoches Registers do not identify Catiche's parents, it is assumed that Father Dupre's identification of her as Louis' natural daughter was provided by her descendants.

54. Marguerite LeRoy, Widow LeComte, to Marie Thérèze Coincoin, and Marie Thérèze Coincoin to Catiche, Natchitoches Parish Records, Docs. 2550 and 2552.

55. French (ed.), *Historical Collections of Louisiana,* III, 94. Mme. Marie St. Denis to Sr. Delissard Jouhannis, Doc. 756, and Sr. de lisard Jouannis to Jⁿ B^{te} Dupre, Doc. 771, Natchitoches Parish Records. It is interesting to note that Dupre's wife was a daughter of the previously mentioned Widow LeComte. Through many generations, the descendants of Marie Thérèze were extraordinarily close to the slaves or freed slaves of the LeComte family.

Upon Dupre's death his widow remarried, but prior to that marriage she sold to her future husband the slaves and land that she had inherited from Sieur Dupre. Among those sold was Françoise, now grown and the mother of three small, half-French, children. This deed of sale and the concurrent inventory of the second husband's estate that was made as part of the marriage contract are the last records that have been found on Françoise. There is no evidence that she or her children were purchased from slavery, although at least one of Françoise's grandsons was eventually manumitted by Dupre's widow and became a part of the Isle Brevelle colony.[56]

Similarly, Marie Thérèze's black son, Jean Joseph, disappears from the records of the post for a considerable length of time. He was purchased by Pierre Metoyer in 1776, at the same time that Metoyer bought from Mme. de Soto his eldest four Franco-African children. No additional record of Jean Joseph can be found for the next seventy-four years, until 1850, when the aged black was buried in the little village of Cloutierville, some twenty-five miles down river from Natchitoches.[57]

There has been found no record which reveals if, when, or by whom Jean Joseph was freed. However, since Marie Thérèze and several of her children so conscientiously bought and freed other family members from the bonds of slavery, and since the burial record did not identify him as the property of any slaveowner, it may be assumed that Jean Joseph was freed at the earliest possible time.

The first six children whom Marie Thérèze bore to Metoyer were technically their father's slaves, but they had long since ceased to be treated as such.

---

56. Widow Baptiste Dupre to Louis Monet, and Marriage Contract of Louis Monet to Widow Baptiste Dupre, in Natchitoches Parish Records, Docs. 1831 and 1839. See Chapter IV for a fuller discussion of this freed slave, Louis Monet, Jr.

57. Mrs. Manuel de Soto to Pierre Metoyer, *ibid.,* Doc. 1161. Burial Book 1, Registers of the Parish of St. Jean Baptiste de Cloutierville (St. John the Baptist Catholic Church, Cloutierville), unnumbered page. Hereinafter cited as Cloutierville Registers.

Neither of these two records identify Jean Joseph by name. The slave sale of 1776 described him only as "one young Negro of ten or twelve years." However, an examination of the civil and ecclesiastical records dealing with the few slaves that Mme. de Soto owned indicates that Jean Joseph was the only male Negro of that age in her household in 1776. The burial record of Jean Joseph stated only that the priest had interred "the body of [blank], brother of Augustin Metoyer, age 85." This unidentified brother could not possibly have been one of Marie Thérèze's Metoyer sons since their dates of death have been firmly established and none died in that year. From the age given for the deceased, it is obvious that he was Jean Joseph.

As a recent authority points out, a slave child of mixed parentage, although not openly recognized, often was given favored treatment and a special position on the plantation.[58] The privileges enjoyed by these Metoyer children were exceptional even to this rule, for they had not only received special treatment from their father but were actually recognized as free within the community.

For example, the twins, Nicolas Augustin and Marie Suzanne, were only nine years old when they served as godparents at the baptism of their young cousin, Nicolas Augustin, the half-French son of Commandant De Mézières' Negro slave, Marie Jeanne. Upon recording their names in the baptismal register, Father Quintanilla identified both young godparents as free.[59] Again in 1795, when Suzanne's eldest son, Florentin, was baptized, Father Juan Delvaux entered into his register that he had baptized a free infant named "Juan Francisco Florentine," son of "Suzanne, free mulatress." Godparents were "Louis, free mulatto," and "Marie Thérèze, free Negress."[60]

In 1793 Pierre Joseph Maes, syndic of the post of Natchitoches, compiled a tax list of all free heads of households and free males over the age of fourteen. Marie Thérèze was listed, along with her eldest Metoyer son who actually was free by that time. Listed with these two was young Pierre Metoyer, now twenty-two but still a slave. His name was scratched through. Apparently Maes first included him on the list, taking it for granted that he was free, but then was corrected by either Pierre or his mother. This list, which purported to include all free male adults or heads-of-households in the parish, indicated the existence of only one other person of color of this standing, a black named Nicolas Docla.[61]

When Marie Thérèze shipped the barge load of tobacco, hides, and bear grease to New Orleans in 1792, Commandant Louis De Blanc indicated on the passport that the barge was manned by two free men of color.[62] Inasmuch as

58. Foner, "The Free People of Color in Louisiana and St. Dominigue," 413.

59. February 9, 1777, Natchitoches Registers, Book 4, p. 308. Upon the partition of slaves of Mme. de St. Denis, De Mézières and his wife had inherited Marie Thérèze's sister, Marie Jeanne; Succession of Wife of St. Denys, in Natchitoches Parish Records, Doc. 205.

60. March 1, 1795, Natchitoches Registers, Book 4, p. 416.

61. Winston DeVille (transcriber), "Natchitoches Tax List for 1793," *Louisiana Genealogical Register,* XVIII (March, 1971), 72.

62. État de la Cargaison, in Holmes Collection.

Marie Thérèze's sons who actually were free at this time were scarcely old enough to undertake such a voyage, in all probability the two boatmen referred to were her older sons who, technically, were still the property of their father, whose bateau they also manned on the trip down river. When Pierre Metoyer finally did free his children, he specifically stated that they "were always in a position to gain escape everywhere they found themselves" and had not attempted to do so.[63] It is obvious from such references that the young Metoyers were treated as free men at the Natchitoches post long before they legally attained that status.

On August 1, 1792, the oldest Metoyer son, Augustin, was given his freedom by his father in accordance with the privilege that Metoyer had reserved for himself in his marriage contract with the Widow Pavie. Three weeks later Augustin was married in the church at Natchitoches to a young, free Franco-African girl named Marie Agnes Poissot.[64] In January of 1795 the fourth Metoyer son, Dominique, also decided to marry, and he too was given his freedom. Four days later, January 19, Dominique was married in the chapel of the parish of St. François to another *femme de couleur libre,* the fourteen-year-old Marguerite LeComte.[65]

In 1801, Pierre Metoyer initiated proceedings to free his remaining three enslaved children, Louis, Pierre, and Marie Suzanne. On April 27 his last will and testament was drawn up at Natchitoches. In the course of this document Metoyer reiterated some of the provisions of his marriage contract, under which he had reserved the right to free his enslaved children at his discretion, and the terms of the annuity agreement which he had made with Marie Thérèze.[66]

It was his intention, Metoyer stated, that when he deemed it advisable to free the last of these children, they, their brothers, and their mother should

63. For example, see Pierre Metoyer to Louis, Manumission, in Natchitoches Parish Records, Book 2, 207–208.

64. Pierre Metoyer to Nicolas Augustin, Manumission, in Natchitoches Parish Records, Doc. 2409; Marriage of Nicolas Augustin to Marie Agnes, August 22, 1792, in Natchitoches Registers, Book 4B, 99.

65. Pierre Metoyer to Dominique, Manumission, in Natchitoches Parish Records Doc. 2584; Marriage of Dominique to Marguerite, January 19, 1795, in Natchitoches Registers, Book 4B, 102.

66. 1801 Will of Claude Thomas Pierre Metoyer (MS in Natchitoches Parish Library).

discharge him from the payment of the annual stipend. He now specified that the date of liberty for the three remaining children completely hinged upon this stipulation. On the day that Marie Thérèze and all of her children annulled the contract, Pierre and Louis would become free and Suzanne would receive conditional freedom. In return, Metoyer expected that, if by unforeseen events the children of his legitimate marriage should become indigent, these children of Marie Thérèze must assist them according to their abilities.[67]

It was Metoyer's desire that his daughter Suzanne should remain under his control until his death. At that time freedom would be given not only to her but to the children she had already produced—Florentin, Marie Suzanne called Suzette, and Marie Aspasie. It would, moreover, apply to all children born to her in the interval between that day and the day of his death. Also in the intervening years, Marie Suzanne was to receive payment for all midwife duties that she performed on his plantation and for any other duties which justified special remuneration.[68]

It was further requested by Metoyer that after his death Marie Suzanne should remain in his household and care for his wife so long as the arrangement was mutually agreeable. Metoyer's youngest son, François Benjamin, was especially entrusted to the care of Marie Suzanne, and the specific request was made of her that she remain responsible for this son, her nursling, both before and after the death of Mme. Metoyer.[69]

Metoyer's will of 1801 contains one further, and puzzling, clause relative to the children of Marie Thérèze. Metoyer declared that his young slave Honoré, son of his black slave Salie, should be sold to none other than Dominique, son of Marie Thérèze, at the price set by the estimators of his estate. However, it was required that Dominique should manumit Honoré prior to his own death. Should Dominique fail to do so, Honoré would revert to Metoyer's estate and would become the inheritance of the legitimate

---

67. *Ibid.* In making this last qualification Metoyer was strictly complying with the enforced legal code of that period. *Las Siete Partidas* required that all freed slaves must assist their former masters if the latter should become impoverished; failure to do so would entitle the former master to reclaim the ex-slave as his property. Moreau L. Lislet and Henry Carleton (trans.), *The Laws of the Las Siete Partidas Which Are Still in Force in the State of Louisiana* (2 vols.; New Orleans, 1820), I, 591–93.

68. 1801 Will of Claude Thomas Pierre Metoyer (MS in Natchitoches Parish Library).

69. *Ibid.*

Metoyer heirs.[70] It may be speculated that this child Honoré, son of Salie, was also the son of Dominique and the grandson of Metoyer himself. There seems to be no other reason for the solicitude which the old French gentleman showed for this slave, one of more than a hundred that he owned.

The conditions set by Metoyer for the manumission of his three children were met in the spring of the year following. In the presence of two witnesses, Marie Thérèze acknowledged that she was now freeing Metoyer of the annuity he had promised her. In final settlement of the promised annuity he was now giving to her the $1,200 equivalent for her to invest as she deemed advisable. In return Marie Thérèze freed Metoyer of all of the terms of the contract, except those that concerned the small plantation he had given her.[71]

Following the execution of this document, Metoyer formally granted freedom to Louis and Pierre. In each document he expressed gratitude for the slave "having always served me faithfully and exactly, always conducting himself to my satisfaction," and stated that he now wished to "recompense him for the good service that he has rendered me, who was in a position to gain escape everywhere that he found himself." In the case of Louis, it was sworn that Metoyer had already verbally given him liberty on January 1, 1801.[72]

The final document executed on this day in May, 1802, was the conditional manumission of Marie Suzanne. It was specifically noted that she had always served Metoyer with zeal, fidelity, and exactness, and that she had by her good service and good attentions saved several lives during various maladies, including the lives of his wife and all their infants.[73] Metoyer further stated

70. *Ibid.*

71. Pierre Metoyer to Marie Thérèze Coincoin, Donation, in Natchitoches Parish Records, Misc. Book 2, pp. 206–207. This document is mislabeled. It should read: Marie Thérèze Coincoin to Pierre Metoyer, Annulment of Donation.

72. Pierre Metoyer to Louis, Manumission, and Pierre Metoyer to Pierre, Manumission, in Natchitoches Parish Records, Misc. Book 2, pp. 207–210.

73. Pierre Metoyer to Marie Suzanne, Manumission, Natchitoches Parish Records, Misc. Book 2, 210–211. It is interesting to note this repetitive theme in documents and tradition dealing with Marie Thérèze and her family. Obviously, medical expertise was a skill highly valued by them, passed from generation to generation. If tradition may be believed, their expertise was based upon African medical practices. Most Africanisms did not long survive the acculturation process of this family. This trait (aside from the perpetuation of the name Coincoin) seems to be the sole example.

that Suzanne had, in fact, nourished with her own milk his youngest son, François Benjamin, and had dry-nursed, reared, and managed his other two children by the Widow Pavie. Upon his death, Suzanne and all her children were to become free. Since slaves were not legally entitled to any property or money, or even the right to work or sell goods for their own profit without the express permission of their master, Metoyer specified that upon his death his heirs and executors would have no claim whatsoever upon any products of Marie Suzanne's industry or upon the savings which she had managed to accumulate by any talent.[74]

Marie Thérèze Buard Metoyer died in the year 1813, thereby freeing Marie Suzanne from her father's wish that she remain with his spouse until her death. Two years later, Claude Thomas Pierre Metoyer was buried beside his late wife in the family's plot in the burial grounds of the parish church.[75] In 1815, at the age of forty-seven, Marie Suzanne Metoyer finally became a free woman.

During the first years of her own freedom, Marie Thérèze Coincoin had labored with but one goal: to earn the sums necessary to purchase her off-spring from the bondage of slavery. With this behind her, the aging black woman did not lessen her toil. Freedom is one of the most basic requisites of humanity, but the poor free man is still yoked to financial and social servitude. In the antebellum plantation society, the passport to real independence was land, slaves, and money. It was these for which Marie Thérèze and her children now labored.

There are no official records that reveal exactly when Marie Thérèze first began to purchase slaves to labor for her. Her only slave purchases on record are those executed for the purchase of her children. It is clear that no slaves were bought prior to 1790 since the church tax list that was compiled that year, placing a poll on every free head of household, every free male over fourteen, and every slave, indicated that Marie Thérèze owned no slaves. Documents executed in 1816 identified twelve of the slaves that she had accumulated by that time and the baptismal records of the church identify four

74. Pierre Metoyer to Marie Suzanne, Manumission, Natchitoches Parish Records, Misc. Book 2, pp. 210–211.
75. Date of death of Metoyer and wife are extracted from tomb markers in the American Cemetery, Natchitoches.

others. Tradition credits her with many more, but numbers are often exaggerated by the passage of time.[76]

Tradition also insists that even though Marie Thérèze purchased other humans and held them in bondage, she always treated her slaves with gentleness, never forgetting that she herself had once been a slave. Marie Thérèze reportedly administered no corporal punishment; misbehavior on her plantation was corrected with imprisonment in the "jail" which she had erected for that purpose on her property.[77] Like most conscientious Catholics of her era and locale, the black mistress also saw to it that her slaves were administered the sacraments of the Church. Except in those years when no priest resided at the post, all slave infants born on Marie Thérèze's plantation were promptly baptized, lest they die "outside the Grace of God." Similarly, slaves who died were taken into the Natchitoches post for burial in the consecrated grounds of the parish church.[78]

In 1807 Marie Thérèze increased her landholdings still further with the purchase of a third tract of land. From the Sieur Jean LaLande she purchased a plantation on Red River, not far from the original tract which Metoyer had given her; the purchase price of five hundred dollars was paid by note due the following March.[79] The old matriarch, however, did not buy this land for her own use. Now in her mid-sixties, she had already begun to turn over her holdings to her children, providing them with a start in life. Three years after the acquisition of the latest property, a neighboring tract exchanged hands; this deed of sale, like all such documents of that period, named the holders of adjoining plantations. In this case, the proprietor of Marie Thérèze's land was identified as Pierre Metoyer, free man of color.[80] It was not until 1814, however, that Pierre Toussaint officially purchased the land from his aging mother and reimbursed her for the sum that she had invested in it.[81]

76. Répartition a L'ocasion de . . . fette le 1r Mars 1790, in Natchitoches Parish Records Collection, LSU; Marie Thérèze Coincoin to [various heirs], Conveyance, in Natchitoches Parish Records Book 3, pp. 524–38; Natchitoches Registers, Books 4B and 5.
77. Interview with Mrs. Coutii, March 24, 1974.
78. Natchitoches Registers, Books 4B and 5.
79. Copie de Vente de Terre, in Natchitoches Parish Records, Conveyance Book 42 (Original Documents), Doc. 501.
80. Louis Verchere to Dominique Rachal, *ibid.,* Doc. 3768.
81. Marie Thérèze Coincoin to Toussaint Metoyer, Sale of Land, *ibid.,* Conveyance Book 3, pp. 308–309.

Even while laboring to build her estate, Marie Thérèze readily assumed her share of responsibility for the welfare of the community in which she lived. When in 1790 the church congregation was faced with the necessity of hiring a carpenter to make repairs and enlargements, Pierre Metoyer as syndic took a census of all inhabitants of the region who were served by the church and assessed one *real* for each free head of household, each free male over fourteen, and each slave. Marie Thérèze, at that time, had no free sons old enough to be taxed and owned no slaves. She was assessed one *real,* but she paid two.[82] In 1793 and 1794 still another list was drawn up of all area inhabitants who had made a contribution of their labor for the benefit of the parish. Among those who had volunteered to work in the parish cemetery was Marie Thérèze.[83]

Although Marie Thérèze and Metoyer had terminated their alliance prior to his marriage in 1788, their friendship continued for many years. It has already been noted that in 1792 they shipped their goods together to the New Orleans market. Further evidence of their continued friendship is provided by the parish records which show Marie Thérèze serving, from time to time, as godmother to Metoyer's slaves. In 1795, for example, the resident priest, Father Delvaux, baptized the infant Juan Bautista Honoré, child of Maria, a slave of Metoyer. Godparents were Marie Thérèze and her Metoyer son Joseph.[84]

Some recent writers have asserted that the children whom Marie Thérèze bore to Metoyer were ashamed of their mother because of her relationship with their father. This assertion reflects an attempt on the part of these writers to project their own morality onto the personalities of these children; certainly, the records do not support this assertion. Regardless of the circumstances surrounding their births, these children clearly maintained their respect and love for their mother for as long as she lived.

There can hardly be more convincing proof of one individual's respect for another than for that individual to desire the other as a godparent to his own child, as a proxy to guide that child's religious development in the event of the parents' deaths. In 1794 the eldest Metoyer son, Augustin, who tradition

82. Répartition a L'ocasion de . . . fette le 1ᵉʳ Mars 1790, in Natchitoches Parish Records Collection, LSU.

83. Role de Corvées et Contributions public, *ibid.,* Folder 1.

84. [no date], Natchitoches Registers, Book 4, p. 423.

claims was a strict moralist, brought his first child to the parish church for baptism; the godmother was Marie Thérèze.[85] From this time, until her death more than twenty years later, Marie Thérèze was to serve as godmother to a number of her grandchildren. The church records also reveal that several of her female grandchildren were given the name of Marie Thérèze, a name which has continued in popularity through all subsequent generations of her descendants. Moreover, tradition holds that her descendants had masses offered in her memory for more than a half century after her death.[86]

The exact date of Marie Thérèze's death is not known. The last records which exist for her are dated in the spring of 1816. On March 9 the old matriarch sold her first homeplace, the small tract given to her by Metoyer, to her neighbor, Jean Baptiste Ailhaud de Ste. Anne.[87] On April 20, nine more documents were presented by her to the parish judge at Natchitoches for filing. By the terms of these documents, executed the previous month, Marie Thérèze transferred to her children and grandchildren twelve slaves which she owned; their total value was $5,250.[88] Each heir who received a slave paid the assessed value. According to the usual practice, the total sum thus raised would have been divided equally among all heirs.

Tradition holds that prior to her death Marie Thérèze also divided the land which had been granted to her "by the King" among the children whom she left behind. Many later documents which relate to this land show that it was divided into ten strips, each with two *arpents* of frontage on the river and a depth of forty *arpents*. This tradition is further supported by the deed of sale from her son Toussaint to his nephew Auguste, dated in March, 1830, in which Toussaint stated that he had acquired the land by "partition made by his mother Marie Thérèze Coincoin between her children."[89]

On December 31, 1817, her son Pierre filed a contract of marriage at Natch-

85. Baptism of Marie Modeste, April 22, 1793, *ibid.,* 119.
86. Interview with Mrs. Coutii, March 24, 1974. Mrs. Coutii's grandmother, Sidalise Sarpy Dupre, the great-granddaughter of Marie Thérèze, was one of those who regularly requested masses to be said for the repose of the soul of their family's matriarch.
87. Marie Thérèze Coincoin to J[n] B[te] Ailhaud Ste. Anne, in Natchitoches Parish Records, Conveyance Book 3, 522–23.
88. Marie Thérèze Coincoin to [various heirs], *ibid.,* 524–38.
89. Toussaint Metoyer to Auguste Metoyer, Sale of Lands and Slaves, *ibid.,* Misc. Book 20, pp. 334–35.

itoches with his second wife in which he identified himself as son of the deceased Marie Thérèze *dit* Coincoin.[90] The death of the matriarch, therefore, occurred between April of 1816, when she filed her last documents, and December of 1817, when Pierre filed his marriage contract. No record of her death can be found in the incomplete church registers which were maintained during that period.

Tradition offers one further detail relevant to the death of Marie Thérèze. In the last months of her life she was living alone; although she was some seventy-four years old, she still insisted upon maintaining her independence, even from her children. Upon learning that his mother was ill, however, Augustin took her to his home to care for her, and it was there that she died. When death occurred, the body was taken the twenty miles or so into Natchitoches for a burial in the cemetery in which her parents, at least two of her children, several of her grandchildren, and Pierre Metoyer were also buried. Tradition also insists that the burial was a fine one.[91]

Although she was forced by the laws of society to defy one of the Christian precepts, tradition still insists that Marie Thérèze was a religious woman. Through the generations her descendants have maintained that their family's matriarch died as a devout Catholic. According to legend she taught her children the Rosary herself, and upon the occasion of their First Communions she gave to each of them a chain of wooden rosary beads which she herself had carved.[92] At least one of these was preserved by the family until well into the twentieth century.[93]

90. Pierre Metoyer and Marie Henriette, Marriage Contract, *ibid.,* Books 2 and 3.

91. Interview with Mrs. Coutii, April 26, 1974. The graves of Pierre Metoyer, his wife, and his two white sons are still to be found, well-marked, in the American Cemetery at Natchitoches. This was the original Catholic cemetery, but was forsaken by the Catholics after the "Americans" began to use it. The markers are concrete, which means they were put there at a later date, probably to replace the earlier iron crosses. The iron or wooden crosses which marked the graves of Marie Thérèze and her children who preceded her in death are no longer extant.

92. Confidential Source to François Mignon, September 3, 1972, Detroit, Michigan. Copy in possession of author. This traditional reference to woodcarving provides another interesting link between Marie Thérèze and her African heritage. According to one authority, inhabitants of the Gold Coast, Dahomey, and Nigeria regions (all three areas which were inhabited by people of the Ewe linguistic group from which Marie Thérèze apparently descended) are noted even today for their highly developed woodcarving skill. Melville J. Herskovits, *The New World Negro* (Bloomington, Indiana, 1966), 118.

93. The Rosary which Marie Thérèze supposedly carved for her youngest son, François, is the one that older family members recall. Its last owner was his great-grandson, Herman ("Gar-

Some versions of the legend describe the "fabulous" heritage that Marie Thérèze Coincoin left her children and attempt to explain it in material terms. But it was not a fully developed estate of thousands of acres that she left to them, an estate whose proceeds would allow them to spend their lives in the pursuit of luxuries and pleasures. A "comfortable" estate would be a more accurate description. It was sizable, consisting of over one thousand *arpents* of land and at least sixteen slaves. If landownership maps of the period may be used as an acceptable guideline, Marie Thérèze's holdings compared well with those of the white inhabitants of the parish and certainly exceeded those of the other free people of color. Moreover, the 1810 census of the parish, the last one taken before her death, shows that only 13 percent of the households had as many or more slaves than Marie Thérèze. Three of the householders who matched or exceeded this number were her children.[94] Even estates of a thousand *arpents* and sixteen slaves, however, are suddenly rendered small when divided among ten heirs.

A great measure of the success which Marie Thérèze did achieve could be attributed to the assistance which she received from the white community. Her entire life is interlaced with kindnesses from such whites as Metoyer and Mme. de Soto and such evidence helps to account for her remarkable story. Yet surely such treatment can only be accounted for by the character and native ability of Marie Thérèze herself.

It would appear that the greatest legacy which Marie Thérèze Coincoin left to her children was the example of determination, loyalty, industry, frugality, and mutual assistance, and the emphasis upon working with the dominant race rather than against it in order to achieve one's goals. It was these qualities, enhanced by innate shrewdness, which enabled her Metoyer sons and daughter to expand the property that she left them into the vast, rich plantations which they came to own on Cane River.

çon") Metoyer of New Orleans. After Herman's death there a number of years ago, the Isle Brevelle family lost track of the Rosary.

94. Third Census of the United States, 1810. This census, which identifies only heads of households, does not list Marie Thérèze by name. Either she was overlooked by the enumerator in his search for households in the rural areas of the parish or else she was included in the household of one of the sons who had twelve or more slaves.

Chapter THREE

Early Development of the
Isle Brevelle Colony

It was the eldest son, Augustin, who led the Metoyers *de couleur* to Isle Brevelle. One by one his brothers followed and, tract by tract, adjacent lands came under their control, by grant, by occupancy, and by purchase. As the years passed the Metoyers of color were recognized more and more as a *famille extraordinaire* by their fellow citizens of Isle Brevelle.

The Isle is not really an island in the commonly accepted sense of that term. More correctly, it is a narrow strip of land some thirty miles in length with three- to four-mile breadth, delineated by a waterway that splits, meanders, and joins again. The channel known as Old River, through which the Red River flowed prior to the 1760s, marks the western boundary of the Isle. The eastern limit is outlined by a channel through which the Red River flowed at the time the Isle was settled. In the 1830s the Red took still another course; the channel to the east of the Isle was then renamed the Cane.

In his 1805 report to authorities at Washington on the Red River valley, Dr. John Sibley indicated that the length of the Isle was divided by a bayou, also called Brevelle, that connected the two rivers. Although both divisions were officially known as Isle Brevelle, it has been a more common practice, from the time of the earliest records, to identify the upper section of the Isle as the Grande Côte, or Côte Joyeuse. It was here that Pierre Metoyer established his plantation and it was here that he installed Marie Thérèze and their children on a sixty-eight-acre tract. The term *Isle Brevelle,* in common usage, was usually restricted to that part of the Isle which lies below the east-west line of the bayou, and it was in this region that the children of Marie Thérèze established themselves.

Sibley reported that Isle Brevelle was named for its earliest settler, Jean Baptiste Brevel, Jr., and cited his source of information as Brevel himself. A native of the Natchitoches post and the son of a Parisian-born trader and his

Indian wife, Brevel married the daughter of a local French officer in 1760.[1] Five years later he petitioned for and received a grant of land from Daniel Pain, the subdelegate at Natchitoches. The only evidence of the grant which remains is its listing in the *French Archives Index* maintained by the Natchitoches Parish clerk of court.[2] The document itself is missing, but apparently the land given Brevel in 1765 was the same land which he settled on the Isle.

Brevel's choice of land was an excellent one. For centuries the Isle had been a flood plain for two sizable rivers, and the deposits left behind formed a soil of such superior quality that after almost a century of cultivation the land was still described as "the most productive cotton growing land in the state" and the "richest cotton growing portion of the South."[3] The natural beauty of the Isle was incomparable. Not even the marks of civilization could spoil its inherent lushness. Father Yves-Marie LeConniat, a transplanted Frenchman, ecstatically referred to it as an "earthly paradise" and described it to a correspondent as: "so rich in lovely vegetation! It overflows with such a variety of natural beauty, natural produce. We have every species, every kind of tree, and in the springtime there are flowers in profusion!... In the woods one really breathes pure balmy air. The sight of the multiple variety of flowers of all different shapes, colors, sizes, is a spectacle to behold! It inspires a person to get down on his knees in recognition of the Creator of all its beauty." Father Yves-Marie did not fail to mention the ticks, or "death-beetles," the lizards, the snakes, and the alligators, but in his piety he explained: "The good God . . . arranged things with balance and equilibrium, the miserable and disagreeable with the beautiful and the lovely, so that man will not become too attached to any of the things of this world."[4]

Despite the natural advantages which the Isle offered, the *habitants* of

1. *American State Papers: Documents Legislative and Executive of the Congress of the United States. Indian Affairs,* I, 727; Marriage of Jean Baptiste Brevel [Sr.] to Anne of the Caddoes, July 27, 1736, Baptism of Jean Baptiste Brevel [Jr.], May 20, 1736, Marriage of Jean Baptiste Brevel [Jr.] to Marie Françoise Poissot, July 14, 1760, all in Natchitoches Registers, Book I.

2. The land patent issued to Brevel was assigned Doc. No. 396 according to the *Index to French Archives.*

3. Orton S. Clark, *The One Hundred and Sixteenth Regiment of New York State Volunteers* (Buffalo, 1868), 150; Harris H. Beecher, *Records of the 114th Regiment, N.Y.S.V.* (Norwich, 1866), 304.

4. Sister Dorothea Olga McCants (ed. and trans.), *They Came to Louisiana: Letters of a Catholic Mission, 1854–1882* (Baton Rouge, 1970), 122–23.

Natchitoches were slow to settle it. In fact, agriculture in general was not a popular means of livelihood among Natchitoches residents. Throughout the French period, colonial settlers of northwest Louisiana clustered, for the most part, at the little village post where they subordinated agriculture to trade. The great distance of Natchitoches from central authority and its proximity to Spanish territory provided the perfect environment for circumvention of restrictive trade laws between the two nations, and the commandants of the post not only condoned smuggling but even engaged in the activity themselves.[5]

The change in government from French to Spanish which occurred in the 1760s was accompanied by a shift in economic emphasis. Trade was deliberately and decisively curtailed by the new officials and a generous land policy was implemented in order to encourage agriculture.[6] Not until they were thereby forced to change their life-styles, over half a century after the founding of the post, did most Natchitoches inhabitants choose lands for plantations. Thus it was that unclaimed lands still remained in the parish when the sons of Marie Thérèze reached maturity in the 1790s.

The first lands chosen by the general populace, not surprisingly, were those nearest the post. When in the 1760s the Red River changed its course and adopted the channel previously known as Little River or Petite Rivière aux Bourguignon (now the Cane), Brevel judiciously appraised the land that lay along the newly adopted channel and chose his lands on the isle formed between the new Red and the old, despite its distance from the post. Another unconventional settler, Lieutenant Louis Mathias LeCourt de Prelle, ventured still further down the new waterway at that same time and settled on a large river bluff in a region known as Rivière aux Cannes.[7]

5. Bridges and DeVille, "Natchitoches in 1766," 146–51.

6. *Ibid.;* Bjork, "Documents Relating to Alexandro O'Reilly," 22; "O'Reilly's Ordinance of 1770," 237–40.

7. The marriage of LeCourt to Marie Jeanne LeRoy, March 1765, in Natchitoches Registers, Book 2, indicates that LeCourt had settled the Rivière aux Cannes (River at the Canes) region by 1765. See also: Heirs of Louis Mathias LeCourt DePrelle to Louis Monet, in Natchitoches Parish Records, Doc. 1848. LeCourt's Bluff is more commonly known by the name of Monette's Bluff. It marks the lower extremity of the stretch of Cane River occupied by the subject colony. Both Lieutenant LeCourt and Sieur Monet, who purchased the bluff region from him, were progenitors of the Cane River colony.

It is interesting to note that a later owner of this bluff tract, Robert McAlpin, is alleged to be the prototype of Harriet Beecher Stowe's villainous slaveowner character, Simon Legree. See D. B. Corley, *A Visit to Uncle Tom's Cabin* (Chicago, 1893).

Of these two newly opened regions, the Isle Brevelle land has since been considered the most productive, but few settlers recognized its potential at the time. Not until the mid-1780s did residents of the post decide to follow Brevel's lead. By 1790, twenty-five years after Brevel's opening of the area, the Isle could claim only twenty-seven free white males over the age of fourteen. The only nonwhites were the forty-nine slaves owned by these men.[8] Not until 1795 did the first *homme de couleur libre* settle on the virgin bottomlands of Isle Brevelle.

It had been three years since Augustin Metoyer had been given his freedom by his father. Already he was twenty-seven and had a wife and two infants to support. With no formal education and apparently no marketable skills, Augustin's only hope for economic advancement lay with the land. His mother had successfully petitioned for a concession the previous year; obviously encouraged by her success, Augustin submitted his own request to the Spanish colonial government. Whereas Marie Thérèze had sought a grant of grazing land in the pine woods that lay across Old River west of her homestead, young Augustin looked downstream to the rich bottomland on lower Isle Brevelle. There he found a vacant tract of the king's domain that suited his needs. On May 6, 1795, the colonial government issued an order authorizing him to settle on the land and to have it surveyed in his name. The first survey of the property indicated that the tract contained 395 acres, a very sizable grant for a young man with no slaves.[9]

Adjacent to Augustin's acquisition was a large section of flat caneland, much larger than the usual Spanish concession, which had been granted in 1789 to a Natchitoches citizen named Silvestre Bossier. Prior to receiving the grant, Bossier had taken slaves to the tract, opened a road, and cleared away a small section of cane. But after receiving title to the land he had abandoned his efforts to improve it and had been forced to surrender his order of survey and settlement. In December of 1795, supposedly, Augustin's ambitious younger brother Louis petitioned Commandant Louis De Blanc for title to the entire tract. Four months later the Spanish governor of Louisiana issued an

8. Répartition a L'ocasion de . . . fette le 1ʳ Mars, in Natchitoches Parish Records Collection, LSU.
9. File B1960, Augustin Metoyer, State Land Records.

order of survey and settlement for all of the requested land, a tract which eventually would be measured at 912 acres.[10]

It was this land which tradition claims was the central plantation of Louis' mother, Marie Thérèze Coincoin, and the center of the Metoyer "empire" on Isle Brevelle. This part of the legend cannot be conclusively proven or disproven. The colonial documents which deal with this plantation indicate that the land was granted to Louis, not to Marie Thérèze. In his 1806 memorial to the United States Board of Land Commissioners, Louis stated that he had "presented a petition to Mr. Louis De Blanc then Commandant of the Post of Natchitoches preparatory to obtaining a 'title in form' . . . that the said commandant certified said land to be Vacant and on the 18th day of May in the year 1795 the then governor of the province of Louisiana gave to your Exponant an Order of survey." [11]

On the surface this statement of Louis', which was accepted by the Board of Land Commissioners, seems to be sufficient evidence of the identity of the recipient of the land. However, Article XXII of the *Code Noir* proclaimed that "slaves can have no right to any kind of property." [12] In May, 1796, when Louis supposedly received this grant, he was still a slave. It was not until 1801 that his father verbally gave him his freedom and not until 1802 that his father executed the legal manumission.[13] Three possible explanations exist for this apparent infringement of the law: the land was not actually granted until after 1802; the land was granted illegally to Louis in 1796; or the land was actually granted to his free mother, as tradition holds, and she privately transferred the property to her son.

The possibility does exist that Commandant De Blanc backdated such a petition for young Louis Metoyer. As one authority has declared, "When the news of the [Louisiana] Cession was received [land policy] was thrown to the winds. Spanish administrative officials connived with American speculators in the perpetration of land frauds by back-dating a large number of blank

10. Memorial of Louis Metoyer, in Opelousas Notarial Records Collection (Archives and Records Service, Baton Rouge), folder dated May, 1796. File B1953, Louis Metoyer, State Land Records.

11. Memorial of Louis Metoyer, in Opelousas Notarial Records Collection.

12. French (ed.), *Historical Collections of Louisiana,* III, 91.

13. Pierre Metoyer to Louis, Manumission, in Natchitoches Parish Records, Misc. Book 2, 207–208.

CANE RIVER COUNTRY

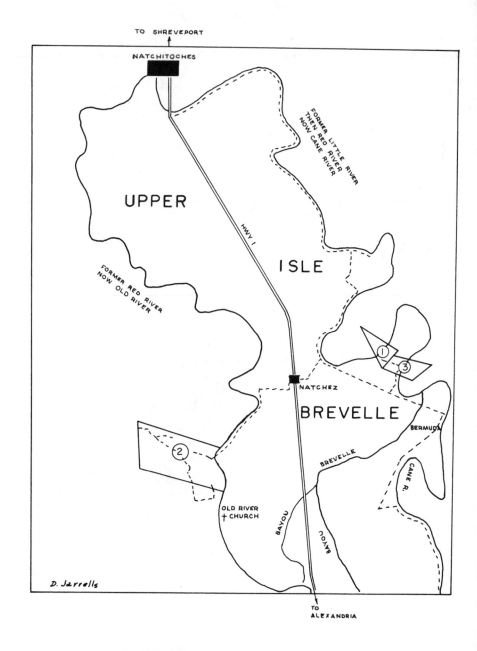

PLANTATIONS AND ROYAL CONCESSION OF
MARIE THÉRÈZE COINCOIN

1. Donation from Claude Thomas Pierre Metoyer
2. Marie Thérèze's Spanish Land Grant of 1794
3. Marie Thérèze's Purchase of 1807

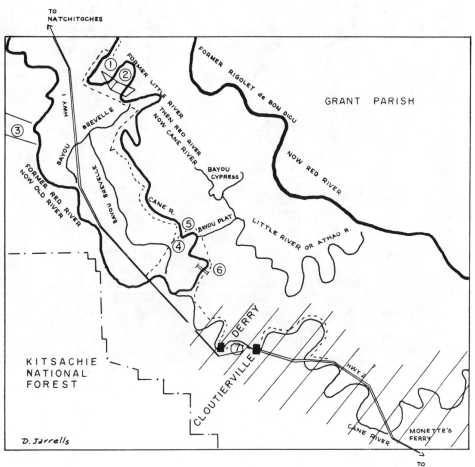

ISLE BREVELLE—PINPOINTING EARLY LAND GRANTS
AND MAJOR POINTS OF INTEREST

1. Homestead given by Pierre Metoyer to Marie Thérèze Coincoin
2. Marie Thérèze Coincoin's purchase of 1807
3. Marie Thérèze Coincoin's Spanish grant of 1794
4. Site of St. Augustine's Church, erected on the 1795 Spanish grant to the Metoyers *de couleur*
5. Melrose Plantation Estate grounds, situated on the 1796 Spanish grant to the Metoyers *de couleur*
6. Usual site of 24-Mile Ferry, located on the 1796 Spanish grant to Dominique Metoyer
7. Shallow Lake Cemetery

The slashed area was known in the eighteenth and early nineteenth centuries as Rivière aux Cannes

Melrose Manor on Cane River

Melrose Manor was built about 1833 for Jean Baptiste Louis Metoyer, a wealthy planter of color of the Cane River colony. Its builder, Seraphin Llorens, was a free man of color from New Orleans who settled on the Isle, married Metoyer's niece, and operated there as a carpenter and farmer for over a half-century. Melrose Manor is the largest of eight remaining structures on the estate grounds of the plantation.

In 1974 the estate grounds of Melrose Plantation were declared a national historic landmark in recognition of the plantation's singular origins and the unique architecture displayed by several of its buildings.

Yucca (*ca.* 1796–1800)

Courtesy of Louisiana Tourist Development Commission
The African House (*ca.* 1800–1833)

Ghana House

Typical of the slave housing provided by Isle Brevelle's planters *de couleur*
is this cabin which stands on the estate grounds of Melrose Plantation. Its
date of construction is unknown, but it is generally believed to be among the
oldest area structures. Elderly residents of the Isle in the early twentieth century
described the cabin then as being "hoary with age" even in their childhood.
Originally erected on the Spanish grant given to Pierre Metoyer, the third son of
Marie Thérèze Coincoin, the cabin was removed to Melrose in the 1930s.
There it was dubbed "Ghana House" by writer-in-residence François Mignon,
in honor of the African slaves who inhabited it.

From a sketch by Deanna Douglas

Early Cane River Plantation Home

Among the antebellum homes that were destroyed on Isle Brevelle in the early twentieth century was this *maison de poteaux en terre*—one of the earliest manor homes erected by the colony. Shortly before its razing, this home was preserved in photograph by the late Mrs. Cammie Garrett Henry. The above pen sketch was made from one of the Henry photographs in the archives of Northwestern State University at Natchitoches.

Portrait by J. Feuille, 1836

Nicolas Augustin Metoyer and the Church of St. Augustine

Although the original chapel no longer remains, a replacement—dedicated to the same saint—stands on the original site. Within the new chapel hangs this portrait of the church's founder.

Emanuel Dupre
Civil War home guardsman of the Isle Brevelle cavalry squadron,
the Augustin's Guards.

Mme. Florentin Conant, Jr. (Née Thérèsine Carles)
Daughter of Dr. Jean André Zepherin Carles and
Marie Rose Metoyer, born 1825.

Grandson and Granddaughter of Marie Thérèze Coincoin

Family tradition identifies the subjects of these oil portraits, taken during the
colony's years of affluence, only as the grandson and granddaughter of the
colony's matriarch. It is believed, however, that the couple is M. and Mme.
Auguste Metoyer, the son and daughter, respectively, of Nicolas Augustin
Metoyer and his twin sister, Marie Suzanne Metoyer.

petitions for grants." [14] Thus, although Louis supposedly received his order of survey and settlement in 1796, there was no survey made of the property during the colonial era. In explanation Louis informed the Board of Land Commissioners that the surveyor of his district had become blind and no replacement had been appointed. He also provided the testimony of a white witness, Antoine Coindet, who verified that Louis held the land by virtue of an order of survey and settlement and that he had inhabited and cultivated the land for fifteen consecutive years prior to the date of his testimony, November 16, 1811. The United States Land Office accepted this testimony and confirmed his title to the land. The issue of his being a slave at the time he supposedly received the grant was not discussed. [15]

The possibility that Louis was in fact granted the land in 1796 in spite of his slave status would suggest conspiracy on the part of the commandant. Although evidence exists that this young slave had been treated as a free man and even identified as such by various individuals prior to his manumission, it does not seem possible that the commandant could have made such a mistake. There were only a handful of free Creoles of color at the Natchitoches post in 1796, and for all of these manumission papers should have been recorded in the carefully preserved and inventoried files of the commandant. In processing Louis' petition for land it is doubtful that the commandant would have certified the land to be free without also determining whether the *homme de couleur* who submitted the petition was likewise free. If Commandant De Blanc did knowingly violate the provisions of the *Code Noir* and colonial land regulations, then in all probability he did so at the instigation of Louis' influential father rather than at the request of the politically impotent young slave.

The third possibility, that the grant was actually issued in the name of Marie Thérèze, who turned it over to her son, provides the only means by which the grant could have been made without subterfuge or chicanery. Marie Thérèze had received a grant of land two years earlier, but Spanish policy did permit "double concessions" provided that the petitioner possessed at least one

14. Gray, *Agriculture in Southern United States,* II, 865.

15. Memorial of Louis Metoyer, in Opelousas Notarial Records Collection; File B1953, Louis Metoyer, State Land Records.

hundred head of cattle and two slaves.[16] Several such double concessions were granted in the Natchitoches area.[17] Although no inventory of Marie Thérèze's holdings exist, it is quite feasible that she could have met these requirements by 1796.

Moreover, such an explanation is not inconsistent with the characters of the people involved. Marie Thérèze and Pierre Metoyer were the founders of a family that has stressed solidarity for almost two centuries. Metoyer provided for his unacknowledged children and did much more for the mother of these children than convention required. As his older children grew to adulthood, Metoyer freed them, but he demanded of these children that they care for their mother if she were in need.[18] As Marie Thérèze grew older she turned over the use of at least two tracts of her land to her sons Pierre and Pierre Toussaint, with no rental contract or legal document of any type to insure herself an income from the property.[19]

In such an atmosphere of family cooperation, respect, and mutual assistance, it is easy to speculate that Marie Thérèze might have sought a grant for her son Louis. The oldest son, Augustin, had become free, married, received his grant of land, and begun to build his fortunes. Dominique, also, had chosen a wife, was freed by his father, and was applying for a grant of his own. It was still five years before Louis was to marry and six before he would be free, but in those intervening years he, too, would have wanted lands of his own to work. Perhaps it was with the help of his mother that Louis obtained his land.

At the same time that Louis supposedly applied for this grant, his younger brother Dominique applied for a similar concession. On May 18, 1796, the same day that the grant was made to Louis, Dominique was issued an order of

16. "O'Reilly's Ordinance of 1770," 239.

17. For example, Jean Baptiste Prudhomme received two grants containing 350 and 766 acres respectively. Sylvestre Rachal's double concession consisted of tracts measuring 322 and 632 acres. Claim files and section maps in the State Land Office reveal a number of similar cases.

18. Metoyer's will of 1801 (MS in Natchitoches Parish Library).

19. It has already been pointed out that when Marie Thérèze purchased the LaLande tract on Red River she turned it over to her son Toussaint. It was also about this same time that she retired from operating her original homeplace. When the U.S. Deputy Surveyor, Joseph Irvin, surveyed this latter tract in 1816 he noted that the land was first claimed by Marie Thérèze but was then being claimed by her son Pierre Metoyer; File A1679, State Land Records. There are on record no deeds of sale or rent contracts by which either piece of land was previously conveyed to these sons.

survey and settlement to a tract on Isle Brevelle two or three miles downriver from his brothers. Dominique, who was definitely eligible for his grant, apparently had no difficulty in finding a surveyor with good eyesight, since a survey dated April 15, 1799, was filed with the United States Board of Land Commissioners in support of his title to this land. Dominique's concession totalled 904 *arpents*.[20]

Marie Thérèze's fourth Metoyer son, Pierre, received a concession of 128 acres on the Isle from the Spanish crown on March 5, 1798, according to the claim which was later filed before the United States Board of Land Commissioners.[21] Here again the question of legality arises. This son was twenty-six years of age at the time he supposedly received his grant, obviously ready to make his own start in life. However, Pierre, like his brother Louis, was not freed until 1802. Tradition does not say that this grant, which was located across Bayou Plat from Louis' land, was once the plantation of Marie Thérèze. Obviously, this grant was either made illegally to Pierre the slave in 1798 or it was actually made several years later and then back-dated. Moreover, the existence of this questionable grant reinforces doubt as to the method by which Louis acquired his tract.

In any event, by one means or another, the Metoyer sons of Marie Thérèze received Spanish colonial grants amounting to 2,075 acres of extremely fertile virgin bottomlands along Red River. After the transfer of Louisiana to American authority in 1803, the Board of Land Commissioners examined all land titles for approval in Washington, and for the next dozen years or so the board continued to accept claims. During this period Marie Thérèze's offspring were confirmed in title to a number of additional tracts, all based upon right by occupany, although the facts of some cases were misrepresented in the interest of the claimant.

Antoine Joseph Metoyer filed a claim for a tract of 640 acres bounding the back side of the grant given his brother Dominique. According to testimony filed in this claim, Joseph had settled and occupied the land for three consecu-

---

20. File B1833, Dominique Metoyer, State Land Records; Survey of Land of Dominique Metoyer, in Opelousas Notarial Records Collection, folder dated May 1796.
21. File B1952, Augustine Metoyer, State Land Records. Although the land was originally granted to Pierre, the claim for the land was filed with the U.S. Land Office in the name of his brother Augustin, who had acquired the property from Pierre by an exchange of property.

tive years prior to December 20, 1803, the day the French officials turned Louisiana over to the American government. Joseph's claim was approved and surveyed at 470 acres. In addition, a claim was filed by Joseph's wife, Marie Pelagie, but the claim was filed under the name of "Marie Pelige," with no indication of the family to which she belonged. The 640 acres that she claimed were located on Bayou D'Ivrogne (Drunkard's Bayou) in the Kisatchie Forest area of Natchitoches Parish, some twenty-five miles, by water route, from the tract claimed by her husband.[22] Testimony in the claims of Joseph Metoyer and his wife Marie Pelagie presents an interesting situation in that Pierre Carey (Quierry, Kerry), a white resident of the parish, testified before the Board of Land Commissioners at Opelousas in the fall of 1813 that both Joseph and Marie Pelagie were heads of households, without mentioning the relationship between them.[23]

The same situation existed in the case of Joseph's brother Pierre and his wife Marie Perine. In addition to the claim which Pierre had filed, Marie Perine claimed 640 acres on Bayou Derbanne. Carey was engaged to testify on her behalf when he traveled to Opelousas to support the claims of the other members of her family. Carey's sworn statement in this claim omitted the fact that Marie Perine was the wife of another claimant and asserted that she, too, was the head of a family.[24] After a considerable dispute over the exact location of her claim and her right to it, Marie Perine's claim was confirmed for 597 acres.[25]

Still another claim based upon "occupancy as required by law" was filed by Toussaint, one of the younger Metoyer brothers. He, too, claimed 640 acres, citing his location as being at the juncture of Bayou Blue with "Little River or River Brosset." Supporting his claim was the same family friend, Pierre Carey, who testified that Toussaint, "[who has] inhabited and cultivated the land for fourteen consecutive years preceding said date, is about thirty-four years of age, and the head of a family."[26] In actuality, Toussaint

22. File R&R 306, Joseph Metoyer, and File R&R 308, Marie Pelige, State Land Records. The identity of Joseph's wife is provided by their marriage record, dated June 1, 1801, in Natchitoches Registers, Book 4-B, 102.

23. *American State Papers: Public Lands*, III, 199.

24. *Ibid.*

25. File R&R 309, Marie Perine, State Land Records.

26. *American State Papers: Public Lands*, III, 199; File R&R 310, Toussaint Metoyer, State Land Records.

was three years younger, which means that he would have been only seventeen when he set out on his own to "inhabit and cultivate" this land. Moreover, neither the church nor civil records of this period show any evidence that Toussaint had a wife or a child. Nevertheless, his claim was confirmed for the amount he had requested.

Adjoining Toussaint's property was an extensive tract of vacant land which was settled by young Florentin Conant, the eldest son of Toussaint's older sister, Marie Suzanne. Upon submitting his claim in 1814, based upon occupancy, Florentin offered the testimony of Michel Papillon, a free man of color who had been freed thirteen years earlier upon the death of his last master, Don Manuel Bermudez y de Soto. Papillon swore that the claimant had resided upon and cultivated the land for about ten years. A second witness, Marcellet Martin, offered testimony that Florentin, "[who has] inhabited and cultivated the land for fourteen consecutive years preceding said date, is about thirty-five years of age, and has no family." [27] Martin was accurate in reference to Florentin's marital status but was very mistaken about his age. Florentin was actually born in 1795. [28] If he began to cultivate his land in 1800 as Martin indicated, or even in 1804 as Papillon testified, Florentin was a mere child when he became a planter. His claim was nevertheless confirmed for 674 acres. [29]

In addition to these successful claims, there were two disallowed claims filed with the register and receiver of the land office by the children of Marie Thérèze Coincoin. Her eldest black daughter, Marie Louise Mariotte, claimed a tract of only 2 *arpents* frontage by a depth of 40 on each side of Red River, a total of 160 *arpents,* contending that she had purchased the land from Antoine Bergeron. Since she was not able to produce any "document of title, or proof of occupancy," her claim was not confirmed. [30] Marie Louise's lack of proof of title is puzzling, since she did, indeed, legally purchase the claimed tract in 1798, and the deed of conveyance executed at that time has been preserved in the notarial records of the parish. [31] Her failure to prove title to a tract right-

27. *American State Papers: Public Lands,* III, 195, 199.
28. Baptism of Juan Francisco Florentine, March 1, 1795, in Natchitoches Registers, Book 4, 416.
29. *American State Papers: Public Lands,* III, 199.
30. *Ibid.,* 78, 84.
31. Antoine Bergeron to Marie Louise *dite* Mariotte, in Natchitoches Parish Records, Doc. 2877.

fully owned partly offsets the gains which the family made when they achieved confirmation of tracts held under dubious titles.

François Metoyer, the youngest son of Marie Thérèze, entered a claim by right of occupancy for 640 acres on Bayou Derbanne in Natchitoches Parish and offered the testimony of Pierre Carey in support of his claim. Carey stated that François had utilized the land as a *vacherie,* which had been supervised by his hirelings for sixteen consecutive years, even though he actually resided on a place that he had bought from his brother. Here again, this claimant appears to have gone into business for himself at a very tender age. In 1797, the year in which he supposedly began his *vacherie* operation, François was only thirteen. The board forwarded his claim to the General Land Office in Washington as a class-nine claim, that is "land occupied as *vacheries;* and whether with or without evidence of occupancy, ought not, in the opinion of the Register and Receiver, to be confirmed." François' claim was dis-allowed.[32]

Upon the transfer of Louisiana to American authority, Marie Thérèze and her family had presented a total of nineteen claims for land. One was based upon a donation, the sixty-eight-acre tract which she had received from Metoyer. Its validity was not questioned. Seven more sizable claims were based upon land purchases which the Metoyer brothers and their half sister had made along Red River (later Cane River). Six of these were confirmed; the seventh was disallowed. The remaining eleven claims were based upon alleged Spanish grants or upon the right of occupancy. Of the ten that were confirmed it is obvious that the supporting evidence provided was valid in only four cases. Marie Thérèze, Augustin, and Dominique received authentic concessions for which they were unquestionably eligible, and there is no evidence of misrepresentation involving Joseph's claim to a tract by right of occupancy. The other six cases, however, contained supporting evidence that was definitely questionable.

In contesting one of these claims, a white neighbor was to state that "this ... is not the first [misrepresentation] of this kind that this family of coloured folks attempt to make."[33] He was correct, but his accusation created

32. *American State Papers: Public Lands,* III, 172, 237.

33. F⁵ Roubieu to [unknown], November 20, 1841, at Natchitoches, in File R&R 309, Marie Perine, State Land Records.

a false impression. The fact is that these questionable claims filed by the Metoyers were not the first such claims made in the parish, or in the state; nor were they to be the last. For example, in the claim of Jean Baptiste Théodore Grillet, white, for 640 acres located above Campti in the northern section of the parish, evidence was introduced that Grillet had cultivated the land for fifteen consecutive years, even though he was only twenty-eight at the time of the testimony. The commissioners disallowed the claim with the observation: "It is very unlikely that the claimant should have established a plantation at thirteen years of age."[34]

Even the complainant who questioned the authenticity of Marie Perine Metoyer's grant (when it conflicted with his own claim to a portion of the same land) had himself filed claims of questionable nature and had assisted his neighbors (including Louis Metoyer) in filing similar claims. Seven years before this objection regarding Metoyer misrepresentations, the Congressional Committee on Private Land Claims had sent to the House of Representatives a report on a number of petitions submitted by residents of Natchitoches Parish. It was the committee's opinion that "some suspicion [is] thrown over the evidence . . . from the fact that these petitioners seem to have sworn generally for each other. The evidence would seem to convey the idea 'if you will swear for me I will swear for you.' " The committee requested that the local land office be authorized to collect testimony relative to these doubtful claims for presentation to Congress.[35]

Although questionable behavior from a community as a whole does not exonerate individual responsibility for such actions, it is nevertheless difficult to censure the ambitious free man or woman of color for employing the same business tactics used by the leading whites of his community. This generation of Creoles, white and colored alike, was the product of an era when Louisiana had been shuffled like a problem child from one national authority to another. With characteristic savoir-faire, they had learned to take care of matters in their own way while governments came and went and struggled for dominance.[36] Especially was this true in the Natchitoches area where the citizens had long been known for their disregard for outside authority.

34. *American State Papers: Public Lands,* III, 209.
35. *Ibid.,* V, 648.
36. It is interesting to note that this particular Creole characteristic generated problems of its own; in fact it caused the American government to view Louisiana as a "problem child" even

Moreover, this generation of Creoles had grown to maturity in a society in which land was free to any ambitious man who was willing to work it. The restrictive land regulations imposed upon them by the new American government left many young men without a means to make their start in life, including such youths as Jean Baptiste Théodore Grillet and Toussaint and François Metoyer, whose older brothers had received generous grants from Spain. To the Creoles of Louisiana, the American policy of purchasing vacant lands from the government undoubtedly seemed more unjust than the expedients which they took to accumulate the land they needed to build upon.

An additional irritant to the claimants of land in the new Louisiana territory was the reduction of size in individual holdings which often resulted from the adjustment of claims. As boundary lines were relocated by American surveyors, many landholders found themselves with less land than they had believed they owned. For example, the grant of Augustin Metoyer, which had been surveyed by the Spanish at 395 acres, was resurveyed by the Americans at only 157 acres. The 640-acre tract for which Joseph filed a claim based upon right by occupancy was surveyed and resurveyed until the boundaries finally decided upon allowed him only 470 acres.[37]

Another source of irritation to Natchitoches landholders was the federal requirement that they file their claims with the register and receiver of the Opelousas land office. As late as 1812, the deputy surveyor of the Natchitoches region, Joseph Irwin, wrote to Register Levin Wailes regarding problems faced by Augustin Metoyer and his mother: "The claimants have engaged the bearer to go forward to your Office to prove what he knows respecting the settlements of these two claims. . . . I write this at the request of the claimants who also wish me to state to the Board of Commissioners the Dificulty [*sic*] they labour under to establish their claims on account of the distance & the Difficulty of finding any person who will leave their habitations to undertake the journey at this season."[38]

---

from the beginning. According to Foner, in "Free People of Color in Louisiana and St. Dominique" (p. 421), "The Americans were generally nervous about taking over a territory whose population had seen frequent changes of government, with loyalties torn between France, Spain, and the United States."

37. File B1960, Augustin Metoyer, and File R&R 306, Antoine Joseph Metoyer, State Land Records.

38. December 9, 1812, at Natchitoches, Joseph Irwin Correspondence, in Chaplin,

The greatest difficulty faced by the Metoyers in the establishment of their claims was the challenge presented to Louis' title by Silvestre Bossier. Although Bossier had been the first owner of the land which Louis had been granted on Isle Brevelle, he had forfeited his title to the land after failing to fulfill requirements exacted of all grantees. In surrendering his order of survey and settlement to the commandant, Bossier had declared that the land was not worth the cost of the half of a bridge which he would have had to erect over neighboring Bayou Plat.[39] By 1806 Louis Metoyer had received title to the land and had made substantial improvements upon it. Bossier obviously regretted having forfeited the land and attempted to regain it. In some way he managed to retrieve his surrendered order of survey and settlement and submitted this to the board as proof of his ownership. Upon learning of his actions, Metoyer engaged the assistance of an attorney, William Murray, to draft for him a memorial setting out the facts regarding Bossier's invalid claim and his own legitimate one. In support of his petition he also secured, apparently through the influence of his father, a letter from former commandant De Blanc verifying that Louis was the rightful owner.

Despite De Blanc's testimony in which he swore "on my religion, my conscience, and my honor, that this declaration is true, that you may be on your guard against those who now wish to claim those titles . . . having lost all right to them," the board of commissioners ruled that Bossier's claim was as valid as Louis'. Their recommendation, which was forwarded to Washington, suggested that Bossier's title be confirmed, since no written evidence of abandonment could be provided. It would then remain for the two claimants to settle the issue between themselves or take the matter to court.[40]

In the end, the courts made the decision. Bossier and his heirs filed suit against Louis to have him evicted from the land and won in district court. Metoyer appealed to the Louisiana Supreme Court, and in the September 1818 term the decision of the lower court was overturned. Louis Metoyer was adjudged to be the rightful owner, and Bossier was charged with the costs of court.[41]

Breazeale, and Chaplin Papers (Louisiana State University Archives, Baton Rouge), Box 1, Folder 1806–1849.

39. *American State Papers: Public Lands,* III, 80.

40. *Ibid.;* Memorial of Louis Metoyer, in Opelousas Notarial Records Collection.

41. *Boissier et al* v. *Metayer,* 5 Mart. (O.S.), 678 (1818).

The adjustment of land claims by the United States government allowed 5,753 acres to Marie Thérèze and her family. Of this total, 68 acres had been given them by Metoyer. The remaining 5,687 acres, an average of 632 per person, had been acquired by Spanish grant or by right of occupancy. It was upon this foundation that the family built its fortunes. With industry and frugality the family members steadily extended their holdings, purchasing one additional tract after the other. Sixteen such purchases were made prior to Marie Thérèze's death, about 1817, bringing the family's total acreage at that time to 10,210, not counting four tracts of undetermined size.[42]

In 1861 a French-born priest in the parish wrote home to his parents, recounting to them the wealth of the local planters and the means by which it was acquired: "With the aid of a negro and a negress, at the most, they started with a little corner in the forest! And now their descendants, despite all their riches are very simple, good affable people."[43] Generally speaking, this rags-to-riches story can be applied aptly to the Isle Brevelle colony; in one significant respect, however, the situation of the Metoyers differed. The sons of Marie Thérèze started their labors alone, without either a "negro or a negress," or even children of sufficient age to assist them in clearing their "little corner in the forest."

The first of the brothers to acquire a plantation, Augustin, was also the first to join the ranks of colonial slaveowners. Living frugally in a small cabin that he erected hastily on his plantation, Augustin managed within two years to accumulate sufficient capital to purchase his first laborer. From a planter of the Rivière aux Cannes settlement, François Davion, he acquired a male Negro of approximately eighteen to twenty years of age, obviously chosen to assist him in clearing his property.[44] From this time (1797) forward, the notarial archives of Natchitoches record Augustin's rapid advancement into the ranks of the largest slaveowners of the parish.

Most such slaves, quite naturally, were purchased for their labor, but a sizable number of purchases were prompted by charity and familial devotion. In 1798, for example, Augustin bought his second slave; but this one was not

---

42. This figure is compiled from the land purchases recorded in the Natchitoches Parish Records and additional purchases itemized in the claims which they submitted to the Board of Land Commissioners for their purchased lands.

43. McCants (ed. and trans.), *They Came to Louisiana,* 134.

44. François Davion to Nicolas Augustin, Doc. 2740, in Natchitoches Parish Records.

a strapping male to help him clear the trees and cane brakes that forested his land but an eight-year-old Franco-African girl named Marguerite who was, in fact, his wife's sister. The purchase price was 261 piasters, and young Marguerite was freed immediately.[45]

In 1800 Augustin paid $300 for his third slave; this one, too, was a child, another natural daughter of his still single and still enslaved brother, Louis. The child's half-French mother, Francesca, was a slave as well; had it not been for Augustin's generous purchase and manumission, the child, Rose, probably would have grown up in bondage also.[46] Again the following year, Augustin paid $600 cash for the manumission of a fifteen-year-old Franco-African girl named Marie Perine—shortly before her marriage to Augustin's brother Pierre.[47]

In 1802, five years after the purchase of his first slave, Augustin bought his second one for labor. This one was a young black female named Jeanne, eighteen years old, with an infant, apparently purchased as a wife for the young male he already owned. A white resident of the Isle, Augustin Fredieu, stood *in solido* with Augustin on the $851 debt which he assumed.[48]

Between 1802 and 1809 Augustin depended upon the natural increase of this couple to enlarge his slave holdings and invested his capital exclusively in land. Apparently he did well, despite limited labor; when he again resumed his purchases of slaves in 1809 he possessed a sizable amount of operating cash. In June of that year, for example, he purchased from Archibald Phillips of Rapides Parish eight "African Negroes" for $3,500 cash: a male of about twenty, five boys aged eleven and twelve, and two girls aged eleven to thirteen. Three of the boys were immediately resold to his brother Louis for $1,350.[49] The following month he purchased another male slave of about twenty, his wife's Franco-African brother Remy. The price was $1,000, and

45. Augustin Metoyer of Succession of Marie LeClerc, Widow Derbanne, *ibid.*, Doc. 2857.
46. Widow LeComte to Nicolas Augustin, November 18, 1800, in Henry Collection, Old Natchitoches Data, No. 279; Baptism of Marie Rose, 1793 [n.d.], in Natchitoches Registers, Book 4, p. 411. The baptismal record does not name Marie Rose's father; family tradition identifies him as Louis, according to Father A. Dupre, Metoyer Family Genealogy.
47. Ambroise LeComte to Nicolas Augustin, Sale and Manumission of Marie Perine. Copy filed in File R&R 309, Marie Perine, State Land Records.
48. Judicial Sale of Property of Mr. Maes, in Henry Collection, English Translations I, No. 2992.
49. Archibald Phillips to Augustin Metoyer, and Augustin Metoyer to Louis Metoyer, in Natchitoches Parish Records, Misc. Book 1, pp. 98–99.

this slave was eventually freed by Augustin "in consideration of faithful service to him rendered."[50] Again the following year he purchased two more slaves from a local planter; the transaction was cash, but the total price was not indicated. One of these slaves, a fourteen-year-old French and African girl named Dorothée, was freed four years later.[51]

Similar slave purchases and manumissions are on record for the brothers and sisters of Augustin. Two such purchases made by Marie Suzanne present a very curious situation. In 1810 she purchased a Negro boy costing $600 from Thomas Parham, a slave trader of Brunswick County, Virginia. The following year she made a similar purchase from a Tennessee trader named Robert Bell.[52] Yet, at the time that Marie Suzanne bought these slaves she was herself a slave. According to the terms of the conditional manumission which her father executed in 1802, she was not to become a free woman until his death; this did not occur until 1815.[53] As in the case of her brothers Louis and Pierre, who allegedly received Spanish grants while still in bondage, Marie Suzanne was also accorded privileges by local authorities which were denied to other slaves.

The census of 1810, the first American census taken in the Territory of Orleans, reflects the growth which the fledgling colony on Isle Brevelle had made. Augustin Metoyer was listed as the owner of seventeen slaves; Louis had fifteen; Pierre, twelve; Dominique, eight; François, three; Joseph, two; and Toussaint, one. Together this made a total of fifty-eight slaves accumulated in twelve years. Of the 259 households enumerated on this census, only 166 owned at least one slave. Of the thirteen other free people of color or free blacks who were listed as heads of households, only four owned slaves; they averaged two each. The census further indicates that, if the population of the parish were divided into family groups by surname, of the resulting 192 family groups only five in the parish owned more slaves than did the Metoyers of

50. Joseph Derbanne to Augustin Metoyer, Misc. Book 1, p. 97; Succession of Marie Le-Clerc, Widow Derbanne, Inventory, Doc. 2857; and Augustin Metoyer to Remy, Conveyance Book 21, p. 109, all in Natchitoches Parish Records.

51. Manuel Derbanne to Augustin Metoyer, Misc. Book 1, pp. 186–87; Augustin Metoyer to Dorothée, Manumission, Book 3, p. 348, both in Natchitoches Parish Records.

52. Thomas Parham to Marie Suzanne, Misc. Book 1, pp. 225–26; Robert Bell to Marie Suzanne, Misc. Book 2, p. 94, both in Natchitoches Parish Records.

53. Pierre Metoyer to Marie Suzanne, Misc. Book 2, in Natchitoches Parish Records; tombstone of Pierre Metoyer, American Cemetery, Natchitoches.

color: the families of Rachal, Lambre, Buard, Prudhomme, and Claude Thomas Pierre Metoyer.[54]

The numerous land purchases which the Metoyers made on Isle Brevelle after 1810 demanded an increasing number of slaves, and in the subsequent years the family steadily enlarged its slave holdings. Conveyances on record indicate the purchase of at least twenty-two slaves between 1810 and 1817. Natural increase added at least nineteen more during this period.[55] In 1778 Marie Thérèze Coincoin had been a thirty-six-year-old freed slave with eleven children; she possessed no home, property, or money. Before her death some thirty-nine years later she had not only succeeded in obtaining the freedom of almost all, if not all, of those children, but she and they had accumulated an estate of between 11,000 and 12,000 acres of land and at least ninety-nine slaves.

Although the foundations of this estate were acquired at no cost other than the surveyors' fees, the rapid progress that the Metoyers made was achieved only through extreme thrift and industry. Frequently, the family purchased goods from the probate auctions of deceased neighbors, but luxury items were not included among these purchases. Land and slaves were their main capital investments, and profits seem to have been reinvested in their plantation operations. The only extravagance that has been credited to them during this period was the journey abroad which tradition claims that Augustin made with his father, touring the cities of France to which he had ancestral ties. This part of the legend has not been documented, but such a trip would have undoubtedly been made at the father's expense. In general, the Metoyers displayed great frugality during the development of their colony. Their way of life was simple; their homes were modest.

In recalling the first home which Louis Metoyer erected on his grant of land, an elderly resident of the area during the early twentieth century described it as "an adobe hut, a small house with but one room, built for the most part by his own hands."[56] This home no longer stands, but two other area dwellings of the same type that were erected during this period are extant,

54. Third Census of the United States, 1810.
55. Natchitoches Parish Records, Docs. 3331, 3810, 3813, 3814, 3815, 3925, 4150, 4178, 4581, 4582, 4633, 3010, and 3012; Natchitoches Registers, Books 5 and 7.
56. Herman de B. Seebold, *Old Louisiana Plantation Homes and Family Trees* (2 vols.; New Orleans, 1941), I, 362.

and excellent descriptions have been provided by an Isle Brevelle resident of the mid-twentieth century, Father J. J. Callahan:

> The Old Convent [is] said to be the oldest building on the river. The date of its construction is of course unknown, but its appearance does not belie its age. The floor is of hard packed clay, and it has a fire place and chimney of native brick. All the rest is cypress with mud filling. . . . the cypress stanchions remain visible in the adobe screen. In the walls of the Roque house the mud is mixed with deer hair; in the Old Convent with Spanish moss, which is today as strong and durable as when it was inserted. It [the Old Convent] is also the most primitive in another sense. It is the only house remaining where there is no attempt at ornamentation. The beams are rough hewn, and the thick boards are just as they were sawed by hand. In later buildings, both boards and beams were hand planed, and every beam that shows in the interior has a bead carved on each side of its face.[57]

Father Callahan's description depicts these earliest homes on the Isle as being crude, indeed, but these structures were not exceptional. Dr. Sibley's report on the urban dwellings in Natchitoches in 1805 was no more flattering; in his words, the town was "meanly built . . . half a dozen houses excepted."[58]

Typical of the more spacious and better class of homes in rural colonial Louisiana is a third extant dwelling on the Isle that dates back to the years of its earliest settlement. This house is the one known as Yucca, which tradition claims was built by Marie Thérèze. Its mode of construction was basically the same as that used for the Old Convent and the Roque house; that is, it was a *maison de poteaux en terre.* Logs were placed upright in the ground to form the framework for the walls. The spaces between the logs were then filled with *bousillage,* the mixture of mud and deer hair or moss. It differed from the more primitive cabins described above in three ways, primarily. First, its construction was of a better quality, indicating that more time and

---

57. J. J. Callahan *et al., The History of St. Augustine's Parish; Isle Brevelle, Natchez, La., 1803–1953; 1829–1954; 1856–1956* (n.p., 1956), 20.

Neither the Roque house or the "Old Convent" of which Father Callahan wrote were built by the Metoyers. The "Convent" was in all probability erected by a retired lieutenant of the militia, Gaspard Roubieu, who settled a tract of unclaimed land on the Isle and lived there with his wife until their deaths, about 1815–1820. At that time the property was acquired by the Metoyer family. Similarly, the Roque House was erected about 1803 by an elderly Negro named Yves *dit* Pocalé, who acquired his freedom at the age of sixty, labored to purchase a small tract of land in the midst of the Metoyer colony on Isle Brevelle, and remained there in close contact with them until his death. His property then became part of the Metoyer holdings.

58. *American State Papers: Indian Affairs,* I, 727.

effort was expended to produce a nicer dwelling. Second, rather than a square one-room cabin, it was an elongated structure of several rooms. Third, its front and back were designed with a spacious veranda extending the full length of the dwelling.[59]

As late as 1812 this style of home was still being constructed in Louisiana; in fact, it was even then preferred, according to one report, since two-story houses were considered unsafe in the "sudden and violent squalls of wind" that characterized Louisiana's weather, and since brick had only just begun to be accepted as a building material for homes. All houses, this account explains, were partly or entirely "surrounded by arcades or piazzas" for coolness.[60] The home in this style which Marie Thérèze allegedly built is believed by one of the foremost authorities on Louisiana architecture to have been built in the late Spanish colonial period, approximately 1796 to 1800.[61]

Although no proof of Marie Thérèze's residence at Yucca has yet been found, it appears to be a definite possibility. The grant of land on which Yucca stands is divided into two sections. On the west side of the river lies a small triangle containing only 53 acres. Across the river to the east is the bulk of the estate, 859 acres. Yucca stands on the east. The earliest survey of this land, made in 1814, and the 1815 survey made of Augustin's neighboring tract, indicate that Louis' home stood on the western section, across the property line from the home of Augustin.[62]

This choice of a site for Louis' residence is puzzling. By 1814 and 1815 Louis Metoyer was a man of means with a considerable amount of cleared land and a number of slaves. If his barns and slave houses were also located on the same side of the river as his home, on that small triangle of land, he would have been faced with the necessity of daily transporting his slaves, animals, and tools across the surging Red River in order to work the bulk of his lands. Reason seems to dictate that his plantation headquarters would have been located on the same side of the river as the bulk of his estate; but would

59. In later years, the ends of the back veranda were enclosed to form two extra rooms.
60. Major Amos Stoddard, *Sketches, Historical and Descriptive, of Louisiana* (Philadelphia, 1812), 328–29.
61. Samuel Wilson, Jr., School of Architecture, Tulane University, New Orleans, to author, July 31, 1973.
62. File B1953, Louis Metoyer, and File B1960, Augustin Metoyer, State Land Records.

Louis not have located his headquarters on the opposite side of the river from his home if there had been a person or persons on the other side of the river to supervise operations there?

Across that river stands Yucca where Marie Thérèze supposedly lived, the house which almost certainly was built during her lifetime. Whether the grant on which it stands was actually issued in her name, or in that of her son Louis, it is still possible that Yucca was her residence, built by her or her son as a new, larger, and nicer family home in the center of the lower Isle Brevelle area where her children were then settling. It would have been an advantageous situation for Louis. Since he remained single for five years after the acquisition of the grant, his mother would have been useful in tending his home. Since he had no children or slaves at that time to assist him in clearing his very sizable grant, his mother's slaves could have provided the necessary labor. The legend does hold that she and her slaves labored to cut this plantation out of the wilderness. Upon his marriage, probably, Louis and his new bride built the little house on the west bank, thereby providing a residence and a point of supervision for both portions of his plantation. At some point between 1815 and 1832 Louis resettled across the river at Yucca.

Beside Yucca stands another building which apparently dates back to the developmental years of the community, a building that is considered to be unique in Louisiana architecture. This little cabin, two stories high, with only one room on each floor, is dominated by a huge roof that drops low and projects twelve feet on all sides like a giant square bowl turned upside down, completely concealing the top story and sheltering the bottom against the most torrential rains. No columns support the heavy roof. A series of horizontal posts are wedged perpendicularly to the wall and the roof's edge. Without a single nail, these posts supported the ponderous roof for a century and a half.

The building strongly resembles a giant mushroom. Its architectural style is usually likened to that found in subtropical Africa or the West Indies. Because of its peculiar shape and the racial origins of the woman who supposedly built it, this house has been known through the years as the "African House." Constructed with bars for windows and no fireplace, it is here that legend says Marie Thérèze incarcerated recalcitrant slaves until they changed their attitude.

By the time that the old family matriarch died, a new generation of Metoyers was reaching adulthood on the Isle. Free lands were no longer available. It was now up to each parent to help his children obtain their starts in life. As these youth began to marry, each was provided with a tract of land, or slaves, or money, or all three, depending upon the assets of the parents and the preferences of the children.

One of the first such donations to the new generation was made in 1817 when Maxille Metoyer, the son of Augustin, married his first cousin, Marie Aspasie Anty, the daughter of Marie Suzanne. Augustin gave to the young couple a tract of land with six *arpents* of frontage "by the depth which it possessed." The tract was located on the lower end of the Isle between the lands of Charles LeMoine and the young couple's uncle, François Metoyer. In addition, Augustin also gave the newlyweds $600 in cash. On the same day, the bride's mother made another donation to the couple. Marie Suzanne had not long been free, and she had not been the recipient of free lands during the colonial era. At this early stage of her economic career, her resources were not as plentiful as those of her twin brother Augustin, but still she made a donation to her daughter and new son-in-law of another $600 in cash.[63]

In subsequent years Augustin, his sister, and their brothers, would make many such donations to their numerous progeny. However, even as the family's wealth increased, the generosity of the parents was tempered with moderation. Enough was given to each child to give him a start in life and a measure of financial security, but no son or daughter was to be given so great a handout as to weaken his initiative or his ambitions. This second generation of Metoyers grew up in households characterized by moderation and industry. Upon reaching maturity each new adult was expected to continue the tradition and to make his own contribution to the development of the Isle.

63. Augustin Metoyer to Maxile Metoyer and Suzanne Metoyer to Marie Aspasie Metoyer [Anty], Donation, Natchitoches Parish Records, Book 6, 252–54.

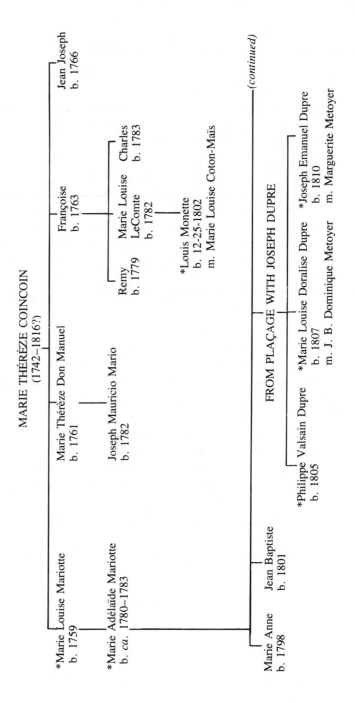

(KNOWN) NON-METOYER DESCENDANTS
OF MARIE THÉRÈZE COINCOIN
For Three Generations
Denoting (with an *) Descendants Who Joined the Isle Brevelle Colony

MARIE THÉRÈZE COINCOIN
(1742–1816?)

*Marie Louise Mariotte
b. 1759

*Marie Adélaïde Mariotte
b. ca. 1780–1783

Marie Anne
b. 1798

Jean Baptiste
b. 1801

Marie Thérèze Don Manuel
b. 1761

Joseph Mauricio Mario
b. 1782

Françoise
b. 1763

Remy
b. 1779

Marie Louise
LeComte
b. 1782

Charles
b. 1783

*Louis Monette
b. 12-25-1802
m. Marie Louise Coton-Maïs

Jean Joseph
b. 1766

FROM PLAÇAGE WITH JOSEPH DUPRE

*Philippe Valsain Dupre
b. 1805

*Marie Louise Doralise Dupre
b. 1807
m. J. B. Dominique Metoyer

*Joseph Emanuel Dupre
b. 1810   m. Marguerite Metoyer

(continued)

72

(cont'd. from page 72)

MARIE THÉRÈZE COINCOIN
(1742–1816?)

*Jean Baptiste St. Ville
b. 1814
m. Marie Cephalide Metoyer

FROM PLAÇAGE WITH
VICTORIN LEVASSEUR

*Marie Felony LeVasseur
b. 1816

*Marie Emy LeVasseur
b. 1816

FROM PLAÇAGE WITH
BARTHELEMY LECOURT

*Louis Toussaint LeCourt
b. 1817
m. Marie Lise Metoyer

METOYER DESCENDANTS OF MARIE THÉRÈZE COINCOIN
For Two Generations
Denoting Introduction of New Family Lines into the Colony

MARIE THÉRÈZE COINCOIN
(1742–1816?)

CLAUDE THOMAS PIERRE METOYER
(1744–1815)

(1)
NICOLAS AUGUSTIN

born: 1-22-1768
died: 12-19-1856
married: 8-22-1792
Marie Agnes **Poissot**
(sister of Marguerite LaFantasy)

Marie Modeste
Marie Louise
J. B. Maxille
Auguste
J. B. Augustin
Marie Pompose m.
  Charles Nerestan **Rocques**
Joseph Augustin m.
  Antoinette **Coindet**
François Gassion m.
  1) Marie Flavie **Mézières**
  2) Rosine **Carles**
  3) Perine **Metoyer**
Marie Suzanne (Suzette) m.
  1) Elisée **Rocques**
  2) Louis Amadée **Morin**

(2)
MARIE SUZANNE

born: 1-22-1768
died: 7-28-1838
placée: *ca.* 1795
Dr. Joseph **Conant**

  Florentin Conant

placée: *ca.* 1798
Jean Baptiste **Anty**

Marie Susanne (Suzette) Anty
Marie Aspasie Anty
Marie Thérèze Carmelite Anty
unnamed male infant
Marie Arsene Anty m.
  Manuel **Llorens**

(3)
LOUIS

born: *ca.* 1770
died: 3-11-1832
married: 2-09-1801
*Marie Thérèze **Lecomte***

Jean Baptiste Louis

(natural children of Louis)
Catiche - placée of
  Étienne **Carles**
Rose m. J. B. **Balthazar-Monet**
placée of: Antoine **Coindet**
        Dr. J. A. Z. **Carles**
        Dr. James **Hurst**

Thérèze m.
  Augustin **Cloutier**
Antoine

(4)
(continued)

MARIE THÉRÈZE COINCOIN
(1742–1816?)

CLAUDE THOMAS PIERRE METOYER
(1744–1815)

(continued)

(cont'd.
from
page 74)

**(4)
PIERRE**

born: *ca.* 1772
died: 6-25-1833
married: *ca.* 1803
Marie Perine **Lecomte**

   Marie Suzanne (Suzette)
   Athanase Vienne (Tanasitte)
   Pierre, Jr.

married: 12-31-1817
Marie Henriette Dorothée
   Monet-Cloutier
   Marie Ozitte m.
     *Neuville **LeCourt**
   Nerestan Pierre
   Auguste Dorestan
   Marie Elise

**(5)
DOMINIQUE**

born: 1776
died: 4-30-1839
married: 1-19-1795
Marie Marguerite **LeComte**

   unnamed male infant
   J. B. Dominique m.
   1) Adélaïde **Rachal**
   2) Marie Doralise **Dupre**
   Joseph Dominique
   Marie Susanne m.
     J. B. Espallier **Rachal**
   Marie Perine m.
     Pierre **Rachal**
   Narcisse Dominique m.
     Marie Cephalide **David**
   Marie Silvie m.
     Joseph Vallery **LeCourt**
     (continued)

DOMINIQUE *(cont'd.)*

   Joseph Ozeme m.
     Catherine **David**
   Marie Louise Theotis m.
     Marin **Rachal**
   Marguerite Arthemise
   Marie Cephalide m.
     J. B. **Mariotte-St. Ville**
   Marie Celine m.
     *Jacques Eloi **LeCourt**
   Louis Dominique
   Jean Baptiste Dominique, *cadet*
   Marie Lise m.
     Louis B. Toussaint **LeCourt**
   Marie Marguerite m.
     Joseph Emanuel **Dupre**
   Ambroise **Chastain**

Boldface surnames denote introduction of new family lines into the colony
*Denotes French-Indian rather than French-African origins
Only out-group marriages are indicated

75

MARIE THÉRÈZE COINCOIN
(1742–1816?)

CLAUDE THOMAS PIERRE METOYER
(1744–1815)

(cont'd. from
pages 74-75)

(6)	(7)	(8-9)	(10)
***	ANTOINE JOSEPH	***	FRANÇOIS

(7)
ANTOINE JOSEPH

born: 1-26-1778
died: 10-09-1838
married: 6-01-1801
Marie Pelagie **LeCourt**

Marie Susanne
Marie Anasthasie
Marie Aspasy m.
   Seraphin **Llorens**
Joseph, Jr.
Marie Deneige
Marie Celina
Marie Elina
Joseph Zenes
St. Syr Hypolite

(10)
FRANÇOIS

born: 9-26-1784
died: 12-28-1862
married: 7-23-1804
Marguerite **Lafantasy**
(sister of Marie Agnes Poissot)

Marie Adélaÿde m.
   Jerome **Sarpy**
Joseph François m.
   Marie Désirée **Coton-Mais**

married: 6-22-1815
   Marie Arthemise **Dupart**

   Oliver
   François Vilcour

***The following children of Marie Thérèze Coincoin and Claude Thomas Pierre Metoyer left no known issue:

(6) Eulalie
born: 1-14-1776
died: 1788–1801

(8) Marie Françoise Roselie
born: 12-9-1780
died: 1780–1783

(9) Pierre Toussaint
born: 10-10-1782
died: 2-17-1863

Chapter FOUR

Background of the Major
Allied Families

Although the Isle Brevelle colony of *gens de couleur libre* was founded by the Metoyers, enlargement of the family circle to include others proved to be a social necessity. Group intermarriage had been most frequent in the early years of the colony. Cousin married first cousin, totally unaware of the genetic hazards of the practice or of their church's proscription against it. In early Natchitoches the forbidden degrees of kinship were not applied to nonwhites. Couples of color were wed with no apparent effort being made to discern if or to what degree they were related.

As the status of the Metoyers improved within their community and they became recognized by society as worthy citizens, not merely freed slaves, a conscientious priest explained to Augustin the church's views on family intermarriages. According to tradition, it was Augustin, the colony's mentor, who then counseled the youth around him to form new marital patterns when they reached adulthood. With Augustin's guidance new blood lines were sought out; those that he approved were introduced into the colony.[1]

Group intermarriage, as it existed on Isle Brevelle, was not uncommon among families such as the Metoyers. Wherever free families of color clustered together for mutual support, especially when they possessed some degree of wealth or status, close marriages were common. For example, John Hope Franklin has pointed out similar marital patterns in North Carolina's Chavis family, quoting an earlier historian who accused them of inbreeding "to an appalling extent."[2]

In actuality, families such as the Metoyers of Louisiana and the Chavises of

1. Interview with Mrs. Coutii, October 12, 1974.
2. John Hope Franklin, *The Free Negro in North Carolina, 1790–1860* (Chapel Hill, 1943), 183, quoting from James Blackwell Browning, "Free Negro in Ante-Bellum North Carolina," *North Carolina Historical Review,* XV (January, 1938), 33.

North Carolina had little choice of mates. Despite the modern trend of blacks to view all men of color as "brothers," and despite the traditional attitude of whites which has tended to lump all nonwhites into a single inferior category, definite class lines have existed in nonwhite society. For the well-to-do free man of color, status, wealth, racial composition, and even religion have been important considerations in choosing a mate.

A study of Metoyer marriages of the colonial and antebellum period reveals that considerable selectivity was exercised. The most obvious criterion which they employed was racial; blacks were systematically excluded by them in the formation of romantic alliances. This was by no means a phenomenon unique to their colony, however; on the contrary, it was a definite characteristic of a large number of the more "aristocratic" families of color. James Hugo Johnston has best explained the rationale of this class: "There were agencies that tended to force many of the mulattoes into a caste apart from the mass of Negro population. When relations of affection existed between the white father and his mulatto children, such fathers were often inclined to consider their offspring not as Negroes but as persons of their blood, and there is evidence that such parents taught their children to consider themselves as better or superior to the members of the servile race."[3]

Adherence to this standard narrowed considerably the field from which the Metoyers could choose their wives and husbands. Within their own parish there was only a small number of free people of color with whom they could mingle socially. Of those available, only a few were considered "acceptable" by them. The settlements of Rapides, Opelousas, Pointe Coupée, Attakapas, St. Charles, East Baton Rouge, and Plaquemines offered small selections, a few of whom possessed a comparable degree of wealth, but no incidences of Metoyer intermarriage with free people of color from these areas can be found.

The city of New Orleans offered the widest choice of peers from whom the Metoyer youth could choose spouses, but here there were several limiting factors. In the earliest years of the colony, when the children of Marie Thérèze were first choosing mates, their economic and social circle did not include New Orleans to any appreciable degree. Their contacts in that city rapidly

3. Johnston, *Race Relations,* 293.

POPULATION GROWTH
OF LOUISIANA'S FREE PEOPLE OF COLOR

Year	Colony	Parish	State
1785	8*	8	1,175
1810	52	181	7,585
1820	75	415	10,476
1830	183	532	16,710
1840	—**	657	25,502
1850	362	881	17,462
1860	411	959	18,647

*This figure includes only the members of the nuclear family and their destined spouses who were already free.
**No accurate tabulation can be made of the colony's population for 1840 since one page of the enumeration of Isle Brevelle for that year is missing.

increased, however, and through the years a number of New Orleans youths were to move up the Red River and settle on Isle Brevelle.

Most New Orleanians of color who migrated to the Isle carried old and proud French names and were well educated. Undoubtedly, it was these factors that earned their acceptance into the Metoyer community, since very few were men of means. With only one exception the New Orleans natives who married on Isle Brevelle were males. The reason, perhaps, may be found in a theory advanced by several Louisiana historians. For example, one writer holds that the free women of color of New Orleans generally disdained alliances with men of their own race as being too "limiting." To become the *placée* of a wealthy French gentleman offered these women advantages that they could never attain as the wives of free men of color, regardless of how wealthy the nonwhite husbands might be.[4]

In addition to the free nonwhite population of Natchitoches and New Orleans, there were two additional groups of people that the Metoyers accepted into their community. According to tradition, several refugees from Haiti appeared on the Isle and became integral parts of the colony. At least three immi-

4. Annie Lee West Stahl, "The Free Negro in Ante-Bellum Louisiana," *Louisiana Historical Quarterly*, XXV (April, 1942), 308, 310, 375.

grants from France also settled there. These were men whose apparently pure French blood precluded their marriages to Creoles of color. Nevertheless, they formed alliances on the Isle, and their children were assimilated into the population.

The children of Marie Thérèze obviously had narrow choice in their selection of mates. When the oldest of these reached maturity, there were hardly a dozen free people of color of all ages at the post, outside of their mother and siblings, although a slightly larger number of slave girls of mixed parentage were available. From these, the Metoyer brothers made their choices. Most of the girls whom they chose were already free, but in a few cases the wife's freedom had to be purchased before the marriage, since none of the siblings would take for his wife a girl in bondage. Class consciousness was already a part of their psychological makeup.

An excellent example of Johnston's theory on the effect that a white father's prejudice had upon the social contacts of his children of color is provided by Marie Suzanne, the eldest daughter of Metoyer and Marie Thérèze. Parish records reveal the presence of no free man of color of appropriate age whom she might have chosen for a spouse. Obviously her father, to whom she was inordinately close, discouraged her contacts with young male slaves. In 1794 Suzanne was twenty-six, still single, and apparently still chaste, since she yet had no children but would soon prove to be quite fertile. Moreover, Suzanne's prospects were growing slimmer with every year that passed.

Early in the previous year there appeared in the parish a white doctor from New Orleans named Joseph Conant. After the doctor expressed a desire to settle in the area, Metoyer sold to him for a nominal sum a plantation three leagues from Natchitoches, complete with a *maison de poteaux en terre,* a storehouse, a garden, and auxiliary buildings. Apparently, the affections of Metoyer's daughter were also part of the transaction. Early in 1795 the twenty-seven-year-old Suzanne gave birth to her first child, a son who was named Florentin Conant.[5]

---

5. Pierre Metoyer to Joseph Conant, Natchitoches Parish Records, Doc. 2518; Baptism of Juan Francisco Florentine, March 1, 1795, in Natchitoches Registers, Book 4; Succession of Marie Suzanne Metoyer, in Natchitoches Parish Records, No. 395.

The match which Metoyer thus made did not last long. Within a year Conant disappeared from local records; whether he died or returned to New Orleans is not known. By 1797, Marie Suzanne had formed a new alliance with a planter of the parish named Jean Baptiste Anty. Her father's role in the formation of this second alliance is not clear, but it is obvious that the arrangement enjoyed his sanction since Suzanne remained under his close control, nursed his children and his wife, and continued to receive special favors from him. Suzanne's alliance with the Sieur Anty was to last for a number of years and resulted in four daughters, all of whom Anty acknowledged even to the point of attending their weddings and signing the marriage registers on those occasions.[6]

In all probability Suzanne's brothers were also guided by their father in their choice of mates. The first three to marry were all manumitted by their father just prior to the marriages, a clear indication that the matches met with his approval. All three chose free women of color for their wives.

Suzanne's twin brother Augustin was married in 1792 to Marie Agnes Poissot, a twenty-two-year-old of half-French, half-Negro extraction.[7] Marie Agnes had been born into the slave household of a nearby planter named Pierre Derbanne; her black mother, Françoise, was the Derbannes' cook. When Marie Agnes was but six years old a neighboring planter named Athanase Poissot acquired her from Derbanne by offering in exchange a black girl of seven years from the Poissot household. Within two months of this transaction Poissot's aging father, the former lieutenant of the militia, Remy

---

6. For example, see Marriage of Jean Baptiste Metoyer to Susanne Anty [date illegible - ca. 1817], Natchitoches Registers, Book 5.

7. August 22, 1792, Natchitoches Registers, Book 4-B, 99; Marie Agnes' age at time of marriage is calculated from date of death given on tombstone, cemetery of St. Augustine's Church, Melrose, Louisiana.

It should be noted that in the early church registers, no surnames were accorded to the wives chosen by the Metoyers. The same is true, in fact, of their husbands; on rare occasions the African name of their mother, Coincoin, was used by the priests as an identifying family name for the brothers. As the years passed and the position of the family improved, the community exhibited a change in attitude. The right to particular family surnames was acknowledged in most of the later civil and ecclesiastical records. Marie Agnes' surname, for example, is provided in such later documents as Marriage of Élise Roques and Marie Susette Metoyer, June 26, 1820, in Natchitoches Registers, Book 11.

Poissot, appeared before the commandant and declared Marie Agnes to be free, promising to rear her conscientiously in the love of God and the faith of the Church.[8]

The manumission of Marie Agnes was not accepted well by the Poissot family—particularly not by the wife of young Athanase Poissot.[9] Within four years Sieur Remy Poissot had to file a second document in which he repeated his manumission of Marie Agnes and indicated at great length that he would go to whatever measures necessary to enforce her freedom over all objections. The manumission was legally recognized, but it appears Mme. Athanase still remained unreconciled to Marie Agnes' freedom and her presence in their home. A contemporary index to notarial records of the post indicates that some ten years after this second manumission Agnes filed charges of ill treatment against Mme. Athanase. The actual proceedings of the suit are no longer on file; thus its particulars and its outcome can only be speculated upon.[10]

It should be noted that tradition has erred in its identification of Augustin's wife. It is occasionally claimed that Marie Agnes was the daughter of an Indian woman and a French-Canadian named Brevelle[11] or Dupre.[12] The only basis for this tradition seems to be the informal genealogy compiled in the late nineteenth century by an Isle Brevelle priest, Father A. Dupre, and deposited in the archives of the Isle Brevelle church. However, the original church records maintained in the archives of the Immaculate Conception Church at Natchitoches, from which Father Dupre apparently extracted most of his information, as well as the civil records of the post, plainly contradict the information on Marie Agnes which he recorded in his genealogy.

Two possible explanations exist for this discrepancy between legend and fact. The priest may have erred in translating the original records, and the community, unaware of his error, perpetuated it through the subsequent gen-

8. Natchitoches Registers, Book 4-B, 99. Succession of Marie LeClerc, Widow Derbanne, Doc. 2857; Pierre Derbanne to Athanaze Poissot, Doc. 1052; Remy Poissot to Agnes, Doc. 1093, all in Natchitoches Parish Records.

9. It is interesting to note that Mme. Athanase Poissot was the young daughter of Mme. Marie de St. Denis de Soto who had befriended Marie Thérèze on several occasions.

10. Remy Poissot to Agnes, Doc. 1357; *Agnes* v. *Mrs. Athanase Poissot*, Doc. 1700.

11. "A Visit to Melrose Plantation with François Mignon," recorded interview, No. B224, in Howard Tilton Memorial Library (Tulane University, New Orleans).

12. Callahan *et al., History of St. Augustine's Parish*, 13.

erations, weaving it into the fabric of their "family tradition." On the other hand, the tradition may have existed prior to the compilation of the genealogy and the priest recorded the tradition as fact. In this event, it is probable that tradition confused the wife of Augustin with the wife of one of his two brothers who married girls of Indian descent. At any rate, there is no existing record of the wife of Augustin which connects her to the Brevelle or Dupre families.

The background of Augustin's wife is doubly important, for one of her sisters married a Metoyer sibling also. As already pointed out, in 1798 Augustin bought and freed his wife's young sister Marguerite. Six years later, at the age of fourteen, Marguerite was married in the Church of St. François at Natchitoches to Augustin's youngest brother, François. Although Marguerite was half-French, no records reveal the identity of her father. After her marriage she assumed the surname of La Fantasy, a name which was used by no other family in the parish or surrounding parishes. Its literal translation seems to indicate that it was chosen for aesthetic appeal rather than to denote paternal ties.[13]

François Metoyer, this youngest son of Marie Thérèze, was the only Isle Brevelle male to marry a free woman of color from New Orleans. His first wife, Marguerite, died only a few years after their marriage. When François remarried he took as his wife a New Orleanian named Marie Arthemise Dupart, the daughter of an educated *femme de couleur libre* of the city named Victoire Mulon.[14] Inasmuch as this marriage took place several months after the *hommes de couleur libre* of Natchitoches reputedly went to New Orleans to assist in the defense of the city against the British, it may be that he was among that group.

In the earliest days of the colony the manumitted Metoyers associated primarily with manumitted slaves of the LeComte family who lived at the upper end of the Rivière aux Cannes settlement, just below the Isle. In 1795,

---

13. Marriage of François to Marguerite, July 23, 1804, in Natchitoches Registers, Book 5; Augustin Metoyer of Succession of Marie LeClerc, in Natchitoches Parish Records, Doc. 2857. Marguerite La Fantasy Metoyer's maiden surname is given in such documents as Marriage of Gerome Sarpy to Marie Adelaÿde Metoyer, June 27, 1820, in Natchitoches Registers, Book 11.

14. June 27, 1815, Natchitoches Registers, Book 5; Succession of Arthemise Dupart, in Natchitoches Parish Records, Succession Book 27, p. 377.

nineteen-year-old Dominique Metoyer married the fourteen-year-old Marguerite LeComte; like Dominique, Marguerite was half-French. Her black mother, Marie, was still a LeComte slave, but Marguerite had been freed by the Widow LeComte only five months before the marriage. Her freedom was granted on the same day, in fact, that Marie Thérèze Coincoin purchased the freedom of the child Catiche from the widow.[15]

On August 24, 1801, Augustin Metoyer reached an agreement with the widow's son Ambroise for the purchase and manumission of another LeComte slave, a fifteen-year-old French and African girl named Marie Perine. The widow had formerly given the girl to her young grandson, Joseph Dupre; as Dupre's guardian, Ambroise contracted the sale of Marie Perine with Augustin.[16] Soon after her manumission, Marie Perine LeComte was married to Augustin's brother Pierre.[17]

A third Metoyer brother with ties to a slave family of the Widow LeComte was Antoine Joseph. His bride, Marie Pelagie, was a quadroon, daughter of a French and African LeComte slave named Marie Magdeleine. Before Pelagie was even eighteen months old, a neighboring planter, Barthelemy LeCourt, paid Mme. LeComte for her (but not for her mother) and promptly manumitted the infant.[18] Throughout her life Marie Pelagie was to use the surname of LeCourt or LaCour. Since the Sieur LeCourt was the father of two other families *de couleur* who intermarried with the Metoyers, it may be speculated that he bore the same relationship to Pelagie.

It was Louis Metoyer who first introduced Indian blood into the family. During this period Indians occupied a very ambivalent position in Louisiana.

---

15. Marriage of Dominique to Marguerite, January 19, 1795, in Natchitoches Registers, Book 4-B, 102; Marguerite LeRoy to Marguerite, Natchitoches Parish Records, Doc. 2551. Marguerite LeComte Metoyer's maiden surname is given in such documents as *M. LeComte, tutrix et al* v. *Marie Susanne Metoyer,* in Natchitoches Parish Records, Succ. Book 12, pp. 175–79.

16. Ambroise LeComte to Augustin, copy of sale filed in File R&R 309, Marie Perine, State Land Records.

17. The marriage record of Pierre and Perine has not been found. The baptism of a daughter in 1804 indicates that the couple was legitimately married by that time. Baptism of Marie Susanne, November 15, 1804, in Natchitoches Registers, Book 5.

18. Marriage of Antoine Joseph to Marie Pelagie, June 1, 1801, in Natchitoches Registers, Book 4-B, 108; Baptism of Pelagie, July 22, 1784, *ibid.,* Book 4, 342; Barthelemy LeCourt to Pelagie, Natchitoches Parish Records, Doc. 1850. Marie Pelagie's surname is given in such documents as Marriage of Zeraphin Llorens to Marie Aspasie Metoyer, August 3, 1820, in Natchitoches Registers, Book 11.

According to the decision rendered in the case of *Adelle* v. *Beauregard,* a free person of color was legally defined as "descended from Indians on both sides, from a white parent, or mulatto parents in possession of their freedom."[19] As a free person of color the Indian was legally free to marry any other free person of color. Yet, since he had no African blood, the law did not prohibit his marriage to a white. Upon his marriage, he shared the status of his spouse.

In 1801 Louis chose for his wife an eighteen-year-old girl named Marie Thérèze LeComte.[20] The records do not indicate whether she was of full Indian blood or only half; her father was not named. It must be noted, however, that she bore a prominent local surname that was not the name of her master, for Marie Thérèze was born into the slave household of the LeCourt family.

Marie Thérèze LeComte's mother, also named Thérèze, was a native of the Cancey nation, a relatively small family of western Indians better known as Kiowa Apache.[21] In describing the nature of this group of Indians, Sibley wrote: "They are attached to the French; are good hunters. . . . They are very particular in their dress . . . the women wear a loose robe resembling that of a Franciscan friar; nothing but their heads and feet are to be seen."[22] Sibley also noted: "Thirty or forty years ago, the Spaniards used to make slaves of them when they could take them; a considerable number of them were brought to Natchitoches and sold amongst the French inhabitants, at forty or fifty dollars a head, and a number of them are still living here, but are now free. About twenty years ago, an order came from the King of Spain . . . and those that were enslaved [were] emancipated."[23]

19. *Adelle* v. *Beauregard,* 1 Mart. La., 183 (1810).
20. Baptism of Marie Thérèze, slave of Sr. LeCourt, December 26, 1783, and Baptism of Marie Celestia, slave of Sr. LeCourt, April 17, 1781, both in Natchitoches Registers, Book 4; Marriage of Louis to Thérèze, February 9, 1801, *ibid.,* Book 4-B. Thérèze's surname is given in such documents as Widow Louis Metoyer to Théophile Metoyer, in Natchitoches Parish Records, Donations Book 30, p. 52.
21. Marriage of Louis to Thérèze, February 9, 1801, in Natchitoches Registers, Book 4-B.
Cancey, Canneci, and Kancei were variant spellings of the name given to the Kiowa Apache by the Caddo Indians of the Natchitoches region and were, consequently, the names by which the Kiowa Apache were known at Natchitoches. It has been estimated that the tribe consisted of only 300 members in 1780. Although chiefly associated with the Kiowas, the Kiowa Apache broke with the parent tribe at one point in their history because of Kiowa unfriendliness to the white man. See John R. Swanton, *The Indian Tribes of North America* (Washington, D.C., 1952, reprinted Grosse Pointe, Michigan, 1968), 296–97.
22. *American State Papers: Indian Affairs,* I, 722–23.
23. *Ibid.*

It was, apparently, the Spanish who brought Thérèze to Natchitoches, where she was purchased by Lieutenant Louis Mathias LeCourt de Prelle of LeCourt's Bluff in the lower Rivière aux Cannes area. By the time of her daughter's marriage to Louis Metoyer, Thérèze was dead; but her daughter was one of that general class of people known as *gens de couleur libre*.[24]

Because of the ambiguity of the Indian's position in colonial Louisiana, and because of the forced emancipation of Indian slaves in the 1780s, some confusion has existed as to whether certain individuals were of Indian or Negro descent. A typical case, and one that involves the Cane River colony, has to do with the uncertain origins of Marie Henriette Dorothée Cloutier, who became the second wife of Pierre Metoyer in 1817 after the death of his first wife, Marie Perine.

Marie Henriette's mother, Dorothée Monet, was baptized at Natchitoches in 1778. The record identifies her only as the natural daughter of Jean Baptiste Dupre's slave, Marguerite. The racial composition of neither Dorothée nor her own mother, Marguerite, was given in the registers of the church.[25] In 1785, after Dupre's death, his widow remarried to a local *habitant* named Louis Monet, but shortly before the marriage she sold to her future husband the estate of her late spouse. Included in the sale was the child Dorothée; the child's mother was not mentioned in the sale or in the subsequent inventories of the property of the newlyweds. Both the sale and the marriage contract inventory identified young Dorothée as a "mulattress."[26]

After Indian slavery was abolished in Louisiana, Dorothée still remained in bondage. It was during this period that her daughter Marie Henriette was born, the natural daughter of a prominent local planter, Alexis Cloutier. Marie Henriette's baptism, and those of her siblings who were born during this period, all identified their mother Dorothée as a "mulattress." It is also noted that even during Dorothée's slavery she had begun to use the surname of her master, a practice not common at Natchitoches.[27]

24. Marriage of Louis to Thérèze, February 9, 1801, in Natchitoches Registers, Book 4-B.

25. Baptism of Atanasio and Dorotea, March 1, 1778, in Natchitoches Registers, Book 4.

26. Widow Baptiste Dupre to Louis Monet, Doc. 1831, and Marriage Contract of Louis Monet and Widow Baptiste Dupre, Doc. 1839, both in Natchitoches Parish Records.

27. For example, see Baptism of Henriette, February 22, 1797, Book 4-B, 39, and Baptism of Dorotea, February 12, 1793, Book 4, both in Natchitoches Registers. See also Alexis Cloutier to Parish Judge, Curator's Bond for Minor Children of Dorothée Monet, Deceased, Natchitoches Parish Records, Book 9, p. 34.

Finally, in the late 1790s, Dorothée was manumitted by the Sieur Monet and given land near LeCourt's Bluff, which Monet had purchased by that time. After the occasion of her manumission, Dorothée formed an alliance with another local planter, and several additional children were born to her. In all of the baptisms of these latter children, the registers of the church identified the mother as Dorothée Monet, "*sauvagesse* of the Canneci Nation." The few civil records which were made of her, however, continued to refer to her as a "mulattress," or a "free woman of color."[28]

The children born to Dorothée before her manumission remained in slavery. In 1810 her fifteen-year-old daughter, Marie Henriette, was purchased from Monet's widow, Marie Louise LeComte Porter, by Pierre Toussaint Metoyer. The terms were $640, on credit; Marie Henriette was declared free. Apparently young Toussaint purchased Marie Henriette with the intention of making her his bride; his plan was not successful. Toussaint did not complete the payment, but returned Marie Henriette to her former owner. The following year the girl's mother, Dorothée Monet, bought her from Mme. Porter for $650 cash and immediately freed her.[29]

When Marie Henriette eventually married, the husband she chose was Toussaint's older, widowed brother, Pierre. Upon Pierre's death almost two decades later, Marie Henriette remarried to another *homme de couleur libre* on the Isle named Émile Dupart. Toussaint remained a bachelor for life. It is apparent, however, that he held no permanent grudge against Marie Henriette for twice spurning him, for there is on record a donation of a slave made to her by Toussaint "in consideration of the love and affection he entertained for Marie Henriette."[30] It is also noted in all of these records that Marie Henriette is consistently referred to as a "free woman of color" or a "mulattress." No record is made of any Indian blood that she supposedly possessed.

28. Files A1794 and B1702, Dorothé Monet, and Section Map, Township 6 North, Range 4 West, Sections 43, 44, and 71, State Land Records. Baptism of Marie Louise Adeline, Marie Louise Adelaïde, and Louis, December 4, 1803, Book 5, p. 12; Baptism of Marie Thérèse Rosalie, October 12, 1805, Book 5; Baptism of Marie Zeline, December 29, 1809, Book 5; Alexis Cloutier to Parish Judge, Book 9, p. 34, all in Natchitoches Parish Records.

29. Mary Louise LeCompte Porter to Toussaint Metoyer, Misc. Book 1, p. 226; Marie Louise LeComte Porter to Dorothée, Doc. 4019, both in Natchitoches Parish Records.

30. Marriage Contract of Pierre Metoyer and Marie Henriette, Books 2 & 3, Marriages & Misc., 1816–1819; *A. P. Metoyer* v. *Henriette Dupard,* District Court Suit 3916; and Toussaint Metoyer to Marie Henriette, Donations Book 30, pp. 10–11, both in Natchitoches Parish Records.

Two possible explanations exist for the discrepancy in racial identification that has appeared in the records dealing with Dorothée and Marie Henriette. On the one hand, it is possible that Dorothée's mother, Marguerite, was an Indian of the Cancey tribe, sold into slavery at Natchitoches, and that her daughter was subsequently identified as a "*sauvagesse* of the Canneci Nation" by right of blood line rather than by actual birth. After the mother's death, Monet purchased the child and kept her in subjection, long after the abolishment of Indian slavery, on the pretext that she was of Negro rather than Indian descent; with no relatives in the area to protect Dorothée's status, such might have been the case. When Monet finally manumitted her, according to this theory, her true race was revealed and she was given property by the aging Monet (who may or may not have been her father) in rectification of the injustice done her.

On the other hand, there is the hypothesis that Dorothée's mother, Marguerite, was actually a Negro rather than an Indian. Dorothée, whom the records classified as a "mulattress," could then have been held in slavery legally. Upon her manumission by Monet (who still may or may not have been her father), an effort could have been made to upgrade her status and that of her children by identifying her as Indian rather than half-Negro.

In the case of Dorothée's daughter, Marie Henriette Cloutier, exact racial composition was to have little effect upon her status, since Henriette married two *hommes de couleur libre* and shared the status of her husbands. However, at least one of her brothers (whose surname was not the same as Henriette's) left Natchitoches in the company of a young girl of pure French descent and succeeded in establishing, elsewhere, his racial identity as white. His children returned to the parish and assimilated into the white population.[31]

In addition to the family of Dorothée, there were two other branches of the Monet family with whom the Cane River colony intermarried. Both were, unquestionably, of African origins. The first male Monet *de couleur* was born about the year 1780; no record of his parentage can be found. The earliest records refer to him under the name of Balthazar or Balthazar Monet, and indicate that in all probability he was free before 1791. The early records also identify him as half-French and half-Negro. Like Dorothée, Balthazar also

---

31. Because of the large number of descendants, long known as white, which this son of Dorothée Monet left in the Natchitoches Parish area, he will not be identified.

became a landed property owner in the Monette's Bluff area. About 1810 he married Marie Rose Metoyer, the teenaged natural daughter of Louis Metoyer whom Augustin had bought and freed in 1800. The marriage was a brief one; Balthazar died soon afterward, leaving Marie Rose two infants and his tract of land. After his death, Balthazar's widow continued to use the surname of Monet for several years, until her formation of a new alliance. Her children, however, dropped the Monet name entirely. Upon reaching maturity they consistently identified their father as Jean Baptiste Balthazar and themselves as Louis and Rose Balthazar. Their descendants have used Balthazar as a surname through all subsequent generations.[32]

Legend disagrees with the records with regard to the origins of this Cane River family. The story is repeated that Balthazar was a native of Haiti, a black who had fought side by side with Toussaint L'Overture. Upon his arrival on the Isle, supposedly, he was greeted with suspicion because of the color of his skin; the Cane River colony thought it more likely that he was a runaway slave. His story, supposedly, was checked into and found to be true; then, because of the great respect which the colony supposedly had for Toussaint, that "great Haitian liberator," his compatriot Balthazar was accepted into the colony. It must be noted that no record can be found to support this tradition, and numerous records contradict it.

The third branch of the Monet family that became an integral part of the Cane River colony was, in fact, directly descended from Marie Thérèze Coincoin. As noted earlier, Marie Thérèze bore a daughter named Françoise in 1763; in 1772 her mistress sold the child to a trader, who promptly resold her at a handsome profit to a local *habitant* named Jean Baptiste Dupre, the same planter who was the first master of Dorothée Monet. In 1782, while the property of Dupre, Françoise bore a daughter of mixed blood who was subsequently known as Marie Louise LeComte.[33]

After Dupre's death, his widow remarried and sold her inheritance from

32. Baptism of Florentin, December 18, 1791, in Natchitoches Registers, Book 4; Third Census of the United States, 1810; Baptism of Marie Rose, daughter of Balthazar Monet, December 6, 1812, Natchitoches Registers, Book 5, No. 1812–45; Marriage of Émile Dupart to Marie Rose Balthazar, July 23, 1829, Natchitoches Registers, Book 11; Rose Metoyer to Louis Balthazar, in Natchitoches Parish Records, Book A, 34.

33. Mme. de Soto to Sieur Delissard Jouhannis, Doc. 765; Sieur de lisard Jouannis to Jn Bte Dupre, Doc. 771; Widow Baptiste Dupre to Louis Monet, Doc. 1831, all in Natchitoches Parish Records.

Dupre to her new husband, Louis Monet. As the years passed, Monet remained in possession of the Franco-African slave, Marie Louise LeComte. On Christmas Day, 1802, the twenty-year-old Marie Louise gave birth to a quadroon son and named him Louis. Sieur Monet subsequently died, and young Louis, who used the surname of Monet rather than his mother's surname, LeComte, was inherited by Monet's widow, Marie Louise LeComte Dupre Monet.[34]

In December of 1824 the Widow Monet, who was by that time also the Widow Porter, petitioned the Louisiana legislature to permit her to free Louis, even though he had not yet attained the legal age for manumission (thirty years). A special bill was introduced in both houses to grant her request, and the bill passed. Although young Louis Monet did not marry into the Metoyer family, he did marry an in-law of theirs; because of his status as great-grandson of Marie Thérèze, he was readily accepted into the community.[35]

In addition to the Monet families, the Rivière aux Cannes settlement included three other main families *de couleur* who were to become an integral part of the Metoyer colony: the Rachals, LeCourts (later spelled LaCour) and Dupres. The first generation sons and daughters of these families were frequently chosen as spouses for the second and third generation Metoyers. Although the Rivière aux Cannes youths were not the equals of those on Isle Brevelle in a financial respect, the white fathers of most of them did provide for them to varying degrees.

The Rachals *de couleur* of Cane River began with a white planter named Jean Baptiste Barthelemy Rachal and his half-French slave, Marie Françoise. In the early years of their alliance the public records did not acknowledge their relationship. In the course of the alliance, however, Marie Françoise was

---

34. Marriage Contract of Louis Monet and Widow Baptiste Dupre, in Natchitoches Parish Records, Doc. 1839; Baptism of Louis, April 10, 1803, in Natchitoches Registers, Book 5.

35. *Journal of the Senate of the State of Louisiana*, 1825, pp. 25, 27, 46; *Journal of the House of the State of Louisiana*, 1825, pp. 39, 71, 75, 83; Marriage of Louis Monette and Marie Louise Cottonmaïs, July 23, 1829, in Natchitoches Registers, Book 11; H. E. Sterkx, *The Free Negro in Ante-Bellum Louisiana* (Rutherford, N.J., 1972), 119.

Sterkx erred in stating that Louis Monette was freed by his mother. Louis' French and African mother did use the name of Marie Louise LeComte, but she was still a slave and played no role in Louis' manumission. The mistress who manumitted Louis, after petitioning the legislature for permission, was Marie Louise LeComte Dupre Monet Porter, a white.

freed, and by the time the last of their six known children was baptized, 1816, Sieur Rachal was publicly acknowledging these children.[36]

In 1817, the eldest of the quadroon Rachals, Jean Baptiste Espallier, married Susanne Metoyer, the daughter of Dominique. Young Rachal indicated in their contract of marriage that he was bringing into the community 300 piasters in addition to a tract of land of five *arpents* of frontage on both sides of Red River. The land had been acquired two days earlier from his father, and was valued at another 300 piasters. The bride was also given 300 piasters in cash by her father, along with a tract of land lying between a plantation owned by him and the land owned by her future spouse. Marie Susanne's tract consisted of only four *arpents* frontage on each bank of the river, but it was valued at 900 piasters. Apparently, her land was of higher quality or was considerably more improved than that of Rachal. The bride's donation was to be considered an advance on her inheritance.[37] If both tracts of land contained the usual depth of forty *arpents* on each side of the river, the young couple began their marriage with 720 square *arpents* of land and 600 piasters in cash. Upon the death of her father, they would inherit more.

At least two other children of Jean Baptiste Rachal and Marie Françoise married members of the Metoyer community. On both occasions Rachal provided them with some degree of financial assistance, although his donations were not as large as those which his children's spouses received from their parents.[38]

The Dupres *de couleur* bore a relationship to the Metoyers before their intermarriage. Their maternal grandmother was Marie Louise Mariotte, the eldest daughter of Marie Thérèze. Their mother, Marie Adélaïde, who was her own mother's slave, had become the common-law wife of a young white Rivière aux Cannes planter named Joseph Dupre.[39]

36. Baptism of Antonio Neres Rachal, January 3, 1816, in Natchitoches Registers, Book 5.

37. Marriage Contract of Jean Baptiste Espallier Rachal and Susanne Metoyer, Books 2 & 3, No. 43; Succession of J. B. E. Rachal, No. 927, both in Natchitoches Parish Records.

38. Marriage Contract of J. B. D. Metoyer and Adelaïde, Books 2 & 3, No. 23, in Natchitoches Parish Records; Marriage of Pierre Rachal to Marie Perine Metoyer, February 8, 1820, in Natchitoches Registers, Book 11.

39. Tradition holds that Adelaïde was of Indian rather than African ancestry. However, the records disagree with this tradition, at least in as far as it regards Adelaïde's maternal ancestry. Her paternal ancestry is not known. Tradition could be reconciled with the records by speculating that Adelaïde was half-Indian and half-African.

In 1810 Dupre became ill; a will was drafted in which he donated $6,400 to his younger half brother, Jean Baptiste Sévère Cloutier, who was his closest legal heir. The remainder of his estate, consisting of slaves, land, livestock, and other goods, was bequeathed to his three natural children, Philippe Valsain, Marie Doralise, and Emanuel (Noel) Dupre. A slave and a sum of money were donated to Adélaïde, the children's mother. In an effort to facilitate the execution of his will he duly acknowledged his children before witnesses.[40] Ordinarily, this procedure should have been legally adequate to guarantee the fulfillment of his wishes. According to one authority, "Whenever a white citizen wished to leave a legacy to an illegitimate offspring [of color] the law required such a person to acknowledge paternity before a notary public in the presence of two witnesses."[41] However, the law also insisted that a natural child of color could inherit no more than one-third of the estate of a white father, and even then only if the father had no legitimate children.[42] It was with regard to this provision of the law that Dupre erred.

After Dupre's death, Adélaïde renounced her share of her inheritance in favor of her children. Dupre's executor, his uncle Ambroise LeComte, proceeded to settle the estate, but a suit was filed against him by Dupre's stepfather, Alexis Cloutier, acting as *curator ad litem* of his son, J. B. Sévère Cloutier. The elder Cloutier petitioned to have the will declared null and to grant Dupre's entire estate to J. B. Sévère. The suit was taken to the state supreme court, and the final decision favored Cloutier. In April, 1816, LeComte delivered to the elder Cloutier $7,000, representing the share of the estate which Dupre had intended to leave his children.[43]

One of the points of controversy in this suit had been the slave status of the legatees. In an effort to remove this obstacle, Marie Louise Mariotte first freed her Dupre grandchildren and then her daughter Adélaïde.[44] The move brought

40. *Philippe Valsain* v. *Cloutier,* in Natchitoches Parish Records, District Court Record, Book 3, pp. 118–26.
41. Sterkx, *The Free Negro in Ante-Bellum Louisiana,* 179.
42. *Ibid.*
43. *Philippe Valsain* v. *Cloutier,* Natchitoches Parish Records.
44. The document whereby Mariotte freed her daughter Marie Adelaïde is not extant; however, it is referred to in a second document, Mariotte to Marie Adelaïde, Donation, in Natchitoches Parish Records, Notarial Book 3, pp. 302–304.

no success. In 1830, when the youngest Dupre child was just short of the age of majority, a family meeting of his "friends and relatives" was called to deliberate on the best course of action that he, as minor legatee of Joseph Dupre, should follow to recover his inheritance. The six "friends and relations" who attended consisted of his older brother, Philippe Valsain Dupre, and five of the most influential whites of the parish: Narcisse Prudhomme, Jean Baptiste Prudhomme, Arnaud Lauvé, Chrisostome Perot and Charles Emmanuel Greneaux.[45]

Acting upon the counsel of these advisors, young Emanuel, his brother Philippe, and sister Marie Doralise, filed suit against Cloutier. According to the petition of the plaintiffs, the $7,000 which Cloutier had received from Dupre's executor in 1816 should be returned to them. Moreover, their petition asserted that their father's plantation of fifteen *arpents* frontage on each side of Red River had been offered for sale at the customary probate auction, where Cloutier had informed the bystanders that he wanted to purchase the plantation for Dupre's children. As a consequence, the bystanders declined to bid against him. Cloutier entered his bid for $200 and was the only bidder. He subsequently resold the land for $2,000. Dupre's children now requested a judgment in their favor of these two sums, $7,000 and $2,000, with 5 percent interest from 1811.[46]

Cloutier countered with the charge that he had already given to the plaintiffs "several slaves . . . out of respect for the memory of Dupre"[47] and that they had already received $5,000 from Dupre's executor. Moreover, Cloutier challenged, they had no right of inheritance at law in the first place. The testator had bequeathed his property to his *children* and since "the Testator was a white man and the Plaintiffs being as they allege themselves persons of colour [they] cannot bring themselves within the term of the will by tracing their paternity."

Cloutier's viewpoint was not shared by the jury. The decree of the court,

---

45. Family Meeting of Friends and Relatives of Noel Dupre, f. m. c., *ibid.*, Book 20, pp. 305–306.

46. *Philippe Valsain* v. *Cloutier, ibid.*

47. Cloutier's claim to have given "several slaves" to the plaintiffs is only partly supported by the records. Only one such donation can be found; see Alexis Cloutier to Marie Doralise, f.w.c., *ibid.*, Doc. 4751.

dated May 28, 1831, ordered the defendant to pay to Dupre's heirs the sum of $6,687, with 5 percent interest from May 3, 1815, until paid, plus the costs of the suit.[48] The judgment against Cloutier, who was described as a wealthy man, was not so harsh, since interest in that period customarily ranged from 8 to 10 percent. Still, assuming that Cloutier repaid the debt immediately, the sum which Dupre's three children were awarded, figured at simple interest, amounted to $14,596.

The Dupre youth were not indigent by any means before the receipt of this inheritance. In 1830 the youngest Dupre, Joseph Emanuel, had married Marie Marguerite Metoyer, the daughter of Dominique. Mlle. Metoyer entered the marriage with $900 in cash. Dupre listed his assets as $1,300, of which he donated $500 to his future wife.[49]

Another Cane River family that the Metoyers accepted into their community were the LeCourts. As previously noted, Joseph Metoyer had married in 1804 a young woman of color who appeared to be the daughter of one Barthelemy LeCourt. This same Sieur LeCourt was later the progenitor of two other families who intermarried with the Metoyers, one family being of French-Indian extraction, and the other French-African.

Barthelemy LeCourt was a son of the French officer Lieutenant Louis Mathias LeCourt de Prelle, who first settled the Rivière aux Cannes area.[50] As a young man Barthelemy formed an alliance, which was to last for many years, with a free Caddo Indian woman named Marie Ursulle.[51] Under the accepted legal definitions of that period, Marie Ursulle was a "free person of color." Her offspring also shared her status. Marriage between whites and Indians was legal under Louisiana law, but LeCourt and Marie Ursulle did not formalize their union. Apparently, their failure to do so led casual acquaintances to assume that marriage between them was illegal, since on one occa-

48. *Philippe Valsain* v. *Cloutier, ibid.*

49. Marriage Contract of Emmanuel Dupre to Marie Marguerite Metoyer, in Natchitoches Parish Records, Misc. Records, Book A, Doc. 457, p. 48.

50. Marriage of Louis LeCourt de Prelle to Jeanne LeRoy and Legitimation of Barthelemy, Jean Baptiste, and Antoinette, March 1765, in Natchitoches Registers, Book 2.

51. Baptism of Marie Louise, *sauvagess,* daughter of Marie Ursulle, *sauvagess* of the Caddo nation, July 6, 1796, in Natchitoches Registers, Book 4, p. 157. This record provides the earliest identification of Marie Ursulle's race.

sion the priest who baptized a child of the couple haphazardly identified the mother not just as a "free woman of color" but as a "free mulattress."[52]

The situation experienced by this family is an interesting one. Their daughter, Marie Louise, was baptized under the customary description of *sauvagesse,* but from the day of her marriage into a respectable white creole family of the area she was never classified as anything but white.[53] Three of her brothers, however, married Metoyers of color and from that time forward were consistently referred to as "free men of color" or as "mulattoes."[54] The only exception occurred at the death of their sister Marie Louise. A family meeting was called to discuss the interests of her minor children; her brothers attended the meeting. Notary Jean Baptiste LeComte, who had long known the family, indicated that the brothers were white in his account of the proceedings, in spite of the fact that at least one of them had already married a Metoyer of color.[55]

After the death of Marie Ursulle, LeCourt formed a new alliance with Marie Adélaïde Mariotte, the former concubine of Joseph Dupre. At least one son was born to this couple, Louis Barthelemy Toussaint LeCourt. Like his Dupre and LeCourt half-siblings, he married into the Metoyer colony.[56]

Above the town of Natchitoches was another, smaller, settlement of free people of color populated mainly by the interrelated families of Grappe, David, and Mézières—most of whom descended from Marie Thérèze's sister, Marie Jeanne Mézières. Three of the second generation Metoyers chose wives from this community.[57] The contract for one of these marriages is still on file.

52. Baptism of Jacques Eloy, December 29, 1809, in Natchitoches Registers, Book 5, No. 1809–67.

53. Marriage of Marie Louise LeCour to Pierre Brosset, October 30, 1813, *ibid.*

54. Marriage of Joseph Valerie, f.m.c., to Marie Silvie Metoyer, in Natchitoches Parish Records, Book C, Notarial, Folios 1–268, Doc. 42; Marriage of Neuville LeCour to Marie Ositte Metoyer, February 15, 1830, Book 11; Marriage of Jacques Eloy LeCour to Marie Celine Metoyer, January 16, 1836, Book 8, both in Natchitoches Registers.

55. Succession of Marie Louise Brosset, née LeCourt, in Natchitoches Parish Records, No. 15.

56. Baptism of Louis Toussaint, November 1, 1817, in Natchitoches Registers, Book 5. Succession of Dominique Metoyer, in Natchitoches Parish Records, Succession Book 12, pp. 175–79, identifies Louis Toussaint as his son-in-law.

57. Marriage Contract of Joseph Ozeme Metoyer and Catherine David, in Henry Collection, Old Natchitoches Data, II, No. 113; Succession of Narcisse Dominique Metoyer, in Natchitoches Parish Records, Succession Book 12, pp. 175–79, identifies his widow as Marie Cephalide

Joseph Ozeme Metoyer, son of "Sieur Dominique Metoyer and Dame Marguerite LeComte," a minor, married Catherine David, the adult daughter of Dame Magdeleine Grappe of Campti. While the groom's property consisted of $300 and a tract of land containing seven *arpents* frontage on the river, the bride brought into the community only "a certain number of animals" valued at $100. Joseph Ozeme gave to her a special mortgage on his property to guarantee her dowry, according to the custom of that time.[58]

After two decades of economic growth, the Metoyer enterprises had expanded to the point that extensive financial dealings were being conducted with business houses of New Orleans. Most probably it was the contacts which were thus formed that resulted in the migration of a number of New Orleans youths to the Isle Brevelle area. Although they had little to contribute in the way of material goods, the young men did possess education and connections with influential New Orleans families.

Most of these youths, apparently, were the illegitimate offspring of well-to-do French gentlemen of the city and their *placées*. Literally, the word means "placed." In old New Orleans it was a special term used for women of a distinctive class. In general, *placées* possessed no more than one-fourth to one-eighth Negro blood; they were of striking beauty and were highly cultured. One English traveler in the city described them as "some of the most beautiful women that can be seen . . . with lovely countenances, full, dark, liquid eyes, lips of coral and teeth of pearl, long raven locks of soft and glossy hair, sylph-like figures, and such beautifully rounded limbs and exquisite gait and manner, that they might furnish models for a Venus or a Hebe to the chisel of a sculptor."[59]

From their childhood, such girls were rigorously trained in the social graces: music, art, literature, dancing, conversation. Many were well educated, some of them going abroad. All were raised in chastity and carefully

---

David; Succession of François Gassion Metoyer, in the Chaplin, Breazeale, and Chaplin Papers, identifies his first wife as Marie Flavie Mézières.

58. Marriage Contract of Joseph Ozeme Metoyer and Catherine David, in Henry Collection, Old Natchitoches Data, II, No. 113.

59. James Silk Buckingham, *The Slave States of America* (2 vols.; London, 1842), 35–38, quoted in Stahl, "The Free Negro in Ante-Bellum Louisiana," 306.

protected until the day that they found a "protector." As a result of their training, visitors to the city noted that they conducted themselves "with more propriety and decorum than the white women." [60]

Upon reaching maturity the young quadroons or octoroons were introduced into society at New Orleans' celebrated quadroon balls. Attendance at these balls was restricted to free women of color and white men of affluence. In addition to providing delightful (but strictly chaperoned) company, the balls also provided the young ladies with the opportunities to display the graces which they had cultivated so carefully. When a young lady's charms had won her an admirer who was acceptable both to her mother and to herself, a mutually satisfactory agreement was reached and a formal contract signed stipulating the manner in which the gentleman would provide for her and their future children. The girl was then feted by her friends, in the same manner in which brides are usually feted. Upon moving into the home established by her "protector," she became *une placée*. [61]

A few such arrangements lasted for a lifetime, some for numerous years, and others for short periods. As long as a *placée* remained faithful, she was esteemed by her peers as honorable and virtuous. Her greatest hope, some allege, was to produce children white enough to pass into that privileged race. Daughters were reared as their mothers had been reared, to become the mistresses of cultured gentlemen. The sons were provided for to varying degrees. Most were well educated, many being sent to France; a few unfortunate ones were said to have ended up in the slave markets. But between these extremes many were placed on plantations in the backcountry of the state. [62] The New Orleans youth who assimilated into the Isle Brevelle population primarily fell into this latter category.

In January, 1818, a twenty-one-year-old *homme de couleur libre* of mixed parentage named Manuel Llorens was married at Natchitoches to Marie Arsene Anty, the quadroon daughter of Sieur Jean Baptiste Anty and Suzanne

---

60. Stahl, "The Free Negro in Ante-Bellum Louisiana," 305–312.
61. *Ibid.*
62. *Ibid.*, 307–308; Donald E. Everett, "Free Persons of Color in New Orleans, 1803–1865" (Ph.D. dissertation, Louisiana State University, 1952), 233–34.

Metoyer. Although young Llorens was a native of New Orleans, his father, Sieur François Llorens, had settled at Natchitoches prior to 1810 with his *placée,* François Nivette, and their children.[63]

In November of that same year Charles Nerestan Rocques—aged twenty, identified as the natural son of Pierre Rocques, white, and Lisette Glapion, free colored, all residents of New Orleans—was married to Augustin Metoyer's seventeen-year-old daughter, Marie Pompose.[64] According to their contract of marriage filed that same day, young Rocques had no assets. His bride took into the marriage an eighteen-year-old "Guineau Negress" valued at 600 piasters and a tract of land of five *arpents* frontage on Isle Brevelle. The total value of her estate was 2,100 piasters.[65]

In 1820 Rocques' brother Élisé, aged twenty-three, married Marie Pompose's fourteen-year-old sister, Marie Susette.[66] The following day another New Orleans native named Jerome Sarpy, the twenty-four-year-old natural son of Sieur Sarpy and Barton Beler, was married to François Metoyer's sixteen-year-old daughter Marie Adelaÿde.[67] Two months later young Seraphin Llorens, whose brother Manuel had married into the community in 1818, was married at Natchitoches to Marie Aspasie Metoyer, the daughter of Joseph.[68]

During the 1820s only two additional free men of color from New Orleans were accepted into the community. Both were named Dupart, and while it is clear that they were not brothers, their exact relationship is unknown. Émile Dupart first appears in parish records in 1824 as a witness to the marriage of Philippe Valsain Dupre. Five years later he also married, choosing as his bride young Marie Rose Balthazar, the only daughter of Jean Baptiste Balthazar-Monet and Marie Rose Metoyer. The marriage record identifies Dupart as the son of Victoire Mulon, a free woman of color of New Orleans. Mme. Mulon was present at the Isle Brevelle wedding and signed the marriage record. This

63. Natchitoches Registers, Book 5; Third Census of the United States, 1810.

64. November 3, 1818, Natchitoches Registers, Book 11.

65. Marriage Contract of Charles Nerestan Rocques and Marie Pompose Metoyer, in Natchitoches Parish Records, Books 2 & 3, No. 87.

66. June 26, 1820, Natchitoches Registers, Book 11.

67. June 27, 1820, *ibid.*

68. August 3, 1820, *ibid.*

Dupart, Émile, was the brother of Arthemise Dupart who married François Metoyer in 1815, the only New Orleans female to marry into the colony.[69]

Leander Dupart, who appeared in the parish at the same time as Émile, married into the colony as well. The wife that he took in 1825 was an orphan named Marie Jeanne Cecile, a free Franco-African girl who was the ward of Augustin Metoyer's son, Auguste. The marriage contract of Leander and Marie Jeanne indicates that he was the son of deceased Lolette Belleaire, a propertied woman of color at New Orleans; it also noted that he would soon be accorded 500 piasters as his share of his mother's succession.[70]

By 1831 another New Orleans native had settled on the Isle, Louis Morin. In the summer of that year he was married to Augustin Metoyer's daughter Marie Suzette, widow of the late Élisé Rocques. Unlike most of the New Orleans youth who migrated to the Isle to seek their fortunes, Morin was a man of property prior to his arrival; his mother, Mme. Sanitte Morin, was herself a property owner. According to the marriage contract which Louis filed with Marie Suzette on the day of their marriage, Morin owned three tracts of land in the city of New Orleans. Two of these were situated in Faubourg Sainte-Marie above the town and the third in the heart of the city. Morin indicated that he had purchased the first tract from Henry Ford, the second at a sheriff's sale, and the third from Joseph Peraltas.[71]

Probably the last New Orleanians to settle on the Isle before the decline of the colony were Firmin Capello Christophe and Oscar Dubreuil. Christophe, a tailor, settled on Isle Brevelle with his family. Upon reaching maturity his children were readily accepted as spouses for the Metoyer youth. Dubreuil, a schoolteacher initially, arrived as a bachelor. It was not long before he had married Marie Celina Rachal from the Cloutierville (Rivière aux Cannes) community, the daughter of Jean Baptiste Espallier Rachal and Marie Susanne

69. Marriage Contract of P. V. Dupre and Marie Doralise Derbanne, in Natchitoches Parish Records, Book 15, 138; Marriage of Émile Dupart to Marie Rose Balthazar, July 25, 1829, in Natchitoches Registers, Book 11.

70. Marriage Contract of Leandre Dupart and Marie Jeanne Cecille, in Natchitoches Parish Records, Book 14, p. 249.

71. Marie Suzette Metoyer, Renunciation, in Natchitoches Parish Records, Misc. Book 19, pp. 268–69; Vᵛᵉ Louis Morin to A. Chateigner, Procuration, DeBlieux Collection (MS in possession of Robert B. Deblieux, Natchitoches), Doc. 342.

Metoyer.[72] Although neither of these men owned much at the time of his arrival upon the Isle, each possessed a skill or a profession that was vitally needed there.

In 1818 Louis Chevalier, a French immigrant from the Department of Haute-Loire, arrived in the United States. By 1830 he had settled on Isle Brevelle with his common-law wife, a free woman of color named Fanny. Tradition holds that Chevalier came to the colony as a teacher, possessing a degree from the Sorbonne or an equally prestigious university.[73] The earliest record of him, dated 1832, indicates that he was a merchant on the Isle at that time, a partner in the firm of Chevalier & Oscar.[74] As his fortunes increased, Chevalier acquired a tract of land across Old River from Isle Brevelle and another on Cane River; he spent the remainder of his life as a planter.[75] Many documents from the 1830 to 1850 period indicate a very close relationship between Chevalier and the Metoyer community.

Before his death Chevalier drafted a will leaving all of his estate to the seven children whom he had by Fanny and naming two influential white friends, the brothers-in-law Michael Boyce and Pascalis Roubieu, as his executors. Chevalier's relative, Dr. Isidore Gimbert of Isle Brevelle, and the remaining heirs in France contested the will. A compromise was reached and the Chevalier children received a settlement of $20,000 in addition to the 500 acres of his Cane River estate that he had purchased in 1851 from the estate of Roubieu's father, François.[76] As a result of this settlement, the Chevalier family was one of the wealthiest with whom the Metoyers intermarried.

In addition to Chevalier, two other French immigrants settled on Cane River. Both formed alliances, in their turn, with the same Creole of color, Marie Rose Metoyer, the widow of Jean Baptiste Balthazar-Monet. Shortly after Balthazar's death, Marie Rose became the *placée* of Jacques Antoine

72. Seventh Census of the United States 1850; interview with Mrs. Coutii, March 24, 1974; Succession of J. B. E. Rachal, in Natchitoches Parish Records, No. 927.

73. Elizabeth Shown Mills, "Certificates of Naturalization, Natchitoches Parish, Louisiana, 1820–50," *Louisiana Genealogical Register*, XXI (March, 1974), 73; interview with Mrs. Coutii, April 26, 1974.

74. Chevalier & Oscar to Celestin Cassa, Statement, in Norbert Badin Papers (Louisiana State University Archives, Baton Rouge).

75. Section Map, Township 8 North, Range 7 West, State Land Records; Seventh Census of the United States, 1850; Succession of Louis Chevalier, in Natchitoches Parish Records, No. 752.

76. *Ibid.*

Coindet, an elderly French-born white who had long been a friend of the Metoyer family. It was Coindet, in fact, who had traveled to Opelousas in 1811 to assist Augustin in proving the title to a tract of land which he was claiming.[77]

In 1822 Coindet died leaving no legitimate direct descendants or ascendants, though there were numerous collateral descendants on the Isle D'Oloron of France. Coindet's will expressed his desire to leave his entire estate to his natural children by Marie Rose. His friend Benjamin Metoyer, a white son of the original Pierre Metoyer, was named executor of the estate.[78] As guardian of her two small children by Coindet, Marie Rose received from Sieur Metoyer cash and property in the amount of $4,878. But the settlement of this estate was soon contested by Coindet's heirs in France. The suit was taken to the district court and was eventually decided in favor of the Coindet heirs in France; Marie Rose was ordered to repay them the sum she had received from Coindet's estate, plus interest, in three annual installments of $1,650 each.[79]

The situation was complicated, in the meantime, by the new *placage* which Rose made with another French immigrant on Cane River, Dr. Jean André Zepherin Carles. In 1824 Rose gave her power of attorney to Carles to assist her in the settlement of Coindet's estate. She also authorized him to build a home on the land which her children had inherited from Coindet. When Rose failed to meet one of her annual installments as it fell due, the Coindet heirs seized the land which Coindet left to his children by Rose, along with the house which Carles built upon the land, and sold both at sheriff's sale.[80]

Dr. Carles died in the midst of the litigation, leaving no property. Marie Rose had attained nothing from her alliances with Coindet and Carles, except the two children that resulted from each of the alliances. All were accepted into the Metoyer community. Rose was not left indigent, however; building upon the estate left her by Balthazar, she had accumulated, by 1830, a total of eleven slaves.[81]

---

77. File B1960, Augustin Metoyer, State Land Records.
78. *Coindet* v. *Metoyer,* Natchitoches Parish Records, District Court Suit No. 942.
79. *Ibid.*
80. Rose Metoyer to J^n A. Z. Carles, D. M., Procuration, No. 109, and Rose Metoyer to J^n P^{re} M^{le} Dubois, Procuration, unnumbered document, in DeBlieux Collection.
81. Marie Rose and Dr. Carles were the parents of two daughters. See Baptism of Thérèsine, December 20, 1826, in Natchitoches Registers, Book 7, and Marriage of Rosine Carles to Fran-

Tradition holds that new blood lines were introduced into the colony in still one other way. Because of their prosperity, the men of this family formed lasting friendships with many of the leading white planters of the parish, and a small number of these planters were, themselves, the fathers of children of color, in addition to their legal offspring. These solicitous fathers, some of whom acknowledged their children publicly, not only freed the children but also worried over the possibility of their sons and daughters "going with the blacks." As a solution to this problem, the planters approached their Metoyer friends and arranged marriages between their offspring.

Documentary support of this tradition is not hard to find. For example, in 1841 François Florival Metoyer, son of Jean Baptiste Augustin Metoyer and his wife Marie Suzette Anty, was married to Marie Thérèse Aspasie Prudhomme. The bride was identified in the marriage registers of the Church of St. François as the natural daughter of J. B. Prudhomme, Jr., a prominent planter on the Côte Joyeuse, and Marie Pompose. Prudhomme signed the register as a witness to his daughter's marriage, along with the bride's brother, Sévèrin Prudhomme. The bride also signed.[82] The marriage record provides no indication of the mother's status. However, the baptismal record of the three-year-old Marie Thérèse, dated 1826, identifies her mother as Marie Pompose, slave of Sieur Prudhomme. The mother's racial composition was not specified in either record.[83]

By the onset of the Civil War the community had grown to include families bearing at least seventeen different surnames. All of these families possessed racial backgrounds similar to that of the Metoyers. There is no case on record during this period in which a member of the family group chose a spouse of pure Negro ancestry. All spouses were chosen from the general category known as *gens de couleur libre,* men and women of part-white and/or part-Indian ancestry.

The full extent of the Indian ancestry claimed by those who allied with the Metoyers cannot be determined. The records indicate that four out-group spouses were definitely of Indian lineage and a fifth and sixth probably were.

çois Gassion Metoyer in Dupre, Metoyer Family Genealogy. Fifth Census of the United States, 1830.

82. February 3, 1841, Natchitoches Registers, Book 12, p. 486.

83. November 3, 1826, *ibid.,* Book 7.

Family tradition claims even more. This, in itself, is not unusual. In discussing racial attitudes of nonwhites in American and Brazilian societies, Carl Degler states: "It is not uncommon . . . for a mulatto, though clearly of Negro ancestry, to assert seriously and insistently that all his ancestors were Indians, for Indian blood does not carry the taint that Negro blood does."[84]

To some degree, Degler's generalization may hold true in application to the Cane River colony, but there are definitely obvious exceptions. Numerous photographs of the early members of the colony depict strong Indian features—even in families whose ancestry cannot be traced, in the records, to any Indian. An excellent example is provided in the family photograph album of Thérèze Sarpy Metoyer.[85] Early in the album appears the portrait of a well-dressed middle-aged woman with pronounced aboriginal features; unfortunately, this portrait, like the others in the album, carries no identification. Examination of Thérèze's ancestry, and even the wives of her brothers, reveals no line to an Indian connection. Since some lines of each individual's ancestry cannot be fully traced, it is presumed that the Indian ancestry entered these families at those points.

An analysis of the background of these families who allied with the Metoyers, as well as of the Metoyers themselves, also discounts another popular generalization—that freed slaves "took" the names of their masters, whether or not they bore any relationship to them. One frequently cited authority on Louisiana's *gens de couleur libre* has quoted an older student on the subject who broadly observed: "As a rule free Negro families took the name of their former masters. A large percentage of these in Natchitoches Parish were named Metoyer, one of the old wealthy white Metoyers having freed some of his slaves. The same is true of the Dupre and Rachal families."[86]

An examination of the background of these three families clearly indicates that the freed slaves who took these names did so because of blood ties. In the case of the Dupres, the *gens de couleur libre* who adopted this surname were never the slaves of any master named Dupre. The same holds true in the case

---

84. Degler, *Neither Black Nor White*, 167.

85. The family album of Thérèze Sarpy Metoyer is now owned by Mrs. Rosa Metoyer Bernard.

86. D. C. Scarborough, Natchitoches, Louisiana, quoted in Calvin Dill Wilson, "Black Masters: A Side-light on Slavery," *North American Review*, CLXXXI (November, 1905), 691–92, and in Stahl, "The Free Negro in Ante-Bellum Louisiana," 321.

of Marie Pelagie LaCour, whose mother was a slave of the LeComte family, in the case of Marie Thérèse LeComte, whose mother was a slave of the LeCourt family, and in the case of Marie Agnes Poissot, whose mother belonged to the Derbannes.

In the case of all manumitted slaves of color in this one parish, prior to the Civil War, there has been found no instance in which such a freed man "took" the name of a master unless there was strong indication of a blood tie. Freed slaves whose white fathers did not claim them, those whose fathers were black, or those who were not aware of their fathers' identities, normally took as a surname the given name of their parent, most commonly their mother. Marie Jeanne Cecille, for example, was the daughter of Cecille; Marie Adélaïde Mariotte was the daughter of Marie Louise called Mariotte; and the children of Balthazar Monet reverted to the use of their father's given name as the family surname.

A further examination of the background of the allied families also reveals that the efforts of the colony's patriarch, Augustin, to reduce inbreeding were not successful. A small number of "outside" families were accepted into the colony; but several of these, it has been noted, already bore some relationship to the Metoyers or to each other. Moreover, the numerous progeny which all of these families produced multiplied faster than the outside society supplied new and "acceptable" matches. Continued inbreeding was inevitable.

When a nonresident of the area, J. W. Thomas, enumerated the population for the census of 1860, he erroneously identified six of the households in this Cane River colony as being of completely white racial heritage, a total of thirty-eight individuals. It is significant to note, also, that Thomas identified several of the pure French households in the area as "mulatto." [87] It is apparent from these mistakes, which were based upon Thomas' personal observation, that a sizable number of the Cane River Creoles of color were actually whiter than an equal number of the true white population. The exclusivity of the colony, coupled with their regular inbreeding, had not only preserved but to a noticeable degree elevated the original family's level on the caste scale, which concurrently improved their status in society.

87. Eighth Census of the United States, 1860, Population Schedule.

Chapter FIVE

In Pursuit of Wealth

The economic activities of the Creoles of Cane River spanned a broad spectrum. Farmers, professional men, merchants, tradesmen, and craftsmen, together they formed an almost self-contained society. The plantations that were mainly devoted to the cultivation of cotton also provided a large percentage of the foodstuffs needed by the community. Other food and supplies were usually purchased from its own merchants. Teachers within the family group instructed each new generation. The people's own craftsmen, both slave and free, supplied the bulk of the skilled labor that was needed; records of the hiring of outside help are rare.

In essence this was a society within a society, and the components of their community differed little from the scheme of the white economic structure in which they operated. Some degree of credit for this circumstance must be given to the temper of the outside society, since Louisiana's legal codes and moral thought provided much more flexibility to the framework in which the third caste could operate. In reviewing the general economic situation of the free man of color, both in the southern slave states and in the northern free ones, one authority concludes:

Generally speaking, the ... economic ... condition of free Negroes was wretched in the extreme. ... In some respects the position of free Negroes was inferior to that of slaves. The latter enjoyed the advantage of the master's protection; were assured a minimum of subsistence, medical attention, and support in old age; and so long as they were well behaved, were regarded with benevolent toleration.

Free Negroes and poor whites were the outcasts of Southern society, but the former were subject to numerous ... disabilities not imposed upon the latter. ... The free Negro was everywhere "regarded with a distrust bordering on apprehension."[1]

1. Gray, *Agriculture in Southern United States,* I, 523–24.

Another authority agrees:

> The early free negroes are not to be thought of apart from slave negroes.... The shifting from one legal category to another left [them] unaltered with respect to fitness for the station they had thereby attained. It did not make them independent of doles from the larders and wardrobes of the whites; it did not essentially change their occupations.... Hence in the economic point of view they were not sharply distinguished ... from those whose status, as the law would have had it, was lower than their own. Their position was anomalous.... They themselves were impotent. They went hither and thither as they were impelled.[2]

In this same vein, another study elaborates: "Because of white prejudice and discrimination, the overwhelming majority of free Negroes were unskilled laborers. Black entrepreneurs found it difficult to obtain capital from white lending institutions. White businessmen were reluctant to employ blacks in skilled or white-collar work, and where they were willing to do so, whites often refused to work with them."[3]

Such generalizations are borne out by numerous incidences. In 1805 a Maryland law denied free people of color the right to sell corn, wheat, or tobacco without first procuring from a justice of the peace a license certifying that the seller was "an orderly person of good character." Not only did this license have to be renewed annually, but subsequent revisions of the law rendered it applicable to almost all farm products.[4] In Mississippi it was illegal for a free nonwhite to sell any goods, whether he acted on his own or as agent for another, outside of the limits of an incorporated town. Even within the limits of a town, he was denied the privilege of selling groceries and liquor, or keeping a house of entertainment.[5] A North Carolina law of 1861 went so far as to prohibit any free person of color from buying, hiring, or apprenticing slaves or from working in any capacity that would put him in a position of control or management over slaves.[6]

2. James M. Wright, *The Free Negro in Maryland, 1634–1860* (New York, 1921), 16–17.

3. John H. Bracey, Jr., August Meier, and Elliott Rudwick (eds.), *Free Blacks in America, 1800–1860* (Belmont, Calif., 1971), 2.

4. Wright, *The Free Negro in Maryland,* 101.

5. Charles S. Sydnor, "The Free Negro in Mississippi Before the Civil War," *American Historical Review,* XXXII (July, 1927), 770.

6. Franklin, *The Free Negro in North Carolina,* 161.

One primary exception existed to these general constraints on the economic activities of free people of color. The *gens de couleur libre* of antebellum Louisiana enjoyed a wide latitude of economic liberties. Few limitations were placed upon their livelihood or their economic competition with whites. They were granted equal protection of property and had the power to make all types of contracts and engage in all business transactions. At least one contemporary Creole of color, a relative of the Cane River colony, firmly declared that he would never live anywhere except in Louisiana. A "colored man," he believed, could make more money in Louisiana than in any of the free states of the North.[7]

One study of the role of the free man of color in Louisiana concludes that "most of the free Negroes in the rural regions . . . eked out pitiful existences at the sufferance of ever-wary whites," although the *gens de couleur libre* of New Orleans enjoyed "strikingly diverse" economic opportunity.[8] This generalization does not hold true when applied to the rural Creoles of color along Cane River. No restrictions were placed upon their diversity, locally, and some of the state-wide restrictions were simply not enforced by local authorities. Not only were the "ever-wary" whites rare in their area, but the Cane River colony enjoyed a level of economic prosperity that sharply contrasts with the general depiction of free men who "eked out pitiful existences."

The economic foundation of the Cane River colony was agriculture. In this respect the colony differed little from the remainder of the parish or the South as a whole. Its staple crop was cotton, the crop favored by the South in general. Its labor was primarily slave labor, worked under the close supervision of each plantation owner, the common practice of the South's middle-class planters. However, an examination of the colony's agricultural activities suggests two distinct factors which accounted in large measure for its degree of success: the quality of its land and the efficient utilization which the people made of it.

The gradual development of agriculture on Isle Brevelle paralleled that of Natchitoches Parish in general. The early crops of indigo, tobacco, and sugar-

7. Sterkx, *The Free Negro in Ante-Bellum Louisiana*, 201; Frederick Law Olmsted, *Journey in the Seaboard Slave States in the Years 1853–1854* (reprinted New York, 1968), 635.
8. Roger A. Fischer, "Racial Segregation in Ante-Bellum Louisiana," *American Historical Review*, LXXIV (February, 1969), 929.

cane gave way to cotton. Some remnants of these early crops managed to survive, but they were retained mainly for home consumption. An indigo sower was one of the items on the succession inventory of Pierre Metoyer in 1833; a tobacco hook was included in the inventory of C. N. Rocque, Jr.'s estate in 1854, and many planters along Cane River maintained a patch of sugarcane for syrup and as a special treat for the children.[9] Throughout most of their period of affluence, however, the farmers of Isle Brevelle favored cotton and corn, the first as a cash crop and the second to feed their families, their slaves, and their animals.

A statistical study of farms within the colony is obstructed by several factors: Although slave tabulations began with the first decennial census, it was not until 1840 that agricultural data was gathered by the United States Bureau of the Census, and even the figures for that year do not include landholdings. The 1850 and 1860 agricultural censuses are much more complete, but factors beyond the people's control had already set the colony on a fast course of economic decline by that time.

The federal census of 1830, despite its lack of agricultural data, provides an excellent synopsis of slaveholding in the colony as compared to that of the general populace. The 58 slaves which the Metoyer colony had owned in 1810 had increased to 287 by 1830. Of this number, 226 were owned by those who bore the surname Metoyer, and 61 were owned by allied families. Augustin and his brother Louis led the colony that year, with each owning 54 slaves. The ninety-nine people of color who lived in households headed by individuals with the surname of Metoyer owned an average of 2.3 slaves for each man, woman, and child. The 3,801 whites in the parish claimed only 3,266 slaves, an average of 0.9 slaves per white. The free people of color who did not belong to the colony held an average of 0.2 slaves each.[10]

In short, the average member of the colony owned 156 percent more slaves than did the average white of the parish and ten and a half times more slaves

9. Gray, *Agriculture in Southern United States,* II, 688, 757; Seventh and Eighth Censuses of the United States, 1850–1860, Agricultural Schedules; Succession of Pierre Metoyer, and Succession of C. N. Rocques, *fils,* in Natchitoches Parish Records, Nos. 193 and 897; Hugh LaCour to author, Shreveport, Louisiana, March 5, 1974 and April 2, 1974; Robert A. Tyson Diary, University Archives (Louisiana State University, Baton Rouge).

10. Fifth Census of the United States, 1830.

than the average free person of color who did not belong to the colony. More-over, Carter Woodson's study of free slaveowners of color throughout the United States in that year reveals that the Metoyers of Isle Brevelle owned more slaves than any other free family of color in the nation. While there were a small number of individuals who owned more slaves than did any individual Metoyer, there was no other family group which even came close to matching the aggregate holdings of those who bore the Metoyer name.[11]

The peak period of Metoyer affluence occurred between 1830 and 1840. Inventories made of several of the estates during these years give a good indication of the size of individual plantations and the extent of their landhold-ings. Pierre Metoyer, one of the less prosperous brothers, died in 1834 leaving a plantation of approximately 677 acres, after having given plantations to each of his seven children at the time of their marriages.[12] The eldest brother, Augustin, who also gave sizable plantations to six of his eight children as wedding presents, divided his remaining holdings between all of them in 1840. The two plantations which he still owned at that time contained 2,134 acres.[13]

As parents divided their holdings between their numerous offspring, the inevitable result was a decrease in the size of individual plantations, a circum-stance that is clearly shown by the 1850 agricultural census. Yet the statistics provided by this census also show that even in decline the members of the colony still held their own in comparison with white planters. Many of the individual members of the group remained among the largest landholders in the parish. François Gassion Metoyer, son of Augustin, had one thousand acres of land, all of which were improved. Only five other planters in the

11. Carter G. Woodson, "Free Negro Owners of Slaves in the United States in 1830," *Jour-nal of Negro History,* IX (January, 1924), 41–85. In compiling his tabulations of free nonwhite slaveowners in Natchitoches Parish, Woodson omitted the household headed by Marie R.[ose] Metoyer, which contained eleven slaves, four children of color, and one white male, in addition to Marie Rose. Apparently, Woodson assumed that the slaves were the property of the white male; in actuality, the white (a North Carolinian named James Hurst) was a propertyless boarder in Marie Rose's home.

12. Succession of Pierre Metoyer, in Natchitoches Parish Records, No. 193. Marriage Con-tract of Athanase Vienne Metoyer to Emelia Metoyer, in Henry Collection, Old Natchitoches Data, II, 87.

13. Augustin Metoyer to His Children, in Natchitoches Parish Records. Donations Book 30, pp. 70–78.

AVERAGE FARM WITHIN THE COLONY
AS COMPARED TO
AVERAGE FARM WITHIN NATCHITOCHES PARISH
1850

	Average Farm in the Colony	Average Farm in the Parish
Improved acres of land	113.3	84.0
Unimproved acres of land	138.9	172.0
Total acres of land	(252.2)	(256.0)
Value of farm	$1,866	$1,664
Value of implements and machinery	$404	$343
Slaves	9.0	9.0
Horses	3.3	3.4
Mules & Asses	2.2	1.2
Oxen	3.4	1.2
Milk cows	4.8	6.0
Beef cattle	4.7	12.0
Swine	6.0	39.0
Sheep	4.2	5.0
Value of animals slaughtered	$30	$61
Ginned cotton (bales)	23.3	18.5
Corn (bushels)	388.9	468.0
Peas & beans (bushels)	1.4	13.7
Irish potatoes (bushels)	.5	4.1
Sweet potatoes (bushels)	22.2	44.3
Butter (pounds)	1.0	35.6
Honey	1.6	9.3
Molasses	*	2.0
Cane sugar (pounds)	*	4.0
Maple sugar (pounds)	*	0.3
Cheese (pounds)	*	0.6
Oats (bushels)	.5	3.8
Rice (pounds)	*	17.1
Garden produce for market (value)	*	$1
Tobacco (pounds)	4.8	5.3
Wool (pounds)	2.0	6.4
Homemade manufactures	$1	$7

*None Reported
Based upon manuscript returns of the Seventh Census of the United States, Slave and Agricultural Schedules.

parish possessed as many improved acres; all were white. There were *no* other large-scale planters, white or nonwhite, who had improved every acre of their land. Four other planters of color on the Isle were proprietors of plantations of more than a thousand acres, improved and unimproved combined: Jean Baptiste Augustin Metoyer, C. N. Rocques, Sr., Marie Suzette Metoyer Morin, and Joseph Augustin Metoyer. Three more members of the colony owned between five hundred and a thousand acres each.[14]

A comparative analysis of the average farm in the colony to the average farm in the parish, based upon the agricultural statistics of the 1850 census (see accompanying table) indicates that the colony stressed the production of their cash crop, cotton, and deemphasized the production of foodstuffs. With the money generated by the sale of their cash crop they purchased necessary food items from their own merchants, thereby fostering other aspects of the Isle Brevelle economy.

The ratio of slaves to acres of improved land within the colony squared with accepted standards. On new ground the average was six acres of cotton and three acres of corn land per slave. More acres per slave could be worked if the land had been previously cultivated.[15] The 5,667 acres of improved land owned by the Metoyers and allied families in 1850 were tilled by 436 slaves, an average of 13 improved acres per slave.[16] Of course, not all slaves were field hands, but neither were all improved lands planted in these two crops.

According to one major study, the production of cotton required 34 percent of the labor time of slaves on cotton plantations. The raising of livestock, including the raising of feed, required about 25 percent. Corn for human consumption utilized 6 percent of the time, and the remaining 34 percent, the same amount of time required for cotton production, was devoted to such miscellaneous tasks as the construction of fences, building, home manufacturing, domestic work, and the raising of other crops.[17]

This southern average does not seem to agree with the labor distribution and crop production patterns of the cotton plantations on Cane River or on at least some other plantations in central Louisiana. An account of a typical antebel-

14. Seventh Census of the United States, 1850, Agricultural Schedule.
15. Joe Gray Taylor, *Negro Slavery in Louisiana* (Baton Rouge, 1963), 68.
16. Seventh Census of the United States, 1850, Agricultural Schedule.
17. Robert William Fogel and Stanley L. Engerman, *Time on the Cross: The Economics of American Negro Slavery* (2 vols.; Boston, 1974), I, 42.

lum cotton plantation in this region was left by Solomon Northup, a slave for ten years in nearby Avoyelles Parish. According to Northup, the agricultural calendar revolved around the production of cotton and corn, in this order: "Ploughing, planting, picking cotton, gathering the corn, and pulling and burning stalks, occupies the whole of the four seasons of the year. Drawing and cutting wood, pressing cotton, fattening and killing hogs, are but incidental labors."[18] Planting season for the staple, according to Northup, was March and April. The fields were prepared with plows pulled by oxen, turning the soil into rows of six-foot widths. A lighter plow followed, making furrows into which seeds were dropped. Next a harrow was pulled over the rows to cover the seeds. In all, two mules or oxen, three slaves, two plows, and a harrow were used in the planting of cotton.

The cotton sprouted in from eight to ten days. Then the first plowing and hoeing began. Not only was it imperative that grass be removed but the cotton had to be thinned into hills about two and a half feet apart. Two weeks later the seedlings were thinned again, leaving only the strongest and healthiest plant in each hill. Two additional hoeings came later, the last about July 1. The hoeing was done by slaves who were paced by a lead worker and driven from behind by a driver or overseer who sported a whip, according to Northup.[19]

In late August picking usually began. An average day's work produced 150 to 200 pounds per slave, although a great variation was exhibited by individual pickers. Five hundred pounds per day was not an impossible goal for a slave with exceptionally nimble fingers. Four pickings were usually required to clean the stalks, the last picking coming as late as January. Excessive spring rains which necessitated replanting could delay the picking season considerably. On the other hand, short crops such as that which occurred in 1841 meant that farmers might finish as much as two months earlier.[20]

18. Solomon Northup, *Twelve Years a Slave,* ed. Sue Eakin and Joseph Logdson (Baton Rouge, 1968), 130.

19. *Ibid.,* 123–24.

20. *Ibid.;* Diary of Dr. McGuire (MS in Henry Collection), 1841, pp. 20–21. It should be noted that Northup's citation of 200 pounds per day as the picking average of slaves is not borne up by Taylor's comprehensive study *Negro Slavery in Louisiana;* Taylor (pages 65–66) concludes that 150 pounds per day was a more accurate average for adults.

Such other crops as corn, sweet potatoes, peas, and beans were tended during time not needed for the cotton crop. The most important of the food crops, corn, was usually planted in February before the onset of the cotton planting season. If February and March were exceptionally cold the corn did not germinate. Still, the planters gambled and sowed the seed early so that the planting of the more valuable cotton crop would not be delayed. In August, after the last hoeing of the cotton and before the first picking began, the leaves were stripped from the corn stalks and laid out to dry for use as animal fodder. The ears of corn were turned down on the stalk for protection against rain until the cotton crop was picked. Only after the cotton was gathered was the corn picked and stored without shucking; shucks were a natural protection against weevils.

After the cotton and corn were gathered, preparations began for the next crop. The stalks were pulled and burned, and plowing began immediately to prepare the field for the next planting. According to Northup most farm animals were allowed to roam the woods, with a minimum of care. The milk cows were worth little since they gave little. The North was mainly relied upon for cheese and butter.[21]

The records of the Cane River plantations indicate a closer parallel to Northup's account of slave labor utilization than to the southern average provided by the previously cited econometric study, especially in the area of livestock and feed production. As previously shown, the average farm in the colony possessed nine slaves in 1850. If 25 percent of its slave labor was devoted to the care of the animals and the production of feed for them, as asserted in the econometric study, then the full-time labor of two slaves and one-fourth of the labor of a third slave would be needed to care for the fifteen livestock which the average farm possessed. This is definitely a disproportionate figure. Many succession inventories of the colony itemized animals "running loose in the woods," as Northup observed, and many cattle and horses were sold at probate auction, sight unseen, because they were also "running loose in the woods."

Exceptions existed, of course. A small percentage of the members of the colony raised a relatively large number of cattle; in 1850, for example, J. B.

---

21. Northup, *Twelve Years a Slave,* 129–31; McGuire Diary, n.d., 1841.

Augustin Metoyer owned seventy-five head of cattle as well as ten work oxen, thirty sheep, and ten hogs. In two cases, hog raising seems to have been the primary agricultural endeavor. Firmin C. Christophe was listed that year as having 50 hogs, 19 head of cattle, 140 bushels of corn, only 20 acres of improved land, and 340 acres of unimproved land. Joseph Rocques had only 20 horses and 25 head of cattle but claimed 60 hogs.[22]

Crop production on the Isle was not always a haphazard enterprise in which each man learned to farm by trial and error or by the advice of his elders. The high value which the colony placed on education was designed not only to enrich the people culturally but to provide them with occupational training. At least one lengthy manual on the latest methods of crop production known in the early nineteenth century has been preserved by the colony, and its pages are well worn.[23]

Although most farming within the colony was conducted on an individual basis, partnerships were sometimes entered into. Augustin Metoyer and Jerome Sarpy, for example. purchased together the plantation of a deceased white neighbor for $19,300.[24] A less amicable partnership was the one formed between Hypolite Chevalier and Joseph François Metoyer who rented a tract of land from Louis Monette's widow on lower Cane River. Metoyer supplied the capital and Chevalier supplied the labor; Chevalier was to receive one-third of the crop. The affair ended in court after a dispute concerning the proper division of the cotton and corn which they produced.[25]

The agreement reached by Athanasite Metoyer and his cousin Jean Baptiste Cloutier in 1852 reflects a different method of handling the profits. Acting as agent for Vial Girard, a white, Metoyer agreed to advance merchandise to Cloutier. In return, Cloutier promised to produce for Girard, on Girard's land, two bales of cotton worth at least $440.[26]

Leases of whole plantations also took place in the community. A typical case was the arrangement between Joseph Augustin Metoyer and his brother

22. Seventh Census of the United States, 1850, Agricultural Schedule.
23. *Le Nouveau Parfait Jardinier; ou L'art de Cultiver* (Paris, 1835), in possession of Mrs. Coutii.
24. Succession of Julien Rachal, in Natchitoches Parish Records, No. 299.
25. *Chevalier* v. *Metoyer,* District Court Suit No. 4668 (1854), *ibid.*
26. Agreement between Jean Baptiste Cloutier and Vial Girard, in DeBlieux Collection.

François Gassion. The original lease was made in September, 1843, and was renewed for three more years in January, 1850. The plantation was leased "with all the slaves, horses, mules, cattle, work oxen, and farming utensils thereon, and also all the cattle and horses belonging to the said Joseph and which may be running at large in the woods."[27]

Similar lease agreements were entered into between free people of color and their white neighbors, with the former usually acting as lessors. The property leased was usually agricultural, but on occasion it included town land and dwellings. Auguste Metoyer rented to Louis Gaspard Derbanne, white, a plantation with all fences and buildings for three years beginning January 1, 1836. Derbanne paid three dollars per acre of cultivable land and agreed to return all buildings and fences in good condition at the end of the lease.[28]

Another renter of Auguste's did not drive as good a bargain as did Derbanne. In March, 1839, William Townsend rented fifty acres from Auguste at the exorbitant rent of $6.75 an acre for a term of one year. Auguste had to take the white to court to collect his rent, and the judge considered the price so high that he cut the debt from $338 to $200. Even after the reduction of the rent, Townsend was unable to pay. The sheriff seized and sold a thirteen-year-old slave in satisfaction of the debt.[29]

An example of a town lease occurred in 1844 between Joseph Metoyer and a white notary and justice of the peace named Alexander Pinçon. Metoyer rented to Pinçon his "lot of ground and buildings" at Cloutierville for one year at the price of fifty dollars. The type of property and its size was not specified.[30]

The basic farm equipment, which was fairly standard throughout the parish, tended toward obsolescence. In fact, a reluctance to adopt new types of equipment had long been a characteristic of the Natchitoches area. In 1805 a federal agent who had been sent to assess the area reported: "Though Natchitoches has been settled almost one hundred years, it is not more than twelve or fifteen years since they ever had a plow, or a flat to cross the river with,

27. Joseph Augustin Metoyer to François G. Metoyer, in Natchitoches Parish Records, Misc. Book FW (also lettered E), 170–71.
28. Auguste Metoyer to Louis Gaspard Derbanne, in DeBlieux Collection, No. 93.
29. *Metoyer* v. *Townsend,* District Court Suit No. 2468 (1840), Natchitoches Paris Records.
30. Joseph Metoyer to Alexander Pinçon, in DeBlieux Collection.

both of which were introduced by an Irish Pennsylvanian, under a similar opposition to the copernican system."[31] Inventories of property in the succession records of white and colored planters during the first half of the nineteenth century provide an excellent cross section of the types of implements used. Such records usually show plows of various types and harrows of wood. Some of the latter had iron teeth. The assessed value of such plows and harrows ranged between fifty cents and a dollar, suggesting their crude nature.[32] The assertion that wooden plows were preferred over cast-iron ones throughout Louisiana and the lower Mississippi valley in the 1850s and 1860s appears to hold true for Natchitoches Parish.[33] These implements were pulled by either mules, horses, or oxen, depending upon the preference of the individual farmer. In the Cane River colony, oxen predominated. Other tools that were inventoried in the various successions included hoes, pickaxes, crosscut and other saws, spades, shovels, rakes, and scythes.

The higher than average value of implements and machinery within the colony that is indicated by the 1850 agricultural census may be attributed in large measure to the high incidence of gins and mills on the plantations. For example, in March, 1840, Augustin Metoyer had two cotton gins, one on the right bank of the river valued at $1,200 and another "with grates" on the left bank worth $2,000. In addition, Augustin's main plantation boasted a "gin for grain" (gristmill) and a pounding mill. These gins were open for use to all of his married children. His sister Suzanne also erected a gristmill and a cotton gin on the plantation that she farmed with her son Florentin Conant. The overall picture provided by the inventories of these two estates is one of unusually progressive plantations. Only a small percentage of the planters in the parish owned and operated cotton gins, and only three gristmills were enumerated in the whole of the parish in 1840.[34]

31. *Message from the President of the United States Communicating Discoveries Made in Exploring the Missouri, Red River and Washita by Captains Lewis and Clark, Doctor Sibley, and Mr. Dunbar* (New York, 1806), 70.

32. Succession of Pierre Metoyer, No. 193, and Succession of Louis Barthelemy Rachal [white planter on Cane River], both in Succession Book 9, p. 4, in Natchitoches Parish Records.

33. Leo Rogin, *The Introduction of Farm Machinery in its Relation to the Productivity of Labor in the Agriculture of the United States during the Nineteenth Century* (Berkeley, 1931), 560.

34. Augustin Metoyer to Children, Donations Book 30, pp. 70–78, Succession of Suzanne Metoyer, No. 355, and Suzanne Metoyer, her Testament, Book 25, pp. 10–11, in Natchitoches Parish Records; Sixth Census of the United States, 1840, Agricultural Schedule.

The operation of a gin was expensive, even after the initial cost of construction was met. For example, S. M. Hyams, a white planter of Natchitoches, paid $54 for fire insurance on his gin in 1852. Repairs were a continual expense. When Augustin Metoyer donated his property to his children in 1840, he specified that the gins were for the use of all the children so long as they contributed their shares to maintenance. The succession of his sister Suzanne noted a payment of $180 for a repair bill on her gin.[35] Yet, the cost of operation and repair was more than offset by the savings. According to the prices of the time, the two gins of Augustin Metoyer and his children would have rendered a saving of $5,764 on the 598 bales of cotton which they produced in the year 1850.[36]

Some of the free people of color within the Cane River colony not only used their gins for their own crops but also provided ginning services for neighbors, white and nonwhite, whose plantations were not large enough to support a gin. Valmont Llorens, Jean Baptiste Espallier Rachal, and Louis Casimere Rachal were among those who supplemented their incomes by ginning and storing cotton for their neighbors.[37]

Most slaves owned by the colony were utilized as labor on individual plantations. However, leases of slaves to other planters as temporary labor did occasionally occur. For example, in 1845 Jacquitte Rachal rented two twenty-eight-year-old slaves, one male and one female, to a white planter named Charles F. Benoist. The price agreed upon was $176 for three years.[38] In the same manner, members of the colony occasionally rented slaves from white neighbors. In an agreement between the Widow Pierre Mission Rachal and the Widow J. B. Brevelle, a white, Mme. Rachal rented a woman from Mme. Brevelle for thirty-nine days at a price of fifty cents per day.[39] Slaves were sometimes owned jointly by free people of color and whites, as in the case of two neighbors, J. B. Espallier Rachal and Victor Rachal, a white. For

35. S. M. Hyams to Sun Mutual Insurance Co. (MS in Chaplin, Breazeale, and Chaplin Collection); Augustin Metoyer to Children, Donations Book 30, pp. 70–78, and Succession of Suzanne Metoyer, No. 355, both in Natchitoches Parish Records.

36. James Hurst to [unknown], January 1843, in Natchitoches Parish Records Collection, LSU; Seventh Census of the United States, 1850, Agricultural Schedule.

37. Succession of Henriette LaCaze and Husband Edmond Duthil, in Natchitoches Parish Records, No. 803; *Dupleix* v. *Gallien*, 21 La. Ann. 534 (1869).

38. Jacquitte Rachal to Ch[s] F. Benoist, in DeBlieux Collection, No. 107.

39. Widow J[n] B[te] Brevelle to Widow P[re] Mission Rachal, in DeBlieux Collection, No. 98.

several years each held a half interest in a slave named Alfred. Most likely the slave had a special skill which both men needed.[40]

In the supervision and treatment of their slaves, a matter which was generally considered to be the personal prerogative of each plantation owner (as long as he did not grossly violate the general laws of the state), most free people of color occupied the tenuous position of "being damned if they did and damned if they didn't." Those who were kind to their bondsmen risked charges from prejudiced whites such as the one who informed Olmsted that the Cane River Creoles of color were "a lazy, beastly set—slaves and all on an equality, socially—no order or discipline on their plantations, but everything going to ruin."[41] On the other hand, if they treated their slaves with firmness and administered punishment when due, others accused the free men of color of being harsh masters "who got out of their slave property all that they could."[42]

These generalizations cannot be validly applied to most slaveowners of the Cane River colony. As with any other group of slaveowners, human property was treated with varying degrees of consideration. Cane River owners who were harsh definitely appear to have been in the minority; and a close examination of the social life and attitudes of the colony certainly belie the statement that slaves were treated as equals.

According to tradition, one of the original Metoyer brothers was a hard taskmaster, but not necessarily with his own slaves. Moreover, the method that he used to obtain the labor of slaves belonging to others was deceptive. Feigning an interest in the purchase of certain slaves, he insisted upon trying them before making a final decision. The borrowed slaves would be put to work on the worst land he had and at exceptionally exhausting tasks that he did not want his own slaves to perform. After completing the work he would return the slaves, claiming that they were poor hands and not worth purchasing. The tradition further holds that this ploy was used on his family as well as outsiders. His brother Louis was deceived twice, but the more perceptive Augustin saw through his younger brother from the start and refused to let him

40. Succession of J. B. E. Rachal, in Natchitoches Parish Records, No. 927.
41. Olmsted, *Journey in the Seaboard Slave States,* 633.
42. Wilson, "Black Masters: A Side-light on Slavery," 689; Stahl, "The Free Negro in Ante-Bellum Louisiana," 347.

have any slaves on trial. Tradition also holds that one female member of the family was "mean" to her slaves. In the opinion of a descendant, however, "The good Lord got even with Tante; her mansion was burned during the Civil War, her second husband ran through her money, and she was forced to live the rest of her days, bedridden, in one of her slave cabins."[43]

If runaway slaves were indicative of ill treatment, then perhaps Cane River owners were occasionally harsh. Louis Metoyer placed an advertisement in the local newspaper in June, 1825, offering a reward for "a mulattoe [sic] slave named Charles, aged about 36." The reward offered was one hundred dollars if captured west of the Sabine River and fifty dollars if captured east of the Sabine.[44] When Joseph Augustin Metoyer died in 1851, one of his slaves, a carpenter named Washington, was sold as "having run away once and having bad sight in one eye but otherwise fully guaranteed." The record does not indicate whether he ran away from Joseph or from a previous master. By contrast, Joseph also had a twenty-eight-year-old male slave named Bossine who was identified as a hunter by occupation.[45] If Joseph was so harsh a master that one slave ran away from him, it is not probable that he would give another slave a gun and send him into the woods to hunt. Masters who were noted for their cruelty were not usually so lenient with their slaves.

Only a few newspapers of the parish are extant for this period, but the numerous legal records that are available contain no other references to runaways. Tradition does hold that there were a few other slaves on the Isle who absconded after punishment and joined the infamous bands of "redbones" who lived in the woodlands; others supposedly abandoned their masters to follow the invading Union army in 1864.[46] One case of the latter is documented in the files of the Southern Claims Commission, but the Negro who fled returned five years later to settle on the plantation of his former master.[47]

---

43. Interview with confidential source, April 26, 1974.
44. *Natchitoches Courier*, July 19, 1825, and the following six weeks.
45. Succession of Joseph Augustin Metoyer, in Natchitoches Parish Records Collection, LSU, Box 11, Folder 47.
46. Interview with confidential source, April 26, 1974. The "redbones" were marauding groups of men and women of mixed racial origins, white, black, and Indian, who inhabited the unsettled areas of the parish.
47. *Emilie Kirkland* v. *United States*, in Records of the Southern Claims Commission (National Archives, Washington), Claim 41317.

As a rule it appears that slaves belonging to the Cane River Creoles of color were treated as well, if not better, than those of the average white planter. Augustin Metoyer and Jerome Sarpy, especially, had reputations for being kind to their slaves. Augustin, it is said, very rarely sold a slave, and the local conveyance records uphold the tradition. Jerome Sarpy, tradition relates, insisted upon excellent housing conditions for his bondsmen; cabins not only had to be kept clean but were whitewashed twice a year, inside and out.[48]

Generally speaking, slave housing on the Isle exhibited a better standard than either the parish or the national average. Robert Fogel and Stanley Engerman's study of slave life, one of the most extensive that has been made, reports that in 1860 the average large plantation enumerated 5.2 slaves per house. In Natchitoches Parish that year the average was four. On plantations belonging to members of the colony, the average cabin housed only three slaves.[49]

The housing which was provided for the Cane River slaves was rudimentary, as was most slave housing, and seems to have been typical of that of the late antebellum period, as described by Fogel and Engerman.[50] After his travels through Natchitoches, Frederick Law Olmsted left descriptions of slave cabins on two large Cane River plantations owned by whites. On the first plantation, he reports, cabins were small, one room to a family, and they were built of plank and chinked with rags and mud. Floors were bare earth, and chimneys were made of sticks and mud. On the second plantation the slave quarters were larger and each had a brick chimney and a front gallery. Such accommodations were rude but comfortable.[51]

The extant slave cabins on land owned during this period by the colony generally fall into the latter category described by Olmsted. Most measured approximately eighteen by twenty feet and were made of logs chinked with mud. They had plank floors, brick or stone chimneys, and windows. The only dirt-floored cabin recalled by the oldest inhabitants was inhabited primarily by

48. Interview with Mrs. Coutii, April 26, 1974; Succession of Augustin Metoyer, in Natchitoches Parish Records, No. 1009.
49. Fogel and Engerman, *Time on the Cross,* I, 115; Eighth Census of the United States, 1860, Slave Schedule.
50. Fogel and Engerman, *Time on the Cross,* I, 116.
51. Olmsted, *Journey in the Seaboard Slave States,* 629–30.

whites and used at one time as a Catholic convent.[52] No older twentieth-century descendant of the colony has been found who can remember any slave cabin with a chimney of sticks and mud.

Fogel and Engerman have concluded that "while such housing is quite mean by modern standards, the houses of slaves compared well with the housing of free workers in the antebellum era."[53] This observation can be validly applied to Natchitoches Parish. In 1860 the family home of one educated white, a former blacksmith and overseer who owned 640 acres of Red River land himself, was described as "a log house 20 X 18 feet, the [attached] storeroom . . . 12 by 8 feet, 6 feet high." Another room for a hired Negro "was same height, and 10 by 6 feet wide. . . . The old house and additions were worth $60."[54] A family of seven inhabited this house.[55]

On several Cane River plantations one cabin, larger than the rest, was set aside as a slave hospital. On Louis Metoyer's plantation, after the family built a large and stately plantation home, their old family home was designated as the hospital. Another hospital recalled by older family members in the twentieth century was located just above 24-Mile Ferry.[56]

According to Fogel and Engerman, the hospitalization of slaves served several purposes. The sick were thereby isolated from the well, minimizing contagion. Special treatment, such as diets, rest, and medication, could be more easily prescribed and administered. Moreover, the immediate confinement and close supervision of those who claimed illness tended to reduce the incidencies of feigned ill health.[57]

The parish records do reflect a small number of lame, sickly, and unsound

52. Callahan *et al., History of St. Augustin's Parish,* 20; interview with Mrs. Coutii, April 26, 1974; see also Chapter III, fn. 58.

53. Fogel and Engerman, *Time on the Cross,* I, 116.

54. *Christy* v. *Spillman,* in Natchitoches Parish Records, District Court Suit No. 5401 (1860).

55. *Ibid.;* Seventh through Ninth Censuses of the United States, 1850–1870, Population Schedules.

56. Hugh LaCour to author, April 5, 1974; interview with Mrs. Coutii, April 26, 1974. Some accounts of the history of Louis Metoyer's plantation claim that the old house called Yucca was first utilized as a slave hospital by a white family who later owned the plantation, rather than by the Metoyers; *i.e.:* "Melrose Manor on Cane River Stands as Relic of World's Strangest Empire," Hammond, La. *Progress,* March 25, 1938. However, descendants of the colony insist that the use of Yucca as a slave hospital was initiated by Louis Metoyer.

57. Fogel and Engerman, *Time on the Cross,* I, 120.

slaves within the colony. The hernias attributed to some of them suggest that heavy manual labor was exacted of them, but here again the records do not indicate how long most of these had been in the colony or whether the condition existed before their purchase. Moreover, hernias have always been an occupational hazard among laborers on cotton plantations and those employed in cotton gins. Even in the twentieth century, the heavy manual work exacted of those who continually handled cotton bales almost inevitably resulted in hernias and serious spinal problems.[58]

Another indication of the concern exhibited by members of the colony for their slaves can be found in slave baptismal records. During the 1820s the parish was without a pastor for a considerable length of time. When a priest arrived in Natchitoches in 1826 he traveled downriver, stopping at every plantation to baptize those whites, free people of color, and slaves who had been born since the last pastoral visit. As the sacraments were administered to the slaves, their names, approximate ages, and sometimes the names of their mothers were entered into the church registers.

At the plantations of the Metoyers, particularly those of Louis, Dominique, Jean Baptiste Augustin, and Suzanne Metoyer, and her son Florentin Conant, the priest was furnished with the exact birth dates of each slave child, even though some were as old as six years. The mother of each child was also identified. Only three of the white planters of the area were able to give exact dates for some of their slaves: Dominique Rachal (who provided the information inconsistently), J. B. Lestage, and Sylvestre Rachal. The latter two were both young planters whose holdings were small enough that such information could be easily kept.[59] Either the Metoyers exhibited better than average concern for their slaves as human beings, or they kept a closer inventory of their property.

The slaves of Isle Brevelle also received special privileges or bonuses, some of which were not unusual within the white community. One of the more common "extras" on southern plantations was a Christmas holiday of varying length, during which a party of one type or another was scheduled. According to one authority the Christmas holidays on cotton plantations usu-

---

58. Jesse Adams, quoted in James G. Andrews, "Let Your Fingers Do the Ginning," *Mid-South* (November 10, 1974), 4–12.
    59. Natchitoches Registers, Book 7.

ally began on the day before Christmas Eve and ended on New Year's Eve. A dinner and a dance were normally scheduled during this interval, and sometimes other varied activities were held.[60]

On the plantation of Augustin Metoyer, Christmas festivities for the slaves centered upon the *papegai*. Several days before the festivities began, the slaves prepared an effigy of a cow, marked into cuts of meat, and the figure was suspended atop a pole. A cow was then butchered. The night of the celebration, a line was drawn forty yards from the effigy, and the slaves aligned themselves behind it. Taking turns, with the eldest going first, the slaves shot at the effigy, aiming at the choicest sections. Whatever cut of unclaimed meat each slave hit on the effigy was the cut he received from the butchered cow. This beef was a very welcome addition to the pork and corn which constituted the usual basis of slave diets in central Louisiana. The customary gift of a bottle of whiskey per slave, along with the usual music and dancing, made Christmas a festive occasion for the slaves on this plantation.[61]

Another common practice which the Metoyers followed was the granting of passes to slaves to visit other plantations or to go to town. Such a pass was given by Auguste Metoyer to two of his slaves, Syphorian and Frank, during the Christmas season of 1850. On the appointed day for their return from George S. Walmsley's at Cloutierville, the slave Frank had not completed his business. Walmsley wrote a note to Metoyer explaining that Frank "leaves his blanket coat unfinished and has some other little affairs to attend to," that the slave wished to return to Cloutierville on New Year's Day, and that he had no objection to the slave's return if Auguste granted permission.[62]

The Creoles of color of Isle Brevelle, like their white counterparts, also granted freedom to valued slaves. In a few cases there appears the possible

---

60. Taylor, *Negro Slavery in Louisiana,* 128.

61. Lyle Saxon, *Children of Strangers* (Reprint New Orleans, 1948), 119–22; interview with Mrs. Coutii, April 26, 1974. Although Saxon's work is presented as a novel, it is based upon actual events in the life of a Cane River family and attempts to portray, as accurately as possible, the life-style of the people. Saxon received most of his information from the late Mrs. Zeline Badin Roque, who grew up in the colony during the period covered by this study, according to Mrs. Coutii, a familiar acquaintance of both Saxon and Mrs. Roque. Northup, *Twelve Years a Slave,* 127.

62. George S. Walmsley to Auguste Metoyer, in Henry Clement Papers, Henry Collection; Taylor, *Negro Slavery in Louisiana,* 131.

motivation of blood relationship or even paternity. But in most cases no relationship existed and in some instances paternity would have been impossible. It appears that the usual deciding factor was "good and faithful service." In one incident in particular the manumission apparently resulted from the close bond of friendship between a slave child and a free child who had grown up together. At the succession sale of the estate of Marie Suzanne Metoyer, her nephew, François Gassion Metoyer, purchased a male slave named Lucas "for his freedom" at the price of $1,500. Lucas was born in 1809, the same year as François Gassion.[63] Apparently no blood relationship existed. Since they were the same age, it is quite possible that the pair were playmates during their childhood.

Most of the slaves freed on the Isle were freed by Augustin. Initially, he had bought and freed family members, one in 1798, another in 1800, and a third in 1801.[64] In 1813 he freed his first nonrelative, a fourteen-year-old French and African girl named Dorothée, whom he had held in bondage for several years. The following month "after necessary advertisement for more than forty days, as required by law," with no opposition voiced by others, Augustin granted freedom to Marguerite, a slave over thirty years of age. In 1835 he manumitted a male named Remy, his wife's brother.[65] In the draft of his last will and testament, he made provisions for the manumission of still another slave. Article Seven of that document stated: "I desire and such is my wish that after my death a small mulattress named Lise, belonging to me and now aged about twelve years, will be freed of the bonds of slavery, and as soon as my testamentary executors judge it convenient, provided that the time of her manumission not be allowed to surpass the time when she will have completed her twenty-first year, or as soon after that as it is possible to do it."[66] In 1851 Augustin sold a twenty-year-old French and African slave girl

63. Succession of Marie Suzanne Metoyer, in Natchitoches Parish Records, No. 355; Seventh Census of the United States, 1850, Population Schedule.

64. Augustin Metoyer of Succession of Marie LeClerc, in Natchitoches Parish Records, Doc. 2857; Widow LeComte to Nicolas Augustin, in Henry Collection, Old Natchitoches Data, II, 279; Ambroise LeComte to Augustin, in File R&R 309, Marie Perine, State Land Office.

65. Augustin Metoyer to Dorothée, Misc. Book 1, p. 225; Augustin Metoyer to mulattress Marguerite, Conveyances, Book 2, p. 179; Augustin Metoyer to Remy, Book 21, p. 109; Succession of Marie LeClerc, Widow Derbanne, Doc. 2857, all in Natchitoches Parish Records.

66. Last Will and Testament of Augustin Metoyer, in Natchitoches Parish Records, Book 25, Notarial Records, 79.

named Marie Lise (four years younger than the Lise above) to his grandson, François Florival Metoyer, with the understanding that she was to be freed. Since François Florival was born in 1820 and the slave in 1831, it is not possible that he was also her father.[67]

At least two of Augustin's brothers also granted freedom to their slaves on several occasions. In 1810 Dominique purchased two slaves, Suzette, eighteen years of age, and her daughter Mary Magdelaine, about one and a half years old, from Mme. Marie Louise Le Comte, white, for $900. The sale carried the stipulation that the child and the mother should be freed after a period of nine years. Any children born to Suzette in that period would be given their freedom at the same time. Dominique also granted freedom in 1825 to another favored slave, Marie Louise, who was about thirty-nine years of age, after advertising his intentions to free her in the local newspaper as the law required.[68]

Louis Metoyer, a brother of Dominique and Augustin, manumitted at least three slaves in his lifetime. In one case, freedom was granted to the natural son of his slave Maria on the day that the child was baptized, June 8, 1815; the child was of mixed racial origins. Five years later he emancipated two female slaves, Baba, about forty-five years old, and Françoise, who was about fifty-five years of age.[69] A blood relationship between Louis and the manumitted infant may be presumed. In the case of the two older slaves, no relationship can be found, and a romantic interest does not appear likely in view of their ages and the fact that he did not free any of their children.

Other free people of color on the Isle, in addition to those bearing the Metoyer name, also manumitted slaves from time to time. For example, Charles N. Rocques, Sr., remembered two of his slaves when he drew up his last will and testament in 1859. A state law passed earlier that year had placed a blanket proscription against all manumissions for any reason. Thus circumvented in his desire to free his slaves Celeste and Reine, Rocques specified in

67. Augustin Metoyer to F. Florival Metoyer, in DeBlieux Collection, No. 388. François Florival's year of birth is calculated from the age given on the Eighth Census of the United States, 1860, Population Schedule.
68. Marie Louise LeComte to Dominique Metoyer, in Natchitoches Parish Records, Doc. 3779; *Natchitoches Courier*, May 24, 1825.
69. Baptism of Antonio, June 18, 1815, Natchitoches Registers, Book 5; Louis Metoyer to Baba and Françoise, in Natchitoches Parish Records, Book 8, p. 231.

his will that these two slaves should be emancipated as soon as the law permitted it.[70]

Philanthropy appears to have been the motivation behind at least one slave purchase on record. In 1834 young Jean Baptiste Louis Metoyer bought from Francisco Gonzales an eighty-year-old Negro slave named Charles. Gonzales had recently purchased the slave from the estate of Louis Barthelemy Rachal, white, and apparently regretted having done so. J. B. Louis reimbursed Gonzales for the twenty dollars that the Spaniard had paid to Rachal's estate and agreed to pay the heirs the remaining ninety dollars of Gonzales' debt for the purchase. The record made no mention of any valuable skill that Charles had, and his advanced age probably made him a poor investment.[71] No evidence of a relationship can be found between the Negro and the Metoyer family. The only apparent explanation for the purchase is sympathy for the old man. Or, perhaps, J. B. Louis already owned a member of Charles' family and had granted his own slave a favor by purchasing the aging relative.

None of these items alone can be considered indicative of the treatment given by the Creoles of color on Isle Brevelle to the slaves who labored for them. Yet, collectively they contradict the generalization that free people of color who owned slaves were harsher masters than were white owners. Indeed, if any general conclusion can be drawn, it is that the Isle Brevelle people treated their slaves in much the same manner as did the whites, no better and no worse. As rising members of the planter class, the Creoles of color worked hard, and they probably worked their slaves the same way, but it is doubtful that they habitually demanded more of their slaves than they could be reasonably expected to give.

In the earliest days of the colony most labor on the plantations was performed by the owners and their slaves. As conditions changed and less land became available, especially near the end of the antebellum period, some young men were forced to begin as laborers and plantation overseers. The job

70. Last Will and Testament of Charles N. Rocques, Sr., in Succession of Charles N. Rocques, Sr., Natchitoches Parish Records, No. 1107; Paul A. Kunkel, "Modifications in Louisiana Legal Status under Louisiana Constitutions, 1812–1957," *Journal of Negro History,* XLIV (January, 1959), 7.

71. Francisco Gonzales to J[n] B[te] Louis Metoyer, in Natchitoches Parish Records, Book 19, p. 328.

of laborer, naturally, was the least desired, since it presented the greatest challenge to advancement. In 1860 the average daily wage for a day laborer in Natchitoches Parish was only $1, with board; a day laborer without board earned $1.25.[72]

Overseers fared somewhat better than laborers. The usual wage for overseers in the Cotton Belt was from four hundred to six hundred dollars per year. Exceptional men could earn as much as two thousand dollars; men of little ability might not gross more than two hundred in cash. In addition, most overseers and their families were provided with food, housing, firewood, and feed for their horses. Occasionally an overseer would be provided a slave for his own use. Of the seven overseers in the Cane River colony in 1860, two obviously were managers of family operations: George Kirkland for his mother-in-law, Widow Auguste Metoyer; and T. L. Metoyer for his mother, Widow Jean Baptiste Louis Metoyer. Employers of the other five are uncertain. One member of the colony, who is listed on the 1860 census as a planter, later indicated that he was employed during this period as a manager for Auguste Predanes Metoyer, and that after Metoyer's death in 1865 he continued in this same capacity for the widow.[73]

The records of the Cane River colony that relate to overseers in the late antebellum period reveal one striking variance from the law. As fears of slave revolts intensified throughout the South, and as a growing number of people were prone to believe that free people of color would incite such revolts, a law was enacted in Louisiana (1852) which called for the presence of at least one white person to every thirty slaves on a plantation.[74] Yet, nowhere in the records dealing with the colony is it indicated that they ever hired whites on their plantations in compliance with this law. Nor is there any indication that charges of noncompliance were brought against them.

Even though agriculture was the foundation of the prosperity of Isle Brevelle, the economic endeavors of the people were not confined to the soil. In

---

72. Eighth Census of the United States, 1860, Population Schedule and Social Statistics.
73. Gray, *Agriculture in Southern United States,* I, 546; Eighth Census of the United States, 1860, Population Schedule; *Jean Conant* v. *United States,* in Records of the Southern Claims Commission, Claim 43566.
74. Alice Dunbar-Nelson, "People of Color in Louisiana," *Journal of Negro History,* II (January, 1917), 64.

partnership with other free people of color or with whites, or both, or in business alone, they engaged in diverse activities supplemental to the plantation economy, such as merchandising, money lending, milling, ginning, blacksmithing, and operating ferry boats.

The usual involvement in merchandising was on the local level. Even then it appears that most of the merchants engaged in such businesses only as a sidelight to their planting operations or as a means to acquire capital for a plantation. The earliest mercantile establishment which has been identified on the Isle was a partnership formed in the mid-1820s by Auguste Metoyer, Charles N. Rocques, and Jerome Sarpy. Operating under the name of Rocques, Sarpy & Company, it was organized for local business only and handled such general merchandise as dry goods and groceries. By mutual consent the partners dissolved the partnership in September of 1827, holding a liquidation sale on Isle Brevelle. The goods were advertised as being "divided into lots to suit planters." It was also requested, by public advertisement, that all who were indebted to or had claims against the firm come forward and settle their business.[75]

After the dissolution of the partnership, Sarpy apparently left the mercantile trade and operated his plantation on a full-time basis, but Auguste Metoyer continued in merchandising. Dealing in a variety of goods, including whiskey, tobacco, dry goods, wine, groceries, medicines, and furniture, he did business with white people of the area as well as with the members of the colony.[76] The majority of the goods that Auguste handled at the Isle Brevelle store came from New Orleans; a major supplier was the New Orleans firm of Jonan, Metoyer & Company, in which Auguste was a partner.

Auguste's business associates in the New Orleans firm were two whites, Antoine Jonan and Emilie Jarreau. In their capacity as cotton brokers, the firm arranged sales of cotton, made purchases for their customers, provided credit, and even paid checks. The records of this business provide evidence of the high quality of the cotton produced on the Isle. For example, on a sale made in June, 1839, the price per pound can be figured to have been 17.5 cents— sharply higher than the average price of 7.5 cents per pound in June of that

75. *Natchitoches Courier,* August 28–October 2, 1827.
76. Auguste Metoyer to various customers, Account Statements, in Henry Clement Papers, Henry Collection.

year which has been reported by one historian of southern agriculture.[77] Another specific comparison is provided by a sale which A. Maurin & Company of New Orleans made for the same planter two months earlier. A shipment of 118 bales went for $7,347, or an average of $62.26 per bale.[78] Although the average per-pound price of this shipment, 14 cents, is significantly lower than the 17.5 cents which Jonan, Metoyer, & Company secured, it is still almost twice the southern average for that year.

The account which Jonan, Metoyer & Company carried for Marie Suzanne Metoyer indicates the broad scope of the firm's services. At the time of her death she owed the company for such items as farming supplies, "nice dry goods," silk stockings ($1.50 per pair), perfume ($5.75 per bottle), "workmanship of a gown," ($4.50), and freight for a bicycle ($1.50). After paying a check for her to C. N. Rocques in the amount of $1,430, the firm recorded a debit for her of $4,470 against credits of $5,442, leaving her a balance of $972. Her account with the house of A. Maurin, by way of comparison, shows that she owed $3,755. Other business transactions of Jonan, Metoyer & Company are reflected by the account rendered to the estate of Marie Louise Metoyer, the wife of Florentin Conant, in 1837. Their bill was issued in the amount of $1,728 for the purchase and shipment of furniture.[79]

After the dissolution of the partnership of Rocques, Sarpy & Company in 1827, Charles Nerestan Rocques continued to do business on his own, and his son followed him into the field of merchandising, dealing in such items as shoes and boots of Moroccan leather, dishes, bags of shot, flintstones, nails, chewing tobacco, powder, percussion caps, plows, cigars, smoking pipes, lumber, and shotguns. In addition to the usual entries, the account of Baptiste LeMoine, white, indicates that the firm had advanced him money to repay loans from other people, including a cotton factor in New Orleans. The presence of eight hundred cigars in the succession inventory of C. N. Rocques, Jr., led one authority to deduce, incorrectly, that Rocques was a cigar maker.

77. *Faures* v. *Metoyer*, 6 Rob. 75 (1843); Dissolution of Partnership between Antoine Jonan and Dame Blanchard (Original document in possession of Mrs. Noble Morin, Natchez, Louisiana); Gray, *Agriculture in Southern United States,* II, 1027; Succession of Marie Suzanne Metoyer, in Natchitoches Parish Records, No. 355.

78. Succession of Marie Suzanne Metoyer, *ibid.*

79. *Ibid.;* Succession of Marie Louise Metoyer, in Natchitoches Parish Records, No. 323.

However, not one of the score of records available locally on this individual contains any reference to his manufacture of this product.[80] Since cigars and whiskey were two of the best-selling products in the Natchitoches area, there was nothing unusual in the presence of these items on the inventory of goods left by Rocques.

Another mercantile firm on the Isle began as a partnership between two members of the colony and two prominent white planters. The firm apparently opened in 1830 under the name of Dupre, Metoyer & Company. Partners were Emanuel Dupre and Jean Baptiste Dominique Metoyer, both free men of color, and Nicolas Gracia and Charles F. Benoist, both white. The exact interests of the two white men were not specified. Presumably they invested a sum in the business, although it is doubtful that their interest was very large. When one of the nonwhite partners, Emanuel Dupre, married in 1830, his contract of marriage listed his assets at $1,300. The total assets of the firm that same year were inventoried at $2,719. The business apparently enjoyed initial success, since in 1831 Dupre and Metoyer bought out their white partners and increased their inventory to $3,306.[81]

In reviewing the activities of the merchants and entrepreneurs in the colony, it is again evident that the increasingly restrictive laws of the state were not enforced on Isle Brevelle. In 1856 a state law was passed which denied free people of color the right to purchase liquor licenses. Yet the account books of the merchant Oscar Dubreuil reveal that during the last week of 1856 he sold over thirty gallons of whiskey to his credit customers. Here again, there is no indication that the penalty of the law was exacted against Dubreuil.[82]

Other members of the colony who operated as merchants at various times were Auguste Predanes Metoyer, Jean Conant, Élisé Rocques, Sarpie Metoyer, Vilfried Metoyer, B. Llorens, and Charles Dupre.[83] No generaliza-

80. Succession of Baptiste Lemoine, and Succession of C. N. Rocques, *fils*, in Natchitoches Parish Records, Nos. 437 and 897; Sterkx, *The Free Negro in Ante-Bellum Louisiana*, 235.

81. Dupre and Metoyer Account Book (Louisiana State University Archives, Baton Rouge); Marriage Contract of Emanuel Dupre and Marie Marguerite Metoyer, in Natchitoches Parish Records, Book A, Records, 48.

82. Robert C. Reinders, "The Free Negro in the New Orleans Economy, 1850–1860," *Louisiana History*, VI (Summer, 1965), 283; [Oscar Dubreuil] Account Book 1856–1858 (MS in Louisiana State University Archives, Baton Rouge).

83. Seventh and Eighth Censuses of the United States, 1850–1860, Population Schedules; interview with Mrs. Coutii, March 24, 1974; *Natchitoches Courier*, March 13, 1826.

tion can be made regarding the success of their enterprises. Some appear to have been quite successful; others, including Auguste Metoyer, eventually lost everything. The credit system on which merchants operated seems to have been the downfall of most of those whose businesses failed. Auguste, for example, who was one of the leaders of the community, was ambitious, industrious, and astute in business. Yet, his business enterprises failed in the panic and depression of the late 1830s, as evidenced by numerous suits against him in the district court. The Civil War was an equally difficult period for the merchants who operated on the credit system. When Auguste Predanes Metoyer died in 1865, the inventory of his estate included seventeen debts owed him that were considered worthless. They totaled $1,424. Seven of the debtors were white.[84] By contrast, however, several white merchants of the parish were also forced out of business entirely by the hardships which attended the war.[85]

Not only did the people of Cane River have extensive interests in mercantile firms, but they operated their own places of entertainment as well. In 1839, for example, Jean Baptiste Espallier Rachal purchased a billiard hall at Cloutierville from a white named Louis Emanuel Gallien. For $1,100 he acquired a lot with 60 feet of frontage by 120 feet of depth, French measure, with "all the improvements such as the building that is found thereon, constructed as a billiard hall, with all the accessories." Neighbors on all sides were white. The document was drafted by the notary in the billiard hall which Rachal was purchasing.[86] In the 1850s and 1860s another member of the community, Oscar Dubreuil, operated a billiard hall at 24-Mile Ferry.[87]

The appearance of very few craftsmen or mechanics within the colony suggests that most such work was done by slaves. The only known carpenters in the community during the early years were Seraphin Llorens and Philippe Valsain Dupre. The contract work which they did for both white and nonwhite planters on the Isle, especially the work of Llorens, reflected a wide range of

84. Succession of Predanes Metoyer, in Natchitoches Parish Records, No. 1360.

85. For example, see "Public Auction of Goods of Antoine Marinovich of Cloutierville," *Natchitoches Union,* May 1, 1862, and "Public Auction of Goods of B. Molina, of Natchitoches," *ibid.,* June 12, 1862.

86. Louis Emanuel Gallien to Jean Baptiste Espallier Rachal, in DeBlieux Collection.

87. J. E. Dunn, "Isle Brevelle," Natchitoches *Louisiana Populist,* February 26, 1897; Mrs. Coutii to author, June 5, 1974.

skills in this trade. In 1836 Llorens contracted with F. S. Lattier, white, for the construction of a cotton gin that both cleaned and pressed the cotton into bales. His fee was six hundred dollars, to be paid by a check drawn on a New Orleans bank.[88]

A building contract held by Llorens and Dupre in 1838 and 1839 involved them in a lawsuit with another member of the community. The two carpenters and their slaves were cutting timber on land they considered to be public domain for the construction of a ginhouse, residence, and other plantation buildings. When Auguste Metoyer informed them that the land actually belonged to him, Llorens and Dupre ignored him. Metoyer filed suit in the amount of $500 and posted a bond in that amount. The judge issued a temporary injunction against the carpenters until surveyor G. W. Morse could establish the boundary line between Auguste's property and the public domain. Llorens obviously thought that $500 in damages was unfair since he had cut only enough timber to make 35,000 cypress shingles worth $10 per 1,000, or a total of only $350. Still insisting that the land was part of the public domain, Llorens filed a counter suit in the amount of $500. The suit was eventually decided in favor of Metoyer.[89]

Seraphin Llorens has also been credited with building the "big house" on the plantation of Louis Metoyer, the best known of the large Metoyer plantation homes that survived into the twentieth century. The much-married Llorens was, by his last wife, the father of Hugh Llorens, who assisted in the remodeling of this house for its white owners in the early 1900s. On many occasions, the son Hugh delighted in telling others that he was not the first in his family to work on this house; in fact, his father had been its builder.[90] No building contract has been found for the house, but the lack of a written contract was not unusual. The Lattier/Llorens contract for the gin was made between a white man and a man of color; an element of distrust was probable. A written contract between Metoyer and Llorens, as members of a closely knit

88. Seraphin Llorens to F. S. Lattier, in DeBlieux Collection, No. 225.

89. *Metoyer* v. *Llorice and Dupre,* in Natchitoches Parish Records, District Court Suit No. 2044 (1839).

90. Hugh LaCour to author, April 5, 1974. Mr. LaCour is a grandnephew of the late Hugh Llorens and was frequently told by Llorens that the latter's father, Seraphin, had "built the big house for Louis Metoyer." Interview with Mrs. Coutii, April 26, 1974.

colony, would be less likely. Nevertheless, the proven fact that Llorens did do this type of work lends credence to the tradition that he was the builder of the house usually called Melrose.

By 1860 the number of carpenters on Isle Brevelle had increased among both the white and the free nonwhite populations. Among those of the latter class who were identified by the census of that year as carpenters were L. B. Chevalier, Magee Grappe, and François Florcal. In addition, succession records indicate that at least two slaves belonging to nonwhites were trained in this skill. The 1838 succession inventory of Marie Louise Metoyer, wife of Florentin Conant, itemizes a slave carpenter, aged thirty-five. Similarly, the 1851 succession inventory of Joseph Augustin Metoyer noted that the slave named Washington, who had run away once and was blind in one eye, was also a skilled carpenter.[91]

Another trade which was practiced to some degree on the Isle was blacksmithing. There were at least two blacksmiths in the community in the 1820s and 1830s, Émile Colson and Leander Dupart. Dupart built and operated a shop on land belonging to François Metoyer at the lower point of the Isle; he also farmed the land for François.[92] It is also probable that François' brother Joseph either was a blacksmith during this period or had a slave with the necessary skill since his succession inventory includes tools of the trade, including a forge and all its appurtenances, a vise, and a turning device. It also itemizes a number of small accounts and notes due to him from other free people of color and whites of the area. The small accounts are indicative of some type of business, and there is no evidence that he was a merchant. Joseph's son, Joseph, Jr., purchased the blacksmithing tools at the succession sale of his father's estate, and his son, Joseph, III, was listed on the 1860 census as a blacksmith. Apparently the skill was passed from the father

91. Eighth Census of the United States, 1860, Population Schedule; Succession of Marie Louise Metoyer, and Succession of Joseph Augustin Metoyer, in Natchitoches Parish Records, Nos. 323 and 692. According to Fogel and Engerman's econometric study of slavery, 11.9 percent of slaves were skilled craftsmen (carpenters, blacksmiths, coopers, etc.). The slave inventories of the Cane River colony do not reveal this high an incidence of skilled slaves, but in the absence of a sufficient number of craftsmen among the free population, it seems likely that they possessed more skilled slaves than those that have been documented. Fogel and Engerman, *Time of the Cross*, I, 39.

92. *Derbanne* v. *Metoyer*, in Natchitoches Parish Records, District Court Suit No. 1097 (1829); *J^h M^ie Rablés* v. *Émile Colson*, in DeBlieux Collection.

through the son to the grandson. L. S. Prudhomme, a freed slave of French and African parentage, was also a blacksmith on the Isle in 1860.[93] In addition to the members of the colony who practiced the smithing trade, three planters owned slaves with the skill: Augustin Metoyer, his nephew Jean Baptiste Louis Metoyer, and the latter's son, Théophile Louis.[94]

One popular trade in the colony which reveals much about the personal characteristics of these people is that of tailor. At least three have been identified between 1830 and 1860 and more than one was in business at one time. Firmin C. Christophe, Sr., settled on Cane River during the 1830s and operated a tailor's shop for approximately three decades. His business must have been small since the 1850 and 1860 censuses place the value of his personal property at only $1,000, which would have been the approximate value of the one slave that he owned. In 1850 the shop was located in Cloutierville, but by 1860 he had returned to the Isle.[95] M. B. Llorens, who owned three slaves and was worth $3,000, was also a tailor in that year. It is possible that these slaves assisted the tailors in the operation of their businesses. Tradition also holds that the versatile Oscar Dubreuil, among his other enterprises, did tailoring for residents of the lower Cane River area.[96]

Related trades which appeared in the colony were those of shoemaker and dressmaker. L. V. Lorance [Llorens] was listed as a shoemaker in 1860. Since he was only twenty years of age and since this trade is not previously found on the Isle, it is probable that he was an apprentice of his neighbor, A. Lourses, a shoemaker from France. Three seamstresses were listed in the colony in that same year: Lodoiska Metoyer, Margaret Monette, and E. Monette.[97]

93. Succession of Joseph Metoyer, in Natchitoches Parish Records, No. 359; Eighth Census of the United States, 1860, Population Schedule.
94. Augustin Metoyer to Children, Donations Book 30, pp. 70–78; Succession of [J. B.] Louis Metoyer, No. 362; Marriage Contract of Théophile Louis Metoyer to Marie Elina Metoyer, Mortgage Record Book 28, p. 277, all in Natchitoches Parish Records.
95. Sixth through Eighth Censuses of the United States, 1840–1860, Population and Slave Schedules. It is interesting to note that in addition to the slave which he claimed on the Natchitoches census, Christophe was also a property holder and tax payer in New Orleans in 1860 and 1861; see David C. Rankin, "The Origins of Black Leadership in New Orleans During Reconstruction," *Journal of Southern History,* XL (August, 1974), 437.
96. Seventh and Eighth Censuses of the United States, 1850–1860, Population and Slave Schedules. Information on Dubreuil provided by his granddaughter, Mrs. Armella Rachal, Natchez, Louisiana, quoted in Mrs. Coutii to author, June 5, 1974.
97. Eighth Census of the United States, 1860, Population Schedule.

Among the miscellaneous trades participated in on a small scale were ceramics and surveying. Tradition holds that one member of the family, Marie Adélaïde Mariotte, was skilled in pottery and provided plates, pots, and vases for the community. The 1850 and 1860 censuses, which are the only ones in which she is listed by name, provide no occupation for her, however.[98] Land survey records from the period of affluence show that several youth of the community assisted the local surveyors during periods when their own farms did not need them. For example, chain bearers for George S. Walmsley from 1840 to 1843 included Émile Colson and Ozeme Dominique Metoyer.[99]

In a country interlaced with rivers and bayous, ferries are often vital to transportation. In Natchitoches Parish there were at least three ferries across Cane River on the main road from Alexandria to the town of Natchitoches. At least two of the ferries were public property, leased annually by the parish at auction. The highest bidder gave his secured note, due at the end of the year, for the amount of his bid plus the interest. Bidders were required to furnish their own equipment, but the equipment was simple. The ferries were operated by a hand wrench, attached to a rope or cable which was tied to the sturdiest post that could be found.[100] Passenger rates were set officially and published in the local newspaper. Rates in 1825, for example, were six and one-fourth cents for one person, twelve and one-half cents for a man and a horse or for a horse and buggy, fifty cents for any four-wheeled vehicle pulled by two horses, and seventy-five cents for a loaded wagon or coach with four horses, including the driver and passengers.[101]

Throughout most of the 1800s these ferries were often operated by free men of color from the Cane River colony. Monette's Ferry (also called 40-Mile Ferry since it was located that distance from the courthouse in Natchitoches) was named for and operated by the family of Louis Monet (Monette), Marie Thérèze's great-grandson, who for several decades owned a plantation at the site.[102]

---

98. Seventh and Eighth Censuses of the United States, 1850 and 1860, Population Schedules; Mrs. Coutii to author, March 31, 1974. Mrs. Coutii is the great-great-granddaughter of Adelaïde Mariotte.

99. File R&R 306, Joseph Metoyer, State Land Records.

100. *Natchitoches Union,* December 25, 1862; Hugh LaCour to author, April 5, 1974.

101. *Natchitoches Courier,* December 26, 1825.

102. Hugh LaCour to author, March 5, 1974.

The second known ferry on the river was located at the village of Cloutier-ville, and at least one member of the colony operated it in the mid-nineteenth century. Young Hypolite Metoyer issued an account statement in 1851 to his white neighbor, Charles Molonguet, for twenty-seven crossings by Molonguet, his slave, and an apparent employee of Molonguet named Louis Gallien. Crossings made with horse and wagon were billed at the rate of forty cents each. Crossings made on horseback were usually twenty cents, while crossings made on foot were only ten cents.[103]

Several members of the colony are known to have operated the 24-Mile Ferry. In the 1850s it was operated by Pierre Metoyer, Jr. In addition to the ordinary flatboat, he also owned three pirogues.[104] Oscar Dubreuil, in addition to being a teacher, merchant, undertaker, tailor, and billiard hall operator, ran the ferry in the 1860s in partnership with his neighbor, Emanuel Dupre.[105] Members of the Dupre family continued to run the ferry long after the Civil War.[106]

The 24-Mile Ferry was an important stopover for stagecoaches and a land-ing for steamboats. Inevitably, a thriving community grew up around it. A stage station, two or three stores, a saloon, and Dubreuil's billiard hall were all established there to meet the needs of the passengers who came through the area. It also appears to have been a point for changing stagecoach drivers, since the censuses of 1850 and 1860 show a driver rooming in a free nonwhite home near the stop. Tradition holds that the ferry site was a steamboat landing as well.[107]

Almost all of the major occupations found within the parish were also found on Isle Brevelle. Only in the professional fields were the members of the colony poorly represented, but this circumstance is to be expected, given their racial heritage. According to one authority, teaching was the only profession in which a significant number of Louisiana's free people of color were in-volved,[108] and this generalization held true on the Isle.

---

103. Hypolite Metoyer to C. Molonguet, Account Statement, in DeBlieux Collection.

104. Succession of Pierre Metoyer, Jr., in Natchitoches Parish Records, No. 902.

105. Succession of Oscar Dubreuil, *ibid.,* No. 1255; Seventh and Eighth Censuses of the United States, 1850–1860, Population Schedules; Dunn, "Isle Brevelle."

106. Interview with Lewis Emory Jones, Natchez, Louisiana, March 16, 1974.

107. Seventh and Eighth Censuses of the United States, 1850–1860, Population Schedules; Mrs. Coutii to author, June 5, 1974.

108. Sterkx, *The Free Negro in Ante-Bellum Louisiana,* 232–33.

The area in which the colony was the least represented was the medical profession. The census of 1850 itemized only two physicians of color in all of rural Louisiana; neither of them was in Natchitoches Parish.[109] However, the fact that no doctor of their race was itemized on the censuses of Isle Brevelle indicates only that no members of the colony had medical degrees. It does not preclude the probability that some of them might have practiced medicine on a small scale. In fact, this probability is strengthened by the fact that the procès-verbal of the sale of the estate of Charles N. Rocques, Jr., included a set of surgical instruments which were purchased by another member of the community, Neres Pierre Metoyer.[110] As in any rural society there were also midwives. Claude Thomas Pierre Metoyer's will of 1801 notes that his daughter, Marie Suzanne, was a skilled midwife, and her grandniece, Sidalise Sarpy Dupre, is recalled as having regularly assisted with deliveries on the Isle.[111] Various others in the community were skilled veterinarians.[112]

Almost all of the activities in which these people engaged were economically profitable, but the most significant fortunes were amassed by those who were full-time planters. As previously noted, all of the earlier generations of the colony gave plantations, slaves, or money to each child upon his or her marriage, yet some of the children of Marie Thérèze Coincoin left sizable fortunes. When Pierre Metoyer died in 1834, his remaining estate was inventoried at $19,969. His sister, Marie Suzanne, was worth $61,600 when she died in 1838, and her nephew Jean Baptiste Louis died the same year leaving an estate valued at $112,761. Dominique, who had supported seventeen children and generously assisted all of those who married before his death in 1839, left property that was inventoried at $42,405. His oldest brother, Augustin, possessed an estate of $140,958 at the time his wife died in 1840, despite the depression which had bankrupted countless Americans during the three preceeding years.[113]

---

109. *Ibid.*

110. Succession of Charles N. Rocques, *fils,* in Natchitoches Parish Records, No. 897.

111. 1801 Will of Metoyer (MS in Natchitoches Parish Library); interview with Mrs. Coutii, March 24, 1974. Mrs. Coutii still owns the voluminous manual on midwifery which her grandmother, Mme. Dupre, used as a guide to her profession.

112. Interview with Tillman Chelettre, Sr., Natchez, Louisiana, October 12, 1974.

113. Succession of Pierre Metoyer, No. 193; Succession of Dominique Metoyer, No. 375; Succession of [Jn Bte] Louis Metoyer, No. 362; Succession of Marie Suzanne Metoyer, No. 355; Succession of Agnes Metoyer, No. 395, all in Natchitoches Parish Records.

An interesting comparison is furnished by an examination of the estate of Augustin's white half brother who had died several months prior to the time Augustin's estate was inventoried. Their father, it may be recalled, was a man of considerable fortune; five years before his death he was the largest slaveholder in the parish, owning 103 bondsmen. At his death his estate was divided between his three white children. In 1839 one of those children, Pierre Victorin, died leaving an estate which contained movables valued at $3,887 and slaves valued at $24,801. Augustin's twin sister, Marie Suzanne, who began her career as a slave midwife, had died the previous year leaving movables worth $1,616 and slaves that brought $25,735 at auction. Augustin's estate, which was inventoried the year following that of his white half brother, contained movables valued at $8,465.50 and slaves worth $44,560.[114]

The legal fees which were paid to settle estates of this magnitude were often sizable. Among the statements of accounts due that were included in Suzanne's succession was a bill from Judge Charles E. Greneaux for $376, representing his share of legal services for filing, recording, and copying of succession records. The settlement of the estate of Pierre Metoyer, the smallest estate owned by the older Metoyers, involved judge's fees of $293, attorney's fees of $200, and administrator's fees of $499, which together reduced the estate by almost $1,000.[115]

Although the wealth of the colony was the exception for men and women of their race, it was not unique, since almost every state claimed a few men of color of comparable wealth. Missouri and Louisiana boasted a number of them. For example, Julius Melbourn of North Carolina, who inherited an estate of $20,000, built it to a peak of $50,000. John Stanley of New Bern, in that same state, began as a barber and amassed a fortune "said at one time" to be worth more than $40,000.[116] An 1858 biographical sketch of Louis Charleville of St. Louis observes: "He was once very wealthy, but his estate has

114. Succession of Pierre Victorin Metoyer, in Natchitoches Parish Records, Succession Book 11, p. 393. A comparison of Pierre Victorin's complete estate with those of his half-siblings is not possible since most of the documents dealing with his succession are no longer on file; only the auction of his movables and slaves is now a matter of record.

115. Succession of Marie Suzanne Metoyer, and Succession of Pierre Metoyer, in Natchitoches Parish Records, Nos. 355 and 193.

116. Franklin, *Free Negro in North Carolina,* 140, 157.

now dwindled down to about $60,000."[117] Antoine Dubuclet of Iberville Parish, Louisiana, was the proprietor of an estate assessed at $206,400 on the 1860 census, and the total free nonwhite population of New Orleans in 1860 has been valued by various historians as $739,890 to $2,000,000.[118]

By way of comparison, the wealthiest man in the Cane River colony was undoubtedly Augustin Metoyer with his estate of $140,958, and the total assessment of the Cane River colony in 1860 was $770,545, a figure which supposedly represented 72 percent of the *true* valuation of the property.[119] Obviously, no individual in the Cane River colony can be touted as being the wealthiest free man of color of his era. However, it is rare to find a group in Louisiana, or in any other state, which boasted as many prosperous men and women or which retained such a degree of wealth for so long a period of time.

Because of their wealth, the men of the colony were accepted, economically, in the highest levels of Natchitoches society. They borrowed and lent cash and stood *in solido* with numerous white planters of the parish. As early as 1815 Augustin signed as security for a white neighbor, François Lavespere, on a note of $1,085 which Lavespere owed. When Joseph Metoyer died in 1838, the inventory of his estate included a note and account due him by his white half brother Benjamin.[120]

Similarly, when the estates of Mme. Desirée Hertzog and Henry Hertzog, white, were opened in 1866, it was noted that they had been indebted to the estate of C. N. Rocques, Sr., in the amount of $3,000 for a number of years.[121] A similar debt was owed to the community by another white Hertzog named Émile. The following year the *Semi-Weekly Times* published a notice of the forthcoming "meeting of the creditors of Émile Hertzog to elect a syndic to represent them in the succession."[122] Jerome Sarpy, Jr., and Nerestan P. Metoyer were elected as joint syndics at this meeting, and two weeks

117. Cyprien Clamorgan, *The Colored Aristocracy of St. Louis* (St. Louis, 1858), 15.

118. Sterkx, *The Free Negro in Ante-Bellum Louisiana,* 208; Erastus Paul Puckett, "The Free Negro in New Orleans to 1860" (M.A. thesis, Tulane University, 1907), 48–49; Reinders, "The Free Negro," 280.

119. Eighth Census of the United States, 1860, Population Schedule.

120. François Lavespere and Wife to Augustin Metoyer, Conveyance Book 37, Doc. 4534; Succession of Joseph Metoyer, No. 359, in Natchitoches Parish Records.

121. Succession of C. N. Rocques, Sr., No. 1107; *Sarpy* v. *Hertzog,* District Court Suit 6489 (1866), both *ibid.*

122. Natchitoches *Semi-Weekly Times,* March 2, 1867.

later the parish clerk certified them to act in this capacity for claimants against both Émile's succession and that of Mme. Desirée Hertzog.[123] Since the creditors of these prominent white planters undoubtedly included other whites as well as the free people of color, it is significant that these two nonwhite creditors were elected to represent the interests of the entire group.

Jerome Sarpy and Nerestan Metoyer also filed suit that same year against another white, Isidore Gimbert, an Isle Brevelle physician. Their legal efforts to recover sums which Gimbert owed them were successful. A judgment was declared against the doctor by the court, and the sheriff seized on their behalf and sold at auction three mules, one wagon, and four pairs of wagon harnesses which had belonged to Gimbert.[124]

On the other hand, the people of the colony were frequently advanced both small and large sums by the white planters of the area, and on some occasions the whites had to take them to court to collect the amounts due. The inventory of the community that existed between Augustin and his wife in 1840 indicated that he was indebted to Emanuel Prudhomme, a white planter of the Côte Joyeuse, for $1,500. Despite the depression which was throttling local economy, Augustin paid his note when it fell due. His son, Joseph Augustin, however, signed in 1843 a note for $310 in favor of Victor Rachal, a white planter from Cloutierville, and was unable to meet his obligation when it came due ten months later. In 1847 Rachal finally brought suit against him to collect the sum and won his case in court.[125]

In examining the financial interchanges between whites and free people of color, one modern study concludes: "Free Negroes frequently engaged in financial and business dealings with White persons. In some instances they borrowed money from White friends and in turn it was not unknown for certain free Negroes to lend money to impecunious White neighbors."[126] In general, this observation is valid. However, it must not be assumed that the majority of the whites or the free people of color who borrowed in the Cane

123. Certification of Jerome Sarpy, Jr., and Nerestan P. Metoyer by J. W. Hamilton, Clerk, in Chaplin, Breazeale and Chaplin Papers, Box 2.
124. *Sarpy and Metoyer* v. *Gimber,* in Natchitoches Parish Records, District Court Suit No. 6336 (1867).
125. Succession of Agnes Metoyer, No. 395; *Rachal* v. *Metoyer, ibid.,* District Court Suit No. 3913 (1847).
126. Sterkx, *The Free Negro in Ante-Bellum Louisiana,* 56–57.

River area did so because they were poor. On the contrary, they were quite often men or women of means. Such people often borrowed for investment purposes and purchased goods on credit. Most of the debts owed by white friends and neighbors to members of the Cane River colony fell into these categories. Rather than rich men helping poor ones, it was usually a case of men of equal standing providing help to each other.

In one respect, the assistance which members of the colony provided was occasionally their downfall. Not only did they lend to whites and borrow from them but they also acted *in solido* for them, signing as security for obligations which whites assumed. In some cases, they later regretted their actions. Jean Baptiste Espallier Rachal, for example, agreed in 1835 to act as one of the sureties for a white neighbor, Jean Baptiste Grandchampt. Grandchampt had been named administrator of the solvent estate of another white, Pierre Baulos; he paid some of the debts of the estate, gave his note for others, and managed to lose a "large balance" which should have been distributed among the heirs of Baulos.

When Grandchampt was found to be insolvent, one creditor of the estate, to whom the administrator had given his note rather than make full payment, brought suit against Rachal in an effort to recover his losses. The codefendant was the widow of a white named Silvestre Rachal who had acted as second surety for Grandchampt. The court of probates ruled that the two Rachals could not be held liable for the debt, but when the case was appealed by the creditor the supreme court of Louisiana decreed that J. B. Espallier Rachal and the Widow Sylvestre Rachal must pay the debt of $1,891.[127]

Incidences such as this, however, should not be interpreted as proof that generosity on the part of the colony was taken advantage of by the whites whom they befriended. The opposite situation also occurred, as in the case of *Chaler* v. *Birtt and Metoyer*. On August 1, 1836, Auguste Metoyer signed two notes in favor of his white in-law, J. B. Anty, for a total of $620 at 10 percent interest. Isaac Birtt, white, signed as surety. Auguste could not meet the payment when it fell due, and Anty died shortly afterward. The administrator of Anty's estate, a prominent white planter of the Isle named Terence Chaler, filed suit against both Metoyer and Birtt in 1839. Metoyer did not

127. *Gillet* v. *Rachal,* 9 Rob. 276 (1844).

contest the case; he had no grounds to do so. Birtt admitted signing *in solido* but insisted nevertheless that he should not be held liable and requested a trial by jury. His request was denied. The court ordered Chaler to collect from Metoyer the sum due, plus interests and the costs of the suit. Another order was issued simultaneously against Birtt, which was to become effective in the event that Metoyer was not able to pay.[128]

The astuteness which members of the colony usually exercised in the conduct of their business was recognized and acknowledged by the community. Jacques LaCaze, a white planter on Little River, left a will in which he named Augustin Metoyer and son Jean Baptiste Augustin as executors of his estate, despite the fact that he left a wife, children, a number of white relatives, and in-laws in the area who could have administered his estate. Another white named Jesse Smith appointed Auguste Metoyer as administrator of his succession which was opened about 1841. When Jacques Dufrois Derbanne and wife died in 1849 and 1850, the court appointed two members of the Cane River colony, Joseph Augustin Metoyer and Emanuel Dupre, to inventory and estimate the Derbanne estate. Even after the Civil War, when the colony had already lost considerable status, Charles Dupre, son of Emanuel, was appointed the administrator of the estate of a white neighbor, Ursin Derbanne.[129]

One indication of the improvement in status which occurred as the Cane River colony progressed economically is reflected by all the documents dealing with the colony that were drafted by the notaries. In the early years of the colony, when the various members purchased property or needed documents executed, they went to the office of the notary or to the home of the white with whom they were doing business, and the notary joined them there. By the 1820s the situation had reversed. The documents executed on behalf of the rank-and-file of the people, as well as their leaders, noted that they were drafted in the homes of the *gens de couleur libre* on Isle Brevelle.

128. *Chaler* v. *Birtt and Metoyer,* in Natchitoches Parish Records, District Court Suit No. 1782 (1838). On the 1830 census, Isaac Birtt (Burke) was listed erroneously as a free man of color, and was included in Woodson's study of slaveowners of this class. However, the numerous church and civil records which exist on Birtt in Natchitoches Parish consistently refer to him as white. Fifth Census of the United States, 1830; Woodson, "Free Negro Owners of Slaves in the United States in 1830," 50.
129. Succession of Jacques LaCaze, No. 139; *Friend* v. *Smith,* Succession Book 12, p. 174; Succession of Jacques Dufrois Derbanne and Wife, No. 669, all in Natchitoches Parish Records; Natchitoches *Semi-Weekly Times,* October 31, 1866.

In 1823, for example, Louis Metoyer sold to his nephew Jean Baptiste Augustin Metoyer a tract of land on Red River for $2,200. The notary recorded that the document was "passed at the domicile of Monsieur Louis Metoyer to which I went upon request of the parties." [130] When the transactions also involved whites, they also frequently went to the homes of the people of color, as in 1848, when Augustin Metoyer sold to a white named Remy McTire (MacTaer) of Campti a tract of land which he owned in the Campti area. McTire traveled the thirty miles to Augustin's home to complete the transaction, and a notary was called to the Isle from Cloutierville to draft the document *"dans la domicile d'Augustin Metoyer."* [131]

The economic status of the Cane River colony was exceptional in American society as a whole. The conditions of racial tolerance and relative acceptance which existed in Louisiana were most certainly prerequisites for such success, but this was by no means the major factor. Toleration never guarantees prosperity, only the right to pursue it. It is the responsibility of the individual to use his rights to make his own degree of success. The people of Isle Brevelle did just that.

The explanation for the success which this colony achieved in their economic endeavors is provided by several features of their economic profile. The higher percentages of improved land on their plantations clearly demonstrate their determination to make the most of whatever they acquired. The broad range of activities in which they participated indicates a desire for self-reliance—a recognition of the need to maintain themselves and their standard of living without dependence upon the increasingly restrictive white society. Their decision to cultivate the most profitable cash crop, while relying upon their own merchants to supplement their food supplies, further reflects their perception of economic principles and their ability to discern the most profitable economic course for their community. In general, perceptive planning, cooperative effort, and unrelenting pursuit of common goals were the main factors which set them apart, economically, from the mass of nonwhites in Louisiana.

---

130. Louis Metoyer to Jean Baptiste Augustin Metoyer, Louis Metoyer Document, 1823 (MS in Louisiana State University Archives, Baton Rouge).
131. Augustin Metoyer to Remy MacTaer, in Natchitoches Parish Records, Notarial Record Book 39, 521–22.

Chapter SIX

The Faith of Their Fathers

The people of the Cane River colony had an enviable reputation. Although exceptions exist for every rule, the majority of the population earned the respect and approbation of all who came into contact with them. The most compelling forces shaping their characters were undoubtedly the Church and their father figure, Augustin Metoyer. In many respects, these forces were one and the same. The people were Roman Catholics, devout in their faith even to the smallest details. Led by Augustin, they established what may well be the oldest church built by and for free people of color in the United States.

In an era in which the whole of Natchitoches Parish suffered from a lack of formal spiritual leadership, Augustin became something of a father confessor to his community. According to tradition he was strict, yet with a piety tempered with kindness that encouraged others to seek his advice and guidance.[1] This tradition is supported by the records. No hint of scandal or indiscretion is attached to his name in any of the civil or ecclesiastical documents, and countless records portray him in the role of family counselor.

The strong presence of religion in Augustin's life can be traced to his childhood. The church registers of 1777 show the nine-year-old Augustin acting as godfather to his cousin and namesake, Nicolas Augustin, a slave of Commandant Athanase De Mézières. In 1781 he served as godfather to an Indian slave child of the Sieur LeCourt. Again in 1783 he acted in this capacity to an infant Negro slave of Mme. Gabriel Buard.[2] From this point on, the registers show

---

1. Confidential source to François Mignon, September 3, 1972, copy in possession of author; interview with Mrs. Coutii, March 24, 1974.
2. Baptism of Nicolas Augustin, February 9, 1777, in Natchitoches Registers, Book 4, p. 308; Baptisms of Maria Modesta and Maria Celesia, April 17, 1781, and Baptism of a small negro of Juana, June 22, 1783, in Natchitoches Registers, Book 4.

him acting regularly in this role. Augustin was, without a doubt, the godfather to more children than any other free man of color in the parish.

According to legend, it was while on continental travels with his father that Augustin first conceived the idea of a church for his people. According to Father J. J. Callahan's history of the parish, "The story goes that Thomas Metoyer had taken his son Augustine [sic] to France in 1801 to visit the homeland of his people, which was in the neighborhood of Lyons. It seems the latter was struck by the organization of French villages whose community life centered about the church. It recalled to his mind that there was no church at Isle Brevelle, and so, after his return, he built one in 1803."[3] However, there is no record of a church having been built on the Isle in that year, and thus is presented the crux of one of the most controversial aspects of the colony's history.

The first known chapel on Isle Brevelle was blessed by the curé from Natchitoches, Father J. B. Blanc, in 1829. Upon his return home, Father Blanc entered the record in his registers:

> The nineteenth day of July of the year 1829. I, the undersigned, pastor of the Church of St. François of Natchitoches, have proceeded to the blessing of a chapel erected on Isle Brevelle on the plantation of Sieur Augustin Metoyer through the care and generosity of the above-named Augustin Metoyer, aided by Louis Metoyer, his brother. The above-named chapel having been constructed to propogate [sic] the principle of our holy religion shall always be considered as a mission of the church of St. François of Natchitoches. The said chapel erected at Isle Brevelle having been dedicated to St. Augustine, shall be considered as under the protection of this great doctor. Done and passed at Natchitoches the twenty-seventh day of July, 1829.[4]

---

3. Callahan *et al.*, *History of St. Augustine's Parish*, 35. Through the years the people have consistently referred to Claude Thomas Pierre Metoyer as "Thomas," even though he always identified himself as Pierre. Perhaps they adopted the practice of referring to their ancestor by one of his less well-known names so as not to offend the white Metoyers who traced their descent from Pierre. As a result of this practice, one version of the legend insists that two Metoyer brothers settled at Natchitoches, one named Pierre and the other named Thomas. Pierre, supposedly, married a French girl at the post and was the progenitor of the white Metoyers of the Côte Joyeuse, while Thomas "married" Marie Thérèze Coincoin and was the progenitor of the Metoyers of Isle Brevelle. The tradition that "Thomas" was from Lyons cannot be supported. The Metoyer "homeland" was actually La Rochelle and Rheims.

4. July 27, 1829, Natchitoches Registers, Book 6, p. 116.

Concerned by the discrepancy between tradition and actual records, Father Callahan questioned in his history of the parish: "If it were built earlier, why had it taken twenty-six years to have it blessed?" Answering his own question, Callahan concluded that the scarcity of priests and the social inferiority of people of color were to blame.[5]

Callahan's conclusion is not convincing. Priests were indeed scarce, but between 1803 and 1829 they made numerous trips to the Isle to perform baptisms and marriages in private homes. For example, on November 15, 1804, several baptisms were performed at the home of Sieur Pierre Jarri, white, on Isle Brevelle, including the baptisms of two children of Pierre and Dominique Metoyer.[6] Callahan felt that this was natural, since the priests of that period would go to the home of a white man before they would visit the home of a colored one.[7] Yet, the records show that it was not long before the priests did go to the Metoyer homes to administer the sacraments. As the influence of the colony increased, the priests regularly visited their homes and plantations, particularly that of Augustin, and whites from the surrounding countryside went there to be married and to have their slaves and their children baptized. But still the registers refer to such events taking place "in the home of Augustin Metoyer," with no mention of the chapel that supposedly stood next door.[8]

It is highly improbable that the priests who made annual or biennial visits during most of the period between 1803 and 1829 would have ignored a chapel for those twenty-six years while they administered the sacraments in the house next door. It was July 19, 1829, when the chapel was finally blessed. Four days later the first marriages were performed there, a quadruple wedding, representing couples of pure French, Spanish, Indian, and mixed ancestry.[9] Two days later still another marriage was performed in the

5. Callahan *et al., History of St. Augustine's Parish,* 37–38.

6. Baptisms of Marie Susanne and Marie Perrine, November 15, 1804, in Natchitoches Registers, Book 5.

7. Callahan *et al., History of St. Augustine's Parish,* 37.

8. For examples, see baptisms dated October 25, 1825, and May 27, 1826, in Natchitoches Registers, Book 5, and Marriage of François Metoyer, Jr., to Marie Desirée Coton-Mais, April 26, 1827, *ibid.,* Book 11.

9. Marriage of Louis Monette and Marie Louise Cottonmaïs, f.p.c., No. 10; Marriage of Étienne LaCase and Caroline LeMoine, white, No. 11; Marriage of Cesaire LeCour and Marie Gertrude Maurine, French-Indian, No. 12; Marriage of Nazario Ortis and Des Neige Aragon, Spanish-French, No. 13, July 23, 1829, all in Natchitoches Registers, Book 11.

chapel,[10] and from that time on the registers of the parish of Natchitoches contain frequent references to sacraments administered in the Chapel of St. Augustine.

In attempting to prove the tradition that the church was built in 1803, Father Callahan offered as evidence a letter belonging to a resident of the Isle which reputedly had been preserved by her family since the date that it was purportedly written, a letter which has been quoted frequently by subsequent writers. The letter reads:

> Cane River
> State of Louisiana
> Isle Brevelle
> 10 June 1803

Mr. Jerome Sarpy
My dear friend and nephew,

I have just returned from New Orleans, and I suspect that you are anxious to have the news. I'll recount it all. Since you are kept to your bed, and I myself am tired after my trip, I send you my faithful servant John Baptist with this message for you. As you know we lived first under our own French government, then under that of Spain, and now we are under the authority of these new people who speak English and travel in wagons covered in white. As we all know these are unquiet times without repose. We shall all pray to our Creator for his blessings. As you know we have already spoken of building a church, and I am sure that with my brother Louis and his knowledge of building, we shall succeed. I shall give the land to the North of my house for the church and for the cemetery. That is what I have always wished to do since I visited the native land of my father in France; Paris, Marseilles, Lyons, in each one of these cities there are churches in every quarter. In one way or another I am sure that having a house of the good God in our midst, our people will live a better life, will love one another, and will live in harmony. I have heard it said that Father La Salle admired the place that I have chosen for the church. Yes, I have also heard that there have been troubles in Haiti. It seems that up to the present time, Toussaint L'Ouverture is unbeaten. I ask myself for how long. He has come up a long way, from coachman to the position he now holds. He has such love for his people and his land. To lose now would break his heart, both his and that of his beloved country.

I am sure that within a week I shall be able to visit you, when we shall have one of our long discussions. I am certain that the church will be finished by the first of August, and I am very grateful to you personally and to James Dupre for offering

---

10. Marriage of Émile Dupart and Marie Rose Baltazar, f.p.c., July 25, 1829, *ibid.*

the main altar. With the aid of all, I know that we shall succeed. Jerome, I beg you to take good care of yourself, and bridle your impetuous temperament.

May Our Father in Heaven bless you.

I remain

Augustin Metoyer
Yucca Plantation[11]

Father Callahan further asserted: "This letter contains within itself evidence of its own authenticity. It is a personal letter to a friend, whom we know otherwise to . . . have been the husband of a niece of Augustine [*sic*]. Notice also the touch of contemporary history. It was the year in which the United States had taken over the territory of the Louisiana Purchase when the settlers were already beginning to pour through Natchitoches."[12]

A comparison of the letter with the well-chronicled historical events which it mentions indicates that the letter in fact contains proof of its own spuriousness. For example, President Jefferson did not sign the treaty ratifying the purchase until October 21, 1803, and the actual announcement of the purchase was not made to the people of Louisiana until November 30, 1803.[13] Moreover, after the purchase, Louisiana was known as the Territory of Orleans until it was granted statehood in 1812. Augustin Metoyer could not possibly have written a letter from the "State of Louisiana" in June of 1803; nor would he have stated in any letter of that date that Louisiana was under American authority.

A second glaring error in the letter is the reference to the "troubles in Haiti" and the statement that Toussaint L'Ouverture was still unbeaten. In actuality, the Haitian leader surrendered in Santo Domingo in June, 1802, and in April, 1803, he died in a French prison.[14] News did travel slowly in the nineteenth century, but it is inconceivable that the latest "news" which Augustin received in New Orleans in June, 1803, could have contained the information that Toussaint L'Ouverture was still unbeaten.

11. Callahan *et al.*, *History of St. Augustine's Parish*, 36.

12. *Ibid.*

13. François Barbe-Marbois, *The History of Louisiana, Particularly of the Cession of that Colony to the United States of America* (trans. from the French, Philadelphia, 1830), 324, 327–28.

14. C. L. R. James, *The Black Jacobins: Toussaint L'Ouverture and the San Domingo Rebellion* (New York, 1963), 330–65.

Then, too, the date of the letter is totally contradicted by the personal family information which it sets forth. The letter is addressed to "Mr. Jerome Sarpy, my dear friend and nephew." Yet, according to the registers of the church, Sarpy did not marry Augustin's niece until 1820, seventeen years after the date of the letter.[15] Moreover, the letter sets forth Augustin's alleged hope that having a church in their midst would enable "our people" to love one another and live in harmony. But, in 1803 the Metoyer colony consisted only of Augustin and his brothers, all of whom worked together extensively and none of whom had children over the age of ten. The family group was not yet large enough or distinct enough to term it "our people"; nor was the colony large enough to need a house of God in their midst to promote harmony between its citizens.

The letter obviously is contrived. When and why it originated can only be speculated. The location of the original letter is not known. One resident of the Isle possesses a handwritten copy; she states that she found this draft in one of the old books given to her many years ago by her mother.[16] During the period in which the letter first surfaced the numerous old and valued books owned by the colony were being borrowed, whenever they could not be purchased, by popular writers who visited a nearby plantation. According to one Louisiana historian, at least two of these writers were renowned practical jokers who had once admitted concocting a spurious "historical story" as a joke on an acquaintance. The possibility does exist that these writers, or others of similar nature, invented this letter, and that it has been innocently perpetuated by other people.[17]

An additional documented incident strengthens the conclusion that the Chapel of St. Augustine was actually built, or completed, in July, 1829. Land surveys of that area indicate that the church grounds straddled the boundary line between two sections. The lower section was confirmed by the American government to Augustin Metoyer, while the upper section was confirmed to François Lavespere. In 1829 Lavespere's widow still resided on the tract. Five months after the church was dedicated, the widow gave power of attorney to

---

15. Marriage of Gerome Sarpy to Marie Adelaÿde Metoyer, June 27, 1820, Natchitoches Registers, Book 11.

16. Mrs. Coutii to confidential source, September 1973, copy in possession of author.

17. Davis, *Louisiana*, 380.

her son-in-law to "act in her stead relative to a certain difference likely to arise between her and Augustin Metoyer, f. m. c., her neighbor, respecting a certain boundary line run between their respective lands."[18] Had the church been built in 1803, with half of it standing on Lavespere's property, it is not likely that he and his wife would have waited twenty-six years to complain about the boundary encroachment. In fact, the mistake would have been discovered and settled, undoubtedly, when the land surveys were made of these two properties in 1814 and 1815.[19]

Regardless of the date when the church was actually built, 1803 or 1829, its construction still warrants recognition as a high point in the lives of the people. It is also indicative of the value placed upon religion by this society. When the parish church at Natchitoches was burned in 1823, the parishioners there went without a house of worship for three years.[20] Finally, a special act of the legislature was passed to permit the citizens of the town to hold a lottery in order to procure the necessary sum for a new church. A ceiling of twenty thousand dollars was put on the lottery.[21] Apparently, the parishioners did not consider themselves financially able to raise the necessary funds for a church, although quite obviously many of them did not mind risking money in a lottery. By contrast, the people of Isle Brevelle set aside a tract of their own fertile land for their church and cemetery grounds and built their church themselves.

In his discussion of this church, Callahan makes an interesting observation that remains relevant whether the church was built in 1803 or in 1829. Callahan cites a quotation from a study of Negro Catholicity and the Jesuit Order which asserts that the first church for Catholics of color in the United States was established in 1860 by Bishop Michael O'Connor of Baltimore in a building purchased by the white Catholics of that diocese. Father Callahan disputes this claim: "It is no reflection on the work of Bishop O'Connor [but] the colored Catholics of Isle Brevelle had their own church . . . before that

18. Widow François Lavespere to Julien Rachal, in Natchitoches Parish Records, Book A, 38.
19. Files B1806, François Lavespere, and B1960, Augustin Metoyer, State Land Records.
20. Beckers *et al., History of Immaculate Conception Catholic Church.*
21. *Journal of the Senate of the State of Louisiana,* 1826, p. 45.

date. . . . And they did not owe their parish to money collected among white Catholics but entirely to themselves."[22]

Undoubtedly, the people of Isle Brevelle also prided themselves on the fact that their church was only the third one that had been established in northwest Louisiana.[23] There had been a church at Natchitoches, intermittently, almost since the settlement of the post. Then in 1816, a white resident of the Rivière aux Cannes settlement, Alexis Cloutier, erected a small chapel on his plantation and donated the chapel and grounds to the Roman Catholic "congregation" of the area. His generosity was not without an ulterior motive, however, since the church was but the first step toward the founding of a town called Cloutierville, which was to be the seat of a new parish that he wanted to carve from Natchitoches.[24] The early registers of the existing Cloutierville church show that the sacraments were administered in Cloutier's chapel only between 1825 and 1829; the mission was then abandoned. Not until 1845 did the congregation reorganize and build an adequate structure.[25] The Isle Brevelle chapel, which was dedicated in 1829, probably drew much of the attendance from the mission church at Cloutierville and may account, in part, for its abandonment that year.

Although the church was built mainly by Louis Metoyer on land donated by Augustin, its furnishings were supplied by the community at large. The spurious letter by Augustin states that James Dupre[26] donated the altar, but tradition generally holds that the altar was given by Marie Suzette Anty, a daughter of Marie Suzanne Metoyer and the wife of Jean Baptiste Augustin Metoyer. Callahan recognizes this tradition, even though it contradicted the letter that he quoted, and states, "They say it cost five hundred dollars, quite a sum for

22. Callahan *et al., History of St. Augustine's Parish,* 40.

23. In the early nineteenth century, all of northwest Louisiana was incorporated in the limits of the parish of Natchitoches.

24. Alexis Cloutié to the Roman Congregation, Donation, in Natchitoches Parish Records, Book 6, Misc., Doc. 142; *Biographical and Historical Memoirs of Northwest Louisiana,* 317.

25. Baptismal Book 1 and Marriage Book 1, Cloutierville Registers; interview with Msgr. Milburn Broussard, Pastor of Church of St. John the Baptist, Cloutierville, August 22, 1970; Msgr. Broussard to author, March 15, 1974.

26. Church and civil records of this period indicate that there was no member of the colony named James or Jacques Dupre, either in 1803 or in 1829.

those days, and came from Europe."[27] The altar continued to be used for over a century, even after the original chapel was twice replaced by newer and larger structures.[28]

Two of the earliest decorations installed in the original chapel were a pair of paintings, one of St. Augustine, the patron saint of the man who conceived the idea of establishing the church and donated the land for it, the other of St. Louis, the patron saint of the chapel's builder. An impressive bell was hung in the belfry above the church's vestibule; its resounding tones could be heard the length and breadth of the Isle.[29] The twelve stations of the cross beautified the interior side walls, inspiring the parishioners to contemplate the burden and the sufferings of Jesus. Each station, it is recalled, was donated by a different member of the congregation.[30]

In 1836 a visiting artist painted Augustin's portrait as he stood on the veranda of his plantation home and pointed through its columns to the church of which he was so proud. In this painting we see a relatively small chapel, containing a single nave covered by a gabled roof on the front of which was erected the belfry tower. The roof extended beyond the walls to cover two galleries running along the sides of the church. According to tradition the galleries served two purposes. The slaves, who were not allowed to sit inside the sanctuary with their masters, attended mass while standing in the galleries. Also, in the event of rain, the galleries were put to use as shelter for the parishioners' carriages.[31]

Three years after the painting of his portrait with the chapel, Augustin Metoyer drafted his last will and testament, in which he explained his purpose in organizing this church:

27. Callahan *et al.*, *History of St. Augustine's Parish*, 42; interview with Mrs. Coutii, April 26, 1974.

28. This altar was finally replaced in the mid-twentieth century. The old altar was "given away"; its present whereabouts is not known. Interview with confidential source, April 26, 1974.

29. The painting of St. Augustine and the original bell still hang in the modern church; the old painting of St. Louis has been "lost" through the decades.

30. Nine of the twelve members of the colony who donated the Stations of the Cross are said to be Leopold Balthazar, Paul Balthazar, Vilfried Metoyer, Emanuel Dupre, Nemour Sarpy, Neres Pierre Metoyer, Carl "Caloot" Metoyer, Sévère Dupre, and Oscar Dubreuil. Mrs. Coutii to author, May 13, 1974.

31. Interview with Mrs. Coutii, April 26, 1974; Callahan *et al.*, *History of St. Augustine's Parish*, 42.

A portion of land of 3/4 *arpent* of frontage by 1 ½ *arpent* of depth, situated on the portion of land above given to my children Joseph and Gassion, at its upper part, does not belong to me. The Church of St. Augustin of Natchitoches was built there by me and my family, principally for our usage, except that I desire, and such is my wish that outsiders professing our holy, catholic, apostolic, and Roman religion will have the right to assist at the divine office in the said chapel and shall enjoy, moreover, all the rights and privileges which I and my family are able to have there. After my death I wish that this portion of land continue to be destined for the preservation of the same church and of a cemetery and that it should never be able to be used otherwise, in any manner or under any pretense that may be; with the privilege to my successors of making officers of the said church the Catholic priests who will suit them and not the others.[32]

Augustin's reference to "outsiders" reflects a curious situation, since the outsiders who attended the Isle Brevelle church were, by and large, whites. Integration of Louisiana's churches (particularly the Catholic churches) was the rule rather than the exception in antebellum Louisiana. However, it was normally the whites who built the churches and permitted nonwhites to attend. On Isle Brevelle the situation was reversed. It was the Creoles of color who organized the church, and when they extended an invitation to the wealthy white planters of the Isle who had no church of their own, the invitation was accepted.[33]

The presence of these "outsiders" was obviously important to Augustin. Upon the completion of his church, his descendants say, he set aside eight pews for the exclusive use of his white friends, located directly behind his own pew that stood in the place of honor before the statue of the Blessed Virgin.[34] For almost two generations whites regularly used these pews, obviously unperturbed by the thought of taking a back seat to a man of color, an unconventional practice even in relatively liberal Creole Louisiana. For Augustin, the establishment of his own church was undoubtedly a symbol of prestige, a measure of affluence and position that few of his white contemporaries could equal.

32. Last Will and Testament of Nicolas Augustin Metoyer, in Natchitoches Parish Records, Book 25, Notarial Records, 77–80.
33. Interview with Mrs. Coutii, March 24, 1974; The Rev. J. A. Baumgartner, "Isle Brevelle," quoted in Stahl, "The Free Negro in Ante-Bellum Louisiana," 362.
34. Interview with Mrs. Coutii, March 24, 1974.

The presence of these outsiders, moreover, provided a legal safeguard for Augustin and his community. As racial tensions heightened in antebellum Louisiana, an increasing number of wary whites looked askance on congregations of free nonwhites gathered for religious or other purposes. Many felt that such meetings provided too convenient a cover for the planning of slave insurrections, which one element of white society believed would be instigated by free men of color. A law was ultimately passed that restricted the congregation of nonwhites, slave or free, for religious purposes. Only if whites were included in their assemblies were the *gens de couleur libre* allowed freedom of worship after that time.[35]

Such a situation could easily have resulted in white assumption of control over the affairs of the Isle Brevelle church. The people would have had no alternative but to accept that control or lose their church when the whites decamped. Descendants of the antebellum colony relate that just such an attempt was made but lacked adequate support.[36] The failure of this alleged attempt, or any other, of whites to wrest control could well be viewed as the ultimate symbol of Augustin's prestige, and a clear indication of the respect which the majority of area whites held for the integrity of the colony.

It is also related that through the years priests from many places, as they were traveling through the region, said mass in the Chapel of St. Augustine. Some came from as far away as New Orleans and even Mexico. It was Augustin, it is said, who paid the priests from his own pocket for their trouble and expense.[37] The identities of most of these priests are not known, but the parish registers at Natchitoches record two such visits made by the bishop from New Orleans. In 1836 the Most Reverend Antoine Blanc made his first pastoral visit to the parish and visited the church on Isle Brevelle which his younger brother had blessed seven years earlier. In the registers at Natchitoches he recorded the visit and noted especially "the condition of decency and cleanli-

35. Stahl, "The Free Negro in Ante-Bellum Louisiana," 376.
36. Interview with confidential source, April 26, 1974. It is also related that on one occasion a white "spy" was found in the loft of the church during services. The "spy," allegedly, was "removed" from the premises by several male members of the congregation and was never seen again. Apparently, the white's disappearance was never conclusively linked to the people of the colony, since no charge against them for such a crime appears in the parish records.
37. Interview with Mrs. Coutii, March 24, 1974; confidential source to François Mignon, September 3, 1972, copy in possession of author.

ness" which he found there.[38] In 1842 the bishop was again in the parish and noted in the registers his visits to three churches, the Church of St. François at Natchitoches, the Church of St. Augustine on Isle Brevelle, and the new Church of the Nativity of the Blessed Virgin at Campti, just north of Natchitoches.[39]

On March 11, 1856, the mission of St. Augustine on Isle Brevelle was decreed by Bishop Auguste Martin of the diocese of Natchitoches to be a parish in its own right. Bishop Martin assigned his own brother, Father François Martin, to be its first resident pastor.[40] Its founder, Augustin Metoyer, died the following December 19, at the age of eighty-eight.[41] He had lived to see the fulfillment of what is said to have been the greatest wish of his old age, the establishment of a parish for his people.

Tradition relates one other story relative to Augustin and his church. After its construction or after the establishment of the parish (tradition varies), Augustin supposedly received a special letter of commendation from the pope which was read to the congregation at high mass. The letter, supposedly, was preserved by a daughter-in-law, Perine Metoyer Dupre, until it was destroyed along with many other old and valuable family heirlooms when "Tante" Perine's home burned.[42]

The spiritual activities of the people began and ended in this church. Newborn infants were taken for baptism to the holy font in the Chapel of St. Augustine as soon as a priest could be brought to the Isle to administer the sacrament to them. On rare occasions when death threatened an infant not yet baptized, the sacrament was administered privately by a family friend or relative. Should the sick one survive, however, a formal baptism still followed in the chapel when a priest next arrived. It was at his baptism than an infant was given his name, a saint's name carefully chosen; thus, at baptism was a child given the model of perfection that he was to follow. For most girls, the first name was Marie, in recognition of the most esteemed model of Christian

38. January 22, 1836, Natchitoches Registers, Book 12.
39. Baudier, *The Catholic Church in Louisiana,* 346.
40. *Ibid.,* 406; Callahan *et al., History of St. Augustine's Parish,* 38.
41. Tomb marker, cemetery of the Chapel of St. Augustine, Isle Brevelle.
42. Callahan *et al., History of St. Augustine's Parish,* 43; interview with Mrs. Coutii, April 26, 1974. A search of the papal correspondence in the Vatican Archives failed to uncover a copy of the letter; Papal secretary, Archivo Segreto Vaticano, to author, April 6, 1974.

virtue. Also at baptism each infant acquired his *parraine* and *marraine*, god-parents whom he grew to love and respect as dearly as his own parents.[43]

Upon reaching puberty, the youth of the Isle received their second sacrament—confirmation. From the bishop himself, upon his periodic visits to the parish, the youth received the Holy Spirit. After his visits to the parish in 1836 and 1842, Bishop Blanc noted that he had confirmed a total of fifty-four youth of the colony.[44]

Most discussions of the religious attitudes of Louisiana's free people of color contain the usual sensational emphasis upon the illicit relations between young women of this class and their white "protectors." One modern writer, for example, discusses this aspect of their society but does note the existence of a second code of morals by observing: "Not all free persons of color entered a state of concubinage. Many of them got married and it was not uncommon for such persons to have their nuptials performed in the churches of Louisiana."[45] However, the general conclusion of this study and that of most historians in this field is that the legitimately married class of *gens de couleur libre* were an elite minority.

Among Cane River's Creoles of color, however, the situation was reversed. Perhaps due to the influence of Grandpère Augustin, who is remembered as a strict moralist, Cane River youths were expected to marry within the church and to pattern their behavior after the strict dictates of their faith.[46] Courting couples were always chaperoned. At dances the girls of good character did not permit the boys even to pay for their refreshments. A walk to the edge of the pavilion where lights were low might be countenanced, but no couple dared leave the pavilion unless accompanied by an older woman.[47]

More often than not, marriages were arranged by the parents, who met and

43. Mrs. Coutii to author, October 5, 1974.
44. Baudier, *The Catholic Church in Louisiana*, 346, 360; Louis Laraboire Morrow, *Our Catholic Faith: A Manual of Religion* (Kenosha, Wis., 1961), 274–75.
45. Sterkx, *The Free Negro in Ante-Bellum Louisiana*, 256.
46. According to a recent sociological study of the colony, 91 percent of the people born before 1865 contracted legal marriages, and most of the remaining 9 percent were youths who died before reaching maturity. See Sister Frances Jerome Woods, *Marginality and Identity: A Colored Creole Family Through Ten Generations* (Baton Rouge, 1972), 78.
47. Interview with Mrs. Coutii, April 26, 1974; Mrs. Coutii to author, April 25, 1974; Saxon, *Children of Strangers*, 44–45.

decided upon the needs of the couple. In general, the preferences of the young people were considered, but in many cases they were not. A typical example is provided by Ambroise Sévère Dupre and his wife Sidalise Sarpy. It was Sidalise's sister for whom Sévère really cared, but she was younger than Sidalise. The fathers, Jerome Sarpy and Emanuel Dupre, conferred, and both agreed that no younger sister should marry until her older sisters had found husbands. Plans for the wedding were then made, with Sidalise rather than her sister as the bride. The young couple made the best of the situation, reportedly, and remained together for the rest of their lives, even though the marriage was not one of choice on their part.[48]

The marriage of Sévère and Sidalise followed the traditional pattern. The youth of the Isle were joined in matrimony at the altar of the Church of St. Augustine. Civil marriages contracted outside the church were uncommonly rare in this period. Instances of divorce or legal separation of bed and board, which did occur even among white Catholics of the parish, were nonexistent in the colony. The unions made at the chapel's altar were expected to last until death.

The church and civil records of the parish reveal that deviation from the moral code outlined by their religion was, in all respects, the exception rather than the rule. Although each family of color did begin with an illicit liaison between a white man and a woman of color, the families thereafter insisted upon contracting legitimate marriages, and for the most part the community standards were upheld by individual members. Most cases of extramarital or premarital liaisons were relationships between females of the colony and men of pure white blood whom they could not marry; most such liaisons also lasted until death claimed one of the partners.

It must not be assumed that the attentions of white men were indiscriminately welcomed by the people as a means of "lightening" their race. During the antebellum years when the colony was accorded respect and prestige, the maintenance of their racial composition through selective marriage was sufficient to preserve their superiority to the black race, and the maintenance of respect from the outside society by adherence to Christian precepts was necessary to their own self-respect. Although the situation was to change after the

48. Interview with Mrs. Coutii, April 26, 1974.

war, as all social and economic conditions underwent drastic alterations, the colony before the war generally spurned the dishonorable attentions of whites.[49]

Aside from the freed slaves, Rose Metoyer and Adelaïde Mariotte, who were the *placées* of a succession of white "protectors" (most of whom died shortly after the initiation of the relationship), the records reveal only rare incidences in which the females of the colony bore children by whites with whom they had established temporary or long-term alliances. Even in such cases, the violation of family standards often had serious impact upon the consciences of the violators. Adelaïde Mariotte, for example, was apologetic for her conduct for the remainder of her life. Apparently fearing that her loved ones would not respect her for her life-style, she repeatedly told her children and grandchildren that she "had disgraced herself to uplift her race."[50] Assuming that personal emotions might have had a certain amount of influence upon her behavior as well, it is still indicative of the attitude of her family group that she felt such a compunction to justify her past actions.

Religious devotion among the people was a private as well as a public matter. The rosary was said at home every night before retiring, and the children were always led in their bedtime prayers by an older adult who knelt with them. The church bell rang the Angelus every morning at six, calling the faithful to daily mass if there was a priest on the Isle, and again at that hour of the evening. Men stopped and doffed their hats at the peal of the bell, and women made the sign of the cross.[51]

All homes had their little altars which were hung prominently on the living room wall. Reflecting the sentiments of the older people whom he recalled, the Louisiana storyteller Harnett Kane wrote: "In each house the altar sparkled beneath the crucifix, and the shrine must be cleaned every day. How would a saint feel if he found dust in which he could write his own name, ahn?"[52]

---

49. For example, refer to the discussion in Chapter VIII relative to the legal suits initiated by the colony against whites who attempted to violate the honor of females of the colony.

50. Interview with Mrs. Coutii, April 26, 1974.

51. Interview with confidential source, April 26, 1974; Mrs. Coutii to author, April 22, 1974.

52. Harnett T. Kane, *Plantation Parade: The Grand Manner in Louisiana* (New York, 1945), 267.

Although many such altars were purchased later from the people during their periods of need, one little altar owned by Sidalise Sarpy Dupre, a daughter of Jerome Sarpy, has been proudly treasured by a granddaughter. Unlike the typical altar found in churches, this home altar resembles more a wall-hung box, shallow at the top, deep at the bottom. The sparkling glass front is a door that opens to provide access to the religious articles stored inside.

All of the holy days on the church calendar were faithfully observed by the people, but the Easter season demanded special devotion. On Holy Thursday and Good Friday all andirons and pokers were moved from fireplaces. It was believed that if on those days iron and fire met, disaster was inevitable. No chickens or any living things were killed, and meat was not eaten between Good Friday and Easter Sunday. Ground was not plowed on those days, since many held to the old belief that drops of the sacred blood of Jesus would appear in the freshly turned earth.[53]

Good Friday was a day set aside for attending to religious obligations. The most pressing necessity was the "making of the Easter duty," the annual confession and penance. After the Easter duty had been performed, the graves in the cemetery behind the church were cleaned and decorated as they had been some six months earlier on All Saints' Day.[54]

Honeysuckle, flowering quince, or other flowers that were in bloom were placed in vases on each grave, along with keepsakes of the deceased which the family had preserved through the years. A lace fan with ivory sticks, a small clock, a rakish hat, a doll, or a fluttering kite would suffice to let the dead one know that he had not been forgotten. In the earliest years, the graves were further decorated with bottles, shells, and other miscellanea of interesting shape and color, arranged in decorative patterns or outlining individual plots.[55]

---

53. Saxon, *Children of Strangers*, 29–31; Hugh LaCour to author, April 22, 1974.

54. Mrs. Coutii to author, April 22, 1974; Saxon, *Children of Strangers*, 30–32; Hugh LaCour to author, April 22, 1974.

55. Saxon, *Children of Strangers*, 30–32; Mrs. Coutii to author, April 22, 1974.

The Isle Brevelle colony, unlike many African descendants in the southern United States, retained almost no African customs or traditions. This religious practice of decorating graves with bottles, shells, and mementoes of the dead appears to be one of the last vestiges. One observer of nonwhite life and customs in the antebellum South recorded: "Negro graves were always decorated with the last article used by the deceased, and broken pitchers and broken bits of colored

Easter Sunday was a day of celebration for the entire community. After mass, coffee was brewed over small fires at the edge of the cemetery, where the people gathered to socialize and celebrate the end of Lenten fast and penance, which would be the occasion of a night of gaiety at the dance which would follow. Amid the chatter, children hid their eggs around the grave markers, while the men gathered with their own gaily decorated eggs, placed their nickle bets, and proceeded with a game of "nip and tuck." Grasping their eggs in the circle formed by the thumb and index finger, each pair of players tapped their eggs together end to end in an effort to crack the opponent's eggs while preserving their own intact. By the end of the day the churchyard and cemetery grounds were covered with white shells.[56]

The Easter gathering and resulting frolic in the cemetery indicated no lack of respect for the dead. On the contrary they were viewed as a means of sharing life once more with loved ones long departed. The Creoles of Louisiana, both white and nonwhite, exhibited a great measure of respect for the deceased. Mother Hyacinthe LeConniat, Superior of the Daughters of the Cross who established a convent in Avoyelles Parish and a second on Isle Brevelle, wrote her brother Yves-Marie in France:

> Nothing equals the care rendered to the dead here. . . . The corpse is wrapped well in white silk. The coffin is of perfect workmanship and is painted on the outside. The inside is padded and lined with velvet or satin, with gold tacks keeping the cloth in place. There is another coffin placed in the bottom of the grave; it is not as attractive as the one that holds the corpse. . . . This is naturally correct because it would be senseless to put the fine coffin in the mud. . . . This beautiful coffin which costs the rich 500 or 600 francs, is transported in a beautiful carriage or hearse. A man on horseback carries a small cross at the head of the cortege. The family and the friends accompany the body, riding in carriages or on horses. They wear on the arm beautiful bows of black lace which cost $2 or $3 apiece. At the church, which is

---

glass." Sara A. Torian (ed.), "Ante-Bellum and War Memories of Mrs. Telfair Hodgson," *Georgia Historical Quarterly,* XXVII (December, 1943), 350–56, quoted in Blassingame, *The Slave Community,* 37. It should be noted that the custom of decorating with bottles and shells did not long survive in the colony. The oldest descendants today have no recollection of the practice, although they do recall the days when keepsakes of the departed ones were placed on the graves during religious seasons.

56. Hugh LaCour to author, April 6, 1974; Saxon, *Children of Strangers,* 42–43.

covered with black, they sing the "Libera Me." No mass. Finally, the burial. All must throw the black crepe into the grave. They erect a fine monument. . . . This sad funeral as I described it to you is first class. If the priest goes to the house to accompany the body to the church, it is $40, and if he does not do this, it is $35. For the second class $25 or $30. For the third class $10 or $15. . . . By means of these stipends the missionary is able to live.[57]

The funerals of the colony were, apparently, first class. For example, the final account rendered by the administrator of the estate of Marie Suzanne Metoyer included a payment to the curé of sixty dollars for her burial in 1838. In 1847 the *marguilliers* of the new Church of St. Jean Baptiste at Cloutierville met to establish the tariffs on burials for that parish and set the rates at eighty dollars for a first-class funeral, thirty for a second-class, twenty for a third-class, and ten dollars for a fourth-class. When J. B. Espallier Rachal died not long afterward, his family paid the Reverend G. Guy eighty dollars for the first-class burial.[58] The hearse to which Mother Hyacinthe referred was furnished the Isle Brevelle community by the jack-of-all trades, Oscar Dubreuil.[59]

Cane River's Creoles of color were buried in four known locations. In the early years, those who lived nearer Natchitoches were taken into the town and buried in the cemetery of the parish church there.[60] Others who lived at the lower end of the settlement were buried in the old Shallow Lake Cemetery near the community later known as Derry. After the establishment of the church and cemetery at nearby Cloutierville, the lower Cane River people almost always used the newer cemetery.[61] Most of the family, however, was buried behind the Chapel of St. Augustine in the heart of their community.

---

57. McCants (ed. and trans.), *They Came to Louisiana,* 60.

58. Succession of Marie Suzanne Metoyer, in Natchitoches Parish Records, No. 355; Memorandum of the Marguilliers, Cloutierville, May 9, 1847, in DeBlieux Collection; Succession of J. B. E. Rachal, in Natchitoches Parish Records, No. 927.

By way of comparison, it may be noted that the son of Jean Baptiste Meuillion, a free man of color of Louisiana who is frequently recognized by modern historians for his wealth, paid only 35 piasters for the requiem mass and interment of his father in 1840; Sterkx, The *Free Negro in Ante-Bellum Louisiana,* 204.

59. Succession of Oscar Dubreuil, in Natchitoches Parish Records, No. 1255.

60. Natchitoches Registers.

61. Interview with Mrs. Coutii, March 24, 1974; Cloutierville Registers, Burial Book I.

Slaves belonging to the colony were not accorded space in the family's burial grounds. Across the road, in the bend of the river, was established the cemetery for slaves. Nothing remains to mark their graves.[62]

The oldest graves in the cemetery of the Chapel of St. Augustine were marked with iron crosses. An occasional wooden cross, painted white with black lettering, marked graves of the less affluent. The most striking graves in the cemetery were the above-ground tombs, miniature white houses about five by seven feet, built to shelter the bodies of the most prominent members of the family.[63] In the place of honor nearest the church was erected one such tomb, with a marble door that identified it as the resting place of Augustin Metoyer and his wife Marie Agnes. After the death of Augustin in 1856 their tomb was twice opened, once for the burial of his favorite son, François Gassion, in the decade that followed, and then again in the early twentieth century to deposit the last remains of that son's third wife, Perine Metoyer Dupre.[64]

For the Creoles of color on Cane River, Catholicity and its precepts were a way of life. Callahan relates that the ancestors of some families in the area came to the Isle as practitioners or teachers of voodoo. Because of one side of the colony's racial heritage, these newcomers assumed the people would be eager students of this particular derivation of African religion. They were mistaken. Their culture made no inroads in the French Catholic society of Cane River, and the newcomers eventually converted to the dominant religion.[65]

Religion, to a large extent, was the cornerstone of Isle Brevelle society. The Angelus of dawn marked the beginning of each new day; the evening peal of bells from their chapel brought that day's labor to an end. The calendar of the church determined their days of work and their days of rest, their days of fast and their days of feasting. The spiritual ties of godparent to godchild were bonds that held the people together as closely as did ties of blood. The influ-

62. Interview with Mrs. Coutii, March 24, 1974.
63. Such tombs were not entirely unique in the parish of Natchitoches, since a handful of affluent whites erected similar monuments. These others, however, have crumbled into decay.
64. Interview with Mrs. Coutii, April 26, 1974. It was Perine Metoyer Dupre who was responsible, more than anyone, for preservation of the legendary stories that the aging Augustin related to her during the years she and her husband cared for him.
65. Interview with confidential source, March 24, 1974; Callahan *et al.*, *History of St. Augustine's Parish*, 28.

ence which their faith held upon these Creoles of color produced results that earned for the colony much of the respect which the outside society accorded it.[66]

66. The religious example set by the early colony has been respected and followed for many generations since. Father Callahan quotes the following accolade to the people made by Bishop Van de Ven of the Alexandria diocese in 1917, at the dedication of the newest church on the Isle: "My dear friends . . . I must tell you that I am proud of you, my dear people, and I can without fear of contradiction, give you as a model for my whole Diocese of Alexandria. Your piety, your generosity, have just accomplished an admirable task—admirable not only because of the size and elegance of style of the building, but admirable especially because of the great sacrifices you have imposed on yourselves to realize it. Your predecessors have set a high standard for you which, if you are their true sons and daughters, you are bound to follow. As the language of your ancestors has it, 'Noblesse oblige.'" Callahan *et al., History of St. Augustine's Parish*, 43.

Chapter SEVEN

Cane River Culture

The economic affluence that the Cane River colony achieved manifested itself in all aspects of the members' personal lives. Large and stately homes, furnished with taste and style, graced many of their plantations. Musical training developed in their youth an appreciation of the arts. Education, even including university study in Europe in some cases, equipped their offspring for a role as southern planters of distinction. All of the social customs and entertainments enjoyed by their affluent white neighbors existed on the Isle, although the social intercourse of the people was largely restricted to the confines of the group. Law and order within the colony was considered by the colony to be their own responsibility and was rigorously enforced by informally chosen but unanimously acknowledged community authorities.

These people were striking in appearance. Old and treasured photographs reflect many attractive faces, both male and female. In most, Caucasian features predominated; bone structure was usually slender and refined. Although shades of complexion varied, a large percentage of the people were fair. Blond and light brown hair was not uncommon, and in more than one case the eyes were said to have been blue. In general, "Latin" would be the most appropriate word to use in describing the people's appearance.

There were exceptions, of course, in which the other elements of their racial heritage were plainly visible. Grandpère Augustin, half-French and half-African, was café-au-lait in color and stockily built with broad features. His grandnephew, Barthelemy LeCour, according to a grandson, was "tall, over six feet, with bronze-colored skin, a long nose, and black hair." LeCour never had to shave. When the little grandson questioned why this was so, his grandfather's Indian heritage was explained to him.[1] A study of LeCour's

---

1. Hugh LaCour to author, March 5, 1974.

ancestry reveals that he was two-sixteenths Indian, five-sixteenths African, and nine-sixteenths French.[2]

In character and personality the people varied widely. There was Augustin, long venerated for his wisdom, and there was François, remembered more than a hundred years after his death as "the strong man." There was Auguste, the ambitious one, who entered every endeavor on a grand scale. There was Rose, the courtesan, the freed slave who started her career with no assets other than her attractiveness, amassed a sizable estate, and ended her life as a servant. There was Oscar, the entrepreneur extraordinaire, merchant, tailor, ferryman, schoolteacher, billiard hall operator, and undertaker. But of them all, the strongest personalities were undoubtedly Augustin and François.

Affectionately called Grandpère Augustin by the community at large, the oldest Metoyer brother was the acknowledged patriarch of the colony. After the death of Claude Thomas Pierre Metoyer and Marie Thérèze Coincoin, Augustin became the head of the family, assuming responsibility for the welfare of all "his people." His word was law; his person was respected. Regardless of how hotly a dispute was being waged by opposing members of the community, when Augustin the arbitrator gave his decision, no one dared to question it.[3] His reputation of effectiveness in controlling deviant behavior within the community is supported by existing records. A search of criminal process records for the parish during this period reveals no conviction of a Cane River Creole of color for any infraction of the law.

The respect which was accorded Grandpère Augustin extended into the smallest incidences of everyday life. A favorite story on the Isle has to do with the fact that in his old age Augustin was fond of sitting on his porch, rocking in his favorite chair, and watching travelers pass on the main road in front of his house. The younger members of the family, with all the haste of youth, were inclined to gallop down that road; but once in sight of Augustin's house they reined their horses to a slow walk. Respectfully they approached. Their

2. Comparisons of racial composition to physical characteristics provide many interesting studies in genetics. For example, Thérèsine Carles (born 1824 of Rose Metoyer and Dr. André Zepherin Carles) was three-fourths French and one-fourth Negro; her hair was light brown and her eyes blue. Emanuel Dupre (born 1807 of Marie Adelaïde Mariotte and Sieur Joseph Dupre) was one-half French, one-fourth Negro, and one-fourth Indian; his hair was jet black, his complexion swarthy, and Indian features were prominent. Sephira Dupre (his daughter by his wife Marie Marguerite Metoyer) was also one-half French, with three-eighths Negro and one-eighth Indian ancestry, but her complexion was fair and her hair a soft blond.

3. Dunn, "Isle Brevelle"; interview with Mrs. Coutii, March 24, 1974.

hats were tipped as they greeted him with a *"Bon jour, Grandpère Augustin"* and awaited his customary reply, *"Bon jour, mes enfants."* Upon receipt of his greeting they slowly walked their horses until out of sight, then whipped the animals again into full speed.[4]

Although the shrewd and pious Grandpère Augustin held the admiration and respect of his people more than any other member of the colony, it was his youngest brother who best captured their imagination. Tradition has preserved almost as many anecdotes relating to young François as it has of the patriarch himself. Although François acquired little in the way of material goods, he was the free spirit everyone in some way wishes he could be. He was the hero, the model for all the youth who wanted to prove their strength and manliness. Francois was the favorite topic of the old men who sat on the gallery of the community store and swapped stories—and of the young who stopped to listen. One of those youths at the turn of the twentieth century later recalled one of the most popular stories of all: François and the bull. The ending of this story conveys François' spirit in that after he has come to the rescue by seizing a raging bull by the horns and pulling him out of the mud, he then shoves the bull in again with the force of one foot, just for the fun of it.[5]

François was reported to have been the strongest man in the region. According to legend, he could take two cotton hooks and carry a five-hundred-pound bale of cotton as easily as an ordinary man could carry a ten-pound bag of flour. When a foundation block had to be replaced under the Isle Brevelle church, François lifted the structure with seeming ease while a new block was slipped into place; no jack was needed.[6] François was so strong, it is claimed, that he could lift a barrel of whiskey, even though he rarely indulged in such stimulants. On one occasion, however, when he had delivered some articles to a Cloutierville resident and had been offered a drink, François decided to make an exception to his usual rule of abstinence. A hogshead of whiskey stood nearby, and when the genial host pointed it out, François reached for it. Putting a hand on either side of the staves, just below the top, he "raised the

---

4. *Ibid.*

5. Hugh LaCour to author, April 6, 1974.

6. *Ibid.;* reminiscences of Duncan Kirkland, January 26, 1922, in Henry Collection, Natchitoches Scrapbook No. 2.

whole hogshead up to the level of his lips, taking one swallow, and then gingerly setting it back on the floor without spilling a drop."[7]

This youngest son of Marie Thérèze Coincoin was also an unpretentious man for whom the simple life had many charms. If he was without a horse and needed to go to town, he was not dismayed. With his shoes tied about his neck, he would walk the more than twenty-five miles from his home on the lower point of the Isle to Natchitoches. Only upon reaching the bridge at the edge of town would he bow to convention and don his shoes before proceeding up Natchitoches' Front Street.[8]

The majority of the people fell between the two extremes of personality marked by Augustin and François. In general, they were cultured; for the most part they were well built. Their health was good, but abstinence from liquors was certainly not the reason for the good health. Most were conscientious Catholics, but few achieved the same level of personal perfection with which their patriarch is credited.

The formation of the characters of these people, as with all people, began in childhood. All children were taught to equate age with wisdom. Parents always knew what was best for their offspring; their authority—and this extended to any legitimate authority—should never be questioned. The precept that children should be seen but not heard was strictly adhered to; when adults visited, the children played outside. All elders were addressed as *Oncle* or *Tante,* whether or not they actually possessed that relationship to the younger person who addressed them. This mark of respect was a lifelong practice, adhered to by adults as well as children.[9]

The respect which was instilled into all the people manifested itself in a still more significant form: self-respect. Members of the Cane River colony did not adopt the stereotyped image of nonwhites forced to subsist under white dominance—shuffling gait, bowed head, subservient demeanor. The members were proud of their heritage, their wealth, their education, their religion, and themselves. Their "curiously erect" posture, their well-modulated

---

7. *Ibid.;* François Mignon to author, April 23, 1974.
8. *Ibid.* Because of his residence on the point of the Isle, François was given the nickname of "Le Pont."
9. Interview with Mrs. Coutii, March 24, 1974; *ibid.* to author, October 5, 1974.

voices, and personal dignity were characteristics that they continued to manifest even after their wealth and position were lost.[10]

The pride and respect that was instilled in the people from early childhood reflected itself even in external trappings such as clothes, accessories, horses, and carriages. Almost all family pictures, many of which were made by leading New Orleans photographers, reflect stylishly dressed ladies and gentlemen. Succession inventories and account statements mirror their taste and their indulgence in the same luxury items enjoyed by wealthier members of the white community. Perfume and silk stockings for the ladies, cologne and expensive beaver hats for the gentlemen, were among many personal items inventoried. Seventy-five-dollar gold watches and one-hundred-dollar carriages were not uncommon.[11]

Like their white counterparts, the wealthy planters of the Cane River colony indulged their egos in expensively procured oil portraits. Four of those preserved by descendants of the colony were featured in a prominent study of American Negro art: the portrait of Augustin, another of his wife, Marie Agnes, and paintings of a dapper Creole man and a beautiful young woman whose identities are uncertain but who are believed to be the grandson and granddaughter of Marie Thérèze.[12] The first of these portraits is life-sized; the others range from two to three feet. One former resident of the area recalled a fifth painting, said to be of François Metoyer,[13] and another twentieth-century resident of the Isle possesses a color photograph of a no longer extant oil portrait of her great-grandmother, Mme. Emanuel Dupre.[14]

10. *Ibid.;* Saxon, *Children of Strangers,* 40; Kane, *Plantation Parade,* 269.

11. Succession of Pierre Metoyer, No. 193; Succession of Suzanne Metoyer, No. 355; Succession of [J. B.] Louis Metoyer, No. 362; Succession of Dominique Metoyer, No. 375; Succession of Agnes Metoyer, No. 395; Succession of Florentin Conant, No. 1049, all in Natchitoches Parish Records. Succession of Joseph Augustin Metoyer, in Natchitoches Parish Records Collection, LSU, Box 11, Folder 47.

12. Cedric Dover, *American Negro Art* (Greenwich, 1960), 62–65. Both Dover and tradition holds that the subjects of these two portraits were grandchildren of Marie Thérèze. A study of the individuals who composed the early colony, their ages and wealth at given periods, and their life styles leads the author to believe that the two subjects are Auguste Metoyer (son of Augustin and Marie Agnes, and a grandson of Marie Thérèze) and his wife, Marie Thérèze Carmelite Anty (daughter of Suzanne Metoyer and Sieur Jean Baptiste Anty, also the grandchild of Marie Thérèze).

13. François Mignon to author, April 8, 1974.

14. Interview with Mrs. Coutii, April 26, 1974.

Still other oils which were once proudly treasured by the people of Isle Brevelle were sold out of the community during their later period of destitution. A number of these were purchased in the early twentieth century by the white owners of a former Metoyer plantation. After viewing these, one visiting newspaperwoman described them as "the finest collection of paintings of people of color in oil, pastel, and prints, in existence."[15]

A solid family relationship was one of the foremost characteristics of the people. When one traveler of the 1850s inquired about them of the driver of his stagecoach, he was so impressed with the reply that he noted in his journal, "He had often staid [*sic*] over night at their houses, and knew them intimately and he was nowhere else so well treated, and he never saw more gentleman-like people. He appeared to have been especially impressed by the domestic and social happiness he had witnessed in their houses."[16]

Although squabbles did occasionally occur, as they do within any society or family group, there were many more incidences of solidarity and mutual assistance. Many examples have already been cited in which the early members of the colony purchased freedom for their less fortunate relatives, but Antoine Joseph Metoyer set the ultimate example for such generosity. In 1818 he paid six hundred dollars to Ambroise LeComte for a "mulatress named Madeleine, Creole of Natchitoches, aged about fifty, in order to give her liberty." Madeleine was his mother-in-law.[17]

Countless other examples exist of the close relationship between members of the colony and of the assistance which they gave each other. When Charles N. Rocques, Sr., died in 1859, it was noted that many of the improvements on his plantation were put there by Jerome Sarpy, Jr.[18] When Augustin Cloutier died about 1837 and left his widow, Thérèze Metoyer, and their children without property, the Indian widow of Louis Metoyer gave the Widow Cloutier the use of a house for life.[19] Vallery Barthelemy LeCour, one of the

15. D. Garber, "History of Melrose Plantation Like Turning Pages of Novel," undated clipping from unidentified Texas newspaper (in private collection of Mrs. Minnie Charleville Mills, Woodlawn, Texas).

16. Olmsted, *Journey in the Seaboard Slave States,* 634.

17. Ambroise LeComte to Joseph Metoyer, in Natchitoches Parish Records, Book 39, No. 481/223.

18. Succession of C. N. Rocques, Sr., *ibid.,* Succession Book 30, p. 219.

19. Widow Louis Metoyer to St. Cyr Metoyer, and Alexis Cloutier to legitimate heirs of Augustin Cloutier, *ibid.,* Donations Book 30, pp. 85 and 41–42.

French-Indian youths who married a daughter of Dominique Metoyer, sold his wife's brother the land that his wife had received as a dowry. Looking after this younger sister's interests, J. B. Dominique wrote into the deed of sale the provision that LeCour must immediately invest the money in another tract of land in order to secure her dowry rights and privileges.[20]

Donations among members of the community occurred with regularity. Almost all children received plantations, slaves, and money as wedding gifts. But many instances occurred in which the recipients of donations were much more distantly related. In 1836, for example, Marie Suzette Metoyer, wife of Louis Morin, made a donation to two nieces by marriage. Among the children whom Marie Suzette had borne to her first husband were two daughters, both of whom had recently died. From the estate that these daughters left Marie Suzette gave $2,443 to two of her late husband's nieces, Clara Berthe, the daughter of Marie Glapion of New Orleans, and Marie Elisa Rocques, Mme. Morin's godchild, the daughter of Charles Nerestan Rocques.[21]

Family solidarity was also clearly evident in the social life of the people of Isle Brevelle. Since they were not white, they were not admitted into the general social affairs of the white community. They were not black, and they would not deign to mingle with that class, slave or free. Since they already had accepted into their community, by marriage, the neighboring free people of color whom they considered to be their equals, they had no avenue for extending their social intercourse beyond their own colony.

As with all Creoles, white or colored, dancing was a favorite entertainment. In this respect, the strict dictates of religion were bent, but not without the sanction of local church authorities. The French-born priest who served the Natchitoches parish as assistant pastor in the 1860s wrote to his parents, expressing his shock at the widespread acceptance of this "evil" which he had found throughout the Natchitoches area: "The Bishop closes his eyes to any harm done there; that is, whenever the dancing takes place in the family circle, he allows it; he does not censure it. They have succeeded in abolishing the

20. Vallery Barthelemy LeCour to Jean Baptiste Dominique Metoyer, *ibid.*, Misc. Records, 1827–1837, Book A, 57.

21. Donation of Marie Suzette Metoyer to Clara Berthe and Marie Elisa Roques, in DeBlieux Collection.

public balls, at least up until now. There are so many reforms to bring about, so many needed." [22]

It has been noted, however, that the Cátholic-oriented society on Isle Brevelle traditionally restricted their dances tó the seasons when festivity was permitted by the Church. A traveler in the area in the late nineteenth century, noting that their customs had not changed in a hundred years, described an old-fashioned dance held on the Isle: "They are fond of dancing, music, and gay dressing. . . . At a dance will be seen a big fire in the yard, and a big pot of gumbo on it, which, with cafe-noir, is served steaming hot to guests at intervals." [23]

A typical dance was announced to the community by two men in a skiff. While one man rowed up one side of the river and then down the other, his companion would blow loudly and clearly on a conch shell to attract the attention of the people who lived along the banks. As crowds gathered on the bank, or as a head appeared in the back door of a solitary house, the announcer would cup his hands and shout a message such as:

> Fais Do-Do!
> Grande danse le soir de Paques a huit heures!
> De la bonne musique, bon temps pour tous!
> Fais Do-Do!
> Au pavilion de Monsieur Monette
> Dimanche a huit heures. Ne manquez pas de venir! [24]

The *"fais do-do"* was the most popular dance of all. Literally, the words meant "go to sleep" but the name was certainly a misnomer. To the rhythm of guitars, drums, triangles, and whatever other instruments were available, to the hand-clapping, finger-snapping accompaniment of the spectators, six couples would take the floor for a Franch version of the square dance, executing all the graceful moves requested by the man who "called the figures." The quadrille waltz was also a popular dance. [25]

Holidays on Cane River were particularly festive occasions, and here again

22. McCants (ed. and trans.), *They Came to Louisiana,* 134–35.
23. Dunn, "Isle Brevelle."
24. Saxon, *Children of Strangers,* 22.
25. *Ibid.,* 43; and Mrs. Coutii to author, April 15, 1974; Hugh LaCour to author, March 5, 1974.

family unity set the pattern for celebrations. As children married and were given a tract from their parents' plantation, they built a small house near the big one of their parents. A cluster of small homes surrounding the "family mansion" inevitably resulted. On such holidays as Christmas and Easter, on birthdays, wedding days, and Church feast days, all children and grandchildren from the smaller homes gathered at the big house for the celebration. A calf or a large "porker" would be barbecued in the yard, then served inside on the vast dining room table with salad, an array of garden vegetables and fruits, coffee, cakes, pralines, popcorn balls, and wine for the women and whiskey for the men.[26]

Among themselves, the people of Isle Brevelle were a gregarious, outgoing, sociable, fun-loving people. Sunday was a day for visiting rather than a "day of rest." When their visits took them to see friends at Campti, Alexandria, or New Orleans, the visits would last for weeks, sometimes months. The hospitality of their Campti relatives was especially memorable; one belle of the antebellum years often fondly recalled in her old age a particular Campti family whom she had frequently visited. When she and the other guests retired for the evening, she related, their clothes were gathered; by the time the guests awoke the next morning all of their garments had been washed, pressed, and hung in their rooms. No matter how many pretty dresses the visiting girls from Isle Brevelle might take with them, they never needed more than one, since their hosts made certain that their clothes were always fresh.[27]

Home life on the Isle was equally sociable, although somewhat quieter. At evening, when the day's work was done, the family gathered on one of their spacious verandas, if the night was sultry, or around the parlor fireplace if the wind blew hard and cold. On the blustery nights the children popped corn over the flickering flames, or the older girls made pralines, and the "old folks" spun their tales of yesteryear, passing on to the young their family's heritage. Then when the children were put to bed, the parents might drink together for an hour or so before retiring, the only time when custom permitted the women of the colony to indulge in "hard liquor."[28]

26. Mrs. Coutii to author, October 5, 1974.

27. *Ibid.;* and Mrs. Coutii to author, April 15, 1974.

28. Mrs. Coutii to author, October 5, 1974. Mrs. Coutii also relates that in the more affluent families, married couples had separate rooms—the master's bedroom and the mistress' bedroom—although this custom did not affect the productivity of the colony.

A variety of other pastimes were popular on the Isle. In the early years, cockfighting and dogfighting were especially popular. Both had almost disappeared by the late nineteenth century, but old men were still alive then who recalled the sports fondly. Pepper, they related, was put under the wings of the chickens to discourage their opponents from pecking them in this vulnerable spot, and soap was rubbed on the birds' necks so that "bill holts" by opposing roosters would be sure to slip.[29]

Succession records from this period provide evidence of two additional methods by which the people whiled away their leisure hours. In 1854 N. P. Metoyer purchased a checker board (also called "draft board and men") and one and a half dozen decks of cards from the probate sale of the estate of C. N. Rocques, Jr., paying $1.50 for the lot. For ten cents Achille Metoyer purchased two decks of cards.[30]

While traveling through Louisiana in the mid-nineteenth century, Frederick Law Olmsted was told: "The Creoles are inveterate gamblers—rich and poor alike. The majority of wealthy Creoles . . . do nothing to improve their estate; and are very apt to live beyond their income. They borrow and play, and keep borrowing to play as long as they can."[31] The people of Isle Brevelle were true Creoles; they thoroughly enjoyed gambling. But most of them, it appears, exercised more prudence than the above generalization indicates. Their estates were certainly not neglected, and it seems that few Creoles of color on the Isle gambled beyond their means. One exception was Emanuel Dupre, who it appears was fast working his way through his wife's inheritance until she resolutely refused to sign over any more property. This was not the end of his gambling, however, for he somehow managed to keep up the practice despite his wife.[32]

Two additional forms of entertainment that were popular on the Isle were

---

29. Hugh LaCour to author, March 5, 1974; Dunn, "Isle Brevelle."
30. Succession of C. N. Rocques, *fils,* Natchitoches Parish Records, No. 897.
31. Olmsted, *Journey in the Seaboard Slave States,* 649.
32. Marriage Contract of Emanuel Dupre to Marie Marguerite Metoyer, Book A, Misc., 48; *Philippe Valsain* v. *Cloutier,* District Court Records, Book 3, pp. 118–26, both in Natchitoches Parish Records; interview with Mrs. Coutii, March 24, 1974.

Apparently, Dupre's gambling did not waste away all of the family fortune. After the disastrous Civil War, he stood financially at the head of the colony. The census of 1870 credits him with real and personal property that was assessed for tax purposes at $15,000; Ninth Census of the United States, 1870, Population Schedule.

fishing and horseracing. Some of the fishing trips took place on a grand scale; their participants numbered as many as seventy to eighty men.[33] The horse races, traditionally, were held at 24-Mile Ferry, where crowds gathered on Sunday afternoons. Refreshment stands offered a wide assortment of foods, such as pies, cakes, anisette, lemonade, and of course coffee. Although the horses usually were not thoroughbreds, many were fast enough to beat the thoroughbreds of a white neighbor that often raced against them.[34]

The women of Isle Brevelle, and the slaves whom they trained, were culinary artists. One visiting newspaperman recalled: "The finest cooks of our State are in Isle Brevelle, and they can beat the San Antonio Mexican making tamales. The Isle Brevelle tamale is made of highly seasoned chopped meats, and meal made from corn treated with lye to remove the husk and pounded in a mortar. Their coffee is unexcelled and if you call at a house, the coffee mill is promptly set agoing, and you are handed a cup of cafe noir, such as you will always remember."[35] This traveler also was impressed with the gumbo, the same "gumbo filet" of which Private Holloway was to write many decades later. According to the earlier visitor, "This gumbo is made from boiling fresh meat or game with pulverized leaves and stems of a dwarf sassafras, which grows on the hills, and whither these people go in great numbers at the proper season to gather it."[36]

Food preparation on the Isle was controlled to a large degree by the seasons. Summer and early fall saw a plentiful supply of fresh garden produce, food which must be preserved to see their families and slaves through the long months of winter and spring. One of the most popular methods of food preservation was drying. Beans, peas, and such legumes dried naturally, but pumpkin, okra, peaches, figs, and the other fruits that abounded on the Isle were sliced and spread on the roof to dry. Onions and peppers were hung on strings; root vegetables such as potatoes were often buried.

Winter was the usual season for slaughtering meat, since the cold was needed to protect it from spoilage during the slaughtering, aging, and process-

33. Testimony of Manuel Llorens, *Roubieu* v. *Metoyer,* in Natchitoches Parish Records, District Court Suit 1395 (1835); Hugh LaCour to author, March 5, 1974.
34. *Ibid.;* Dunn, "Isle Brevelle."
35. Dunn, "Isle Brevelle."
36. *Ibid.*

ing. Hams and bacon were smoked; other cuts of pork would be cooked and packed in big crocks. As long as lard was poured on top, the cooked pork never spoiled. Both pork and beef were used to make *taso,* a Cane River favorite; cut into cubes, covered with salt and a large quantity of red pepper, the meat was laid out to dry, then packed away in a moisture-proof container.[37]

The health of the people appears to have been excellent. When Olmsted appeared in the parish, the first person who mentioned the Creoles of color on Isle Brevelle swore that "they had sore eyes, and lost their teeth early, and had few children, and showed other scrofulous symptoms, and evidences of weak constitutions." After inquiring extensively and meeting the people themselves, Olmsted observed: "I think this gentleman must have read *De Bow's Review* and taken these facts for granted, without personal knowledge; for neither my own observations, nor any information that I could obtain from others at all confirmed his statement."[38]

This gentleman's comments to Olmsted, however erroneous, reflected a somewhat popular generalization. Even in Jamaica, a prestigious historian in the latter part of eighteenth century recorded as fact his opinion that "some few of them [people of color] have intermarried with those of their own complexions but such matches have generally been defective and barren. They seem in this respect to be actually of the mule-kind, and not so capable of producing from one another as from commerce with a distinct White or Black."[39] As late as 1927 a Harvard scholar, under the heading of "New Lights on Evolution," repeated this same postulation: "The sterility of hybrids has been long and even popularly known, as witness the cases of the mule and the mulatto."[40]

The people of Isle Brevelle, like people of color everywhere, proved this generalization false. The original six Metoyer brothers, who married girls of similar origins, averaged eight children each. The census of 1850 indicates

37. Interview with Mr. and Mrs. Tillman Chelettre, Sr., Natchez, Louisiana, October 12, 1974.
38. Olmsted, *A Journey in the Seaboard Slave States,* 633.
39. Edward Long, *The History of Jamaica* (3 vols.; London, 1774), II, 355, quoted in Edward Brathwaite, *The Development of Creole Society in Jamaica, 1770–1820* (Oxford, 1971), 177.
40. Edward C. Jeffrey, "New Lights on Evolution," *Science,* LXV (May 13, 1927). 459.

that the average family in the colony had four children living at home; to this number must be added the children who had died before the census or who were already married. Also, most of the families tabulated were still in their childbearing years, which meant that their families were still not complete.[41]

But Olmsted was not the only antebellum observer who reached the conclusion that people of color were just as capable of reproducing their own kind as were members of any other "race." A West Indian planter of the early nineteenth century recalled in his journal: "I think it is Long who asserts, that two mulattos will never have children; but, as far as the most positive assurances can go, since my arrival in Jamaica, I have reason to believe the contrary, and that mulattos breed together just as well as blacks and whites." This journalist destroyed his image as an "enlightened" observer, however, when he continued with "but they are almost universally weak and effeminate persons and thus their children are very difficult to rear."[42]

Olmsted's first informant in the Cane River area had made essentially the same observation in application to the Cane River colony. However, the inquisitive traveler inquired still further of local residents and came away with an entirely different view of the colony's physical state. According to Olmsted, other whites in the parish expressed the opinion that "they enjoyed better health than the whites living in their vicinity," and declared that they "could not recollect a single instance of those indications of weak constitution."[43]

Few records exist which show ill health among these people. The census of 1850, which tabulated incidences of ill health or disability, enumerated only twenty members of the Cane River colony in this category, approximately 5 percent of the population.[44] Most of the extant account statements rendered by doctors of the area were rendered for services to those who were on their deathbeds.

Intermarriage between close relatives, especially repeated intermarriage, is a practice in which few families have indulged without serious genetic consequences. Poor eyesight and mental instability are two of the more common

41. Seventh Census of the United States, 1850, Population Schedule.
42. M. G. Lewis, *Journal of a West India Proprietor, Kept During a Residence in the Island of Jamaica* (London, 1834, reprinted 1929), 94–95.
43. Olmsted, *A Journey in the Seaboard Slave States,* 633.
44. Seventh Census of the United States, 1850, Population Schedule.

results. Yet, for the first seventy years of the colony's existence, only one case of insanity and one of blindness are known to have occurred.[45] Neither of the afflicted had parents who were related. In 1842 Philippe Dupre was interdicted by the court as a result of his recent derangement; his brother Emanuel was appointed curator of Philippe and of Philippe's property. As required by law, Emanuel signed a bond guaranteeing honest administration of the estate until his brother regained his mental faculties; a white friend, Dr. Thomas A. Morgan, signed an equal bond as his surety. Whether or not Philippe recovered is unknown; by 1850 he was dead.[46] The records mention no cases of blindness, but tradition holds that one family member, Marie Adelaïde Mariotte, was totally blind in her old age.[47] One case of hermaphroditism is also reported.[48]

Yellow fever and smallpox were constant threats, as they were throughout the region. The yellow fever epidemic of 1853 which struck Natchitoches Parish reportedly resulted in many deaths on Isle Brevelle. The only known victims of the epidemic are Ambroise Azenor Metoyer and his wife, Marie Lilette Sarpy, who died in October of that year after the epidemic had begun to wane. A partial list of those who died from the fever in the region was published in a contemporary newspaper, but it included only those victims from the white community.[49] Occasional incidences of smallpox also are recalled; as was the custom elsewhere, in case of death by smallpox the home and all belongings of the afflicted were burned to destroy the germ.[50]

The low incidence of disease among the people of this area is surprising when one considers the nature of the country they lived in. A northern soldier who spent almost a month in the region during the Civil War wrote in his diary: "Lying in the woods, we begin to be seriously annoyed with the insects

45. The census of 1850, which recorded cases of insanity, revealed no instances in the colony at that time; Seventh Census of the United States, 1850, Population Schedule.
46. Succession of Philippe Valsain Dupre, interdict, in Natchitoches Parish Records, No. 630; Seventh Census of the United States, 1850, Population Schedule.
47. Mrs. Coutii to author, March 31, 1974.
48. Interview with confidential source, April 26, 1974. The victim's abnormality, it is related, did not prevent her from marrying and leading an otherwise normal life.
49. Interview with Mrs. Coutii, April 24, 1974; Succession of A. A. Metoyer and Wife, in Natchitoches Parish Records, No. 841; Blaise C. D'Antoni, "Some 1853 Cloutierville Yellow Fever Deaths," *New Orleans Genesis,* XXXV (June, 1970), 261–62.
50. Interview with Mrs. Coutii, April 24, 1974.

and vermin incident to this country. Many of the men are suffering from the effects of the wood-tick, which bore themselves into the flesh, causing inflammation and running sores. Scorpions are not unfrequent [*sic*] to this region, the sting of which is fatal."[51] Echoing these sentiments, Father Yves-Marie of Natchitoches wrote to his former pastor in France of the "death-beetles," the flies, and the mosquitoes which constantly assailed him. "I really believe it is in this country that Beezlebub has established his kingdom."[52]

The one feature of Cane River life which most impressed visitors was the quality of the plantations and homes. The captain of the steamboat *Dalmau,* which regularly stopped in the area, observed: "The plantations appeared no way different from the generality of those of white Creoles; and on some of them were large, handsome, and comfortable houses."[53] Only one of the large plantation homes is still extant: the one built for Louis Metoyer, supposedly in 1833, by Seraphin Llorens. Old residents of the late twentieth century remember six more, all of which were destroyed early in their lifetimes: the home of Augustin Metoyer; a similar home belonging to his son Jean Baptiste Augustin; the spacious manor house of Jerome Sarpy, at the upper end of the Isle; the "eleven-room mansion" of Emanuel Dupre and his wife Marguerite Metoyer, which stood across from the 24-Mile Ferry; the home of Oscar Dubreuil at the site of the ferry; and the nearby home of the merchant Vilfried Metoyer. An eighth large antebellum home, officially described as a "mansion house," was the residence of Auguste Metoyer and his wife Melite Anty; this home was lost in a lawsuit before the Civil War. Another large house of the same general style, reportedly, belonged to Estelle Morin Metoyer, the granddaughter of Augustin. According to tradition, it was destroyed during the war.[54]

51. Elias P. Pellet, *History of the 114th Regiment, New York State Volunteers* (Norwich, N.Y., 1866), 224.
52. McCants (ed. and trans.), *They Came to Louisiana,* 122.
53. Olmsted, *Journey in the Seaboard Slave States,* 633.
54. Interview with Mrs. Coutii, March 24, 1974; Hugh LaCour to author, April 5, 1974; Natchitoches, 1920, Scrapbook, in Henry Collection; *Anty* v. *Adlé,* 9 La. Ann. 490 (1854).
The one extant home, that of Louis Metoyer, is known today as Melrose and in 1974 was declared a National Historic Landmark. Now owned by the Association for the Preservation of Historic Natchitoches, it is in the process of being restored.

In general, builders of houses on the Isle used three different construction methods: *bousillage, brique entre poteaux,* and round logs chinked with mud. Homes built during the colonial and territorial periods, such as those described in Chapter III, were usually of *bousillage.* By the second decade of the nineteenth century the two-story manor house built of *brique entre poteaux* (brick between wood) was gaining in popularity. By the time of the Civil War all of the "mansion houses" belonging to the community were constructed in this way. Only the homes of the poorer people and those of the slaves were constructed, usually, of logs chinked with mud. Most houses and stables were fitted with equipment to protect them from lightning.[55]

One Cane River native described the antebellum plantation houses as being large and two-storied. The bottom floor served as an above-ground basement. Living quarters were on the second floor where the breezes blew cooler and the mosquitoes were less apt to hover. Since flooding was occasionally a threat to houses built near the river, the first floor exterior walls were usually of brick, and brick pillars supported the veranda that was invariably built outside the second floor. High, wide steps provided access to the main living area. On many homes the verandas were L-shaped, extending the length of one side as well as the front; in some cases, the verandas extended down both sides of the home, or even on all four sides. Bay windows were not uncommon.[56]

Kitchens, invariably, were built detached from the main house, to prevent heating the living quarters in summer. Some houses, such as that of Emanuel Dupre, sported a backyard barbeque grill, equipped with a long iron rod on which porkers or calves were speared for cooking. Augustin Metoyer's yard boasted two pigeon houses, appraised at ten times the value of a slave cabin. This was a feature found on few white plantations of the area.[57]

All "better homes" in the colony were graced with a lane of whitewashed

---

55. Hugh LaCour to author, April 5, 1974; McCants (ed. and trans.), *They Came to Louisiana,* 120; Stoddard, *Sketches of Louisiana,* 328–29.

56. Hugh LaCour to author, April 5, 1974. Variations on the general theme occurred, of course. For example, at Melrose and some no longer extant homes that are still recalled, the wide, single, center-front stairway was foregone in favor of two small stairways at either end of the ground floor veranda.

57. Interview with Mrs. Coutii, March 24, 1974; and Mrs. Contii to author, October 5, 1974; Succession of Agnes Metoyer, in Natchitoches Parish Records, No. 395.

oak or cedar trees, a status symbol among planters in the parish. Six cedars lined the entranceway to the Dupre home, and an even larger number set off the estate grounds of the Sarpy plantation home. According to an 1890 history of the parish, the Sarpy manor house was "a large and commodious one, being 130 feet long by 80 feet wide. The yard in which it stands contains a fine cedar grove, and overlooking, as it does, the beautiful Cane River it is one of the most beautiful country seats in the parish."[58]

In discussing the homes of this type that he had seen before they were razed in the twentieth century, Callahan wrote: "What called most for ornamentation were the mantels and fireplaces. The wood-work extended from floor to ceiling, and here the craftsman showed his skill. It is all honest wood and honest work. Some of the wood is native, some mahogany. The designs are simple, but elegant. There is no overcharging of ornament, no useless detail. Even now, in some of these old buildings, despite years of neglect, the woodwork of these fireplaces and mantels gives indication of its former beauty."[59]

Quite often special features were constructed in the interior of the homes to accommodate them to Louisiana's climate. In the dining rooms, for example, large clover-leaf boards called *punkahs* swung from the ceilings above the long dining tables. Ropes, similar to the chains of twentieth-century swag lamps, dropped into easy reach on the other side of the rooms. Pulls on these ropes, by slave children usually, caused the *punkahs* to swing rhythmically, cooling the diners and fanning the flies from the food.[60]

The interiors of the homes were usually furnished in accordance with the general architectural styles of the buildings. Succession inventories of those who lived in smaller homes indicated sparse furnishings. Inventories of the larger homes almost all reflected quality and taste. The succession of Mme. Florentin Conant, which was opened in 1837, indicated that she and her husband had recently purchased new furniture costing $1,728, an extremely im-

58. Interview with Mrs. Coutii, March 24, 1974; *Biographical and Historical Memoirs of Northwest Louisiana*, 353. By the time this 1890 description was written, the Sarpy home had proceeded through a succession of owners and had become the home of a new member of the colony, Carroll Jones, Sr.

59. Callahan *et al.*, *History of St. Augustine's Parish*, 23.

60. Hugh LaCour to author, April 5, 1974.

pressive amount for furniture in a period when four-poster beds could be purchased for as little as $10 to $25. The inventory of her estate also included a sizable amount of other furniture. When J. B. Louis Metoyer died the following year, his furnishings included a mahogany bookcase valued at $60, one of the most expensive bookcases found on any succession inventory, white or nonwhite, in the parish. Most of the furniture in his home was made of mahogany or cherry rather than the inexpensive native cypress. When his son Théophile Louis married in 1843 the furnishings of his home included a piano.[61]

The probate sale of the succession of C. N. Rocques, Sr., in 1859 included a steam bathtub that was purchased by the Widow Jean Baptiste Metoyer for $100 and a stove which was adjudicated to Rocques' widow for $30. A carpet from the Rocques home was bought at the sale by a local white physician, Isidore Gimbert, and the inventory of Predanes Metoyer's home included an iron safe where he kept his valuables. An organ and two clocks, one of which was valued at $35, were in the estate left by Augustin Metoyer and his wife. The succession of C. N. Rocques, Jr., inventoried a special set of children's dishes, and numerous successions boasted sterling silver flatwear and serving pieces.[62]

Most of the fine furniture owned by the family was passed through successive generations until the reversal of family fortunes forced the sale of much of it. Pieces which remain in the area include a huge oak table with a lazy Susan built into the center, a demitasse set, a marble-top dresser, and a grandfather clock, all of which once belonged to Augustin Metoyer. Another lazy Susan of silver is said to have been owned by his son Jean Baptiste Metoyer.[63] A piano of unusual and impressive design which formerly belonged to the colony was purchased in 1970 for prominent display in the restored manor house of an early family of white planters on the Côte

61. Succession of Marie Louise Metoyer [Mme. Florentin Conant, Sr.], No. 323; Succession of [J. B.] Louis Metoyer, No. 362; Théophile L. Metoyer and Marie Elina Metoyer, Marriage Contract, Mortgage Records, Vol. 28, pp. 276–79, all in Natchitoches Parish Records.

62. Succession of Charles Nerestan Rocques, Sr., Succession Book 30, p. 225; Succession of Agnes Metoyer, No. 395; Succession of C. N. Rocques, *fils,* No. 897; and Succession of Predanes Metoyer, No. 1360, all in Natchitoches Parish Records.

63. François Mignon to author, April 8, 1974.

Joyeuse.[64] Recalling the huge old four-poster beds that his family once owned, one twentieth-century descendant offered the following description: "Posts on beds are about eight inches square at the bottom to about 4" × 4" at the top with a canopy (tester) that rests on the four posts. Side rail is about 18 inches wide. There is a large key to lock the side rail to the head and foot boards. The mosquito bar hung from a long rod around the bed inside the tester. The bar rod had rings all along two sides which slipped over the rods so the bar could be pulled back when not in use."[65]

Another descendant recalled that the oldest chairs preserved by the family were straight backed and covered with deer hide; later, cowhide was used. Her mother had inherited a marble pestle for crushing herbs and spices and an iron clock that "rang so loud you could hear it across the river."[66] An early cypress armoire of the locally-made variety, which has been preserved by the Morin, Roque, and Chelettre families, boasts straight, clean lines that complement its petite size; round wooden pegs hold the armoire together, their perfection marking the work of a proud craftsman.[67]

One of the most treasured items preserved by twentieth-century descendants is a small crystal mug with an ivory bust of Napoleon. It seems there had been eight originally, brought back from France by Jerome Sarpy when he accompanied Augustin on the latter's last trip abroad. The set was divided when Sarpy died, and each of the mugs was inherited by a different child.[68]

Of all the refinements and advantages which the people enjoyed, the one which they undoubtedly appreciated the most was their education. Many of the Creoles of color on the Isle in fact possessed a higher level of education than did many of the whites with whom they did business. Numerous business documents show the signature of a person of color in beautiful, flowing script set beside a white man's mark of a cross.

Only one of the first-generation Metoyers, Pierre, was able to sign his

64. *Natchitoches: Oldest Settlement in the Louisiana Purchase, Founded 1714* (Natchitoches, 1973), 49. This piano is to be found in the living room of the home called Cherokee, which is open for public display during the area's annual tour of homes.

65. Hugh LaCour to author, April 5, 1974.

66. Interview with Mrs. Coutii, April 26, 1974; and Mrs. Coutii to author, April 15, 1974.

67. This cypress armoire is now in the possession of Armeline Roque (Mrs. Tillman) Chelettre.

68. Interview with Mrs. Coutii, April 26, 1974; and Mrs. Coutii to author, April 15, 1974. The present whereabouts of only one of these mugs is known; the others were sold by the people to collectors during their period of need.

name. The family's early illiteracy was not unusual in that era, however. An 1803 report on affairs in Louisiana complained that there was no college at all in the colony, only one public school (at New Orleans), and only a few private schools. "Not more than half of the inhabitants," it was reported, "are supposed to be able to read and write, of whom not more than two hundred perhaps are able to do it well." [69]

Despite their general illiteracy, the original Metoyer siblings recognized the importance of education and made certain that their children received as much as they could provide for them. How and by whom the first children of the Isle were educated is not known, but when these children became adults, about 1820, all but one of the males were literate. The majority of the females of this second generation could not sign their names, and most of the other free people of color of Natchitoches Parish with whom they intermarried labored under the same handicap. Emanuel Dupre was an exception. Of the third generation, all the males and almost all of the females were literate. The signature of Widow C. N. Rocques, Jr., in 1854, is particularly revealing. Signing a document as guardian of her minor children, she wrote *"Marie Anaïs Metoyer, pour moimême et pour enfants mineurs"* in beautiful, perfect script, far better than that of the notary who drafted the document. [70]

In most southern states teaching a person of color, free or slave, to read and write was considred a crime. In Louisiana such instruction was tacitly tolerated but not publicly encouraged. Public schools came into existence in Louisiana in 1841, but none of them admitted children of color. The 1850 census of Natchitoches Parish noted the existence of only one public school with one teacher to whom $320 was paid as a salary. The 1860 census enumerated forty public schools, one male college, and one private female academy. [71] None of these schools were located on the Isle. In all cases during

---

69. *An Account of Louisiana*, 33.

70. Succession of C. N. Rocques, *fils*, in Natchitoches Parish Records, No. 897.

71. Stahl, "The Free Negro in Ante-Bellum Louisiana," 357–59; Rodolphe Lucien Desdunes, *Our People and Our History*, trans. and ed. by Sister Dorothea O. McCants (Baton Rouge, 1973), 137n; Seventh and Eighth Censuses of the United States, 1850–1860, Social Statistics.

The statistics provided by the 1850 census also reveal that 15.8 percent of the colony's population had attended school within the year (even though the existence of their school was not recorded). Statewide, only 6.9 percent of the nonwhite population had attended school for any time at all during the previous year. J. B. D. DeBow (comp.), *Statistical View of the United States* (Washington, 1854), 154.

this period the instruction which the children of the colony received was private.

Tradition holds that one of the earliest teachers on the Isle was the French immigrant Louis Chevalier, who took a free woman of color as his lifelong common-law wife. Chevalier supposedly held a degree from a major European university, perhaps the Sorbonne.[72] No records can be found to prove or disprove this tradition. The earliest teacher on the Isle who has been identified was Nicolas Charles LeRoy, a native of Versailles, who came to the United States in December, 1828, at the age of forty-four, having "crossed the ocean in order to live in a free country and to be more independent."[73]

Upon his arrival in Natchitoches Parish, LeRoy found employment on Isle Brevelle,[74] but by 1841 he had left the community to teach the children of the wealthy white planters on the Côte Joyeuse. Although he quit their service, LeRoy apparently remained on friendly terms with members of the colony. A letter written by him to Auguste Metoyer in 1841 began with *"Mon cher Auguste,"* proceeded to convey his regards for the addressee's wife and young daughter, and was signed *"votre tout devotée."*[75]

The apparent successor to LeRoy was Bernard Desormes Dauphin, the first of several free men of color who are known to have taught on the Isle at various times during the antebellum years. Dauphin's tenure was not a long one. In 1843, shortly after his marriage to Marie Barbe Melisine Metoyer, this serious and sensitive young scholar was buried in the little cemetery on Isle Brevelle. In his memory, the grieving community carved an epithet on his tomb that reveals not only Dauphin's character, but also something of the values held by the people of the Isle: *"Son amour pour la literature refleches-sair les plus rares vertus."*[76]

---

72. Interview with Mrs. Coutii, April 26, 1974.
73. Elizabeth S. Mills, "Certificates of Naturalization, Natchitoches Parish, Louisiana, 1820–1850," 91; Last Will and Testament of Nicholas C. LeRoy, Succession No. 922, in Natchitoches Parish Records.
74. Succession of Pierre Metoyer, in Natchitoches Parish Records, No. 193. The final account of Pierre's administrator reported the settlement of the deceased's account with LeRoy for his teaching services in the local school.
75. Seventh Census of the United States, 1850, Population Schedule; Charles LeRoy to Auguste Metoyer, April 1, 1841, in Auguste Metoyer Papers, Louisiana State University Archives, Baton Rouge.
76. Desdunes, *Our People and Our History,* 51–52; Marriage Contract of Bernard Dauphin and Marie Barbe Melisine Metoyer, in Natchitoches Parish Records, Book 32, p. 22; Callahan *et al., History of St. Augustine's Parish,* 29.

The memorial to Dauphin was an appropriate one. This gifted young man of letters was one of seventeen of Louisiana's most cultured Creoles of color whose works appear in the small and now-rare anthology, *Les Cenelles*. In presenting a selection of Dauphin's work, the editor muses: "As to the clarity of thought, as well as the purity of the language, nothing in these selected poems surpasses the excellence of the strophe here produced." [77]

ADIEUX

Dearest one, why have you
So soon dispelled the transports of my love?
Do you remember the days when you were so enamored
And you promised me a happiness without regret?
Adieu, good-bye, pardon if my faithful heart
Cannot detach itself from you;
I am going to pay today with my life
For the happy day when I received your trust.

> Good-bye, from the celestial vault of heaven
> I will watch over your destiny;
> There will end the unhappiness of life,
> Which already approaches its end;

When tormented by a secret pain,
Your fickle heart will recognize the sorrow
Come, pray to God at my tomb, please
For there you will be reborn to happiness.
And the Eternal One hearing your prayer,
In memory of our past love,
Will place a flower on the marble tomb
Which will cover my dried remains;

> Good-bye from the celestial vault of heaven,
> I will watch over your destiny;
> There will end the unhappiness of life,
> Which already approaches its end.

Other *hommes de couleur libre* of New Orleans followed Bernard Dauphin at the school on Isle Brevelle. Oscar Dubreuil, who taught in the early 1850s, and Firmin C. Christophe, Jr., who taught in the early 1860s, were both natives of New Orleans, the city whose culture all of Louisiana envied. Native

---

77. Desdunes, *Our People and Our History,* 51.

sons, as well, served as tutors to the youth of the Isle. Émile Chevalier, the oldest son of Louis Chevalier and his *placée* Fanny, and Oscar Dupre, son of Emanuel Dupre and Marie Marguerite Metoyer, had studied in their childhood under Louis Chevalier and LeRoy. Upon reaching maturity they became teachers themselves.[78]

In the earliest years, education upon the Isle was almost totally French oriented. Jean Baptiste Dominique Metoyer and Emanuel Dupre, members of the second generation, were both educated men, but when in 1839 a document was drafted for them in the English language, it was necessary for the notary to record that he had read the document to them and translated it into French before they signed it. However, in less than one generation, a large percentage of the members of the colony became fluent in both of these languages.[79]

In discussing the type of education provided in the Isle Brevelle schools, Callahan described an old handwritten textbook owned by the late Jean Conant:

> The first and larger part . . . is a complete treatise on Bookkeeping, both single and double entry. It explains the theory and gives examples illustrating the whole process. It is the completest treatise in the whole book, evidently important for the education of future planters and merchants. The manuscript is beautifully written; at first sight it looks like a steel engraving. Students got a broad idea of commerce, transactions are noted with Paris, Rouen, Nantes, Metz, Perpignan, as well as with New Orleans and Mexico.
>
> The rest of the manuscript is also important and interesting. The instruction in this part is catechetical. It consists of a series of questions and answers on various subjects. They are so divided as to give a general cultural knowledge. The titles are: The Sphere, Geology, Civics, Astronomy, Geometry, Greek and Roman History. The title, The Sphere, is concerned with the general geography of the globe, the countries of Europe, then particularly France and the United States, as of the time it was written. The list of presidents ends with Jackson. There are only a few torn pages giving examples of arithmetic. The whole course covered what might be called general information from the Great Wall of China to where sugar cane originated and its travels to reach the United States. Many of the questions would stump

78. Seventh and Eighth Censuses of the United States, 1850–1860, Population Schedules; interview with Mrs. Coutii, March 24, 1974.

79. J. B. D. Metoyer, *cadet,* to Em¹ Dupre, in DeBlieux Collection; Olmsted, *Journey in the Seaboard Slave States,* 634. According to Olmsted's informants, the people spoke "French among themselves, but all are able to converse in English also, and many of them are well educated."

the college graduate of today. The teacher of those days would make a marvellous quiz-master on televison; but I dare say he would not have to give away much money.[80]

Other textbooks that were used on the Isle covered a variety of subjects, and included such publications as: *Civil Code of the State of Louisiana* (1838); Alexandré Dumas, *Mémoires d'un Médecin la Comtesse de Charny* (1856); M. Noel & M. Chapsal, *Leçons D'analyse Grammaticale* (1838); A. G. Maillet, *Traité Complète des Verbes Irrégulières, Simples et Composés de la Langue Anglaise* (n.d.); *McGuffey's Third Eclectic Reader* (n.d.); *Le Nouveau Parfait Jardinier; Ou L'art de Cultiver* (1835); *Histoire Romain depuis la Fondation de Rome* (1831); *Les Aventures de Télémaque Fils d'Ulysse* (1850); Smith, *English and French Dictionary* (n.d., but published in Paris); and *A Pilgrimage to the Holy Land* (1832).[81]

Upon the completion of their education on the Isle, some young men apparently were sent to the North or to France for a year of university study. Among those who are credited with receiving a year of continental education were Sévère Dupre, Arnould Conant, and Vilfried Metoyer. Young Vilarco Llorens was also sent abroad, it is reported, but suffered an acute case of homesickness and returned to Louisiana almost immediately.[82]

According to one modern writer, whatever organized education for free people of color existed in Louisiana was usually provided by the church.[83] In 1856 the religious leaders of Louisiana took an interest in the education of the free people of color on Isle Brevelle. In that year, Bishop Martin declared the mission of Isle Brevelle to be a parish in its own right and purchased from a white resident of the Isle a small house and a tract of land on which a school could be established. The Daughters of the Cross, who had established a convent for girls in Avoyelles Parish the year before, were invited to open a mission school on the Isle, and the order accepted. In 1856 Mother Superior Hyacinthe LeConniat, of the house at Avoyelles, wrote to her brother in

80. Callahan *et al., History of St. Augustine's Parish,* 30.
81. All of these books, which were owned by Ambroise Sévère Dupre and his wife Sidalise Sarpy, now belong to their granddaughter, Mrs. Coutii.
82. Callahan *et al., History of St. Augustine's Parish,* 29; interview with Mrs. Coutii, March 24, 1974.
83. Stahl, "The Free Negro in Ante-Bellum Louisiana," 359.

France about the new plans: "Our first mission house will be in Ile Bre-velle.... Father Martin has charge of this mission and the population is all mulatto. These are people of leisure and many of wealth and means. The Bishop bought us a house with sixty acres of land there. It will form a small establishment for three or four Sisters. As soon as the finances of our Bishop permit, he will fix the house, which right now is in mighty poor shape. We will go there when things are repaired." [84]

By January, 1858, the school had opened its doors. Mother Hyacinthe again wrote her brother:

> The Ile Brevelle house is progressing well. We have already twenty-seven pupils and in the spring we will have forty or fifty more for sure. This is a simple school—a modest school. The students pay $4 a month, that is twenty francs and something. Next year, we will take some boarders. The people of this parish, al-though they are very rich, are disdained by the white people who do not want the mulattoes in their schools. So, here we will have only mulattoes. These good people gave us $1,100 to $1,200 to build two houses. We have here more land than in Avoyelles. One of the classrooms has been transformed into a chapel. The Blessed Sacrament is reserved there. Father Martin who is but one mile from us had the kindness to come three or four times last week to say Mass for us. [85]

The physical work on the school was still not completed, however. At this time the church authorities were awaiting two thousand pieces of lumber which had been ordered from New Orleans to make tables for the classrooms, a refectory, some benches, a partition in the chapel, and a floor for the house. Two gardens were being laid out. [86]

The mission school, which had been named St. Joseph Convent, soon out-grew its accommodations. By 1859 there were from 120 to 130 girls enrolled. Moreover, the school was located a mile from the church, and the sisters found that much too far to walk to daily mass in the summer heat and winter cold. Funds were raised and new buildings were erected beside the church.

---

84. McCants (ed. and trans.), *They Came to Louisiana,* 41, 43; Callahan *et al., History of St. Augustine's Parish,* 32; Baudier, *The Catholic Church in Louisiana,* 409; Sigmond Kieffy to Auguste Martin, in Natchitoches Parish Records, Book 49, p. 504.

The home which the bishop purchased for the Daughters of the Cross is the one discussed as the "Old Convent" in Chapter III. With no floor other than the dirt on which it stood, this was the most primitive house on the Isle.

85. McCants (ed. and trans.), *They Came to Louisiana,* 72–73.

86. *Ibid.,* 71–72.

With the enlarged space it became possible to accept as boarders the girls who lived too far from the school to commute daily. Additional nuns were brought in as enrollment increased.[87]

Through 1862 the school flourished, but as war conditions brought increased hardships and financial reverses, the enrollment of St. Joseph Convent nosedived. Federal troops established themselves on the Red River and made communication even more difficult between the mother convent at Avoyelles and the mission on Isle Brevelle. The mother superior obtained from one general a promise of safe conduct for any provisions which she sent to the nuns on the Isle, but the mission convent was doomed. By December, 1863, the school had closed.[88]

Almost a century later, the resident priest on the Isle was to observe: "The people of Isle Brevelle have a traditional respect for education."[89] This observation is a valid one. The succession inventories of those who died in the antebellum era itemize many lots of books and other items indicative of their educational training. The succession of C. N. Rocques, Jr., in 1854 included three lots of books which sold for $3. The number of books in each lot was not indicated, but the inventory of property belonging to the schoolmaster LeRoy in that period included six hundred volumes valued at $60, or ten cents per volume. At this rate, the three lots belonging to Rocques would have contained some thirty books. Also sold from Rocques' estate was a fifteen-volume set entitled *Esprit de Enciclopédie,* which was purchased by another member of the colony, Edward Séveran, for $15. The inventory and appraisement of the estate of Auguste Predanes Metoyer in 1865 included one lot of books valued at $6, a *Colton's Atlas* at $8, a writing desk, and a secretary.[90]

Although the quantity and value of such private libraries were small by modern standards, they were significant in the mid-1800s. The census of 1870 indicates that in the whole of the parish there were only twenty-three private libraries, including those of lawyers and clergymen, with an average of 107

87. *Ibid.,* 83–84, 143; Callahan *et al., History of St. Augustine's Parish,* 32.

88. Baudier, *The Catholic Church in Louisiana,* 432.

89. Callahan *et al., History of St. Augustine's Parish,* 29.

90. Succession of C. N. Rocques, *fils,* No. 897; Succession of Nicholas Charles LeRoy, No. 922; Succession of Predanes Metoyer, No. 1360, all in Natchitoches Parish Records.

books. The five-shelved bookcase of C. N. Rocques, Sr., which at the time of his death in 1859 was valued at $40.50, could easily have held this many books. The $60 bookcase in the 1838 succession of J. B. Louis Metoyer probably held many more.[91] Judging from the number of Metoyer estates which possessed sizable quantities of books, it is quite possible that a large percentage of those private libraries in the parish in 1870 were located on Isle Brevelle.

Even those homes with only a few books of value were still among the elite minority. According to Olmsted, one fellow traveler in Louisiana informed him that "he might travel several days, and call on a hundred planters, and hardly see in their houses more than a single newspaper apiece, in most cases; perhaps none at all; nor any books except a Bible, and some Government publications, that had been franked to them through the post-office, and perhaps a few religious tracts or school-books."[92]

By and large, the Cane River colony of free people of color enjoyed a standard of living that certainly equaled that of the well-to-do middle-class white planters of their era, and perhaps in a sense of quality excelled that of the very wealthy upper class, if one contemporary observer is to be believed. Olmsted's traveling companion also convinced him that the middle-class southern planter who was worth $40,000 enjoyed a far more gracious life than a planter worth $300,000.[93]

Olmsted, in fact, provides the best and most concise evaluation of the personal lives of the colony that was recorded by any contemporary: "If you have occasion to call at their houses . . . you will be received in a gentlemanly manner, and find they live in the same style with white people of the same wealth."[94]

In 1795, when Augustin Metoyer began the Isle Brevelle colony, he was a recently manumitted slave, a penniless twenty-seven year old with a family to support. He had no education, no marketable trade, and no property except for

91. Ninth Census of the United States, 1870, Social Statistics; Succession of C. N. Rocques, Sr., Succession Book 30, p. 225, and Succession of [J. B.] Louis Metoyer, No. 362, all in Natchitoches Parish Records.
92. Olmsted, *Journey in the Seaboard Slave States*, 652.
93. *Ibid.*
94. *Ibid.*, 634.

the raw land that the Spanish crown had recently given him. Within sixty-five years—less than one lifetime—his family completely vanquished the stigmas of slavery, illegitimacy, illiteracy, and poverty.

The various comments on the colony that Olmsted recorded, comments made by all classes from stage driver to merchant to riverboat captain, emphasized the same quality: the *gentlemanly* behavior and life-style of the people. The basis for their transmigration into the ranks of "gentlemen" was clearly their wealth. The fortunes they accumulated proved their astute business judgment and won for them the respect of that element of society which valued this in a person. Their wealth enabled them to have their own church, which not only was a status symbol and brougnt wealthy whites into their midst, but did much to improve public opinions on their morality. Their wealth bought them finer plantations, finer homes, and finer carriages, and earned for them the approval of industrious whites and the envy of less fortunate ones. But most significantly, the wealth of the people brought them education and culture, the two factors which proved to be the bridge between the colony and the more genteel element of whites that dominated parish society.

Chapter EIGHT

Racism and Citizenship

With astute planning and diligent application of their talents, Cane River's Creoles of color acquired wealth and culture. In their best years they ranked financially in the highest levels of Natchitoches society. They possessed a superior education and set excellent examples in both refinement and religious devotion. They had overcome the handicaps posed by slavery, poverty, illiteracy, and illegitimacy, but they were still *gens de couleur libre*. The most formidable difficulty they faced remains to be examined: the exercise of the rights of citizenship. What role did these people play in a society that measured citizenship by the coloring of skin? What degree of prejudice did they suffer because of the measure of black blood which they still possessed? What political and social privileges were allowed them because of their white heritage? And, most important, in a society that pitted black against white, where lay the allegiance of the in-between people of this third caste who lived on Isle Brevelle?

In 1832, when the Isle Brevelle colony was in its peak of affluence, a South Carolina appeals judge ruled that nonwhites "belong to a degraded caste of society; they are in no respect on an equality with a white man. According to their condition they ought by law to be compelled to demean themselves as inferiors, from whom submission and respect to the whites, in all their intercourse in society ought to be demanded."[1] A Tennessee judge in 1839 agreed: "Free Negroes have always been a degraded race in the United States . . . with whom public opinion has never permitted the white population to associate on terms of equality, and in relation to whom, the laws have never allowed the immunities of the free white citizen."[2]

1. Theodore Brantner Wilson, *The Black Codes of the South* (University, Ala., 1965), 27.
2. *Ibid.,* 36.

"But, we are not Negroes," the people of Isle Brevelle always have argued; "we are *gens de couleur libre.*" To them a clear distinction exists, but this distinction is not one that society has acknowledged readily. According to Carl N. Degler, "Historically, in the United States any person with Negro ancestry has been considered a Negro, even if he appeared to be white. In the days of slavery as later, in the days of legal separation, a Negro was defined in law and in custom as anyone with a certain amount of Negro ancestry—usually one-eighth." [3] Most of the people of Isle Brevelle, since the inception of the colony, have fallen within this legal definition—if only barely.

Recognizing the validity of racial views such as that held by the Isle Brevelle colony, Degler continues: "Although all Americans, white and black, grew up with and accept without question that definition of a Negro, there is no inherent logic in it. There is no reason why a person with half his ancestry white and half black should be defined as a Negro. With equal logic he could be defined as a white, or more precisely as a half white, half black. . . . No other country in the New World, with the exception of Canada, follows the United States in defining a black man as anyone with a measurable amount of Negro ancestry or 'blood.' " [4]

Degler's assessment of American racial attitudes is borne out by countless documents. In general, all laws enacted that dealt with the free Negro also applied to the free part-Negro; and in many cases legislation affecting slaves was likewise construed to include the free nonwhite, regardless of exact racial composition. The Georgia civil code of 1861, for example, held that "the free person of color is entitled to no right of citizenship, except such as are specifically given by law. . . . All laws enacted in reference to slaves, and in their nature applicable to free persons of color, shall be construed to include them." The Georgia penal code of that year went still further and decreed: "All Negroes and mulattoes are deemed, and are hereby declared to be 'prima facie' slaves, and it rests upon those alleging freedom to prove it." [5]

Clearly, the laws of the antebellum United States accorded no special privileges to a nonwhite simply because he possessed some measure of white blood. In general, the privileges of citizenship were granted on an all-or-

3. Degler, *Neither Black Nor White*, 101.
4. *Ibid.*, 102.
5. Wilson, *The Black Codes of the South*, 35, 38.

nothing basis. By contrast, America's neighbors in the New World (excepting Canada) have traditionally recognized the third caste and have accorded it a special role in society. In comparing the United States to one South American country, Degler notes that in the latter "the mulatto or mixed blood in general, occupies a special place intermediate between white and black; he is neither black nor white. No such place is reserved for the so-called mixed blood in the United States; a person is either a black or a white."[6]

For the free nonwhite in South America, the recognition of this third caste has offered what Degler terms an "escape hatch," a special social level into which the part-black can flee in order to escape the nonentity and social servitude of blackness, a more privileged level that offers the opportunity to share the rights and responsibilities of citizenship. Within the United States there has existed only one society that has recognized to any extent the existence of an intermediate racial category and has attempted to accord to it any comparable level of citizenship. That one exception has been Creole Louisiana.

The French-Spanish, Roman Catholic heritage of Louisiana produced an entirely different set of racial concepts from that which developed in the predominantly Anglo-Saxon Protestant societies of the other American colonies. Consequently, when Creole Louisiana was inducted into the American states, the immediate result was a clash of racial concepts and ideals. Several decades of ideological conflict followed, but inevitably "English attitudes and institutions . . . triumphed over Spanish-French resistance, and Anglo American ideals and prejudices were superimposed on Latin Louisiana."[7] Those who lost the most in the conflict were the members of the third caste. The people of Isle Brevelle and their counterparts at New Orleans, Opelousas, East Baton Rouge, and thousands more scattered throughout the rural areas of the state lost their political and social "escape hatch."

An anlysis of the legal status of the colony and the interracial relationships which affected them shows clearly the unusual role which Louisiana's third caste played, in contrast to the situation in other regions. In 1715, for example, the state of Maryland enacted a law permitting quite indiscriminate arrest

6. Degler, *Neither Black Nor White*, 107.
7. Johnston, *Race Relations*, 231.

of free nonwhites; those who were unable to prove satisfactorily that they were not runaways were returned to their last master or sold into servitude to pay the costs of their detention and trial.[8] By contrast, as long as the free man of color in French colonial Louisiana "complied with the rather mild regulations governing their conduct, they enjoyed the same economic and legal privileges as White persons."[9]

While Virginia in 1757 prohibited free Negroes or part-Negroes from bearing arms in the state militia,[10] Louisiana not only outfitted two complete units of free men of color in New Orleans[11] and permitted free nonwhites at the other posts to join local units, but she went so far as to arm slaves and gave them the opportunity to defend the territory in exchange for their freedom.[12]

By 1793 Virginia had on her statute books a law prohibiting free people of color from entering the state.[13] At this same time, Spanish Louisiana welcomed all settlers, regardless of color, and made generous grants to all free heads of households who sought them, whether they were white, black, or *gens de couleur libre*. It was this lenient policy of the colonial Louisiana government which enabled Marie Thérèze and her children to accumulate their initial holdings in land. Had they been forced to labor until they had saved sufficient cash to purchase the 5,753 acres which the Spanish government allowed them, it is doubtful that the family would have achieved any significant foothold in society.

Although the racial policies of colonial Louisiana were extremely tolerant in comparison to those in the other North American colonies, it is not to be assumed that they were completely indiscriminatory. On the contrary, interracial marriages were flatly prohibited, and the Spanish ordinances went so far as to forbid women of the slightest color to show excessive attention to their dress. Such items popular among stylish Creole ladies as feathers, jewelry,

8. Wright, *The Free Negro in Maryland*, 109.
9. Sterkx, *The Free Negro in Ante-Bellum Louisiana*, 34.
10. Franklin, *The Free Negro in North Carolina*, 193.
11. Governor Bernardo de Galvez reported to Madrid in 1779 that these two companies "behaved on all occasions with as much valor and generosity as the white soldiers." Alice Dunbar-Nelson, "People of Color in Louisiana," Part II, 374.
12. *Ibid.*, 370, 374; Foner, "Free People of Color," 416; Elizabeth Shown Mills, "Natchitoches Militia of 1782," *Louisiana Genealogical Register*, XX (September, 1973), 216, notes the presence on this roll of one "Zacherie," a free man of color at the Natchitoches post.
13. Franklin, *The Free Negro in North Carolina*, 193.

caps, and mantillas were specifically proscribed for free women of color. Their heads, in fact, were required to be bound at all times in a handkerchief, or *tignon*.[14]

In general, colonial Louisiana accorded the free man of color most rights of citizenship but drew the line at full social equality. This was the society into which the Cane River colony was born and the society to which they tenaciously clung. Long after Louisiana had become a part of the United States, they continued to refer to themselves as "French citizens."

With the transfer of Louisiana to the United States, the position of the free man of color became increasingly restricted. The Americans were exceedingly apprehensive over the existence of a "large, wealthy, *armed* free colored community." To them it was "painful and perplexing" to envision "the formidable aspect of the armed Blacks and Mulattoes officered and organized."[15] Despite at least one recommendation that it was "worth the consideration of the government [that free people of color] be made good citizens," the new regime proceeded to revise Louisiana's black code in order to align it more closely with those of the other American states.[16]

In 1806, the first American revisions in the black code appeared, limiting the privileges of all men of color, slave or free. Strict immigration laws were passed to prevent an influx of more free people of color from the French West Indies. Those already in Louisiana were required to appear before authorities and give proof of their freedom or be classed as runaway slaves. Any free people of color carrying guns were required to carry also their freedom papers.[17]

In 1808 the territorial legislature decreed that all public documents referring to free people of color must contain the words "free man of color" or "free woman of color" or the appropriate abbreviation after the surname of the individual. In 1812, when Louisiana was granted statehood, suffrage was limited to whites. During the next half-century many additional restirctions were

14. Charles Gayarré, *History of Louisiana* (4 vols.; New Orleans, 1903), III, 179.
15. Clarence E. Carter (ed.), *The Territorial Papers of the United States* (Washington, 1934–), Vol. IX; *The Territory of Orleans, 1803–1812* (Washington, 1940), 139, quoted in Foner, "Free People of Color," 421. Italics in Foner.
16. Foner, "Free People of Color," 421.
17. Sterkx, *The Free Negro in Ante-Bellum Louisiana,* 161.

placed upon the free Creole of color, denying him such rights of citizenship as military and jury service and taking from him various social and economic privileges.[18]

Such changes were not always readily accepted, even by the white Creole population. According to one authority, "When the ancient customs and traditions conflicted with the [new American] code, there were many in Louisiana who sought to evade and nullify the law." Indeed, the conflict between French tradition and American law became so serious that at one point a judge was forced to rule that the *"decisions of the courts of France"* were no longer legally binding in Louisiana.[19] Obviously, the people of Isle Brevelle were not alone when they continued to regard themselves as "French citizens."

Creoles of color enjoyed several important advantages, even under the Americanized black code, that were frequently denied to free people of color in other states. According to one judicial decision, "as far as it concerns everything, except political rights, free people of color appear to possess all other rights of persons, whether absolute or relative. . . . They . . . may take and hold property by purchase, inheritance or donation; they may marry, and as a consequence, exercise parental authority over their children; they may be witnesses; they may stand in judgement, and they are responsible under the general designation of "persons" for crimes."[20]

One of the basic advantages which the free man of color held in Louisiana was the presumption of freedom versus presumption of bondage. In direct contrast to the rulings in Georgia and in most other states that a man of color was considered to be a slave until he proved himself to be free, the supreme court of Louisiana ruled in 1810: "Considering how much probability there is in favor of the liberty of these persons, they ought not to be deprived of it upon mere presumption."[21] As late as 1845 this ruling was upheld by the same court: "Ever since the case of Adelle *vs*. Beauregard it has been the settled doctrine here, that persons of color are presumed to be free. . . . The

---

18. Stahl, "The Free Negro in Ante-Bellum Louisiana," 316, 327; Gray, *Agriculture in Southern United States,* I, 524.
19. Johnston, *Race Relations,* 231. Italics added.
20. Quoted in Paul A. Kunkel, "Modifications in Louisiana Negro Legal Status," 4.
21. *Adele* v. *Beauregard,* 1 Mart. La., 183 (1810).

presumption is in favor of freedom, and the burden of proof is on him who claims the colored person as a slave."[22]

A second privilege not usually accorded to American nonwhites that the *gens de couleur libre* occasionally enjoyed was the right to bear arms in defense of their country. In the War of 1812, for example, the free men of color in Louisiana were allowed to form militia units, as their ancestors had done in colonial days, to assist in the defense of New Orleans against the British. Special authorization of the governor was given the Creoles of color in Natchitoches Parish to form an auxiliary unit of no more than eighty-four men, provided that they furnished their own arms and horses. Only those who possessed property worth at least one hundred dollars were allowed to participate in this enterprise. Since the Metoyer colony on Isle Brevelle represented 45 percent of the households headed by free people of color in the parish and 73 percent of the property owners in this category, it is reasonable to assume that they also made up a large percentage of the patriots who formed this militia unit.[23]

Between 1824 and 1832 free nonwhites in Maryland were entirely denied the privilege of owning firearms.[24] Other states adopted measures that were almost as drastic. One early twentieth-century study of Louisiana's *gens de couleur libre* asserts that they suffered the same restriction. A later study, however, contends that they were able to own weapons but were not permitted to carry them unless they also carried their freedom papers.[25]

This latter interpretation of the law appears to be more valid, since almost every succession within the Cane River colony of Creoles of color inventoried guns and ammunition, sometimes in large quantities and often of considerable value. Since many of these items were auctioned at succession sales conducted by the sheriff of the parish and attended by whites, and many such items were purchased under these conditions by the various members of the community, it is improbable that ownership was illegal. Moreover, since the

22. Helen Tunncliff Catterall, *Judicial Cases Concerning American Slavery and the Negro* (5 vols.; Washington, 1932), III, 571.

23. Sterkx, *The Free Negro in Ante-Bellum Louisiana,* 182–84; Third Census of the United States, 1810.

24. Wright, *The Free Negro in Maryland,* 106–107.

25. Stahl, "The Free Negro in Ante-Bellum Louisiana," 318; Sterkx, *The Free Negro in Ante-Bellum Louisiana,* 161.

Metoyer colony was well known in the area, it is doubtful that the regulation requiring the possession of freedom papers on one's person was enforced unless members traveled elsewhere.

Another onerous restriction which was placed on the free nonwhites throughout the United States did definitely apply to Louisiana's *gens de couleur libre*. The South Carolina appeals court ruling that free nonwhites "belong to a degraded caste [and] ought by law to be compelled to demean themselves as inferiors" [26] had its counterpart in the Americanized black code of Louisiana: "Free People of Color ought never to insult or strike white people, nor presume to conceive themselves equal to the white, but on the contrary, they ought to yield to them in every occasion, and never speak or answer to them but with respect, under the penalty of imprisonment, according to the nature of the offense." [27]

The people of Isle Brevelle were keenly aware of this discriminatory clause in the law. They fought it with the best weapons that their wealth and relative independence afforded them: quiet dignity and strict formality in their dealings with whites. One less well-to-do relative of theirs, the "handsome, light coloured young barber" whom Olmsted interviewed on board the steamship *Dalmau*, offered the following insight into their personality and attitude: "They rather avoided white people. . . . They were uncertain of their position with them, and were afraid, if they were not reserved, they would be thought to be taking liberties, and would be subject to insults, which they could not very well resent." [28] On the other hand, the relative indicated that there were some whites whom the people knew quite well and with whom they were very much at ease. [29]

On at least one occasion, one of the craftsmen of the colony was accused of violating this strict code of interracial behavior. Joseph Marie Rabalais (Rablés), a white resident of the area, filed charges of attack and battery against the blacksmith Émile Dupart in 1828 with the Cloutierville justice of the peace, Jean Pierre Marie Dubois. According to Rabalais' accusations, he had visited Dupart's blacksmith shop, seeking repayment of the five dollars that

26. Wilson, *The Black Codes of the South,* 27.
27. Kunkel, "Modifications in Louisiana Negro Legal Status," 4.
28. Olmsted, *Journey in the Seaboard Slave States,* 636.
29. *Ibid.*

Dupart owed him. Dupart responded to his polite request, Rabalais alleged, with menacing words and actions, advanced toward him, struck him in the face, and knocked his hat to the ground.

Witnesses were present at the alleged affray: one member of the colony, Jean Baptiste Louis Metoyer, and one white, Lestan Langlois. Both witnesses swore under oath that unpleasant words indeed had been exchanged, that Dupart took a step toward Rabalais, and that the latter's hat then fell of its own accord. Neither witness believed that the blacksmith actually struck the white. The extant records in the files of this justice of the peace do not reveal the outcome of the case, but the parish records at Natchitoches indicate no conviction or sentence against Dupart.[30]

One of the most serious rights of citizenship that were denied free non-whites, not only in the South but in much of the North as well, was the privilege of testifying in court against a white man. They were, in fact, prohibited from even instituting a suit against a white in most states before the Civil War.[31] By contrast, the Creole of color was permitted free access to the courts of law in Louisiana. Not only was he entitled to defend himself in court against whites, but he could bring charges against whites as well. His testimony was accepted in every type of legal case.[32] As late as 1850 the supreme court of Louisiana pointed out that in many areas of the state the free men of color were "respectable from [*sic*] their intelligence, industry, and habits of good order. Many . . . are enlightened by education and . . . [are] large property holders." The word of such people, the court decreed, should be accepted without hesitation by any court or jury.[33]

Numerous court records exist in which the people of Isle Brevelle exercised this legal privilege. They sued or were sued by whites, gave testimony against whites, or swore out complaints against them for advances toward the females of their family. One major clash between members of the two races occurred in 1835, involving Augustin Metoyer and a white neighbor with an equally

30. J^h Me Rablés *contra* Émile Dupart, *h.d.c.l.,* in DeBlieux Collection.
31. Herbert Aptheker (ed.), *A Documentary History of the Negro People in the United States* (New York, 1951), 26; Sydnor, "The Free Negro in Mississippi," 7–8.
32. Stahl, "The Free Negro in Ante-Bellum Louisiana," 315–19.
33. Catterall, *Judicial Cases,* III, 601.

forceful personality, François Roubieu. Both Metoyer and Roubieu claimed title to a tract of land. Roubieu filed suit in the district court charging that Metoyer had

> ... without right caused an ex-parte survey to be made of his lands and has run what he pleases to call the division line between your Petitioner and himself in such a manner as not only to deprive your Petitioner of two hundred acres of land but to render the remainder of little value ... has actually taken possession ... and has cut and destroyed timber to the great injury of your Petitioner's property. That from the diminished quantity of value of your Petitioner's tract of land, owing to the illegal conduct of said Augustin Metoyer, your Petitioner has been forced to discontinue the building of a cotton gin on said land, which would have been of great use to your Petitioner not only in preparing his own crops for market, but in ginning the crops of his neighbours. That being deprived the use of this tract of land your Petitioner had to forego an opportunity of selling another Plantation which he has, though offered a fair price.... Petitioner avers that he has suffered damages in the amount of ten thousand dollars, for which he claims judgement against the said Augustin Metoyer.[34]

Augustin soon filed a countersuit against Roubieu averring that he had been in quiet and peaceable possession of the land for ten years before Roubieu decided to claim it. Moreover, the white planter had gone on the land, allegedly, on several occasions and removed great quantities of cypress and other timber for which Metoyer felt that he should receive compensation. In addition, Metoyer sought an injunction prohibiting Roubieu from committing any further damage to the property. Upon Metoyer's agreement to post a bond in the amount of five thousand dollars the injunction was issued by the judge.

The cases remained on the court docket for four years. Numerous testimonies were heard from whites and from members of the colony; several of the whites who testified did so on Metoyer's behalf. A considerable number of delays were granted to Roubieu in order that he might have additional time to settle technicalities that arose in the conduct of his case. Within a year, Roubieu's attorneys had abandoned his cause and were actually handling Metoyer's defense against Roubieu's suit, as well as the prosecution of Metoyer's suit against Roubieu. In 1838 the cases were consolidated and the

---

34. *Roubieu* v. *Metoyer*, District Court Suit 1395 (1835), in Natchitoches Parish Records.

jury ruled in favor of Metoyer.[35] Roubieu filed a motion for a new trial on the grounds that the verdict was signed by the foreman of the jury after its dismissal, and the motion was granted.

The new trial opened early the following year. After the jury was impaneled, Roubieu noted that a large percentage of the jurors had served during the previous trial and requested their dismissal. This request was likewise granted. The second trial had been in progress for eighteen days when the white planter's attorneys apparently convinced him that he had no chance of winning. His counsel moved to have the case dismissed, as in the case of a nonsuit, with their client to pay the costs of trial. Again the motion was granted. Augustin received no reimbursement for the damages which Roubieu had inflicted upon his property or for the legal expenses he had incurred. On the other hand, he had successfully defended himself against the $10,000 damage suit filed against him by the white, and his right to the possession of the property was confirmed.[36]

One of the most onerous consequences of the nonwhite's inability to testify against whites in most other states was his inability to defend the virtue of his wife, his sisters, or his daughters. The *gens de couleur libre* of Louisiana did not suffer this restriction, and the justice of the peace courts on Cane River clearly show that the free people of color on the Isle did not tolerate untoward conduct toward their females. Several incidences are documented in which legal action was taken to protect the young ladies on Isle Brevelle from the abuse of white neighbors.

In 1829, for example, young Marie Mariotte, who was herself the child of a *placage* between a white man and a woman of color, filed charges against a white neighbor for the improper advances which he was making to her. As a result, the neighbor was forced to post a $100 bond, along with his surety, to guarantee that he would "be quiet and peaceable with every person in the aforesaid State of Louisiana and particularly with Mademoiselle Marie, daughter of Adelaïde Mariotte, f.w.o.c." for a period of six months. Again in 1844 Manuel Llorens filed extensive charges in the same court against another

---

35. It is interesting to note that the all-white jury consisted of several of Roubieu's friends and in-laws. The foreman of the jury, in fact, was a brother of one of Roubieu's witnesses, Lemant Chaler, who was employed as Roubieu's overseer.

36. *Roubieu* v. *Metoyer.*

white neighbor who had attempted to force his attentions upon Llorens' young daughter. The white was required to post bond in the amount of fifty dollars, but only for a period of three months.[37]

Although Louisiana's free people of color possessed the right to bring suits against whites, to defend themselves against suits by whites, and to bear witness against whites, they were in general politically impotent. One authority points out: "Louisiana free Negroes were never allowed direct participation in the affairs of government to the extent enjoyed by white citizens. They were, nevertheless, permitted a kind of left-handed representation through the right of petition."[38] At least once during the antebellum period the Isle Brevelle people exercised successfully this right of petition.

A white planter of the Rivière aux Cannes area, Alexis Cloutier, had donated a portion of his plantation as grounds for a community church in 1817 and then proceeded to divide the surrounding land into lots. Several streets were laid out in what was to be the new town of Cloutierville, which the ambitious Cloutier planned to have designated as the seat of a new parish which he hoped to have carved from the extensive boundaries of Natchitoches. Also included in the new parish would be Isle Brevelle. In January, 1825, Cloutier's friend, Placide Bossier, the state senator from Natchitoches Parish, presented to the state legislature several petitions from "his constituents" seeking the division of the parish.[39]

The boundaries of Natchitoches were indeed extensive in this period. Some citizens, such as those in the Allen settlement in the northern portion of the parish, were required to travel as much as eighty-four miles to the parish seat at Natchitoches to conduct official business. Several outlying segments of the parish's population desired to have their areas made into new parishes. But the residents of Isle Brevelle, who lived from ten to thirty miles from the parish

---

37. *Mme. Marie, f.w.o.c.* v. *Victorin Levasseur* and *Manuel Llorens* v. *Firmin Lattier*, in DeBlieux Collection.

38. Sterkx, *The Free Negro in Ante-Bellum Louisiana*, 170.

39. Alexis Cloutier to the Roman Congregation, in Natchitoches Parish Records, Donation, Book 6 Misc., Doc. 142; Germaine Portré-Bobinski and Clara Mildred Smith, *Natchitoches: The Up-to-Date Oldest Town in Louisiana* (New Orleans, 1936), 206; *Journal of the Senate of the State of Louisiana*, 1825, pp. 55–60. Numerous documents in the DeBlieux Collection represent sales of lots in Cloutierville which were made by Cloutier in the 1820s; all refer to the various streets laid out on the plat filed with the parish clerk. This plat is no longer extant.

seat and had good roads, saw no need to be split from the mother parish. Moreover, they already had been taxed for the construction of the parish buildings at Natchitoches and were not eager to be taxed again for the construction of similar buildings in a new parish.[40]

Within three weeks of Bossier's move, a protest petition from the citizens of Isle Brevelle, both white and nonwhite, was presented to the legislature. Bossier, who strongly favored the division, attempted to render the petition impotent by declaring to his colleagues:

> This document, which your committee are at a loss to know by which name to qualify, is signed by twenty-odd persons, the majority of whom . . . [are] free men of colour and other persons having no political rights.
>
> Your committee will forbear making any commentary on the disrespectful terms of this address to the first body politic of this state, nay they will acknowledge that they have given to it all the weight that could have been attached to a petition of our constituents drafted in proper language.[41]

In reporting legislative proceedings, one publication, the *Commercial Journal,* repeated Bossier's identification of the signers of the petition as "free men of colour and other persons having no political rights." Moreover, the *Journal* editorialized strongly against the "disrespectful and menacing" action that this class had taken against the legislative body. This chastisement, which placed a blanket indictment upon the white signers of the petition and unfairly criticized the men of color who did have the legal right of petition, did not go unnoticed by the population of Isle Brevelle. A lengthy letter appeared in the *Natchitoches Courier* in response to this editorial, signed simply "An Inhabitant of Isle Brevelle."[42]

The author of this response "respectfully" pointed out that the signers represented members of both races who possessed "the largest share of taxable property" in the proposed parish and who would therefore shoulder the burden of the expenses for the institutions of the new parish, just as they had been taxed to pay for the buildings of the existing one. "Such a division," the writer claimed, "would be injurious to their interests, and . . . it was only

40. *Journal of the House of the State of Louisiana,* 1827, p. 49; *Natchitoches Courier,* March 13, 1826.
41. *Journal of the Senate of the State of Louisiana,* 1826, 61–62.
42. *Natchitoches Courier,* March 13, 1826.

prayed for by some intriguing persons with the only view of increasing their fortunes."[43]

Those who desired the parish division, the author further asserted, were proclaiming that the desires of the free people of color on Isle Brevelle did not matter since they had no political rights. Yet, the author alleged, these same people had "employed fraud" to obtain the signatures of the people of color on the original petitions for the division. Now that the free people of color had ample opportunity to consider the serious ramifications of the move and had expressed explicit opposition to it, their rights were being challenged by the same people who previously had courted their support. The people of color were "to be taxed, and to pay without being consulted or daring to say a word."

In closing, the writer of the protest asserted that the signers of the controversial petition opposing the new parish represented "the *unanimous* wish of the taxable part of its population," both whites and free people of color, and that they had "used the language which free men have the right to use, whenever they think they are about to be wronged by an arbitrary and oppressive measure."[44]

The following month another sharp criticism of Bossier's conduct in the senate appeared in the *Courier*. This writer, also from Isle Brevelle, accused Bossier of numerous misrepresentations in the issue. The senator's statement that the petition contained only about twenty-odd signatures, "the majority of which were those of free men of color, enjoying no political rights," was again challenged. There were, in fact, forty signatures in all, and these forty represented all of the taxable inhabitants of the Isle, except for three men who were absent at the time. Only fourteen of the forty were actually free men of color, and all fourteen were described as "heads of families, and respected for their morality, good conduct, and industry, most of them paying very heavy taxes and to whom, although they do not enjoy political rights, we cannot contest that of petitioning." The writer further asserted that the Natchitoches commissioners appointed by the senate the previous year to study the division had not been convened and that one member of the committee, a resident of

---

43. *Ibid.*
44. *Ibid.;* italics in original.

Rapides, had issued an opinion in their names, a fact which Bossier allegedly attempted to conceal. The senator had, in short, "betrayed the interests of his constituents" on Isle Brevelle.[45]

A weak rebuttal by Bossier sparked another sharp criticism from the author of the first letter.[46] Finally, three months after the submission of the "disrespectful" petition, thirty-nine of its signers submitted to the *Courier* an open letter to Bossier that was filled with glowing praise but plainly reeked of "disrespectful" sarcasm:

> To what extent, illustrious Senator, are we not indebted to you, for the zeal with which you have defended our rights in a question somewhat delicate, which has lately been agitated in the Senate. . . . What a display of thanks do we not owe you for the friendly advice . . . on the course we ought to pursue, considering our color and our little weight in the political balance. Infatuated as we were . . . we might perhaps have persisted in our folly, with pretensions even to the right of Petition, a right proscribed, and granted even only to characters of influence. . . . We even found ourselves in spite of our prompt repentance, at the threshold of being dragged from our firesides, filed off in detachments, handcuffed . . . and paraded with all the display of criminal misdemeanor. . . . In this critical moment who has saved us? . . . Whose generous voice was heard in our behalf? . . . Come then worthy Representative of a people who are already covered with shame for having had the folly to dare and speak or even think for themselves, on a subject which interested them about which they have no right. . . . Come then and receive the recompense . . . of your fellow citizens of this county on the approaching occasion on which you demand only the right of continuing to extend toward us your fostering care and protection.[47]

The "approaching occasion" to which they referred was the upcoming senatorial election in which Bossier was running as an incumbent. The "recompense" given to Bossier on election day was a sound defeat. His subsequent contest of the election results was quickly squelched.[48] The parish division proposal had lost its staunchest supporter in the legislature. Moreover, a resident of upper Isle Brevelle won a seat in that same election. Not only was he an opponent of the division, but he, Benjamin Metoyer, was also

45. *Ibid.*, April 17, 1826.
46. *Ibid.*, May 1, 1826, and May 8, 1826.
47. *Ibid.*, May 22, 1826.
48. *Journal of the Senate of the State of Louisiana,* 1827, pp. 3–4, 20–21.

the half brother of seven of those free men of color who signed the "disrespectful" petition.

Upon taking his seat in the house, Metoyer was appointed to a committee to study the division proposal. The majority opinion of this committee ruled against any parish division "without some evident necessity, as the expenses of the state are thereby necessarily increased." Since the proposed division also "would be equally injurious to those who petition for, and to those who oppose it," the committee recommended its rejection. Their recommendation was adopted by the house, and the proposal was subsequently dropped by the senate as well.[49]

The people of Isle Brevelle, working hand in hand with their white friends and neighbors, had won a smashing political victory. Could they have done it alone without the aid of the white citizens? Probably not. Since they were opposing the interests of the political leader of their parish, they would have been branded by him as troublemakers with no political power. On the other hand, it is also doubtful that the whites could have succeeded in this issue without the free men of color, since their support enabled the whites to set forth their position as representative of the unanimous wish of the taxpaying citizens of the area involved. The people of Isle Brevelle, in short, held the balance of political power in this issue.

The details of this case clearly illustrate the nebulous political status accorded these free people of color. Their initial support of the position favored by those in power was not merely accepted but actively (and apparently fraudulently) sought. When they turned their support against those in power, the banner of white supremacy was waved and "disrespect for authority" was raised as a battle cry to turn public opinion against their efforts to defend their rights.

Throughout the antebellum South, one of the most crucial issues of race relations was the allegiance of the free nonwhite. Did his sympathies lie with the whites who allowed him freedom or with the bondsmen who shared his racial heritage? Would he encourage his "blood brothers" to revolt and seize freedom for themselves, or would he align himself with white slaveowners to

---

49. *Journal of the House of the State of Louisiana*, 1827, p. 49; *Natchitoches Courier*, February 27, 1827.

protect the institution of slavery? In general, the southern slaveowner held grave doubts over the loyalty of free nonwhites to the current social and economic system; because of these doubts, the "freedom" of the free nonwhite was curtailed severely. Only in Louisiana did there exist a sizable population who believed in an affinity between all free men regardless of color, and the black code which the white Creoles enforced reflected that basic trust.

The people of Isle Brevelle were typical of most free nonwhites in Louisiana in the sense that a large percentage of white "blood" flowed in their veins. Of the 17,462 free nonwhites in Louisiana in 1850, only 20 percent were of pure African heritage; 80 percent bore some degree of white ancestry.[50] The problem of racial affinity undoubtedly caused inner conflict for many of these people. As James Hugo Johnston succinctly points out, "Problems of racial relations are exceedingly complex, but there can be no more intricate problem than that of the relation of the mulatto to the two races whose blood, in varying proportions, united in his veins."[51]

For the people of Isle Brevelle, as with many Louisiana Creoles of color, the conflict was not only racial but class-oriented as well. Occupations, incomes, education, and even religion were important considerations in each man's determination of personal allegiance. Inevitably, for the people of the colony and many of their counterparts these various factors ruled out any ideological affiliations with blacks or slaves. As Johnston further observes, "Some of these people, possessing so much more of white than of Negro blood and with traditions that separated them from the Negro, could not think of themselves as part of the Negro race. With their inheritance and in their peculiar environment, they developed caste attitudes that were very strong and that seem to explain some of the seeming contradictions in Negro life."[52]

In the earliest years of the colony, when the original Metoyer siblings were growing to maturity, a considerable degree of social interaction existed between them and all other people of color—black, part-black, and Indian, free and slave. A measurable degree of African heritage was evident in their actions and their culture. As the social and economic status of the colony progressed, however, an inevitable chasm appeared, irrevocably severing the

50. DeBow, *Statistical View of the United States,* 83.
51. Johnston, *Race Relations,* 298.
52. *Ibid.,* 296.

colony from propertyless or low-income blacks and from the socially and culturally inferior slaves of all shades. Ultimately, the last vestiges of their African heritage disappeared from their culture and their life style. In short, the evolution of the colony precisely followed the pattern theorized by Melville J. Herskovitz: "Culture-change differs in degree and intensity with the socio-economic position of the individuals that make up a given Afroamerican society." The various subcultures that Herskovitz examined displayed the same characteristics as those on Isle Brevelle: Africanisms disappeared from the social framework of those subcultures as their position as a whole in American society increased.[53]

The cultural rift between the third-caste society of Isle Brevelle and the black/slave society that they left behind them was evident in all aspects of their lives—in their religion, their economic pursuits, and their social activities. As previously pointed out, African religious practices were not tolerated. The Roman Catholicism professed by white Creoles was the *only* religion which was acceptable to the colony. In the conduct of their business affairs, the people allied themselves with whites, as business partners, as sureties, as lessees and lessors. *Only* in the earliest years of the colony did any of the people work with free blacks in any economic enterprise, and even in this period such contacts were rare.

The most obvious cleavage between Cane River's *gens de couleur libre* and area free blacks or slaves occurred in the social arena. Dancing, for example, was a pastime in which all classes of Creole society reveled—the French, the African, the free man, and the slave. The *style* of dancing was the differentiating factor between the classes. "In Louisiana," one nineteenth-century observer recorded, "the slaves have Sunday for a day of recreation, and upon many plantations they dance for several hours during the afternoon. . . . The general movement is in what they call the Congo dance."[54] The Isle Brevelle plantations were no exception, but for the African descendants who lived in the manor houses, the style of movement was decidedly French; the quadrille waltz and the *fais do-do* replaced the Congo dance.

---

53. Herskovits, *The New World Negro,* 77.
54. Isaac Holmes, *An Account of the United States of America* (London, 1823), quoted in Blassingame, *The Slave Community,* 32.

The rigid barrier between the classes of nonwhites on Isle Brevelle was most evident at the matrimonial altar. In contrast to situations which existed elsewhere, no instance appeared throughout the history of the colony in which a Cane River Creole of color was wed to either a black or a slave. Both represented castes that were culturally, socially, and economically inferior, and marriage beneath one's caste was a taboo that none of them dared to breach in this period.[55]

Numerous studies of Louisiana's *gens de couleur libre* have discussed the social stratification based upon percentage of white "blood" that often characterized this society. H. E. Sterkx, for example, holds that "the Griffe looked down upon the pure Negro; the Mulatto regarded the Griffe as inferior and in turn was spurned by the Quadroon; while the Octoroon refused any or little social intercourse with those ethnically below himself."[56] Such social stratification would have been possible in such metropolitan areas as New Orleans, which possessed a very large free nonwhite population. In a community such as Isle Brevelle, however, these arbitrary social levels and the resulting ostracism or acceptance of individuals at each level would have been impossible for a number of reasons. The limited size of the population and the interdependence of the people for economic security and social identity were inescapable factors; indeed, the very fact that all of them bore close and often complicated blood relationships forestalled any such stratification.

The social hierarchy which existed on Isle Brevelle, if indeed it could be termed such, was considerably more subtle and was based not upon shades of skin as much as upon the number of years which an individual was removed from slavery. The attitude was not an uncommon one, as Degler reminds us: "Just as the white of threatened status may trace his lineage to the Mayflower and seek refuge in the Daughters or Sons of the American Revolution, so the Negro may boast that his family were freed Negroes earlier than others were, or that his parents 'had money.'"[57] This concept, in essence, was the basis for whatever social discrimination existed in the colony.[58]

---

55. After the Civil War, this attitude did gradually, but slowly, change. Saxon recounts one revealing Cane River song about a postwar father whose daughter had brought "disgrace" upon him; this song ended with the refrain: "I wouldn't mind the fellow if his skin was yellow, but Mary's run away with a coon." Saxon, *Children of Strangers*, 47.

56. Sterkx, *The Free Negro in Ante-Bellum Louisiana*, 247.

57. Degler, *Neither Black Nor White*, 168.

58. In the post-Civil War period, when all men of color suddenly became free and allegedly

The exclusivity of the colony in its intercourse with other nonwhites definitely limited its social scope, since by law and custom the *gens de couleur libre* were prohibited from seeking social equality with whites. Still, in many respects the dictates of law and custom were bent frequently by Creoles, white and colored, who found bonds in spite of their varying shades of skin.

The degree of friendship which existed between whites and members of the colony can only be measured in relative terms. The most prominent study of Louisiana's Creoles of color concludes that their social status was "just above the slave level." Both legislation and custom in the Creole state "specifically relegated the free Negroes within its borders to an inferior social status and were based primarily upon the idea that such persons were never and could never be equal to White persons just because of their Negro ancestry."[59]

In general, the social intercourse between races that was discussed by the above study, and most others, took place in four areas: gaming, male sports, the quadroon balls of New Orleans, and concubinages. Desegregation in these areas was not tantamount to acceptability in the eyes of all white Creoles, however. The subtleties involved in the white code of behavior guarding such social congresses were explicitly revealed in 1857 by a New Orleans Creole who served in the state senate. "If out on a hunt," he swore to his colleagues, "he might set and take refreshments at a free colored man's table, he would never shake hands with one of them because there was social contagion at the touch."[60]

Social intercourse between the whites of Natchitoches Parish and the free people of color on Cane River does not appear to have been as restrictive or as ambiguous as this observation would indicate. At all stages of the colony's development, numerous records exist which reflect a cordial interchange and mutual acceptance between them and *certain* whites of their area.

"equal," this conceptual discrimination became even more pronounced. Deprived of their former wealth and status, the colony prided itself—and justified the continuance of its social superiority—upon this factor alone. Indeed, more than one twentieth-century descendant of the colony uses this one standard as the discriminating factor between their people and members of the black or Negro race. A black or Negro in essence, is considered to be one whose ancestors were freed by the Emancipation Proclamation, whereas the colony, and their counterparts in other areas, were *gens de couleur libre*—free, wealthy, property owners and slave owners in the antebellum society. For a detailed examination of this social concept within the colony, see Woods, *Marginality and Identity,* especially pages 53–54, 61, 198–226.

59. Sterkx, *The Free Negro in Ante-Bellum Louisiana,* 240, 283.
60. *Ibid.,* 246.

The registers of the church provide the bulk of the available records reflecting the social relations between the colony and their white neighbors. When Dominique and Marguerite Metoyer took their eldest son into the post for baptism in 1797, the friends who accompanied them to act as sponsors for the child were Jean Baptiste LeComte, a prominent white youth of the Rivière aux Cannes area below the Isle, and Marie Françoise Himel, a young French and German Creole who lived near Marie Thérèze's first homeplace.[61] When Dominique's brother Joseph married Pelagie LeCourt in 1801, his best man was Antoine Himel, and a young white lady of the neighborhood, Mlle. Frederick, was the bride's maid of honor.[62]

When Louis Metoyer married Marie Thérèze LeComte, an Indian, that same year, his best man was a white named Julien Besson; the bride's brother stood for her.[63] In 1836 when Eloy LeCourt, another youth of French-Indian extraction, married Marie Celine Metoyer, daughter of Dominique, one of the witnesses who signed the church registers was Charles LeRoy, the white schoolteacher on the Isle.[64] When François Florival Metoyer married Marie Thérèse Aspasie Prudhomme in 1841, the official witnesses at the wedding included one of the most prominent planters of the parish, Jean Baptiste Prudhomme, Jr.[65]

By the same token, when two white residents of the Isle Brevelle area, Emanuel Brevel and Marie Clarisse Chelettre, married in the Chapel of St. Augustine, witnesses were the groom's father, Balthazar Brevel, and two Creoles *de couleur,* Jerome Sarpy, Jr., and Pierre Metoyer.[66] The marriage of Étienne LaCaze and Caroline LeMoine, white, was also performed in the chapel, and official witnesses were Louis Monette and Cesaire LeCourt of the Cane River colony.[67] These instances cited represent only a small percentage

61. Baptism of male infant of Dominique and Marguerite, [illegible] 29, 1797, in Natchitoches Registers, Book 4-B.
62. June 1, 1801, *ibid.,* 108.
63. June 9, 1801, *ibid.*
64. January 16, 1836, *ibid.,* Book 8.
65. February 3, 1841, *ibid.,* Book 12. According to tradition, the men of this white Creole family were particularly close to the Metoyer colony. Church and civil records seem to bear out the tradition.
66. March 13, 1838, Natchitoches Registers, Book 12, p. 392.
67. July 23, 1829, *ibid.,* Book 11.

of such occasions in which the white and nonwhite Creoles of the area stood for each other in the reception of the sacraments.

The legal records of the parish contain a limited number of references to fraternization between the colony and whites of their area. Most of these records, naturally, pertain to the handful of interracial concubinages which existed, since this form of fraternization was the most likely to bring legal recriminations. However, a few indirect references to other types of social intercourse are recorded. For example, while testifying in a case before the district court in 1835, Manuel Llorens recalled a fishing party he had attended in 1818 in company with Augustin Metoyer and "seventy or eighty others."[68] Llorens did not indicate whether the other participants were white or free men of color, but it is obvious that a large number must have been white since the free nonwhite population of the area hardly could have mustered so many men at that time.

Other legal records of the parish reflect situations in which honest friendships obviously existed between members of the two castes, a friendship that may or may not have included fraternization. For example, in 1840 when Auguste Metoyer was in serious financial difficulty, he received the following letter from a white resident of the Cloutierville area:[69]

Rivière aux Cannes
May 10, 1840

Mr. Auguste Augustin Metoyer

I received your letter of yesterday, in which you ask me to join you to go to the Post tomorrow. It is impossible for me to make the trip at this time . . . [to] help in the arrangement of your affair with Baptiste Adlé. I am inclined as much as possible towards your arrangement and because of this I make you the offer of making a $3,000 payment on the property you sold me. For a long time I have been in torment over this affair, it is of importance that we end it.

Your very devoted
p^{re} LaCour

---

68. *Roubieu* v. *Metoyer*.

69. Henry Clement Papers, Henry Collection. Since a number of the people descended from a family of white LeCourts/LaCours, who openly acknowledged the relationship, it should be noted that the Pierre LaCour in the record above did *not* belong to the same LaCour family that spawned the people of the colony and that no blood ties fostered his friendship with Auguste Metoyer. Three distinct families of the surname LaCour/LeCourt, from three distant areas of France, were among the settlers of early Natchitoches.

Another incident reflecting friendship between the colony and their white neighbors occurred in 1838 when seventy-year-old Marie Suzanne Metoyer became ill and the doctor prescribed leeches. A white neighbor, Narcisse Prudhomme, rode into Natchitoches to purchase them from a local drug firm and paid for them out of his pocket. He was, of course, reimbursed later by the administrator of Suzanne's estate.[70]

Family tradition within the colony holds that there was a great deal of fraternization between the males in the colony and white Creole males of equal standing, particularly the wealthy planters of the Côte Joyeuse. Dining, card-playing, hunting, fishing, and horseracing are the most commonly mentioned forms of "socializing" that occurred.[71] One Creole of color, Emanuel Dupre, was later described by his daughter-in-law, Sidalise Sarpy Dupre, as having "nothing but white friends," with the exception of his business partner, Dubreuil.[72] Tradition also holds that the white males not only visited in the homes of the people of the Isle, but that the males of the colony were welcomed in the white homes during the antebellum period.[73]

The one contemporary travel account which specifically mentions the colony quotes various white citizens of the area who were on friendly terms with the people and were familiar with their hospitality. None were identified by name and the hospitality was spoken of only in general terms; few details regarding the nature or extent of the social intercourse with the colony were provided. Other information given by this traveler, however, indicated that the Metoyers generally exercised a considerable degree of prudence and selectivity in fraternizing with whites.[74]

In general, the degree of "acceptability" and social status which the people of Isle Brevelle enjoyed, or the degree of racism to which they were subjected, depended upon the element of society that was judging them. Those whites who did not know them well, or who possessed preconceived ideas regarding the inferiority of the "mongrelized race" of half-caste people, were prone to indict them. Not uncommon were such broad generalizations as that

70. Succession of Marie Suzanne Metoyer, Natchitoches Parish Records, No. 355.
71. Interview with confidential source, April 26, 1974.
72. Mrs. Coutii to author, June 5, 1974.
73. Interview with confidential source, April 20, 1974.
74. Olmsted, *Journey in the Seaboard Slave States,* 636.

expressed by that champion of white supremacy, Timothy Flint: "The mulatto or free born negro as a rule was worthless or in other words he was too lazy to work for himself. The facts are the mixture then as to-day produced a race unfitted or incapacitated to do hard work of any kind. Many of them would marry a slave, and would work with his wife as one, but they were always tractable and peaceably inclined, and yet when freedom came to them all they developed the meanest traits of both races."[75] Some whites who did now the people, who perhaps envied them their prosperity and culture and were disdained as "poor white trash" by the colony, in turn disdained the people of color. Some wealthy whites who were, perhaps, self-made men, *nouveau riche,* and unsure of their own social standing, were apparently ambivalent, friendly as long as their interests did not conflict.

An evaluation of the background of people whom the records and tradition hold to have been true friends of the colony reveal that they fall into two general categories. First, there was the small planter, content with his lot and holding no envy toward those who possessed more, basically charitable and willing to recognize the good in all men. On the other hand, there was the wealthy planter, aristocratic although his ancestors might not have been, financially and culturally equal (and sometimes superior) to the people of the colony, and confident of his own social standing. It was this type of Creole who informed Olmsted that the people were "honest, and industrious, and paid their debts quite as punctually as the white planters and [are] . . . good citizens in all respects."[76]

The role of the free man of color in antebellum society was indeed a tenuous one. In most states, men of this class were looked upon as a "pariah group." In Louisiana, they were more or less tolerated by the "American" element, and it is doubtful that even this marginal toleration would have existed had it not been for the fact that so many of the white Creoles felt a closer affinity with the Catholic, French-speaking *gens de couleur libre* than

75. James T. Flint, "Reminiscences of the Long Ago" (MS in Henry Collection), 2. Flint also categorically stated that there existed but one exception to the observations made above: Carroll Jones of Rapides Parish. After being devastated by the Civil War, Jones settled on Isle Brevelle, converted to Catholicism, rebuilt his fortunes, and soon became one of the most prominent men in the Cane River colony. *Biographical and Historical Memoirs of Northwest Louisiana,* 353; interview with Mrs. Coutii, March 24, 1974; interview with confidential source, April 26, 1974.

76. Olmsted, *Journey in the Seaboard Slave States,* 634.

they did with the English-speaking Protestant migrants from the "American" states. Moreover, the affinity of the white Creoles for the Creole of color was generally returned in kind, and therein lay the basis for most of the privileges allowed the Louisiana nonwhite.

Johnston has evaluated the singular role of the free nonwhite in American society very precisely: "The free mulatto found himself in a peculiar and intricate environment. His happiness and success depended upon his ability to adjust himself to his environment. Had he failed to adjust himself to the intricate social system that surrounded him, he would have been driven from the slave country. The fact that so many of these people prospered in spite of the complications of their lives must be regarded as proof of their individual worth." [77]

The free man of color on Isle Brevelle very adeptly "adjusted himself to his environment." The initial liberality of colonial Louisiana and the reluctance of white Creoles to change their system provided the *gens de couleur libre* on the Isle with privileges that their counterparts in other states did not enjoy. The colony used these privileges, and their accompanying quasi-citizenship, to full advantage. Their astute business judgment earned for them economic equality, and the education and culture which they acquired proved to be the entry to a limited degree of social parity between the men of the colony and well-to-do whites.

The wealth which reinforced their civil status also divorced the colony from the vast majority of Americans who shared their African heritage. Tenuous bonds of blood were irrevocably broken by diverging cultural patterns. Sharp variances in economic progress delineated contrasting courses of behavior. The people of Isle Brevelle certainly did not fit the Sambo image which many people entertain of the antebellum free man of color. Relatively independent, economically speaking, the Cane River Creole could afford to adopt aloofness and reserve as a part of his character. There was no financial necessity to efface himself for the sake of harmony with the dominant society on which the poorer man was dependent for his livelihood.

77. Johnston, *Race Relations*, 312.

Most significantly, the people of Isle Brevelle were concerned with their political rights and kept abreast of legislation which affected them.[78] If any white attempted to take advantage of them, they knew their ground and stood it. If the white then took them to court over the issue, they hired counsel and fully defended themselves. Likewise, if any white infringed upon their rights, they had no qualms about filing suit against that white and trusting the outcome to the judgment of a white jury. Clearly, however limited their citizenship may have been, the Cane River Creoles used it to full advantage.

78. For example, one of the books preserved by a descendant of the colony is a well-worn copy of *Civil Code of Louisiana* (Baton Rouge, 1832).

Chapter NINE

Economic and Social Decline

The economy of the Cane River colony had grown steadily until the late 1830s, but at that point the trend reversed. The aggregate wealth of the colony did continue to increase until the Civil War, reflecting the growing population and the rising value of property, but the individual holdings in land and slaves, the most basic and most tangible capital investments they possessed, declined.

The colony contained 174 people in 1830; by 1860 its population had swelled to 411. In 1830 the colony owned 276 slaves; by 1850 the number had risen to 436, but in the decade that followed it declined to 379. While the total population increased 136 percent in the three decades between 1830 and 1860, aggregate slave holdings of the colony increased only 37 percent.[1]

Landholdings reflected a similar pattern. The federal censuses prior to 1850 did not indicate the size of farms, but an examination of land conveyances on file in the parish indicates that in the 1830s the colony's holdings fluctuated between 13,000 and 15,000 acres. By 1850 this figure had fallen to 12,615, and a decade later a larger population could claim only 7,736 acres.[2]

Despite the decline in land and slave holdings and the increase in population that occurred in the colony between 1830 and 1860, few of the families actually suffered economic hardship. On the contrary, the average Creole of color on Cane River was still a man of substantial means by any comparative standard. With relation to other free people of color, the average Cane River Creole was exceptionally wealthy. John Hope Franklin's study of free people

1. Fifth Census of the United States, 1830; Seventh Census of the United States, 1850, Slave Schedule; Eighth Census of the United States, 1860, Population and Slave Schedules.
2. Seventh Census of the United States, 1850, Agricultural Schedule; Eighth Census of the United States, 1860, Agricultural Schedule.

POPULATION AND SLAVE HOLDINGS OF THE COLONY
IN RATIO TO PARISH TOTALS, 1790–1860

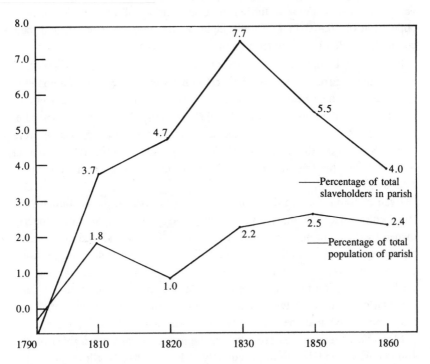

The relatively stable lower line represents the colony's total population in relation to the total population of the parish. In 1790, the colony constituted less than half of one percent of the area's population. By 1860, the colony's population was still only 2.4 percent of the parish total.

Offering sharp contrast, the upper line represents the colony's percentage of the total number of slaves owned in the parish. In 1790, the budding colony held no slaves. By 1830 they owned 7.7 percent of the parish's total, although they constituted a significantly smaller percentage of the total population. In 1860, despite three decades of declining wealth, the colony still possessed a disproportionately large percentage of the area's slave property.

of color in North Carolina indicates that the assessed per capita wealth of that class in 1860 was $34. By contrast, the per capita wealth in the Isle Brevelle colony, using the assessed valuation provided on the census schedule of that year, was $1,875. Franklin further indicates that out of a total free nonwhite population of 30,463 in 1860 only eight owned any slaves at all, and their cumulative holdings amounted to a mere twenty-five.[3]

In Sterkx's comprehensive study of Louisiana's free people of color, it is noted that the free nonwhites of Natchitoches were the wealthiest among the rural parishes, their wealth amounting to "over $750,000." The Metoyer colony possessed the bulk of this wealth; their property, in fact, was assessed at $770,545. By comparison, the free nonwhites of St. Landry Parish were worth $640,000, those in Point Coupée possessed property valued at $480,000, and the free men of color in Plaquemines were worth a combined total of $330,000.[4]

Even in comparison to the white Creoles of Louisiana, the declining Cane River colony made an impressive showing. The assessed value of the property owned by the eighty-nine families in the colony in 1860, $770,545, reflected an average estate of $8,658 per family. The parish and state averages were $4,399 and $2,074 per family, respectively. Despite three decades of gradual decline, on the eve of the Civil War the average family in the Cane River colony was worth twice as much as the average family in the parish and four times as much as the average family in the state.[5]

Moreover, the averages provided by the *assessed* valuations given on the 1860 census schedules do not accurately reflect the true worth of any of the individuals. The assessed valuations given in that year represented only 72 percent of the true valuation of that property; therefore, the true economic worth of the average Metoyer family was actually $12,025, and the true value of the colony's real and personal property was $1,070,201.[6]

In 1830, 82 percent of the families within the colony were landowners. By 1860 only 44 percent fell into that category. Still, the average family on Cane River fared better than the statewide average in a comparison of acreage

3. Franklin, *The Free Negro in North Carolina,* 17, 157, 159.
4. Sterkx, *The Free Negro in Ante-Bellum Louisiana,* 238.
5. Eighth Census of the United States, 1860, Population Schedule.
6. *Ibid.;* Francis A. Walker, *A Compendium of the Ninth Census* (Washington, 1872), 639.

owned. According to Sterkx, "the great majority" of free nonwhites in Louisiana were landless and were forced to earn their livelihood as farm laborers, whereas Roger W. Shugg asserts that three out of five families, white and nonwhite, in the state in that year owned no land at all. In fact, over half the landholdings in Louisiana, Shugg relates, were farms under fifty acres in size and over half the white inhabitants owned no slaves.[7]

In general, the decline which the colony experienced occurred mainly in two periods: the depression of the late 1830s and early 1840s and the years of Civil War and Reconstruction. Both were eras of general destitution in which men of all races suffered economic disaster. After both periods the stronger members of the white race were able to rebuild. The men of color, however, faced an entirely different situation.

The depression of the 1830s was not unforeseen by cautious men. Toward the end of the period of economic boom that dominated the 1820s and early 1830s, it was obvious that the nation was headed for difficulties. In January, 1837, a north Louisiana physician wrote: "Property have [*sic*] taken a very sudden rise here within the last year, caused principally by speculators from Vicksburg coming in to play the same wild game here they did there. Credit is buying everything. How it will end is yet to be determined."[8] In May he answered his own query:

> Every species of property has fallen. The bubble has burst and half the large Merchants in the world have failed and the Banks refused to pay specie.... Thousands are thrown out of employment and families want bread, which, with all the necessities of life, has risen to an enormouse price, and no money to buy with, or such as they have is paper depreciated & passing at from 15 to 25 percent discount.... even [this] is of no use ... unless it is the notes of the Pennsylvania U.S. Bank.... many farmers owning 100s of 1000s ... are without the means of buying the necessary food for their slaves and horses.[9]

The economic depression lingered for almost a decade in Louisiana. The spring of 1839 brought a drought; it was months before the planted seed could

7. Sterkx, *The Free Negro in Ante-Bellum Louisiana,* 217; Roger W. Shugg, *Origins of Class Struggle in Louisiana: A Social History of White Farmers and Laborers During Slavery and After, 1840–1875* (Baton Rouge, 1939), 8, 86.
8. McGuire Diary, 13.
9. *Ibid.,* 13–14.

germinate and crops were considerably short as a consequence. In 1840 the land on Cane River was inundated; the wake of the flood brought a drove of caterpillars that ate their way through half of the crops. By 1841 cotton was down to nine cents a pound and continued to decline. Mercantile houses were failing all over the state. By early 1842 most banks were dealing exclusively in specie, depreciating the paper currency issued by municipalities. By May of that year all but four banks in the state had gone broke. Many shared the sentiment of the physician who wailed: "Ruin appears before all who are in debt." True to his fears, hopes of economic recovery in Louisiana were dashed that year when the bud worm destroyed the cotton crops south of the Red River. By the summer of 1843, cotton was selling at a new low of four to six cents a pound.[10]

Through 1846 the economic woes of Louisiana's agricultural-based economy continued as the caterpillars, floods, and droughts took their turns on the crops.[11] In company with a large percentage of Louisiana's planters, the Cane River colony during the 1830s had dealt heavily in credit. They were no more prepared for the decade of disaster than were most other classes of Louisiana's society. All experienced economic problems, and some suffered financial ruin.

The records of the district court in this decade clearly show the economic disaster which Natchitoches Parish experienced. The number of suits rose sharply as planters without funds sued their debtors in hopes of raising money to pay their creditors. The two largest banks in the state, the City Bank of New Orleans and the Union Bank of New Orleans, both of which did extensive business with planters of Natchitoches Parish, filed 275 suits in the district court at Natchitoches during this period. Most of these were against planters of substantial means. Only three suits were against members of the colony: two against Auguste Metoyer and one against his brother Joseph.

The records of the court from 1837 through 1846 further show that members of the colony filed thirteen suits against people who owed them money and that they were, in turn, named defendants in thirty-three general lawsuits,

---

10. *Ibid.*, 19–27; James Hurst Letter.
11. James L. Watkins, *King Cotton: A Historical and Statistical Review, 1790 to 1908* (reprinted New York, 1969), 197.

most of which were for the recovery of debts. Twenty-three of these lawsuits were directed against four members of the colony, and two of these four, Auguste and Théophile Louis Metoyer, were practically destroyed by the resulting litigation.[12]

The difficulties faced by Auguste provide an interesting example of individual decline within the colony. This case by no means can be called average, but on the other hand it was not an isolated example. There were other individuals who were placed in a comparable situation. As already shown, Auguste was a merchant, the sole owner of one firm located on the Isle and a partner in another firm in New Orleans. He was also a planter, owning approximately two thousand acres in the area of the Cane and Little rivers. His financial judgment was respected. Various residents of the parish named him as administrator of their estates; others, including whites, gave him their powers of attorney to conduct their business for them. But he was overextended in his financial obligations at the time the depression began. The credit system under which he and countless others operated was the instrument of his defeat.

In January of 1837, when such concern was being expressed with the speculative prices of real estate, Auguste purchased a plantation from a white planter named Baptiste Adlé. For $50,000 he acquired approximately four hundred acres of land with the plantation home and its furnishings, farm buildings and improvements, and fifteen slaves. In payment, Auguste gave Adlé three secured notes, each for $16,666.66 payable May 1, 1837, March 31, 1838, and March 31, 1839. Auguste's cousin, Jean Baptiste Louis Metoyer, cosigned as surety. The nation's finances collapsed; Auguste did not meet even the first of his scheduled payments. Adlé promptly filed suit against Auguste and his cousin.[13]

In an effort to meet his obligations to Adlé and other creditors and to pay current plantation and business expenses, Auguste sold his land that was not mortaged—at depression prices. A plantation of 301 acres, for example, was

12. Index to the Records of the District Court, in Natchitoches Parish Records.

13. *Adlé* v. *Metoyer, ibid.*, District Court Record Book (Oct. 1830–April 1840), 399. When Auguste's financial difficulties began, his white partner in New Orleans, Antoine Jonan, severed their partnership and formed a new business alliance with a well-to-do white matron of that city. Yet, by 1842, Jonan was bankrupt also. Dissolution of Partnership of Antoine Jonan and Dame Blanchard, Morin Papers (MS in possession of Mrs. Noble Morin, Natchez, La); *Faures* v. *Metoyer,* 6 Rob. 75 (1843).

purchased by the white planter Lestan Prudhomme for only $377. Auguste's father, Augustin Metoyer, advanced him $23,031, but only $11,700 of the money thus raised went to Adlé. A series of writs of seizure were issued against Auguste at Adlé's instigation, but each time Auguste succeeded in obtaining delays. Finally, Adlé offered to buy back the $50,000 plantation for $18,200, and in May, 1843, Auguste accepted the offer. Approximately $20,000 still remained on the debt.[14]

Auguste's personal financial affairs were closely connected to those of his wife. As with most husbands of this period he controlled Melite's very sizable inheritance and dowry. In an effort to protect her interests from his creditors, Auguste deeded to her several pieces of property in December, 1843, and February, 1844, and Melite obtained the legal separation of her property from that of her husband. The remainder of Auguste's holdings were seized by Adlé. Auguste was left with nothing, but the debt still was not cleared.

The white planter's efforts to recover his losses from those allied with Auguste met with considerable difficulty. Adlé had won a judgment in his favor in the suit which he had filed against Auguste's surety, Jean Baptiste Louis Metoyer. However, Jean Baptiste Louis had died during the course of the litigation, and his heirs appealed the decision to the supreme court of the state. The decision of the lower court was reversed, and the heirs were declared not responsible for Auguste's debt.

In the meantime, Adlé had filed another suit against Mme. Auguste Metoyer and succeeded in obtaining the seizure and sale of the property which her husband had deeded to her. The supreme court also reversed this decision, in 1850, and ordered the return of the property.[15] Mme. Auguste then filed her own suit against Adlé for damages amounting to $19,440, which represented the rent on slaves and land, the value of a slave lost by death, the loss of crops and building materials, and the "value of a mansion house" removed from the land by Adlé. This suit was also taken to the supreme court, and the final ruling was in favor of Mme. Auguste.[16]

---

14. Auguste Metoyer to Lestan Prudhomme, Notarial Record Book 25, pp. 351–352; Augustin Metoyer to Children, Donations Book 30, p. 74; Auguste Metoyer to J. B. Adlé, Notarial Record Book 34, p. 199, all in Natchitoches Parish Records; *Adlé* v. *Metoyer,* 1 La. Ann. 254 (1846); *Adlé* v. *Anty,* 5 La. Ann. 631 (1850).

15. *Adlé* v. *Anty,* 5 La. Ann 631 (1850); *Adlé* v. *Metoyer,* 1 La. Ann. 254 (1846).

16. *Anty* v. *Adlé,* 9 La. Ann. 490 (1854).

The entire litigation left Auguste penniless, dependent entirely upon his wife's dowry and inheritance for his livelihood. By the time of his death in 1859 he had succeeded in rebuilding his personal estate only to $2,144. This sum, less estate expenses, was assigned to the heirs of Adlé in payment of the balance of the debt. No inheritance was left for his one daughter.[17]

The depression of the 1830s affected most of the other members of the colony, if to a lesser degree. Most of the suits filed against them represented small sums, such as the suit filed by A. Rivarde & Company, a brokerage firm of New Orleans, against Louis Dominique Metoyer in 1842. The brokers had carried forward a balance of $464 on Louis Dominique's account from the previous year and had advanced additional funds to make his crop in 1842. Interest on these sums brought the total due to $1,321. When poor agricultural conditions resulted in a short crop again that year and Louis Dominique sent only fifteen bales of cotton for sale, Rivarde & Company credited his account with the $567 which those bales brought in the depressed market and filed suit for the remaining balance.[18]

A much smaller suit was instigated against a less well-to-do member of the colony, young Charles Coton-Maïs. The court ruled in favor of the creditor and ordered the constable to collect the sum due or seize as much movable property as necessary to pay the $45.96 debt. The constable returned the writ of seizure to the court with a notation that he had served the notice and that the defendant had refused to pay, but that he had "not been able to find any movable property to seize."[19]

Many similar suits were filed against numerous citizens of the parish during this period. Some people, both poor and wealthy, planter and tradesman, were wiped out; but the majority managed to survive and began the task of rebuilding their estates. Most of the Cane River colony of Creoles of color also managed to survive the crisis without losing all that they owned, but none of them escaped without a significant reduction in their estates. Even those who held on to their land and slaves suffered the loss of savings.

For a variety of reasons, moreover, recovery of these losses was not as easy for the Creoles of color as it was for many of the whites. As noted by one

---

17. Succession of Auguste Metoyer, in Natchitoches Parish Records, No. 1015.
18. *Rivarde & Co.* v. *Metoyer, ibid.,* District Court Suit No. 3603.
19. Writ of seizure to William Cannon, constable, in DeBlieux Collection, No. 127.

Louisiana historian, nonwhite entrepreneurs "declined in number and prosperity [after] the 1830's—their's was a lost cause."[20] Nor was the situation in
Louisiana unique; Franklin reports the same situation in North Carolina and
concludes: "The remarkable decline . . . suggests the increasing economic and
political difficulty that the free Negro was encountering."[21]

Other major factors which prevented further economic expansion by the
colony were population increases and geographical confinement. As new generations grew to maturity and the older members of the colony died, original
holdings were divided and subdivided among the numerous progeny. The
description of the small tract owned by Emilie Kirkland in 1867 is suggestive
of the divisions that occurred: "one half of the four-fifth of the piece of a
certain tract of land."[22]

Moreover, the opportunities for the young to purchase additional land became increasingly slim. By the 1830s almost all of the land of any value was
in private hands. The only vacant lands which remained for sale by the government were the swamp and hill lands, most of which were considered
worthless.[23] As individual members of the colony fell into debt and their lands
were seized, a small percentage was purchased at the sheriff's auctions by
other members of the colony. Most of the seized lands, however, fell into the
hands of the creditors who held the mortgages.

People have faced similar situations throughout the course of American
history; and, as space became limited, they sought new lands in the West.
Many of the younger members of white families in Natchitoches followed that
practice, pushing into the unsettled areas of northwest Louisiana and crossing
the Sabine to settle in Texas. For the people of the colony, however, this
solution to their population explosion was not practical. Free men of color
enjoyed a position in Louisiana that few of their counterparts enjoyed elsewhere in the United States. To leave Louisiana for the newly opened lands in
Texas would have meant a loss of rights, a loss of status, and even more
limited opportunity. In fact, to leave Natchitoches Parish, where they were

20. Reinders, "The Free Negro in the New Orleans Economy," 285.
21. Franklin, *The Free Negro in North Carolina*, 161.
22. Natchitoches *Semi-Weekly Times*, March 2, 1867.
23. Olmsted, *Journey in the Seaboard Slave States*, 628.

known and respected, even to settle elsewhere in the state, would have resulted in the loss of much of their prestige.

It would be impossible to assess accurately the economic difficulties faced by the wealthy free people of color on Cane River without a comparison of the colony to the equally close-knit community of wealthy white planters on upper Cane River. These white planters suffered the same financial distress during the depression. The growth of their plantations was limited by the same geographical confinement. In the main, their youth did not migrate westward in search of better opportunities. Yet, these white families suffered no general decline such as that which characterized the colony of Creoles of color.

Apart from the obvious political and legal advantages which the white families enjoyed, there is one main factor which seems to provide the explanation for the diverging paths of two societies that up to this point had displayed strikingly similar patterns of economic development. For the most part, the white families produced a smaller number of offspring than did the Isle Brevelle colony of Creoles of color. Moreover, there were found among the whites several families of considerable wealth, and the progeny of these families habitually intermarried in order to consolidate and strengthen their families' fortunes.

On the other hand, the offspring of the original Metoyer siblings had almost no financial peers with whom they could marry. With but few exceptions the spouses whom they chose, although they were of similar racial background, were of significantly lower economic standing. Each new marriage to an individual outside of the colony produced a reduction in per capita wealth. To a large extent the colony indulged in the same inbreeding that their wealthy white friends practiced, but not consistently enough or soon enough to prevent the decline.

Still another factor which contributed to the decline of the colony was the transfer of Louisiana to American authority. The black codes were almost immediately revised to bring them more closely in line with American concepts, and they continued to be revised throughout the antebellum period. Every revision resulted in less freedom and less opportunity, economically, socially, and politically, for the free man of color.[24] The change in govern-

24. Sterkx, *The Free Negro in Ante-Bellum Louisiana,* 160–99.

ment also brought an influx of new settlers into the parish, rapidly depleting the supply of available land and closing in the borders of the Cane River colony.

The attitude of the colony toward the new government and the mutual suspicion between them and their new neighbors were also significant factors in the decline of the society. For many years the people did not believe that the new government would prove to be permanent. Their original mother country, France, had given them to Spain, but eventually she had taken them back. She next gave them to the United States, but it would be only a matter of time, they felt, before this transaction would be rescinded also. Consequently, these people displayed little eagerness to adapt to the conditions of American life. By the late antebellum period the younger members had acknowledged the necessity of learning the English language, but their common language and their culture remained French.[25]

Moreover, an element of distrust developed between the two cultures. Tradition relates that members of the colony had greeted the better class of Americans with the same friendliness that they had always exhibited toward the white Creole planters of the area and that they were pleased when this attitude was reciprocated. The colony learned too late, it is claimed, that the American white and the Creole white held different opinions of them and that the Americans were interested in their friendship only as long as they could profit from it.

At a friendly game of cards, for example, the Americans supposedly insisted upon high stakes. Those members of the colony who displayed more eagerness than skill at poker found that they had lost their property rather than the few dollars that they had cheerfully lost to the Creole whites.[26] Such legends are difficult to prove or disprove. Legal records did not usually indicate the reason a note or mortgage was given, but it is probable that at least a few incidences of American greed occurred, even if the extent of their prevalence cannot be determined.

As the ideological, cultural, and economic conflict between Creole and

25. Olmsted, *Journey in the Seaboard Slave States,* 634; interview with Mrs. Coutii, March 24, 1974.
26. Dunn, "Isle Brevelle;" interview with confidential source, April 26, 1974.

American societies increased in the state, the more "sensitive" free Creoles of color began to migrate. Most settled in France, including a few from the Isle. One or two of the Cane River Creoles are said to have settled in Canada and the island of Martinique.[27] In 1844, the *United States Magazine and Democratic Review* lauded the equal rights and status of the free man of color in Latin America and urged the American nonwhite to emigrate:

> In Mexico and in Central America, and in the vast regions still further south, the negro is already a free man—socially as well as politically the equal of the white. Nine tenths of the population there is made up of the colored races; the Generals, the Congressmen, the Presidents are of mixed blood.
>
> Let the emancipated negro find himself on the borders of Mexico and the States beyond, and his fate is no longer doubtful or gloomy. He is near the land of his fellows where equal rights and equal hopes await him and his offspring.[28]

Among those from the Isle who are said to have taken this advice and moved to Mexico in search of fortune and equality are Omar Chevalier and his wife Augusta Dupre. In Mexico Chevalier entered the shipping business, but his career was a short one. After the births of two children, Chevalier died; his young wife returned with the children to the Isle.[29]

The depression had dealt the colony its first severe blow and left it reeling throughout the 1840s. In the 1850s the general economy of the nation made a definite upswing, but Creoles of color hardly shared the rising prosperity. "The fifties," one Louisiana historian notes, "was a period of white hostility, restrictive laws, and declining economic opportunities" for the man of color. The gradual but continual decline of the Cane River colony was but a reflection of nationwide circumstances.[30]

The Civil War plummeted the people of the colony into complete economic, social, and political ruin. The eruption of the war undoubtedly presented their society with its greatest dilemma. A northern victory promised the people social and political equality; it also would eliminate their unique status

---

27. Reinders, "The Free Negro in the New Orleans Economy," 284; Mrs. Coutii to author, April 15, 1974.

28. "The Re-Annexation of Texas; in its Influence on the Duration of Slavery," *United States Magazine and Democratic Review*, XV (July, 1844), 14.

29. Interview with Mrs. Coutii, April 26, 1974.

30. Reinders, "The Free Negro in the New Orleans Economy," 285.

and might well contribute to their economic destruction. As a general rule, Louisiana's *gens de couleur libre* had always been known for their patriotism to their state;[31] but this patriotism undoubtedly reflected a degree of expediency since unpatriotic free people of color would have aroused the ire of the whites who lived around them.

Although the sympathies of a small portion of the Cane River population were later questioned, the colony publicly favored the Confederacy throughout the conflict. They deprived themselves and their families to help maintain Confederate forces. They volunteered their services for whatever uses the Confederacy had for them. They ultimately lost their slaves and suffered deprivations at the hands of the invading Union army. Their role in the war, in fact, differed only slightly from that of white Creole planters. Yet the war had a far greater adverse effect on them than it did on any other segment of Natchitoches society.

Cane River's population, white and nonwhite, entered the war in difficult circumstances. The drought of 1860 turned that year's corn crop into "a disastrous failure." One traveler in the parish noted on the eve of the war: "The planter's stock will show their ribs this season, for 'stock never fattens on bought corn,' especially when prices are at the figure that they are and will be hereabout."[32]

The outbreak of the conflict totally disrupted Louisiana's economy. The nature of the war, of course, proscribed the continued sale of southern cotton to northern factories. The New Orleans port was blockaded early in the struggle, thereby preventing the export of Louisiana's primary commodity to foreign markets. Increasing transportation problems resulted in shortages of food and other basic supplies.

In view of the blockade and the food shortages, the planters of Natchitoches were exhorted as early as 1862 to raise provisions rather than cotton. Not only was it necessary for each family to be self-sufficient, but its assistance was also demanded in providing food for the troops and for the wives and children left behind by the volunteer soldiers. Also, the sale of provisions would provide planters with sufficient cash to pay their taxes.[33]

31. John D. Winters, *The Civil War in Louisiana* (Baton Rouge, 1963), 34.
32. J. W. Dorr, "A Tourist's Description of Louisiana in 1860," *Louisiana Historical Quarterly*, XXI (October, 1938), 1170.
33. *Natchitoches Union,* November 21, 1861, and April 17, 1862.

Compliance with the exhortation was thwarted by natural disasters. By Christmas of 1862 the outlook was gloomy indeed in the parish. "The drought of last summer ruined crops," the Natchitoches newspaper reported. "Many have no corn to fatten hogs and thus have no meat. No money, but if they did, the price of everything is so high they could buy little."[34]

Despite the shortages that prevailed, the Cane River plantations still were called upon frequently to provide forage for the Confederate troops. Major General Richard Taylor noted in dispatches from the parish that he drew his forage from the families along the Cane.[35] General Alfred Mouton sent the Confederate officer Felix Pierre Poche into the area to find flour for his troops. In 1864, Confederate General Hamilton P. Bee was ordered to draw his provision from the plantations along the Cane River as long as his cavalry occupied the valley.[36] That same spring, a Union soldier commented that while the majority of the men in the Cane River area were away fighting the war, the women, children, and slaves were producing foodstuffs on their land to feed "large forces of the enemy."[37]

Whether this aid was given freely by the Cane River colony of Creoles of color is uncertain. While attempting to obtain reimbursement after the war for goods taken by the Union forces, several of the people were questioned as to the extent of their contributions to the "enemy." All claimants asserted then that they had not willingly aided the Confederacy. Gassion Metoyer, Jr., for example, claimed that the Rebels "took" seven or eight head of horses and mules and about ten head of cattle, in addition to corn and fodder. He was not paid for the animals, although he was occasionally reimbursed for the feed. In those cases in which the troops did not volunteer payment, he swore, he "dared not ask for payment." Enos Richmond, the special agent sent by the Southern Claims Commission to investigate the claims filed by the colony against the United States, reported: "It is true a few of the free Col'd men in this parish did aid the Confederates by contributions and service. But as for

34. *Ibid.*, December 18, 1862.

35. *War of the Rebellion: A Compilation of the Official Records of the Union and Confederate Armies* (130 vols; Washington, 1880–1901), Series I, XXXIV, 505, 561.

36. Bearss, E. C. (ed.), *A Louisiana Confederate: Diary of Felix Pierre Poché* (Natchitoches, 1972), 101; Richard Taylor, *Destruction and Reconstruction: Personal Experiences of the Late War* (New York, 1890), 181.

37. John Scott, *Story of the Thirty-Second Iowa Infantry Volunteers* (Nevada, Iowa, 1896), 127–28.

the claimants in this case they did nothing to aid the Confederates further than pay the tax in kind which was required by a Confederate levy."[38]

It would seem, however, that the records of the proceedings of such claims cases hardly provide an unbiased view of the people's loyalty. They suffered heavy losses at the hands of both governments. There was no hope of recovering any of the losses from the defunct Confederate States of America. When the victorious Union assumed control of Louisiana's administration, Union sympathies became politically expedient. Certainly, when the Union government agreed to reimburse "loyal" citizens for losses suffered, loyalty became an economic necessity for hard-pressed members of both races in the parish.

In addition to supplying forage and foodstuffs to the Confederacy, the colony also participated in state work programs. In October, 1862, a statewide order of the governor appeared in the Natchitoches newspaper directing planters to help harvest the crops of the families of the volunteers who needed assistance. It further stated that all men over forty-five years of age (and therefore exempted from military duty) must donate their labor and that of their slaves to build defenses on the rivers in Louisiana, especially the Red.[39]

In November of that year a specific order was issued to Natchitoches Parish by the governor to furnish 300 male slaves between the ages of eighteen and forty-five for work on the Red River defenses. Urgency was emphasized when the headquarters of the Western District at Alexandria requested that the police jury of Natchitoches "take immediate steps" to comply with this order. Among the sixteen prominent planters of the parish who sent slaves to labor on the Red River fortifications were four Metoyers of Isle Brevelle.[40]

At least four members of the colony personally worked on fortifications for the Confederacy. The Morin brothers—Charles Arnould, Charles Bajolia ("Bi-jo") and François ("Pasoose")—worked on defenses at Alexandria, while their brother-in-law, Gassion Metoyer, Jr., was sent to work at Shreveport. Charles Arnould labored for a month before paying $500 to A. H. Pierson, a Natchitoches attorney, to obtain his exemption so that he could return home and assist his widowed and aging mother in the operation of her

---

38. *Gassion Metoyer* v. *United States,* in Records of the Southern Claims Commission, Claim 43576.

39. *Natchitoches Union,* October 9, 1862.

40. *Ibid.,* November 27 and December 11, 1862.

plantation. Gassion Metoyer later stated that he worked at Shreveport for "a month or more" before being excused. There is no indication of the length of service of Charles Bajolia and François Morin, but it may be assumed that they served longer than their brother. The four individuals, naturally, swore later that they contributed their labor under duress and succeeded in convincing the agent of the Southern Claims Commission of the validity of this contention.[41]

One contribution to the war effort that appears to have been strictly voluntary was the donation of salt to be sent to the men who were working on the Red River defenses. A meeting was held at the Saline Salt Works north of Natchitoches to secure donations, and those who attended donated a total of 232 bushels. The local newspaper published a partial list of the donors, representing a contribution of 38 bushels, and at least three of the fifteen names on the list were free people of color.[42]

Louisiana's *gens de couleur libre* were not drafted into the regular Confederate army, or even accepted as volunteers, since the law prohibited them from regular military service. However, the people of Isle Brevelle, as did their New Orleans counterparts, organized military units during the Civil War. Sterkx noted the existence of one such unit in Natchitoches Parish, but in actuality there were two.[43] Both were organized early in the war and were composed, for the most part, of descendants of Marie Thérèze Coincoin.

A cavalry squadron, called the Augustin Guards, was organized under the direction of Henry Hertzog, a wealthy white planter of the Isle. The cavalry not only earned the praise of the white community for serving the area loyally and usefully but also for its ability on the drill field. An observer who attended one of its drills described the maneuvers:

> The squadron of cavalry, so skillfully trained by Dr. Burdin, was admirable in its uniformity and precision. The firm commands and good cadence of the captain, and the other officers; the intelligent enthusiasm exhibited by all the soldiers; the excellent horsemanship by the squadron; all contributed to amaze the public who had

41. *Suzette A. Morin, deceased* v. *United States,* and *Gassion Metoyer* v. *United States,* in Records of the Southern Claims Commission, Claims 13578 and 43576.

42. *Natchitoches Union,* December 11, 1862. Only the first initial is given for most of the names on this list, so it is impossible to determine whether some of the donors were free people of color or white.

43. Sterkx, *The Free Negro in Ante-Bellum Louisiana,* 213.

come to attend these maneuvers. For us who have often attended cavalry drills in Europe, we wonder how, in so little time, these men have been able to attain this degree of perfection.[44]

The Cane River infantry company of free people of color, called Monet's Guards, was composed of seventy-six men under the direction of Henry Hertzog's brother Hypolite, of Adolphe Prudhomme, and of other prominent white planters who were numbered among the friends of the colony. The drill performance of the infantry did not merit the same praise that the cavalry earned from the representative of the Natchitoches *Union* who viewed their exercises: "The company of infantry, newly formed, has need of practice, but we are convinced that having a little, their drills will be executed with as much precision as in the cavalry."[45] The infantry, apparently, did make a sincere effort toward improvement. When *Casey's Infantry Tactics for the Instruction, Exercise, and Manoeuvers* appeared on the market the following year, a copy was acquired by one member of the company.

The identities of only a few members of these units are known. Ambroise Sévère Dupre, the owner of *Casey's Infantry Tactics,* served in Monet's Guards. His father, Emanuel Dupre, was a member of the cavalry squadron. Other residents of the Isle who are said to have been members of one unit or the other were J. Emanuel Dupre, Jr., and his brothers Charles, Nelson, and Leandre, Vilfried Metoyer, Robert Llorens, Arnould Morin, Nemour Sarpy, Arnould Conant, and François Morin.[46] The men in both companies were required to furnish their own equipment, since Louisiana did not outfit the home guard units organized by *gens de couleur libre.*[47]

In congratulating the two companies, the Natchitoches *Union* observer expressed the opinion that they would make "excellent patrols at the coast and

44. *Natchitoches Union,* December 26, 1861, and May 1, 1862. The observer who praised the cavalry's performance so highly, editor Ernest Le Gendre, was an excellent critic. A French immigrant to Louisiana, Le Gendre had been exiled because of his military role in the Revolution of 1848. Such praise from so qualified an observer is noteworthy.
45. *Natchiotches Union,* December 26, 1861, and May 1, 1862.
46. Mrs. Coutii to author, April 15, 1974; interview with Mrs. Coutii, April 26, 1974. Sévère's copy of Casey's manual and Emanuel's cavalry sword are both owned today by Mrs. Coutii.
47. Winters, *Civil War in Louisiana,* 35.

contribute to maintaining the public tranquility."[48] The reference to the "coast" is not clear. It could have been used to refer to the Cane River area below Natchitoches which was commonly called the Côte Joyeuse or Joyous Coast. In view of later developments, however, the references could also have been to either the Gulf Coast or to the German Coast, which lay immediately above New Orleans.

In March, 1862, the police jury of Natchitoches appropriated six hundred dollars "to defray the expenses of the volunteers, and their families, composing the company of the free colored persons of this parish, going to New Orleans for the defence [sic] of that city." The money was to be given to Henry Hertzog, who apparently was to accompany them. In addition to the lump sum appropriated for expenses, each volunteer was to receive a twenty-five dollar bonus, which was only half the bonus given to white volunteers. By May 1, 1862, the unit still had not departed, but the Union noted that it was going to New Orleans soon to join the Native Guards under Colonel Felix Labutut.[49] It is not indicated whether these Natchitoches units had volunteered for state service or had been called by the state.

It appears that the two units from the Cane River colony did not reach New Orleans before it surrendered to the Union forces. However, the names of four men from the colony appeared on the rolls of the 1st Regiment of Native Guards at New Orleans: Paul Balthazar, Hypolite Metoyer, Jules Chevalier, and Firmin C. Christophe.[50] Apparently, these men had gone to New Orleans on their own initiative to join the guard unit there before the organization of those on the Isle.

Although the Augustin Guards and Monet's Guards saw no action against the enemy, they were allowed to take part in the military funeral of one of their white neighbors which was held in Cloutierville. Young Felix Chaler had died of typhoid fever at Maysville, Arkansas, in 1861, after distinguished service at the Battle of Oak Hill. Six months later his body was returned to the Isle. With two white companies of the parish, the two companies of free men of color met and escorted the body to the Church of St. Jean Baptiste for a

48. *Natchitoches Union*, December 26, 1861, and May 1, 1862.

49. *Ibid.*, March 27 and May 1, 1862.

50. Andrew B. Booth (comp.), *Records of Louisiana Confederate Soldiers and Louisiana Confederate Commands* (3 vols.; New Orleans, 1920), I, 113; II, 325, 332; III, 956.

funeral mass. Captains Pierre Brosset and J. Janin of the white companies each fired a farewell shot "into the grave of the hero." The two companies of *gens de couleur libre* then fired their salutes over the grave.[51]

Although some members of the colony later found it politically and economically expedient to portray themselves as Union sympathizers, their alleged sympathies did not prompt them to enlist in the Union army. A handful of free men of color from the parish and a large number of slaves joined the Union ranks in the spring of 1864 when the federal army swept through Natchitoches Parish, but no members of the Cane River colony are known to have been included in this number. The 1890 special census of Union veterans and widows enumerated a veteran called "Louis Metoyer alias Johnson" who had enlisted in March, 1864, and had served in the 4th U.S. Cavalry for two and a half years. Metoyer, or Johnson, in all probability, was a slave since there was no Louis Metoyer in the colony in 1864 of an appropriate age to see military service. Quite possibly, he was the same former slave who called himself "Henry Johnson Top of the Garden No. 9 Come to Town" and who, during the early twentieth century, was generally known in the area as a Union veteran.[52]

One member of the Cane River colony did provide a service to the Union cause, but the records disagree as to whether this service was voluntary or compulsory. In one of his depositions before the Southern Claims Commission, Charles Bajolia Morin testified: "In 1864, on the retreat of the army from Mansfield I voluntarily acted as a guide for the Union army, and piloted them by short cuts through the swamps to Cloutierville. The distance around by the main road was 19 miles and the way I took them it was about 9 miles. I was never paid for those services, never asked for any pay, was not compelled to do so, did so voluntarily." Yet, in another statement to the commission, Morin recounted the incident in a slightly different manner: "The federal

51. *Natchiotches Union,* January 9 and March 6, 1862.
52. 1890 Special Census; Hugh LaCour to author, March 5, 1974. According to LaCour, his maternal grandfather, Joseph Leonard Prudhomme, also fought on the Union side, but Prudhomme was not a member of the colony at that time. A distant relative of the people named Victor David is also reputed to have served, but David belonged to the Campti community of free people of color and did not settle in the Cane River colony until after the war.

troops took me as a guide on their way down to Alexandria, and turned me loose at Monette's Ferry."[53]

The Red River Campaign, which brought the Union troops into Natchitoches Parish, dealt the deathblow to the economy of the Cane River colony. As the invading Union forces pushed northward through the parish the army's line of march followed the course of the Cane River. As they retreated through the parish a month later, after the expedition's defeat at the battles of Mansfield and Pleasant Hill, they followed the same general course. The campaign failed, but not before the Cane River area was devastated completely.

It was the Confederates who initiated incendiarism on Cane River. Suspecting that the Federals had begun the campaign as cover for raiding the most lucrative cotton stores in Louisiana, the Confederate military leaders ordered the destruction of all cotton stored on every Natchitoches plantation before it could be seized by the enemy. Many gins and other buildings in which planters had stored their cotton were destroyed by the fire brigades. Not infrequently, sparks from the burning buildings ignited plantation homes as well.[54] One Confederate soldier who traveled the main road from the lower Isle to Natchitoches recorded in his diary that "the road all the way to Natchitoches . . . was a solid flame. My heart was filled with sadness at the sight of those lovely plantations in flames, and to see the work of honest industry and perseverance of those good old Creole planters destroyed in the twinkling of an eye."[55]

The Union army followed closely on the heels of the Confederates, and a large number of the northerners later commented on the state of affairs that they found along the Cane. One soldier observed that the troops "were like the Israelites of old, accompanied by a cloud (of smoke) by day, and a pillar of fire by night."[56] An officer later wrote: "No language which I can com-

---

53. *Suzette A. Morin, deceased,* v. *United States,* in Records of the Southern Claims Commission, Claim 13678.

54. Testimony of Lt. F. L. Grappe, C.S.A., *Charles C. Bertrand* v. *The United States,* in Records of the French and American Claims Commission (National Archives, Washington), Claim No. 345.

55. Bearss (ed.), *A Louisiana Confederate,* 102.

56. John A. Bering and Thomas Montgomery, *History of the Forty-Eighth Ohio Veterans Volunteer Infantry* (Hillsboro, Ohio, 1880), 129.

mand can convey to one not there an idea of the ruin and confusion that we saw.... I speak of *ruin* in connection with the planters' property, and of *confusion* in reference to the Negroes. The blacks followed us in droves... mounted on mules which they had stolen."[57] The "ruin" on which most of the northern soldiers did not comment, however, was that which their own forces committed. One of the few who did make reference to the matter reported that "orders were given to destroy all property which could not be carried."[58]

The Union rampage was extremely violent on the retreat down river. War has always brought plunder and destruction to the invaded, but the vindictiveness vented upon the Cane River valley shocked even the despoilers. Union General William B. Franklin was "mortified" at the behavior of his fellow soldiers; calling their behavior "disgraceful to the army of a civilized nation," he offered a $500 reward for evidence to convict the guilty parties. One federal soldier on the march later recalled the incidents with disgust and termed it "a lasting disgrace" to the Union command that committed the atrocities.[59]

A Confederate general who pursued the retreating Federals later wrote: "The destruction of this country by the enemy exceeds anything in history. For many miles every dwelling-house, every negro cabin, every cotton gin, every corn-crib, and even chicken-houses have been burned to the ground; every fence torn down and the fields torn up by the hoofs of horses and wheels of wagons.... In pursuit we passed the smoking ruins of homesteads by which stood weeping women and children. Time for the removal of the most necessary articles of furniture had been refused."[60] In his memoirs, Henry Watkins Allen, the Civil War governor of Louisiana, recollected that "along the river from above Campte to the [mouth of Cane River] . . . the enemy had taken or destroyed nearly every eatable thing, and what little they left, our own pursuing troops generally appropriated. Thus, those who had laid up abundant supplies for the season, suddenly found themselves deprived of their

---

57. John M. Gould, *History of the First-Tenth-Twenty-Ninth Maine Regiment* (Portland, 1871), 434.

58. Edward B. Lufkin, *History of the Thirteenth Maine Regiment* (Bridgton, Me., 1898), 87.

59. Pellet, *History of the 114th Regiment, N.Y.S.V.*, 229; Winters, *Civil War in Louisiana*, 365–66.

60. *Ibid.;* Taylor, *Destruction and Reconstruction*, 193.

last ear of corn and pound of bacon by one army or the other. Starvation literally stared this part of our population in the face." [61] In reviewing the specific situation of the *gens de couleur libre,* Governor Allen noted: "They have suffered heavily in the war, and, in many instances, have been made the special objects of brutal treatment by the enemy." [62] Governor Allen's assessment accurately applied to the colony. Although the people belonged to the nonwhite race for whose rights the North supposedly fought, they suffered the same devastation which was wrought upon the families of the white Confederate soldiers.

Many stories of the destruction wrought by Federal troops against the people of Isle Brevelle have been recounted by their descendants ever since the war. Dishes and household utensils were smashed, stolen, or scattered. Food was taken or thrown on the ground, even the milk for babies. Livestock was butchered or stolen, saddles and harnesses burned. Horses were appropriated, plantation machinery, buildings, and homes were destroyed, and many slaves were driven off or enticed away. Members of the colony buried their valuables, just as their white neighbors did. Some of the items, it is related, were buried in the cemetery and never recovered; jewelry inherited from Augustin, reputedly, was included among the valuables thus lost. One resident of Cane River, Barthelemy LeCour, saved his last barrel of syrup by rolling it three miles to hide it on Little River.

A portion of the Church of St. Augustine was destroyed, reportedly, as well as part of the "eleven room mansion house" of Emanuel and Marguerite Dupre. Even the portrait of Augustin did not escape the vindictiveness of northern troops. One officer, tradition holds, queried the descendant in whose home the portrait proudly hung: "Was he a slave owner?" When the Creole lady replied *"Oui, Monsieur,"* the officer drew his sword and slashed the portrait from top to bottom. [63]

---

61. Sarah A. Dorsey, *Recollections of Henry Watkins Allen* (New York, 1866), 279–80.
62. *Ibid.,* 382.
63. Callahan *et al., History of St. Augustine's Parish,* 27; interview with confidential source, April 26, 1974; interview with Tillman Chelettre, Sr., October 12, 1974; interview with Mrs. Coutii, March 24, 1974; Mrs. Coutii to author, April 15, 1974; Hugh LaCour to author, February 19, 1974. The portrait of Augustin remained damaged for a half century until the white proprietress of a former Metoyer plantation offered to have it repaired at her expense in exchange for the privilege of hanging it in one of her plantation homes.

Many of these traditions are borne out by existing records. In the claim filed with the French and American Claims Commission by a French citizen residing at Cloutierville, it was reported that the Union troops burned a ten-mile swath on the lower Cane, an area that was heavily populated by outlying members of the colony. The testimony further indicated that the first plantation burned after the troops left Cloutierville was that of a free man of color, L. G. Rachal, who lived two miles below the town. From the Rachal plantation to Monette's Ferry, only two plantations were spared. In a lawsuit between two white residents of the area that was prosecuted after the war, reference was made to the cotton gin of Louis Casimere Rachal, which also was burned during the Red River Campaign.[64] Yet, even though the members of the colony who lived in this area suffered extensive damages, none of them filed suit after the war for recovery of their losses.

There were, in all, thirty-six claims filed with the Southern Claims Commission by residents of Natchitoches Parish who reported they had been Union sympathizers. Only six of the applicants were members of the Cane River colony: Jerome Sarpy, Emilie Kirkland, the estate of Suzette A. Morin, Gassion Metoyer, Jr., and Jean Conant, acting for himself in one case and as guardian of the orphaned children of Auguste Predanes Metoyer in another.[65]

From these six claimants, the Union army allegedly took 40 horses, 16 mules, 141 beef and milk cows, 26 oxen, 16 hogs, 2 sheep, 320 fowl, 3,500 bushels of corn, over 400 bottles of wine, and 13,000 pounds of fodder. In addition, several wagons and sets of harnesses, saddles, chains, flour, sugar, lard, coffee, bacon, pickled beef, and blankets were carried away by Union troops. In making camp the soldiers destroyed fences and used over 4,000 cypress fence rails for firewood.[66]

Undoubtedly, the losses were exaggerated somewhat. The people knew, in all probabili:y, that the government would not pay them in full for all losses claimed. Since they expected a compromise, it is likely that they adjusted

64. *Bertrand* v. *United States; Dupleix* v. *Gallien,* 21 La. Ann. 534 (1869).
65. *Jerome Sarpy* v. *United States,* Claim 43582; *Emilie Kirkland* v. *United States,* Claim 41317; *Suzette A. Morin, deceased,* v. *United States,* Claim 13578; *Gassion Metoyer* v. *United States,* Claim 43576; *Jean Conant, Tutor for Annie Metoyer and Others* v. *United States,* Claim 43566; *Jean Conant* v. *United States,* Claim 43565, all in Records of the Southern Claims Commission.
66. *Ibid.*

their losses upwards. However, if they did do so, their claims probably still did not approach the full extent of their losses. Most accounts of the deprivations suffered by Cane River residents, documented and alleged, emphasized that the greater portion represented "useless and wanton destruction of valuable property" by straggling soldiers. Requests for compensation for this kind of depredation were not even accepted by the commission; it considered only claims for food and animals that were "officially" appropriated. The six claimants in the Cane River colony estimated that the "officially appropriated" goods were valued at $19,015. In 1877 the commission finally approved 41 percent of the damages sued for and authorized payments totaling $7,716 to the six claimants.[67]

In describing the destruction committed by the individual soldiers, Charles A. and Charles B. Morin informed the commission that half of their corn was wasted on the ground, trampled by animals, and "scattered through the country."[68] Soldiers slaughtered Jerome Sarpy's hogs in his yard, carried off the fat ones, and left the poorer ones in the yard to rot.[69] After the troops scattered Gassion Metoyer's animals, he and his stepson, Sylvestre Metoyer, "went all through the woods . . . and only found one cow."[70] They made no estimate of their total losses.

The main portion of the Isle Brevelle colony escaped the extreme devastation that was wrought upon their relatives who lived on the lower Cane below the Isle. The main road from Alexandria to Shreveport, which the Union forces took on their ascent through Natchitoches Parish, followed the course of the Cane through the heart of the colony. It was on this ascent that most of the depredations on the Isle occurred. By a stroke of fortune, or design, the central colony was spared the incendiarism that characterized the Union's retreat.

When the troops entered the area generally termed "the Isle," they enlisted the aid of Charles Bajolia Morin to guide them by way of shortcuts to Cloutierville. This route left the main road and bypassed many of the homes.

67. *Ibid.*, Beecher, *Record of the 114th Regiment, N.Y.S.V.*, 328; Pellet, *History of the 114th Regiment*, 225.

68. *Suzette A. Morin, deceased,* v. *United States,* and *Jerome Sarpy* v. *United States,* in Records of the Southern Claims Commission, Claims 13578 and 43582.

69. *Jerome Sarpy* v. *United States, ibid.,* Claim 43582.

70. *Gassion Metoyer* v. *United States, ibid.,* Claim 43576.

Whether Morin volunteered to show the troops the shortcuts out of loyalty or from an ulterior desire to protect his people's property, or whether he was actually pressed into service, cannot be determined. Nevertheless, Morin probably was to a great degree responsible for saving many of the homes on the upper Cane. If the troops had taken the main road, the homes and other plantation buildings on the Isle would undoubtedly have suffered the same fate as those on the lower Cane.

Of all the families in the colony, only six filed claims for damages. Certainly the other families suffered comparable losses. It is not likely that the thousands of soldiers who invaded the Isle singled out only a half dozen homes for pillage and forage. It is not clear from the records why the others did not also file claims. The only apparent explanation lies in the issue of loyalties. Indeed, loyalty seems to have been the most important factor in all of the claims cases.

Proof of sympathy for the Union cause was mandatory, but in all of the claims filed in Natchitoches Parish the usual "proof" offered was nothing more than the testimony of other alleged loyalists, the majority of whom also filed claims. Each of the six claimants from the Isle testified for each other, and in one case the testimonies of two white loyalists from Cloutierville were offered also. In the claim of Emilie Kirkland, Dr. S. O. Scruggs, the family physician, swore: "She was a colored woman, and I took it for granted that her sympathies were with the Union, as were all the free mulatoes [sic] in her neighborhood, they could not have been otherwise in as much as they were deprived of the rights of citizenship, and understood that the successful termination of the war, would guarantee to them both their civil and political rights. . . . All the mulatoes [sic] in what is called the Island were looked upon as in sympathy with the Union."[71] Gervais Fontenot, whose father-in-law, Baptiste Adlé, had fought a legal battle of many years' duration against Emilie's parents, Auguste and Melite Metoyer, testified also on Emilie's behalf. She and her deceased husband, George Kirkland, were loyal supporters of the Union cause, he swore, as were "all the colored in that neighborhood."[72]

---

71. *Emilie Kirkland* v. *United States, ibid.,* Claim 41317.
72. *Ibid.*

The proclaimed Union sympathies of the colony were accepted without reservation by the local special commissioner who had been appointed to take testimonies in these claims. Louis V. Marye, a French immigrant who had been a grocer in Natchitoches for many years before his retirement, reported: "There is very little doubt that all the colored population in the 'Isle Brevelle' settlement were loyal to the Union cause. They were educated and knew that the success of the Union cause would better their social position." [73] Enos Richmond, the special agent sent by the claims commission to make an unbiased report, was not as convinced of the people's loyalty. Noting that a few of them "did aid the Confederates by contributions and service," Richmond finally concluded that they appeared "to have been as loyal as the[y] could be in their situation." [74]

A review of the statements made in these cases reveals that Richmond did have some basis for his doubts. Charles A. Morin, for example, swore to his Union sympathies, but his testimony also revealed that he had attempted to hide his property from the Union forces. Believing that the Federals were approaching on the east bank of the river, he hastily drove his herd of cattle to the woods on the west bank. Upon reaching the other side Morin was greeted by another army unit, whereupon he "gladly" gave his cattle to the hungry soldiers. [75] Testifying on behalf of Widow Kirkland, F. Azenor Metoyer indicated that he, too, had suffered losses but had not filed a claim for damages because "he did not regret the loss of his slaves and other property . . . [as] he was fully compensated in the benefits he had received in the civil rights obtained and actually declined proving up his claims for these reasons, stating that he . . . willingly gave his property taken from him to the government." [76]

Azenor's testimony sharply illustrates the sentiments of the Isle Brevelle people. Its theme is the same theme that dominates all protestations of loyalty: the expectation that a Union victory would result in improved civil, social, and economic rights. The sincerity of such a hope cannot be doubted; consequently, each individual's loyalty undoubtedly was divided to some degree by the war. Most of the colony realized that a Union victory would mean the

---

73. *Ibid.*
74. *Suzette A. Morin* v. *United States, ibid.*, Claim 13578.
75. *Ibid.*
76. *Emilie Kirkland* v. *United States, ibid.*, Claim 41317.

complete destruction of their economy, the basis of their livelihood, and their special status as *gens de couleur libre*. On the other hand, this special status was still below that of whites, and the Union promise of equality was undoubtedly enticing. For the most part, the people appear to have favored the Confederacy, as tradition holds, but whatever despair they felt with defeat was undoubtedly tempered, initially, by the promise of a better life following the Union victory.

Such expectations were not fulfilled. The devastating war and the disappointing Reconstruction which followed constituted the main factors in their economic and social decline. In the decade after 1860 the value of individual holdings in the colony plummeted from $8,648 per family to a drastically lower $1,116. In 1860, the average worth per family was four times the state average, despite the economic decline that had already occurred in the colony, but by 1870 the average family worth had fallen to 28 percent below the state average of $1,602. The extent of the colony's decline becomes even more obvious when one considers the fact that the 1870 averages included thousands of former slave families that had little or nothing.[77]

Denied the use of slave labor, crippled by the loss of the sizable investment which this labor represented, struggling to survive in the turbulent economy produced by the war, and lacking capital with which to hire free labor, the people had no alternative but to return to the fields themselves. In 1870 there were three times as many farm laborers in the colony as there had been just ten years before. Total landholdings had fallen to 5,169 acres; 67 percent of the households owned no land at all. The total worth of the 121 families in the colony was assessed at $135,098.[78] Augustin alone had been worth more than that forty years earlier.

The most crushing blow of all was undoubtedly the realization that their economic sacrifice had been in vain. The improved status and equal rights to which Azenor Metoyer alluded were but fleeting and illusory benefits. For almost a dozen years following the close of the Civil War, Radical politicians held control of Louisiana's legislature and almost succeeded in destroying all legal distinctions between Louisiana's white and nonwhite residents. Non-

77. Eighth and Ninth Censuses of the United States, 1860–1870, Population and Agricultural Schedules.
78. *Ibid*.

whites were enfranchised, miscegenation laws were abolished, public schools for children of all races were ordered, and racial discrimination on public conveyances and in public facilities was forbidden.[79] Application of the letter of the law was not so easily enforced, however. Civil and political privileges in many instances, particularly in Natchitoches Parish, were only token.

The people of Isle Brevelle were among the first nonwhites in the parish who registered to vote.[80] Moreover, the leaders of the colony were active supporters of the National Republican Union Club. The role which they were allowed to play in this political organization, however, was only nominal. One public announcement of a meeting in 1867 provides a typical look at the composition of the club. Nine nonwhites, including eight from Isle Brevelle, were listed in attendance. Only one nonwhite, however, was identified as a committeeman, and all other positions of leadership, the major positions, were held by whites.[81]

Similarly, nonwhites in Natchitoches served in various capacities as minor public servants during the decade of Reconstruction, but their participation was by no means representative of their numbers. The census of 1870 enumerates 7,312 whites to 10,953 nonwhites in the parish. Yet, in the seven years between 1865 and 1871, inclusive, only four of the forty citizens elected to serve terms on the parish police jury were nonwhite. Only one, Theodore Monette, was actually a member of the Isle Brevelle colony.[82] Similar tokenism was evident in other local governing agencies. N. P. Metoyer, for example, was elected in 1872 to serve as the only nonwhite on the seven-member board of the Immigration Bureau.[83] Five years later an unidentified

79. Germaine A. Reed, "Race Legislation in Louisiana, 1864–1920," *Louisiana History,* VI (Fall, 1965), 379–82.

80. Numerous descendants of the colony have proudly preserved the registration certificates of their ancestors who registered in 1866 and 1867.

81. Natchitoches *Semi-Weekly Times,* May 22, 1867. The eight from Isle Brevelle who attended this party's meeting were Emanuel and Charles Dupre, Jerome Sarpy, Jr., Azenor and F. Metoyer, François Raphael, John B. Vienne, and George Kirkland. Charles LeRoy, a shoemaker from the town of Natchitoches, was the only nonwhite committeeman.

82. Walker, *Compendium of the Ninth Census,* 25; *Biographical and Historical Memoirs of Northwest Louisiana,* 302. The other nonwhite members of the police jury were Emile Silvie, J. B. Vienne, and Charles LeRoy. Both Silvie and Vienne resided in the Isle area but were not actually part of the colony at this time.

83. *Biographical and Historical Memoirs of Northwest Louisiana,* 302.

Metoyer *de couleur* was recorded as a member of the ten-man parish school board.[84]

Even this nominal participation in local government by the Cane River Creoles of color was short-lived. A predominantly white Democratic legislature took control of the state's government in 1877, and the era of "Redemption" from Reconstruction was begun. By 1878 white Democrats in Natchitoches Parish were already publicly proclaiming that "they were not worthy to be called white men if they could not do away with fourteen or fifteen radical leaders."[85] From this point forward, no nonwhite in the parish was elected to any public position, and their exercise of civil rights was marked by steady regression. According to the most authoritative study of reconstructed Louisiana, "Politically, socially, and economically the status of the vast majority of Louisiana [nonwhites] . . . declined for a half-century after 1877. There was to be little or no improvement in their condition for three quarters of a century."[86]

The reversal of political trends after 1877 left the average nonwhite of Louisiana in circumstances still basically better than the slavery he had endured before the war. For the people of Isle Brevelle, however, the loss of political fortunes was the ultimate blow. The special status which the people had previously enjoyed as *gens de couleur libre* was passé under the new system. Instead of being elevated to a position of full citizenship and equality with whites, as they had fervently hoped, the people of Isle Brevelle were now hopelessly submerged in the new mass of black freedmen.

84. Edward Jewett Brown, "History of Education in Natchitoches Parish" (M.A. thesis, Louisiana State University, 1932), 21.

85. Marguerite T. Leach, "The Aftermath of Reconstruction in Louisiana," *Louisiana Historical Quarterly*, XXXII (July, 1949), 651.

86. Joe Gray Taylor, *Louisiana Reconstructed, 1863–1877* (Baton Rouge, 1974), 507.

Epilogue

Throughout the remainder of the nineteenth century Cane River's Creoles of color suffered economic deprivation and increasing social degradation. They were soon abandoned by all but their closest white friends, and with the passing of years even these relationships withered. Moreover, the establishment of a church on the plantation of a white planter of the Côte Joyeuse drew away the whites from the Chapel of St. Augustine. The contacts of the people became almost exclusively limited to the confines of their own society.

Only a small number out of this group emerged from the Civil War in comfortable circumstances. These few, including such men as Emanuel Dupre, who was by far the wealthiest member of the colony in 1870, became the new leaders of the community. For even these men, however, the passing of years brought a steady diminution of fortunes. Each new generation resulted in a further division of property holdings until many families owned no more than narrow strips of land. Large plantation homes were lost along with the land on which they stood. Those members of the colony who managed to hold their land but could not afford the upkeep on their large houses moved into the cabins formerly occupied by their slaves. The "mansion houses" were torn down, and the bricks and lumber sold for whatever they would bring. The expensive furniture and other inherited heirlooms were the last vestiges of earlier wealth to be parted with. The hugh four-poster beds and ceiling-high armoires literally filled the rooms of the little cabins, but not until all other resources were exhausted did the people succumb to the clamor of the eager collectors who coveted these items.

The decline of the colony's economy and status was accompanied by a similar decline in educational opportunities. The children of the Isle did not deign to go to school with the blacks who attended the new public institutions after the war. Their parents could ill afford to send them to the private academies which their upper-class white neighbors supported; nor could they afford private tutors any longer. The Daughters of the Cross reopened their convent on the Isle at the close of the war and continued to operate it for many decades, with only one lapse of several years. Education in the church-sponsored school, however, covered only the primary grades. The general level of education within the colony fell sharply.

With each new reversal, the Cane River colony became more and more a society within a society. More than ever its members withdrew into themselves, insisting upon self-reliance and group solidarity as a defense against the ambivalence of outsiders. Indeed, one organization, the *Societé des amis unis de L'Ile Brevelle,* was formed in 1889 for the specific purpose of providing mutual succor and of raising the morale of its membership.

As the parish moved rapidly toward Americanization, the colony clung tenaciously to its French heritage, to the Creole culture that was for all practical purposes the last remaining tie between their postwar society and the life they had once known. But throughout their tribulations, the people never lost their pride. "It's blood that counts," they taught their children, and parents instructed the young ones concerning the virtue, integrity, and superiority of the blood they had inherited from their genteel ancestors.

By the arrival of the twentieth century, younger members of the colony had begun to disperse, hoping to find more opportunity in the industrial cities than they could find on the small tracts of land that barely supported their parents. Many settled in the larger cities of Louisiana. A number went to the industrial areas of the North and the West Coast. A few, whose complexions and predilections were already white, assimilated into the white population, but the majority of migrants settled together in the cities and founded small colonies there. Yet, regardless of where the people lived or worked, Isle Brevelle was still their home. Ties to the Isle and to the families there remained strong, and many of those who died in distant places expressed a last wish to be buried on the Isle.

In the twentieth century the plight of the "forgotten people" began a very slow and very gradual turn for the better. The most significant factor which influenced the people of the colony early in this period was the settlement among them of a white family of unusual character. The plantation known as

Yucca or Melrose, which had been lost in 1847 by young Théophile Louis Metoyer, had passed through a succession of white owners until it was inherited in 1898 by a prominent white planter, John Hampton Henry, who settled with his family in the long-neglected manor house. While Henry devoted his time to the expansion of the plantation, his wife, "Miss Cammie," turned her efforts to the restoration of the plantation buildings and to the development of the estate as a literary and cultural center. Fascinated by the people around her, "Miss Cammie" used their lives and their legends as the theme of her endeavors. Early Cane River crafts were revived at Melrose. Paintings, furniture, heirlooms, and mementos of the colony were gradually acquired and displayed in the manor house, as well as in the auxiliary buildings on the plantation. The library was stocked with published and unpublished works that explored all aspects of Louisiana life in general and Cane River life in particular.

From the 1920s through the mid 1940s, Melrose was known as a veritable gold mine for writers, painters, and others interested in the arts. "Miss Cammie's" hospitality was always extended to anyone sincerely interested in the area. As leading writers of that era—William Faulkner, Lyle Saxon, Roark Bradford, and a number of their colleagues—visited the Cane River plantation, they too were fascinated with the unique society that existed on the river and with the legends and traditions that the people had preserved. Many of them explored the colony's literary resources and used the materials they gathered in their own works. One of these, the imaginative François Mignon, not only built his literary career upon this theme but also devoted his life to the promotion of the Cane River way of life.

Inevitably, varying degrees of literary license were exercised in the dramatization of Cane River legends, and the traditions of the people acquired a certain amount of embellishment. In a few cases, these embellishments were repeated so often that the people themselves experienced some difficulty in distinguishing them from the original version. However, the damage thus done to the basic legend has been more than offset by the attention which these stories has focused upon the heritage of the "forgotten people." In 1974 the extant buildings of Melrose Plantation were officially declared a national historic landmark in recognition of the unique history which they possessed and the *societé nonpareil* which created them.

The twentieth century has not only seen a revival in public awareness of the colony and public recognition and respect for its heritage, but it also has brought definite attempts to provide the economic, political, and social opportunities long awaited by its people. Many of the industrious and self-sacrificing parents of the twentieth century have succeeded in providing excellent education for their children. The descendants of the colony now include physicians, attorneys, college administrators and educators, and a number of other professionals. The progress in civil rights during the third quarter of the century has provided these highly qualified men and women with excellent opportunities for advancement in private enterprise, public service, and politics. Most significantly, the changing mores of American society are making "social equality" a distinct possibility instead of a frustrating illusion.

The Cane River people who took Private Holloway into their homes and touched him with their kindness still exist. The same names still dominate the Isle. The same graciousness is extended to their visitors. Their coffee, tamales, and gumbo are even yet the envy of many Creole cooks, and the savory dinners that they serve during the area's annual October fair lure to the Isle scores of connoisseurs who seek to recapture the flavor of the past.

The Chapel of St. Augustine has remained the center of community life. The French heritage of the colony is still cherished, and the people's pride in their ancestry is perhaps stronger than ever. The farms of the colony, despite lasting economic difficulties, reflect increased prosperity. With continued progress in the present direction, the Cane River Creoles and their countless relatives who have spread from coast to coast will no longer have to consider themselves America's "forgotten people."

Bibliography

Primary Sources

MANUSCRIPTS

Immaculate Conception Church, Natchitoches, La.
  Registers of the Parish of St. François, 1729–1870.
Department of Archives, Louisiana State University, Baton Rouge
  William Aull Letter, 1833.
  Norbert Badin Papers, 1829–1837.
  Chaplin, Breazeale, and Chaplin Papers, 1806–1904.
  [Oscar Dubreuil] Account Books, 1856–1858, Isle Brevelle.
  Dupre, Metoyer & Company, Account Book, 1830–1837, 1873.
  James Hurst Letter, 1843.
  Joseph Irwin Correspondence.
  Adeleda Metoyer Papers, 1845–1897.
  Auguste Metoyer Papers, 1835–1846.
  Louis Metoyer Document, 1823.
  Natchitoches Parish Surveys Collection, 1808–1837.
  Natchitoches Times Subscription List, 1864–1867.
  Pauline Roque Letter, 1859.
  Gerome Sarpy Documents, 1852, 1876.
  Miles Terrell and Family, Papers, 1859–1929.
  Robert A. Tyson Diary, 1863–1864.
Natchitoches Parish Library, Natchitoches, La.
  Claude Thomas Pierre Metoyer, Last Will and Testament, 1801.
Northwestern State University, Eugene P. Watson Memorial Library, Natchitoches.
  Cammie G. Henry Collection
  Jack D. L. Holmes Collection
  Safford Collection
Private Collections
  Coutii Papers, 1803–1943. In possession of Mrs. Lee Etta Vaccarini Coutii, Natchez, La.

DeBlieux Collection. In possession of Robert B. DeBlieux, Natchitoches.

Morin Family Papers. In possession of Mrs. Noble Morin, Natchez, La.

St. John the Baptist Church, Cloutierville, La.

Registers of the Parish of St. Jean Baptiste, 1825–1880.

St. Landry Catholic Church, Opelousas, La.

Registers of the Parish of St. Landry des Opelousas, 1776–1805.

OFFICIAL RECORDS - UNPUBLISHED

Book of Patents. State Land Office, Baton Rouge.

Jack D. L. Holmes Collection, Microfilmed Documents Relating to Natchitoches and Adjacent Territory, Papeles de Estado, Archivo Historico Nacional de Seville, Eugene P. Watson Memorial Library, Northwestern State University of Louisiana, Natchitoches.

La Rochelle Actes de Enterrement, Mariage, et Naissance. Archives of the Department of Charente-Maritime, La Rochelle, France.

Louisiana State Land Records. State Land Office, Baton Rouge.

Natchitoches Parish Records. Office of the Clerk of Court, Natchitoches.

Natchitoches Parish Records, 1734–1905. Louisiana State University, Department of Archives.

New Orleans Mortgage Archives. Civil Courts Building, New Orleans.

New Orleans Notarial Archives. Civil Courts Building, New Orleans.

Opelousas Notarial Archives. Archives and Records Service, Baton Rouge.

Papeles Procedentes de Cuba. Archivo General de Indias, Seville, Spain.

Records of the French and American Claims Commission. National Archives, Washington, D.C.

Records of the Southern Claims Commission. National Archives, Washington, D.C.

U.S. Bureau of the Census, Third through Ninth Censuses, State of Louisiana, 1810–1870, Agricultural, Population, and Slave Schedules, and Social Statistics. National Archives, Washington, D.C.

U.S. Tract Book. State Land Office, Baton Rouge.

Works Progress Administration. Survey of the Federal Archives in Louisiana. County-Parish Boundaries in Louisiana. Typescript prepared in 1939 and housed in Department of Archives, Louisiana State University, Baton Rouge.

Works Progress Administration. Survey of the Federal Archives in Louisiana. Alphabetical and Chronological Digest of the Acts and Deliberations of the Cabildo, 1769–1803. Ten-volume typescript prepared in 1939 and housed in New Orleans Public Library.

OFFICIAL RECORDS - PUBLISHED

Acts Passed at the First Session of the First Legislature of the Territory of Orleans, 1806. New Orleans: n.p., 1807.

American State Papers: Documents Legislative and Executive of the Congress of the United States. 38 vols. Washington, D.C.: Gales & Seaton, 1832–1861.

An Account of Louisiana, Being an Abstract of Documents in the Offices of the Department of State and of the Treasury. Philadelphia: William Duane, 1803.

Carter, Clarence E., ed. *The Territorial Papers of the United States.* 27 vols. Washington, D.C.: Government Printing Office, 1934–.

Civil Code of the State of Louisiana. New Orleans: J. C. De St. Romes, printer, 1825.

Code Noir ou Loi Municipal Servant de Reglement. New Orleans: A. Boudousquie 1778.

Compiled Edition of the Civil Codes of Louisiana. Baton Rouge: State of Louisiana, 1940.

Historic American Buildings Survey, 1941. Washington, D. C.: National Park Service, 1941.

Journals of the House of Representatives of the State of Louisiana, 1825–1827.

Journals of the Senate of the State of Louisiana, 1825–1827.

Lislet, Moreau L., and Henry Carleton, trans. *The Laws of Las Siete Partidas Which are Still in Force in the State of Louisiana.* 2 vols. New Orleans: James M'Karaher, printer, 1820.

Martin, François Xavier. *Term Reports of Cases Argued and Determined in the Superior Court of the Territory of Orleans, 1809–1823.* 12 vols. New Orleans: n.p., 1854.

———. *Louisiana Term Reports, or Cases Argued and Determined in the Supreme Court of that State.* 8 vols. New Orleans: n.p., 1823–1830.

Message from the President of the United States Communicating Discoveries Made in Exploring the Missouri, Red River and Washita, by Captains Lewis and Clark, Doctor Sibley, and Mr. Dunbar. New York: A. & G. Way, printers, 1806.

Moore, Thomas O. *Annual Message of Governor Thomas O. Moore to the Twenty-Eighth General Assembly of the State of Louisiana, January, 1864.* Shreveport, La.: n.p., 1864.

Morgan, Thomas G., ed. *Civil Code of the State of Louisiana, with the Statutory Amendments, from 1825 to 1853, Inclusive.* New Orleans: J. B. Steel, 1853.

Reports of Cases Argued and Determined in the Supreme Court of the State of Louisiana. 19 vols. New Orleans: n.p., 1831–1841.

Reports of Cases Argued and Determined in the Supreme Court of Louisiana. 52 vols. New Orleans: n.p., 1846–1900.

Robertson, Meritt M., comp. *Reports of Cases Argued and Determined in the Supreme Court of Louisiana.* 12 vols. New Orleans: n.p., 1842–1846.

Walker, Francis A. *A Compendium of the Ninth Census (June 1, 1870).* Washington, D. C.: Government Printing Office, 1872.

The War of the Rebellion: A Compilation of the Official Records of the Union and Confederate Armies. 130 vols. Washington, D. C.: Government Printing Office, 1880–1901.

NEWSPAPERS

Alexandria, La., *Daily Democrat Times,* April 21, 1970.
Chicago *Tribune,* August 1, 1943.
Hammond, La., *Progress,* March 25, 1938.
Natchitoches *Courier,* 1825–1827.
Natchitoches *El Mexicano,* 1813.
Natchitoches *Semi-Weekly Times,* 1866–1867.
Natchitoches *Times,* 1972–1973.
Natchitoches *Union,* 1861–1862.
Natchitoches *Weekly Populist,* February 26, 1897.
New Orleans *Times-Picayune,* June 4, 1970; January 23, 1972; July 2, 1972.

CONTEMPORARY BOOKS, PERIODICALS, AND MISCELLANEOUS SOURCES

American Cemetery, Natchitoches.
Bacon, Edward. *Among the Cotton Thieves.* Detroit: Free Press Steam Book and Job Printing House, 1867.
Bartlett, Napier. *Military Record of Louisiana, Including Biographical and Historical Papers Relating to the Military Organizations of the State.* Baton Rouge: Louisiana State University Press, 1964.
Bearss, E. C., ed. *A Louisiana Confederate: Diary of Felix Pierre Poché.* Natchitoches: Northwestern State University, 1972.
Beecher, Harris H. *Record of the 114th Regiment, N.Y.S.V.* Norwich, N.Y.: J. F. Hubbard, Jr., 1866.
Bering, John A., and Thomas Montgomery. *History of the Forty-Eighth Ohio Veterans Volunteer Infantry.* Hillsboro, Ohio: Highland News Office, 1880.
Bjork, David K. "Documents Relating to Alexandro O'Reilly and an Expedition Sent Out by Him from New Orleans to Natchitoches, 1769–1770." *Louisiana Historical Quarterly,* VII (January, 1924), 20–39.
Bolton, Herbert Eugene, *Athanase De Mézières and the Louisiana-Texas Frontier, 1768–1780.* 2 vols. Cleveland: Arthur H. Clark Co., 1914.
Booth, Andrew B., comp. *Records of Louisiana Confederate Soldiers and Louisiana Confederate Commands.* 3 vols. New Orleans: n.p., 1920.
Bridges, Katherine. "Natchitoches in 1726." *Genealogical Register,* VIII (September, 1961), 37–39.
Bryner, Cloyd. *Bugle Echoes: The Story of Illinois 47th.* Springfield: Phillips Bros., 1905.
Buckingham, James Silk. *The Slave States of America.* 2 vols. London: Fisher, Son, & Co., 1842.
Cartwright, Samuel A. "Diseases and Peculiarities of the Negro Race." *De Bow's Review,* IV (1851), 64–69.

Catterall, Helen Tunncliff, ed. *Judicial Cases Concerning American Slavery and the Negro*. 5 vols. Washington, D. C.: Carnegie Institute, 1932.

Cemetery of the Chapel of St. Augustine, Isle Brevelle, La.

Clamorgan, Cyprien, *The Colored Aristocracy of St. Louis*. St. Louis: n.p., 1858.

Clark, Orton S., *The One Hundred and Sixteenth Regiment of New York State Volunteers*. Buffalo: Printing House of Matthews and Warren, 1868.

D'Antoni, Blaise C. "Some 1853 Cloutierville Yellow Fever Deaths." *New Orleans Genesis*, XXXV (June, 1970), 261–62.

DeBow, J. B. D., comp. *Statistical View of the United States. Embracing its Territory, Population—White, Free Colored, and Slave—Moral and Social Condition, Industry, Property, and Revenue; the Detailed Statistics of Cities, Towns, and Counties; Being a Compendium of the Seventh Census; to which are added the results of every previous census, beginning with 1790, in comparative tables, with explanatory and illustrative notes, based upon the schedules and other official sources of information*. Washington, D.C.: Beverly Tucker, 1854.

DeVille, Winston. *Louisiana Troops, 1720–1770*. Fort Worth: American Reference Publishers, 1965.

———. "Natchitoches Tax List for 1793." *Louisiana Genealogical Register*, XVIII (March, 1971), 72–73.

Ditchy, Jay K., trans. "Early Census Tables of Louisiana." *Louisiana Historical Quarterly*, XIII (April, 1930), 205–29.

Dodd, Donald B., and Wynelle S. *Historical Statistics of the South, 1790–1970; A Compilation of State-Level Census Statistics*. University, Ala.: University of Alabama Press, 1973.

Dorr, J. W. "A Tourist's Description of Louisiana in 1860." Edited by Walter Prichard. *Louisiana Historical Quarterly*, XXII (October, 1938), 1110–1214.

Dorsey, Sarah A. *Recollections of Henry Watkins Allen*. New York: M. Doolady, 1866.

Ewer, James K. *The Third Massachusetts Cavalry in the War for the Union*. Maplewood, Mass.: Wm. G. J. Perry Press, 1903.

Flinn, Frank M. *Campaigning with Banks in Louisiana*. Lynn, Mass.: Thos. P. Nichols, 1887.

French, B. F., ed. *Historical Collections of Louisiana*. 5 vols. New York: D. Appleton & Company, 1851.

Gould, John M. *History of the First-Tenth-Twenty-Ninth Maine Regiment*. Portland: S. Berry, 1871.

Hanaburgh, D. H. *History of the One Hundred and Twenty-Eighth Regiment, New York Volunteers*. Poughkeepsie: Press of the Enterprise Publishing Co., 1894.

Hill, Roscoe R. *Descriptive Catalogue of the Documents Relating to the History of the United States in the Papeles Procedentes de Cuba Deposited in the Archivo General de Indias at Seville*. Washington, D. C.: Carnegie Institute, 1916.

Holmes, Isaac. *An Account of the United States of America*. London: Caxton Press, 1823.

Holmes, Jack D. L. *Honor and Fidelity: the Louisiana Infantry Regiment and the Louisiana Militia Companies, 1766–1821*. Birmingham: n.p., 1965.

Kinnaird, Lawrence, ed. *Spain in the Mississippi Valley, 1765–1794*. 3 vols. Washington, D. C.: Government Printing Office, 1949.

Kneeland, Dr. Samuel. "The Hybrid Races of Animals and Men." *De Bow's Review*, XIX (1855), 535–39.

Le Page du Pratz, Antoine-Simon. *The History of Louisiana*. Trans. from the French, London: T. Becket, 1774. Reprinted at New Orleans: J. S. Harmanson, 1947.

Lewis, M. G. *Journal of a West India Proprietor, Kept During a Residence in the Island of Jamaica*. London: John Murray, 1834. Reprinted 1929.

Long, Edward. *The History of Jamaica*. 3 vols. London: T. Lowndes, 1774.

Lubbock, Francis R. *Six Decades in Texas*. Austin: Ben C. Jones and Co., 1900.

Lufkin, Edwin B. *History of the Thirteenth Maine Regiment*. Bridgton, Me.: H. A. Shorey and Son, 1898.

Martin, François Xavier. *The History of Louisiana from the Earliest Period*. 2 vols. New Orleans: I, Lyman and Beardslee, 1827; II, A. T. Penniman & Co., 1829.

McCants, Sister Dorothea Olga, ed. and trans. *They Came to Louisiana: Letters of a Catholic Mission, 1854–1882*. Baton Rouge: Louisiana State University Press, 1970.

Menn, Joseph Karl. *The Large Slaveholders of Louisiana—1860*. New Orleans: Pelican Publishing Co., 1964.

Mills, Elizabeth Shown. "Certificates of Naturalization, Natchitoches Parish, Louisiana, 1820–1850." *Louisiana Genealogical Register*, XXI (March, 1974), 85–93.

———, ed. and trans. *Natchitoches, 1729–1803; Abstracts of the Catholic Church Registers of the French and Spanish Post of St. Jean Baptiste des Natchitoches in Louisiana*. New Orleans: Polyanthos, 1977.

———. "Natchitoches Militia of 1782." *Louisiana Genealogical Register*, XX (September, 1973), 216–18.

Northup, Solomon. *Twelve Years a Slave*. Edited by Sue Eakin and Joseph Logsdon. Baton Rouge: Louisiana State University Press, 1968.

Olmsted, Frederick Law. *Journey in the Seaboard Slave States in the Years 1853–1854*. New York: Dix and Edwards, 1856. Reprinted New York: Negro Universities Press, 1968.

———. *The Cotton Kingdom: A Traveller's Observations on Cotton and Slavery in the American Slave States*. Edited by Arthur M. Schlesinger. New York: Alfred A. Knopf, 1953.

"O'Reilly's Ordinance of 1770." *Louisiana Historical Quarterly*, XI (April, 1928), 237–40.

Paris, Comte de (Louis Philippe Albert d'Orleans). *History of the Civil War in America*. 4 vols. Philadelphia: Porter & Coates, 1875–1888.

Pellet, Elias P. *History of the 114th Regiment, New York State Volunteers*. Norwich, N.Y.: Telegraph & Chronicle Press Print, 1866.

Porteous, Laura L., trans. "Index to the Spanish Judicial Records of Louisiana." *Louisiana Historical Quarterly*, VI–XXXI (1923–1949).

Powers, George W. *The Story of the Thirty-Eighth Regiment of Massachussetts Volunteers*. Cambridge: Dakin & Metcalf, 1866.

Scott, John. *Story of the Thirty-Second Iowa Infantry Volunteers*. Nevada, Iowa: n.p., 1896.

Shorey, Henry A. *The Story of the Maine Fifteenth*. Bridgton, Me.: Press of the Bridgton News, 1890.

Smith, Walter G. *Life and Letters of Thomas Kilby Smith*. New York: G. P. Putnam's Sons, 1898.

Stoddard, Major Amos. *Sketches, Historical and Descriptive, of Louisiana*. Philadelphia: Mathew Carey, 1812.

Stuart, James. *Three Years in North America*. 2 vols. New York: J. and J. Harper, 1833.

Taylor, Richard. *Destruction and Reconstruction: Personal Experiences of the Late War*. New York: D. Appleton and Company, 1890.

Torian, Sarah A., ed. "Ante-Bellum and War Memories of Mrs. Telfair Hodgson," *Georgia Historical Quarterly*, XXVII (December, 1943), 350–56.

Tunnard, W. H. *A Southern Record: The History of the Third Regiment, Louisiana Infantry*. Baton Rouge: n.p., 1866. Reprinted Dayton, Ohio: Morningside Bookshop, 1970.

Willey, Nathan. "Education of the Colored Population of Louisiana," *Harper's New Monthly Magazine*, XXXIII (1866), 246–50.

LETTERS AND INTERVIEWS

Letters to the Author:

Archivo Segreto Vaticano, Secretary of, Vatican City, April 6, 1974.

Broussard, Msgr. Milburn, Cloutierville, La., March 15, 1974.

Coutii, Mrs. Lee Etta Vaccarini, Natchez, La., various dates 1974–1976.

LaCour, Hugh, Shreveport, La., various dates, 1974.

Mignon, François, Natchitoches, La., various dates, 1974.

Vansina, Dr. Jan, Madison, Wisconsin, May 12, 1973.

Wilson, Samuel, Jr., New Orleans, La., July 31, 1973.

Other Letters:

Confidential source to François Mignon, Detroit, Mich., September 3, 1972.

Coutii, Mrs. Lee Etta Vaccarini, Natchez, La., to Sister Frances Jerome Woods, September, 1973.

Interviews:

Broussard, Msgr. Milburn, Cloutierville, La., August 22, 1970.

Chelettre, Tillman, Sr., and Armeline Roque Chelettre, Natchez, La., October 12, 1974.

Jones, Lewis Emory, and Gloria Sers Jones, Natchez, La., March 16, 1975.

Mignon, François, "A Visit to Melrose Plantation with François Mignon," recorded interview, Melrose, La. Produced Alexandria, La., 1967. No. B224, Howard-Tilton Memorial Library, Tulane University, New Orleans.

Secondary Sources

BOOKS

Aptheker, Herbert, ed. *A Documentary History of the Negro People in the United States.* New York: Citadel Press, 1951.

Barbe-Marbois, François. *The History of Louisiana, Particularly of the Cession of that Colony to the United States of America.* Trans. from the French, Philadelphia: Carey & Lea, 1830.

Baudier, Roger. *The Catholic Church in Louisiana.* New Orleans: A. W. Hyatt, printers, 1939.

Beckers, Henry F. *et al. A History of Immaculate Conception Catholic Church, Natchitoches, Louisiana, 1717–1973.* Natchitoches: n.p., 1973.

Biographical and Historical Memoirs of Northwest Louisiana. Nashville: The Southern Publishing Co., 1890.

Blassingame, John W. *The Slave Community: Plantation Life in the Antebellum South.* New York: Oxford University Press, 1972.

Bracey, John H., Jr., August Meier, and Elliott Rudwick, eds. *Free Blacks in America, 1800–1860.* Belmont, Cal.: Wadsworth Publishing Co., Inc. 1971.

Brathwaite, Edward. *The Development of Creole Society in Jamaica, 1770–1820.* Oxford: Clarendon Press, 1971.

Cable, George W. *The Creoles of Louisiana.* New York: C. Scribner's Sons, 1884.

Callahan, J. J., *et al. The History of St. Augustine's Parish; Isle Brevelle, Natchez, La.; 1803–1953; 1829–1954; 1856–1956.* Natchitoches: n.p., 1956.

Chambers, Henry E. *A History of Louisiana.* 3 vols. New York: American Historical Society, Inc., 1925.

Corley, D. B. *A Visit to Uncle Tom's Cabin.* Chicago: Laird & Lee, 1893.

Davis, Edwin Adams. *Louisiana: A Narrative History.* Baton Rouge: Claitor's Book Store, 1961.

Degler, Carl N. *Neither Black Nor White: Slavery and Race Relations in Brazil and the United States.* New York: Macmillan Company, 1971.

Desdunes, Rodolphe Lucien. *Our People and Our History.* Translated by Sister Dorothea Olga McCants. Baton Rouge: Louisiana State University Press, 1973.

Dover, Cedric. *American Negro Art.* Greenwich: New York Graphic Society, 1960.

Fogel, Robert William, and Stanley L. Engerman. *Time on the Cross: The Economics of American Negro Slavery.* 2 vols. Boston: Little, Brown & Co., 1974.

Fortier, Alcée. *A History of Louisiana*. 4 vols. New York: Manzi, Joyant & Co., 1904.

————. *Louisiana: Comprising Sketches of Parishes, Towns, Events, Institutions, and Persons, Arranged in Cyclopedic Form*. Madison, Wis.: Century Historical Association, 1914.

Franklin, John Hope. *The Free Negro in North Carolina, 1790–1860*. Chapel Hill: University of North Carolina Press, 1943.

Frazier, E. Franklin. *The Free Negro Family: A Study of Family Origins Before the Civil War*. Nashville: Fisk University Press, 1932.

Gayarré, Charles E. *History of Louisiana*. 4 vols. New Orleans: Armand Hawkins, 1903.

Gray, Lewis Cecil. *History of Agriculture in the Southern United States to 1860*. 2 vols. Washington, D.C.: Carnegie Institute, 1933. Reprinted, Gloucester, Mass.: Peter Smith, 1958.

Herskovits, Melville J. *The New World Negro*. Edited by Frances S. Herskovits. Bloomington, Ind.: Indiana University Press, 1966.

James, C. L. R. *The Black Jacobins: Toussaint L'Ouverture and the San Domingo Rebellion*. New York: Vantage Books, 1963.

Johnson, Ludwell H. *Red River Campaign: Politics and Cotton in the Civil War*. Baltimore: Johns Hopkins Press, 1958.

Johnson, Robert U., and Clarence C. Buel, eds. *Battles and Leaders of the Civil War*. 4 vols. New York: The Century Co., 1887–1888.

Johnston, James Hugo. *Race Relations in Virginia and Miscegenation in the South, 1776–1860*. Amherst, Mass.: University of Massachusetts Press, 1970.

Jordan, Winthrop D. *White Over Black: American Attitudes Toward the Negro, 1550–1812*. Chapel Hill, N.C.: University of North Carolina Press, 1968.

Kane, Harnett T. *Plantation Parade: The Grand Manner in Louisiana*. New York: Wm. Morrow & Co., 1945.

Kerby, Robert L. *Kirby Smith's Confederacy: The Trans-Mississippi South, 1863–1865*. New York: Columbia University Press, 1972.

Mignon, François. *Plantation Memo: Plantation Life in Louisiana 1750–1970, and Other Matter*. Baton Rouge: Claitor's Publishing Division, 1973.

Mills, Gary B. and Elizabeth S. *Melrose*. Natchitoches: Association for the Preservation of Historic Natchitoches, 1973.

Morrow, Louis Laraboire. *Our Catholic Faith: A Manual of Religion*. Kenosha, Wis.: My Mission House, 1961.

Natchitoches: Oldest Settlement in the Louisiana Purchase, Founded 1714. Natchitoches: Association of Natchitoches Women for the Preservation of Historic Natchitoches, 1973.

Phares, Ross. *Cavalier in the Wilderness*. Baton Rouge: Louisiana State University Press, 1952.

Portré-Bobinski, Germaine, and Clara Mildred Smith. *Natchitoches: The Up-to-Date Oldest Town in Louisiana*. New Orleans: Dameron-Pierson Co., Ltd., 1936.

————. *Natchitoches; Translations of Old French and Spanish Documents*. N.p.: n.p., 1928.

Quarles, Benjamin. *The Negro in the Civil War*. Boston: Little, Brown, 1953.

Read, William A. *Louisiana French*. Baton Rouge: Louisiana State University Press, 1931.

Rogin, Leo. *The Introduction of Farm Machinery in Its Relation to the Productivity of Labor in the Agriculture of the United States During the Nineteenth Century*. Berkeley: University of California Press, 1931.

Rousseve, Charles B. *The Negro in Louisiana: Aspects of His History and His Literature*. New Orleans: Xavier University Press, 1937.

Russell, John H. *The Free Negro in Virginia, 1619–1685*. Baltimore: Johns Hopkins Press, 1913.

Saxon, Lyle. *Children of Strangers*. Boston: Houghton Mifflin Co., 1937. Reprinted New Orleans: Robert L. Crager & Co., 1948.

Seebold, Herman de B. *Old Louisiana Plantation Homes and Family Trees*. 2 vols. New Orleans: n.p., 1941.

Shugg, Roger W. *Origins of Class Struggle in Louisiana: a Social History of White Farmers and Laborers During Slavery and After, 1840–1875*. Baton Rouge: Louisiana State University Press, 1939.

Sterkx, H. E. *The Free Negro in Ante-Bellum Louisiana*. Rutherford, N.J.: Fairleigh Dickinson University Press, 1972.

Surrey, N. M. Miller. *The Commerce of Louisiana During the French Regime, 1699–1763*. New York: Columbia University Press, 1916.

Swanton, John R. *The Indian Tribes of North America*. Washington, D.C.: Government Printing Office, 1952. Reprinted, Grosse Pointe, Mich.: Scholarly Press, 1968.

Tannenbaum, Frank. *Slave and Citizen*. New York: A. A. Knopf, 1947.

Taylor, Joe Gray. *Louisiana Reconstructed, 1863–1877*. Baton Rouge: Louisiana State University Press, 1974.

————. *Negro Slavery in Louisiana*. Baton Rouge: Louisiana Historical Association, 1963.

Watkins, James L. *King Cotton: A Historical and Statistical Review, 1790 to 1908*. N.p.: James L. Watkins and Sons, 1908. Reprinted, New York: Negro Universities Press, 1969.

Wesley, Charles Harris. *Negro Americans in the Civil War: From Slavery to Citizenship*. 3 vols. New York: Publishers Co., Inc., 1967.

Wilson, Joseph T. *The Black Phalanx; A History of the Negro Soldiers of the United States in the Wars of 1775–1812, 1861–1865*. Hartford: American Publishing Co., 1888.

Wilson, Theodore Brantner. *The Black Codes of the South*. University, Ala.: University of Alabama Press, 1965.

Winters, John D. *The Civil War in Louisiana*. Baton Rouge: Louisiana State University Press, 1963.

Woodman, Harold D. *King Cotton and His Retainers; Financing and Marketing the Cotton Crop of the South, 1800–1925*. Lexington: University of Kentucky Press, 1968.

Woods, Sister Frances Jerome. *Marginality and Identity: A Colored Creole Family Through Ten Generations*. Baton Rouge: Louisiana State University Press, 1972.

Woodson, Carter G., comp. and ed. *Free Negro Owners of Slaves in the United States in 1830, Together with Absentee Ownership of Slaves in the United States in 1830*. Washington, D. C.: The Association for the Study of Negro Life and History, 1924.

———. *The Negro in Our History*. Washington, D.C.: The Associated Publishers, Inc., 1928.

Wright, James M. *The Free Negro in Maryland, 1634–1860*. New York: Columbia University Press, 1921.

PERIODICALS

Andrews, James G. "Let Your Fingers Do the Ginning." *Mid-South,* November 10, 1974.

"Auction Slated at Plantation." New Orleans *Times-Picayune,* June 4, 1970.

Arena, C. Richard. "Landholding and Political Power in Spanish Louisiana." *Louisiana Historical Quarterly,* XXXVIII (October, 1955), 39–54.

Bridges, Katherine, and Winston DeVille. "Natchitoches in 1766." *Louisiana History,* IV (April, 1963), 145–59.

Browning, James Blackwell. "Free Negro in Ante-Bellum North Carolina." *North Carolina Historical Review,* XV (January, 1938), 23–33.

Burns, Francis P. "The Spanish Land Laws of Louisiana." *Louisiana Historical Quarterly,* XI (October, 1928), 557–81.

"Cluster of Treasures Along Cane River." New Orleans *Times-Picayune,* July 2, 1972.

Cruzat, Heloize H., trans. "Louisiana in 1724." *Louisiana Historical Quarterly,* XII (January, 1929), 121–33.

De Gournay, P. F. "The F.M.C.'s of Louisiana." *Lippincott's Monthly Magazine,* LIII (1894), 511–17.

Dorr, J. W. "A Tourist's Description of Louisiana in 1860." *Louisiana Historical Quarterly,* XXI (Ocotber, 1938).

Dunbar-Nelson, Alice. "People of Color in Louisiana." *Journal of Negro History,* I (October, 1916), 361–76; II (January, 1917), 51–78.

Dunn, J. E. "Isle Brevelle." Natchitoches *Louisiana Populist,* February 26, 1897.

Dunn, Milton, "History of Natchitoches." *Louisiana Historical Quarterly,* III (January, 1920), 26–56.

Everett, Donald E. "Free Persons of Color in Colonial Louisiana." *Louisiana History,* VII (Winter, 1966), 21–50.

Fischer, Roger A. "Racial Segregation in Ante-Bellum Louisiana." *American Historical Review,* LXXIV (February, 1969), 926–37.

Foner, Laura. "The Free People of Color in Louisiana and St. Dominigue: A Comparative Portrait of Two Three-Caste Societies." *Journal of Social History,* III (Summer, 1970), 406–30.

Garber, D. "History of Melrose Plantation Like Turning Pages of Novel." (Undated clipping from unidentified Texas newspaper in collection of Mrs. Minnie Charleville Mills, Woodlawn, Texas).

Jeffrey, Edward C. "New Lights on Evolution." *Science.* LXV (May 13, 1927), 458–62.

Kunkel, Paul A. "Modifications in Louisiana Negro Legal Status under Louisiana Constitutions, 1812–1957." *Journal of Negro History,* XLIV (January, 1959), 1–25.

Leach, Marguerite T. "The Aftermath of Reconstruction in Louisiana." *Louisiana Historical Quarterly,* XXXII (July, 1949), 631–717.

McCloy, Shelby T. "Negroes and Mulattoes in Eighteenth-Century France." *Journal of Negro History,* XXX (July, 1945), 276–92.

"Melrose." *Louisiana REA News* (July, 1953), 11.

"Melrose Manor on Cane River Stands as Relic of World's Strangest Empire." Hammond, La., *Progress,* March 25, 1938.

Mignon, François. "Sale of Plantation Biggest in History." Alexandria, La., *Daily Town Talk,* April 21, 1970.

Mills, Elizabeth S. "Marie Therese, the Metoyers, and Melrose." *Proceedings of the Seventeenth Annual Institute of the Louisiana Genealogical and Historical Society* (Baton Rouge, 1974), 13–25.

Mills, Gary B. "Cane River Country, 1860–1866." *Proceedings of the Seventeenth Annual Institute of the Louisiana Genealogical and Historical Society* (Baton Rouge, 1974), 1–12.

Mills, Gary B. and Elizabeth S. "Marie Therese and the Founding of Melrose: A Study of Facts and Fallacies." Natchitoches *Times,* July 29, August 5, 12, 19, 1973.

Nardini, Louis R. "Legends About Marie Therese Disputed by Local Historian and Author." Natchitoches *Times,* October 22, 1972.

Ocariz, Juan José Andreu. "The Natchitoches Revolt." Translated by Jack D. L. Holmes. *Louisiana Studies,* III (Spring, 1964), 117–32.

Ousler, Loree. "Portrait of Carmelite." Natchitoches *Times,* October 11, 1973.

Porter, Betty. "The History of Negro Education in Louisiana." *Louisiana Historical Quarterly,* XXV (July, 1942), 728–821.

"Preservation Group Given Deed to Melrose Plantation." New Orleans *Times-Picayune,* January 23, 1972.

Rankin, David C. "The Origins of Black Leadership in New Orleans During Recon-struction." *Journal of Southern History,* XL (August, 1974), 416–40.

Reed, Germaine A. "Race Legislation in Louisiana, 1864–1920." *Louisiana History,* VI (Fall, 1965), 369–92.

Reinders, Robert C. "The Decline of the New Orleans Free Negro in the Decade before the Civil War." *Journal of Mississippi History,* XXIV (January, 1962), 88–98.

———. "The Free Negro in the New Orleans Economy, 1850–1860." *Louisiana History,* VI (Summer, 1965), 273–85.

Russ, William A., Jr. "Disfranchisement in Louisiana (1862–1870)." *Louisiana Historical Quarterly,* XVII (July, 1935), 555–80.

Shoen, Harold. "The Free Negro in the Republic of Texas." *Southwestern Historical Quarterly,* XXXIX (April, 1936), 292–309; XL (October, 1936), 85–114; (January, 1937), 169–99; (April, 1937), 267–89; (July, 1937), 83–108.

Shugg, Roger Wallace. "Suffrage and Representation in Ante-Bellum Louisiana." *Louisiana Historical Quarterly,* XIX (April, 1936), 390–406.

Stahl, Annie Lee West. "The Free Negro in Ante-Bellum Louisiana." *Louisiana Historical Quarterly,* XXV (April, 1942), 301–396.

Sydnor, Charles S. "The Free Negro in Mississippi Before the Civil War." *American Historical Review,* XXXI (July, 1927), 769–88.

Thomas, William J. "Louisiana Creole French, Black or White?" *Wichita State University Bulletin,* XLIX (February, 1973), 15–26.

Touchstone, Blake. "Voodoo in New Orleans." *Louisiana History,* XIII (Fall, 1972), 371–86.

Wesley, Charles Harris. "The Employment of Negroes as Soldiers in the Confederate Army." *Journal of Negro History,* IV (July, 1919), 239–53.

Wilson, Calvin Dill. "Black Masters: A Side-light on Slavery." *North American Review,* CLXXXI (November, 1905), 685–98.

Woodson, Carter G., ed. "Beginnings of Miscegenation of Whites and Blacks." *Journal of Negro History,* III (October, 1918), 335–53.

———. "Free Negro Owners of Slaves in the United States in 1830." *Journal of Negro History,* IX (January, 1924), 41–85.

THESES AND DISSERTATIONS

Brown, Edward Jewett. "History of Education in Natchitoches Parish." M.A. thesis, Louisiana State University, 1932.

Constantin, Roland Paul. "The Louisiana 'Black Code' Legislation of 1865." M.A. thesis, Louisiana State University, 1956.

Everett, Donald E. "Free Persons of Color in New Orleans, 1803–1865." Ph.D. dissertation, Tulane University, 1952.

Gallien, Charles Stanley. "Melrose: A Southern Cultural and Literary Center." M.A. thesis, Northwestern State University of Louisiana, 1966.

Hymes, Valery. "A History of Navigation of the Red River from 1815 to 1865." M.A. thesis, Louisiana State University, 1939.

Puckett, Erastus Paul. "The Free Negro in New Orleans to 1860." M.A. thesis, Tulane University, 1907.

Reddick, Lawrence D. "The Negro in the New Orleans Press, 1850–1860: A Study in Attitudes and Propaganda." Ph.D. dissertation, University of Chicago, 1939.

Vincent, Charles. "Negro Leadership in Louisiana, 1862–1870." M.A. thesis, Louisiana State University, 1966.

Index

265